EXPLORING AND TEACHING THE ENGLISH LANGUAGE ARTS

EXPLORING AND TEACHING THE ENGLISH LANGUAGE ARTS

Fourth Edition

STEPHEN TCHUDI
University of Nevada, Reno

DIANA MITCHELL
President, Michigan Council of Teachers of English

An imprint of Addison Wesley Longman, Inc.

New York • Reading, Massachusetts • Menlo Park, California • Harlow, England
Don Mills, Ontario • Sydney • Mexico City • Madrid • Amsterdam

Acquisitions Editor : Virginia L. Blanford
Development Manager: Arlene Bessenoff
Editorial Assistant: Allison Stone Wolcott
Marketing Manager: Renee Ortbals
Electronic Page Makeup/Project Coordination and Text Design: WestWords, Inc.
Cover Design Manager: Nancy Danahy
Cover Designer: Joseph DePinho
Cover Photos: © Richard Hutchings
Full Service Production Manager: Eric Jorgensen
Manufacturing Manager: Denise Sandler
Printer and Binder: Maple-Vail Book Manufacturing Group
Cover Printer: Coral Graphic Services, Inc.

Library of Congress Cataloging-in-Publication Data

Tchudi, Stephen, 1942—
    Exploring and Teaching the English Language Arts / Stephen Tchudi, Diana Mitchell —4th ed.
      p   cm.
    Rev. ed. of: Explorations in the teaching of English. c1989.
    Includes bibliographical references and index.
    ISBN 0-321-00215-6
    1. English language—Study and teaching.   2. Language arts.
  I. Mitchell, Diana.   II. Tchudi, Stephen, 1942– Explorations in the teachings of English.   III. Title.
PE1065. T36   1998
428′ .007—dc21   98-7341
                                           CIP

Please visit our website at http://longman.awl.com

ISBN 0-321-00215-6

  345678910—MA—0100

Dedication

Stephen Tchudi dedicates this book to the late Wallace W. Douglas: teacher, advisor, mentor, friend.

Diana Mitchell dedicates this book to Susan Tchudi: teacher, advisor, mentor, friend.

CONTENTS

PREFACE

Attached to the deceptively simple title "Teacher of English" or "Teacher of Language Arts" are responsibilities that could tax the capabilities of a dozen specialists in diverse fields. It is not enough that the English/language teacher takes on two-thirds of the three Rs; beyond the teaching of fundamentals of literacy, he or she must be a reading consultant and diagnostician, literary critic, writing instructor, writer, librarian, reader of books, media specialist, linguist, psychologist, and counselor.

Given the complexity of the task of "teaching" literacy, it is tempting for teachers to look for *the method,* a clear-cut, no-nonsense approach that will reduce complexity and bring serenity. It is also tempting for the writers of a book on the teaching of English/language arts to develop a formula for instruction, a compendium of rules and "sure fire" lesson plans purporting to solve the teacher's dilemma.

This book does not offer such formulae, although it does present what we regard as a consistent, integrated approach to the English/language arts. Our writing draws on contemporary research, our observation of other teachers and classes, as well as our combined fifty years of experience teaching middle school, high school, and college English. What we offer is not a set program for teaching but a description of integrated, research-based principles for the teaching and learning of language, accompanied by numerous examples drawn either from our own experiences in the schools or from the professional literature.

We see *Exploring and Teaching the English Language Arts* as a source book for the teacher/learner, the teacher of *any* age and *any* amount of experience who wishes to explore systematically his or her approach to teaching the English/language arts in the elementary, junior high/middle school, or secondary classroom. Our book is a starting point for individual experimentation that, we believe, will help teachers discover and refine their own sets of methods for teaching.

The heart of the book is a series of Explorations—some problems to think about, talk over, and do—that appear at the close of each chapter. These are not ordinary discussion questions or homework assignments; they are open-ended suggestions that both prospective and experienced teachers can explore as a way of seeking information and ideas about the teaching of English. We know from responses to earlier editions of this book that teachers can use the explorations to build a repertoire of teaching ideas and strategies; more important, when faced with new challenges and opportunities, they can improvise and apply their understandings in fresh, original, and pedagogically valid ways.

This is the fourth edition of this book, and for the most part, we've stayed with what has worked in terms of content and structure. We begin with an historical/documentary overview of literacy education in this country that we think is important background for any teacher, new or experienced, because it provides a context for myriad current issues and problems. A key chapter (1) then examines current English language arts theory and our "experiential" model, followed by a discussion of the integrated curriculum (2). Two additional chapters set the stage for teaching by discussing ways of creating instructional units (3) and creating a classroom community (4). The reader is thus positioned to begin collecting, designing, and planning materials for his/her classroom from the start.

Despite our commitment to integrated teaching, with writing flowing from reading and vice versa, and with "English" naturally making links across the curriculum, we nevertheless subdivide our more specific discussion of teaching approaches and strategies into the familiar "tripod" of literature/reading (5–7), writing (8–9) and language (10). These are followed by chapters that discuss ways of expanding the traditional content of the English language arts through work in oral English and drama (11) and multimedia (12). We then finish with a discussion of assessment, evaluation, and grading (13), emphasizing ways of integrating assessment naturally into a multidisciplinary, integrated literacy curriculum.

The order of chapters in this book reflects an order of teaching that we have generally pursued in our own "methods" courses. We think that a grounding in theory is extremely important, and thus we encourage readers to think of some of the larger issues—goals, standards, curriculum—before taking up the theory and pragmatics of teaching literature, composition, oral language, drama, and media. The order of the text also encourages readers to think from the start about integrated curriculum and about designing their own, integrated teaching units. However, we also recognize that methods instructors and readers certainly have their own ideas about a teaching/reading order. With that in mind, we have designed the chapters to stand on their own, by and large. obviously the chapters on literature 5-6-7 are designed as a sequence, as are the two on teaching writing 6-9. We recommend that all readers begin with the theoretical background in Chapter 1. Some readers may want to move directly from that chapter into the classroom-specific, "methods" chapter, which focus closely on classroom instruction, reserving the chapters on curriculum (2) and unit building (3) for later. We should add, too, that our own teaching in the methods course has generally been linked to a variety of field experience or internship courses, so that students are working in the schools even while considering methods of instruction on the university campus. Such correlated experiences obvious shape not only how readings are sequenced, but whether the book is used more as a reference book than as a text for cover-to-cover reading.

Readers familiar with earlier editions of this book will find a number of new and expanded features:

- the early emphasis on curriculum integration.
- a new chapter on creating classroom community.
- updated reading references for children and young adults.

- discussion of the role of national standards in curriculum development and planning.
- expanded material on oral English and drama, with emphasis on integrating them into the curriculum.
- continued exploration of the grading/evaluation dilemma, providing strategies for teachers to derive grades and mark papers while still maintaining strong support for their students' efforts.

Despite its many rewards, English/language teaching is sometimes difficult, painful, lonely work, a topic we explore briefly in the Coda to this book. Teaching can cause stomach aches, headaches, heartaches, and sleepless nights. *Exploring and Teaching the English Language Arts* is intended to support the teacher who is willing to take some risks in the interest of better teaching and who will engage in trials and experiments to find more effective ways of helping students become literate in the fullest and best sense.

We would like to thank the following reviewers who have made valuable contributions to the fourth edition of *Exploring and Teaching the English Language Arts:*

M. Linda Broughton, Florida State University
Linda P. Cavazos, University of Nevada, Las Vegas
Ruth K. Duncan, St. Leo College
Flo Denny Durway, Louisiana State University
Jeanne Gerlach, University of Texas at Arlington
Linda Goldsmith, Nova Southeastern University
Sheila Gullickson, Moorhead State University
Mary A. Haug, South Dakota State University
Terry Martin, Central Washington University
William J. McCleary, State University of New York at Cortland
Don Melichar, Central Missouri State University
Jamie Myers, Pennsylvania State University
Joseph Potts, California State University–Long Beach
Mary Ann Tighe, Troy State University
Rex Veeder, St. Cloud State University
Monica Weis, Nazareth College

We also deeply appreciate the interest and support of Ginny Blanford and Allison Wolcott at Addison Wesley Longman, Pat McCutcheon, the Project Manager for WestWords, and C. R. Batten, copyeditor. We also want to acknowledge the help and support of all the people at Addison Wesley Longman and WestWords who have been involved in making this book a reality.

A DOCUMENTARY HISTORY OF TEACHING THE ENGLISH LANGUAGE ARTS

"Those who cannot remember the past are doomed to repeat it."

—George Santayana
The Life of Reason (1905)

"A people's speech is the skin of its culture."

—Max Lerner
America as a Civilization (1957)

You have probably encountered philosopher George Santayana's observation that those who don't know their history are doomed to repeat it. It may have been quoted to you by history teachers as a way of persuading you of the value of their discipline and to urge you to pass the course so as not to have to repeat History 101 yourself. We agree with Santayana on the importance of knowing one's history, but in the instance of the English language arts, we think there's an even more important reason for beginning a book of this kind with a modest history lesson. As linguists and philosophers have long pointed out, language is a uniquely human achievement. Although there is some debate about whether animals have "true" languages—bird whistles, dolphin chirps, chimpanzee signing, and your favorite dog doing what it's "told"—there's little debate that human uses and applications are unique. The complexity of our language is shown by the thickness of our dictionaries, by the volume of words we consume and create every day of our lives, by our arguments and quarrels, our debate and reasoning, our whoopin' and hollerin', our whispering secrets, our telling jokes. As Max Lerner has observed, human language is "the skin of its culture," the symbolic manifestation of what the human race has been in the past, is now, and is in the process of becoming.

There are parts of the history of language teaching that we surely hope you as a teacher will not be doomed to repeat. We hope that nobody will require you to teach sentence diagramming as part of some vaguely historical notion that it was good for grandma and grandpa, so we ought to teach it to children today. We hope you won't feel it necessary to acquire a red pen or pencil and exhaustively mark every last error on every last student paper, a procedure that our history and research have shown to be unproductive and hurtful. We hope you won't tell your students to take Latin thinking it will teach them English grammar, and we hope you won't push difficult classics of literature on students on the grounds that it's somehow good discipline for them or the only way they can discover their own cultural history.

Rather, we hope you'll join us in celebrating the fact that as a teacher of the English language arts , you are part of a tradition that goes back thousands of years, whose origins, in fact, are lost in prehistory, the times for which there is no linguistic record.

TRADITIONS IN LITERACY

Language teachers have been part of the power structure of historic Egypt, Greece, and Rome; the subject of language has been granted a central, even dominating role in schooling for as long as we know its history. In his book *Voices from the Past,* Merrit Ruhlen observes,

> Inasmuch as written language, so far as anyone knows, is only about 5,000 years old—and spoken language by itself leaves no historical trace at all—one might imagine that language would have little to tell us about human pre-history. But in fact it can tell us a great deal, not only about languages that existed long before the invention of writing, but also about the prehistorical migrations that led to the present distribution of the world's languages. (p. 3)

In this book, we won't go into the history of languages, particularly English, in any great details, though we would urge every English language arts teacher to take a good course in language history or to read some of the books that we suggest at the close of this chapter. English, as you may know, is an especially rich language in a polyglot sort of way, and a study of its history can help you understand, for example, why English spelling is so complex and inconsistent (leading to numerous ill-fated efforts over the years to reform it); why our language is so rich in synonyms drawn from all over Europe with their bases in Scandinavian language, the Germanic languages, the romance languages; and how the "grammar" of English, that you so naturally use every time you speak, has evolved over the past 1,400 years.

Linguists and anthropologists observe that oral language is generally acquired surprisingly easily in *any* society, with the help of tutoring from parents, family, and community members. (Note, for example, that you and every other member of your family came to school talking successfully, without the benefit of any formal instruction or schooling.) As linguists remind us, *spoken* language is *the* language, and *writing* is simply a representation of speech. Nevertheless, writing, because of its relative permanence and its high visibility, has always attracted a great deal of attention, and we find that just about as soon as scripts emerged in the world—about 3500 B.C. by most accounts—teachers of scripts emerged.

In his history, *Writing: The Story of Alphabets and Scripts* , Georges Jean argues that in Egypt, scribes held a particularly important and powerful position, for they possessed the important, almost mystical power to record words, words of literature, the utterances and decrees of the kings, national history, hymns and poetry, homages to the dead, scientific and medical information, astronomical discoveries, and so on. "The Egyptian scribes were, of course, masters of the art of writing," Jean explains, "and therefore masters of teaching—for teaching meant almost exclusively the teaching of writing" (p. 39). Much of the teaching methodology, he reports, was rote work:

> The art of writing was taught through dictation and the copying of exercises, initially using the cursive script and later, hieroglyphs. Corporal punishment was considered an effective means of education, if one is to believe the Egyptian saying: "A boy's ears are on his back; he listens when he is beaten." (pp. 39–40)

A tradition of rote work dominates much of literacy education for its first millennium, and much of that instruction focused on what we would today call encoding and decoding skills—how to decipher words on the page, how to get words down on the page. There was not a great deal of interest in "imaginative" or "creative" writing or on reading for pleasure or satisfaction, two important themes of this book. The Greek writer/scribe, for example, had to master the sophisticated skill of recognizing letters in undifferentiated strings, for nospaceswereplacedbetweenwords.Writing flowed from one side of the page to another, then reversed direction at the end of a line and came back the other way—a form of script that was named after agricultural plowing where the farmer, reaching the end of a row, turns around and goes in the other direction.

Literacy in Greece was taught by a writing master or *grammatistes,* which gives a strong hint as to the nature of instruction. Learning to read and write was analytic—meaning that the language was broken down into its component parts for mastery—and we can only assume that learning was tedious. Students—boys for the most part—learned the alphabet (the word itself derived from the Greek *alpha* and *beta*) from beginning to end, from *alpha* to *omega.* Students then progressed to syllables and then to words of one syllable, two syllables, and three syllables—a pattern of instruction that, as we'll see, was to influence literacy instruction powerfully for the next two thousand years. Grammar was next in the instructional hierarchy, followed by rhetoric, the latter primarily focusing on oral language and public speaking.

Despite the apparent rigidity of this curriculum (and we will have much to say about the problems with this bits-to-whole approach to literacy in future chapters), it was linked to a remarkably rich educational system. Greek education placed strong emphasis on reading the classic poets and playwrights, Homer, Pindar, Aristophanes, and others. Older learners studied these texts thoroughly as a way of knowing their cultural heritage. Greek education also emphasized physical skills and powers (culminating in both the first Olympics and in warfare) as well as a kind of streetwise application of knowledge, for example, constructing speeches on all sorts of civic and moral issues. The Greek student not only knew grammar and rhetoric and the classics, but constantly sought application of that knowledge in society.

Indeed, for the Greeks, literacy and ethics were closely linked. In his famous book describing his ideal society, *The Republic,* Plato would ban rhetoric teachers on the grounds that they merely taught argument for the sake of argument, not from deeply rooted understanding of ethics and truths. He stereotyped his rivals, the Sophists, so successfully that even today "sophistry" means verbal trickery, mere "rhetoric." In fact the Sophists were also concerned about knowledge and ethics, but unlike Plato (and more like modern thinkers), they didn't believe that humans could arrive at absolute or certain truths.

Many of those concerns, as well as a valuing of the classics in literature, were adapted by the Romans, including placing high value on literacy as a core of education. The Roman rhetorician Cicero, for example, made a strong case for the orator, not as a sophist or snake-oil salesman, but as one of the most broadly educated people in the community, one who was deeply familiar with traditions and customs but who also had developed skill at learning in many fields and could thus master new material well enough to deliver sound orations on it.

In his *Institutes of Oratory,* Quintillian, another Roman rhetorician, spoke in depth about the teaching of language and described some practices that, like traditions in grammar, were to be passed on to schoolchildren for literally thousands of years. He favored translation exercises, for example, where young scholars would translate Greek texts into Latin, with particular interest in creating proper, even eloquent Latin forms, rather than literal or word-for-word translations. Students would write paraphrases and abstracts of the words of great writers and would complete exercises and practice declamations. Often students would be given broad problems, "Did so-and-so behave properly?" and asked to argue the case, generating long lists of arguments and frequently embellishing those arguments through careful application of metaphors and other figures of speech. Although this course of instruction was difficult, and, we suspect, often tedious, Quintillian also spoke of the qualifications and skills of the teacher in language that sounds remarkably familiar:

> Let him adopt, then, above all things, the feelings of a parent toward his pupils, and consider that he succeeds in the place of those by whom the children were entrusted to him. . . . Let his austerity not be stern, nor his affability too easy, lest dislike arise from the one, or contempt from the other. . . . Let him not be of an angry temper, and yet not a conniver at what ought to be corrected. . . . In amending what requires correction, let him not be harsh, and least of all, not reproachful; for that very circumstance, that some tutors blame as if they hated, deters many young men from their proposed course of study. (Cited in Bizzell and Herzberg, p. 299)

From the Greeks and the Romans (as you've heard many times before) a great many of these traditions were passed to England and thence to the United States. Through the Middle (sometimes erroneously called the "Dark") Ages, classical learning went through a series of declines and resurgences, often in competition with the

Christian church, which had its own body of wisdom that it valued and held to be antithetical and superior to many of the pre-Christian classics. For our purposes, it is especially important to note that the medieval universities developed a curriculum that centered on literacy. The first tier of study was called the *trivium,* whose three components were *grammar, rhetoric,* and *dialectic* (or logical argument). After students had mastered literacy skills they moved to the next tier of the *quadrivium,* whose four components were arithmetic, geometry, music, and astronomy. While that second array of subjects seems a bit eclectic from a modern perspective, it is critical to note that literacy was perceived as a gateway to higher order learning.

TEACHING THE MOTHER TONGUE

At the beginning of the European and English renaissance period in the fifteenth century, the printing presses of Johannes Gutenberg and others, coupled with the Protestant Reformation, created a vast interest in literacy, especially literacy in the vernacular, one's native language, rather than the classical languages. Books, monographs, pamphlets, and broadsheets prospered all over England, and it's no coincidence that some of the most revered and honored writing in English emerged at this time. Building on the tradition of Geoffrey Chaucer, one of the earlier writer/poets to compose in English rather than a non-native tongue, Francis Bacon, William Shakespeare, John Donne, John Locke, and others composed and were published in English. It's also no coincidence that during this renaissance scholars first began to write grammars to describe the English tongue, and it is no coincidence that the lowest schools came to be called "grammar" schools, a term that was in use in the United States until quite recently. Thus it is not surprising that at this same time, we see the production of the first textbooks for use by English-speaking students. Modeled closely on their Greek and Latin forbears, these texts took an analytic approach to the language, breaking it into its component parts for mastery in a pattern that went from small pieces to the comprehensive whole.

When the colonists fled from England to the New World and inscribed the date of 1642 on Plymouth Rock, their possessions included this long tradition of interest in literacy and models for instruction. By 1648, the colonists in Massachusetts demonstrated their interest in education by passing a law that every community of

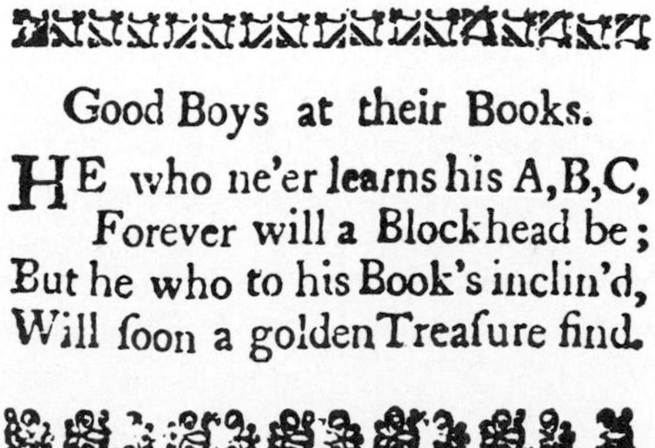

Good Boys at their Books.

H E who ne'er learns his A,B,C,
    Forever will a Blockhead be;
But he who to his Book's inclin'd,
Will soon a golden Treasure find.

Figure P.1   From the *New England Primer*

more than fifty families must provide instruction in the 3Rs of reading, writing, and arithmetic. Our choice for a starting point, then, of literacy instruction in America, is the little poem shown. It is one of the earliest efforts to motivate children to learn by extolling the virtues of literacy. *The New England Primer* was closely patterned after English textbooks and carried the imposing subtitle of *An easy and pleasant Guide to the Art of Reading, Adorn'd with Cuts. To which are added, The Assembly of Divines and Mr. Cotton's CATECHISM.* The values of reading—the "Golden Treasure"—promised to the children of New England were two-fold. First, reading (like its sister R, 'rithmetic) equipped a young person with the skills to function effectively in business. Second, and more important, the art of reading prepared a child to understand and receive religious instruction. As we'll see, these twin strands—reading as functional skill and reading for culture and values—continue to this day, sometimes contesting one another, sometimes seen as working in harmony.

The instructional strategy—the "pedagogy"—of the *Primer* went back over two thousand years to the pattern followed by the Greeks. The alphabet was taught and retaught with a variety of poems and mnemonic devices: A—"In *Adam's* Fall/We sinned all"; F—The idle *Fool*/Is whip't at School." (The latter suggests that instructional methodology might not have changed much from the Greeks either; literacy learning was seen as a rote skill requiring considerable discipline, and if that discipline were not forthcoming spontaneously from the young scholar, it would be administered by the teacher.)

This instruction in the alphabet was an elementary version of what we know today as "phonics," showing the relationship between written letters and their pronounced sounds. The *Primer* presented all such relationships as essentially invariable, ignoring the evolution of English spelling in its idiosyncratic complexity, where, for example, the sound of "F" as in Fool can also be represented "ph" (as in phonics), "gh" (enough), "ft" (soften) and even "v" (as in Chekhov). The *Primer* then taught syllables, essentially all possible vowel-consonant combinations such as (ab, ac, ad, af), then "Words of One Syllable," "Words of Two Syllables," up through "Words of Five Syllables"—a sequence of instruction that ranged from "fire" to a five syllable pronunciation of "for-ni-ca-ti-on."

Following this course of instruction, which would, in theory, equip the young person to read just about every word in the language, the *Primer* presented "The Lord's Prayer," "The Dutiful Child's Promises," "Lessons for Youth," Biblical excerpts, and the Catechism, or "Spiritual Milk For American Babes, Drawn out of the Breasts of both Testaments, for their Souls Nourishment." In its way, the *New England Primer* was a remarkably compact, one-volume curriculum—ordered, sequential, with clear-cut aims and outcomes. In our time, researchers have come to challenge the letter-to-syllables-to-words approach to teaching, arguing, among other things, that Colonial children may have learned to read in spite of this method, rather than because of it. But there can be little doubt that generations of children learned to read more or less successfully through a course of instruction solidly based on the *New England Primer* and its Greco-Anglo roots.

For many years, instruction in literacy centered on books like *The New England Primer.* Much instruction centered in home or "dame" schools, and few children received more than rudimentary instruction in English, while the academies and colleges still concentrated their language teaching on Latin and Greek. It was still widely assumed that higher literacy in one's mother tongue was a more or less natural acquisition, that once one had one's basic skills down, that reading and writing instruction was over with.

Much of the reading material young people consumed was overtly didactic, intended to teach morals, religious matter, and ethics, and for many years, textbooks drew directly on the *New England Primer* as a pedagogical model. After the American revolution, however, several interesting new trends emerged. One was interest in a uniquely American language, particularly as promoted by Noah Webster in his spellers, books that sold phenomenal numbers of copies. The "progressive," "eclectic" readers of William Holmes McGuffey were also a best selling, uniquely American contribution to education, offering a mix of moral advice and natural wisdom that prompted some "back-to-basics" advocates to actually reintroduce them into schools in the late twentieth century.

Another important post-revolutionary trend was the secularization of books and reading materials, breaking the domination of religious instruction as directly related to literacy. Many books, were, in fact designed for home instruction. One especially famous book for reading at home was *Goody Two-Shoes*, by H. W. Hewit, a book that has left its heroine's name imprinted in our language. "Goody" was a remarkably well-behaved child whose actual, but metaphorical name was Margery Meanwell. She

Figure P.2 Title page and text from a McGuffey Reader.

was shod with her nickname after expressing great joy over a new pair of shoes given to her by a clergyman, Mr. Smith. Goody/Margery was precocious in seeing how wise a man was Rev. Smith and astute in seeing that she could follow his model and teach herself:

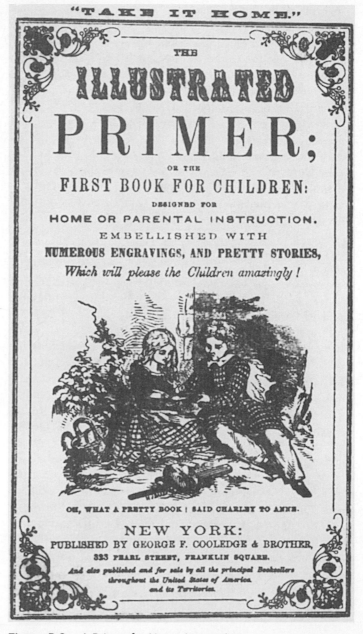

Figure P.3   *A Primer for Home Instruction*

Little Margery saw how good and how wise Mr. Smith was and concluded that this was owing to his great learning; therefore she wanted, of all things, to learn to read. For this purpose she used to meet the little boys and girls as they came from school, borrow their books, and sit down till they returned. By this means she soon got more learning than any of her playmates.

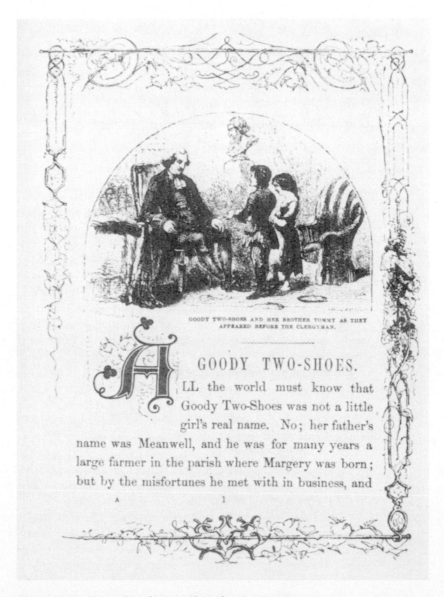

Figure P.4   From *Goody Two-Shoes* by H. W. Hewit.

Later, Goody participated in the dame school tradition by teaching other children to learn to spell and read, once again following the alphabetic method. Goody carved out shapes of the letters of the alphabet to teach those to her friends, then went through the syllables (*ba, be, bi, bo, bu*), and moved to full words. Because a book like *Goody Two-Shoes* was read aloud to children, parents were supplied with a basic course in "methods of teaching reading" simply by following the stages used by the precocious Goody in her own course of instruction.

The impulse toward public education for all students (as opposed, particularly, to the more selective system of British education, where a "public" school is actually what we would call "private") is deeply rooted in American culture. Initially only elementary school education was mandated, but the nineteenth century saw rapid growth in establishing secondary private academies and, eventually public high schools, and many of our state universities carry a founders' date in the mid- to late 1800s.

Especially important for our purposes is to note that literacy has been at the center of that democratic education: Knowing how to read and write is regarded as an unwritten bill of rights for all Americans.

CREATING A TRADITION

The movement toward literacy was soon extended beyond the basics of reading and writing (or, more accurately, word recognition and spelling). In his "Proposals for an Academy," Benjamin Franklin included recommendations for increased attention to the teaching of English at the secondary school level, and his own academy in Philadelphia emphasized English instruction for young men about to enter commercial life. Although English is today perceived as one of the humanities, allied with the fine arts and classics, it had to fight its way into the curriculum allied with "practical" skills in opposition to traditional education in Latin and Greek. Study the announcement in Figure P.5 (a document that is especially interesting because someone also used it as a piece of blotting paper; note the reversed writing two-thirds of the way down the page). The "primary department" of this school covered the basic elements of learning (not unlike the concept of the medieval "trivium"), including geography, and arithmetic, but dominated by the skills of literacy: grammar, reading, spelling, and writing. Some "advanced study" in those areas was also included as part of the Union School's aim to have "scholars. . . in this School, fully prepare themselves for *College,* as well as obtain a thorough education," and it's interesting that those advanced studies are called "the English branches." Although Greek, Latin, and French were offered along with chemistry, algebra, and geometry, the inclusion of a "practical" course in "surveying" provides important evidence of a shift away from a purely classical education under the rubric of "English."

Although there was some lamenting of the loss of tradition through the new emphasis on the English branches, the clear trend in the nineteenth century (and in the twentieth, for that matter) was toward education that, while paying due allegiance to classical traditions, was squarely aimed at preparing people to function in practical ways in society.

The mention of "grammar" in the Union School flier allows us to touch briefly on the history of that curricular mainstay, for from the first, and well ahead of the intro-

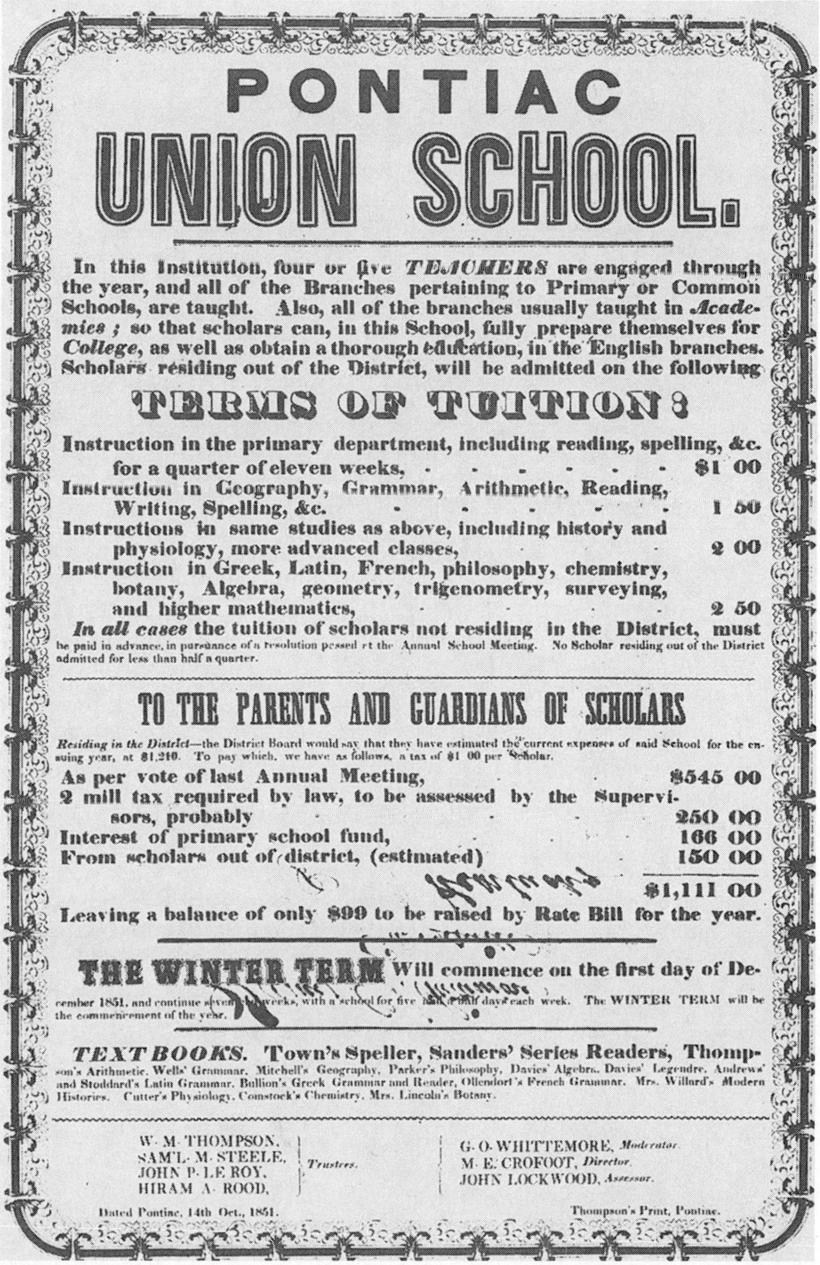

PONTIAC UNION SCHOOL.

In this Institution, four or five *TEACHERS* are engaged through the year, and all of the Branches pertaining to Primary or Common Schools, are taught. Also, all of the branches usually taught in *Academies*; so that scholars can, in this School, fully prepare themselves for *College*, as well as obtain a thorough education, in the English branches. Scholars residing out of the District, will be admitted on the following

TERMS OF TUITION:

Instruction in the primary department, including reading, spelling, &c. for a quarter of eleven weeks,	$1 00
Instruction in Geography, Grammar, Arithmetic, Reading, Writing, Spelling, &c.	1 50
Instructions in same studies as above, including history and physiology, more advanced classes,	2 00
Instruction in Greek, Latin, French, philosophy, chemistry, botany, Algebra, geometry, trigenometry, surveying, and higher mathematics,	2 50

In all cases the tuition of scholars not residing in the District, must be paid in advance, in pursuance of a resolution passed at the Annual School Meeting. No Scholar residing out of the District admitted for less than half a quarter.

TO THE PARENTS AND GUARDIANS OF SCHOLARS

Residing in the District—the District Board would say that they have estimated the current expenses of said School for the ensuing year, at $1,210. To pay which, we have as follows, a tax of $1 00 per Scholar.

As per vote of last Annual Meeting,	$545 00
2 mill tax required by law, to be assessed by the Supervisors, probably	250 00
Interest of primary school fund,	166 00
From scholars out of district, (estimated)	150 00
	$1,111 00

Leaving a balance of only $99 to be raised by Rate Bill for the year.

THE WINTER TERM Will commence on the first day of December 1851, and continue [illegible] weeks, with a school for five [illegible] half days each week. The WINTER TERM will be the commencement of the year.

TEXTBOOKS. Town's Speller, Sanders' Series Readers, Thompson's Arithmetic, Wells' Grammar, Mitchell's Geography, Parker's Philosophy, Davies' Algebra, Davies' Legendre, Andrews' and Stoddard's Latin Grammar, Bullion's Greek Grammar and Reader, Ollendorf's French Grammar, Mrs. Willard's Modern Histories, Cutter's Physiology, Comstock's Chemistry, Mrs. Lincoln's Botany.

W. M. THOMPSON,
SAM'L. M. STEELE,
JOHN P. LE ROY,
HIRAM A. ROOD, *Trustees.*

G. O. WHITTEMORE, *Moderator.*
M. E. CROFOOT, *Director.*
JOHN LOCKWOOD, *Assessor.*

Dated Pontiac, 14th Oct., 1851.

Thompson's Print, Pontiac.

Figure P.5 Announcement of the terms of tuition and taxation for an early public secondary school, 1851. Michigan History Collection.

duction of literature and composition, the schools taught English "Grammatickally." By the early 1900s, a number of grammar books were competitors in American schools, and by 1819 Princeton introduced a requirement for knowledge of grammar for college admission.

The grammarian whose books came to dominate in the schools was Lindley Murray, whose name became so synonymous with grammar instruction that students came to speak of studying their "Murray." Murray's grammar centered on mastery of parts of speech, followed by sentence analysis. His main pedagogical tool was "parsing," a form of sentence analysis that was said to discipline the mind while teaching students to speak and write "with propriety." Murray's work continued the moral tone of the primers and linked the use of language to proper human conduct. Murray said that as an author, he wanted "to promote in some degree":

> the cause of virtue, as well as of learning: and with this view, he has been studious, through the whole of the work, not only to avoid every example and illustration, which might have an improper effect on the minds of youth; but also to introduce, on many occasions, such as have moral and religious tendency. His attention to objects of so much importance will, he trusts, meet with the approbation of every well-disposed reader. If they were faithfully regarded in all books of education, they would doubtlessly contribute very materially to the order and happiness of society, by guarding the innocence, and cherishing the virtue, of the rising generation. (Cited in Geller, p. 75)

What an astonishing burden to place on the teaching of grammar! When, in our time, we sometimes wonder why people become so indignant over "improper grammar," we must remember the attitudes of a Lindley Murray and the importance he placed on purity and propriety in language. Nor was Murray alone in his interest in "guarding the innocence" of young people. Whether through literature, writing, or grammar instruction, English language arts teachers have long been perceived (and have often perceived themselves) as being defenders of the language against the onslaughts of barbarians, including their own students.

As a footnote in this fleeting look at grammar instruction, we must not leave out the contribution of Alonzo Reed and Brainerd Kellogg, who, in 1877 introduced the sentence diagram in their textbooks. Convinced that parsing of the sort practiced by Lindley Murray was not useful, they favored "the simple map, or diagram" that would:

> enable the pupil to present directly and vividly to the eye the exact function of every clause in the sentence, of every phrase in the clause, and of every word in the phrase—to picture the complete analysis of the sentence, with principal and subordinate parts in their proper relations. It is only by the aid of such a map, or picture, that the pupil; can, at a single view, see the sentence as an organic whole made up of many parts performing various functions in various relations.

They cautioned, confidently, that "analysis by diagram often becomes so interesting and so helpful that, like other good things, it is liable to be overdone." Generations of students to follow were to temper their teachers' enthusiasm for the sentence diagram by finding them difficult and obscure, rather than bringing about the clarity of understanding claimed by Reed and Kellogg.

More important, perhaps, is that the sentence diagram became a symbol for an attitude toward language instruction, one based in grammar, that said, essentially, that the understanding of grammar—the parts of English syntax—was not only

54   THE SENTENCE AND THE PARTS OF SPEECH

Analysis and Parsing

1. Ah! anxious wives, sisters, and mothers wait for the news.

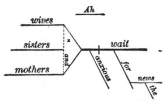

Explanation. The three short horizontal lines represent each a part of the compound subject. They are connected by dotted lines, which stand for the connecting word. The × shows that a conjunction is understood. The line standing for the word modifier is joined to that part of the subject line which represents the entire subject. Turn this diagram about, and the connected horizontal lines will stand for the parts of a compound predicate.

Oral Analysis. *Wives, sisters* and *mothers* form the compound subject; *anxious* is a modifier of the compound subject; *and* connects *sisters* and *mothers.*

Parsing. *And* is a conjunction connecting *sisters* and *mothers; ah* is an interjection, expressing a sudden burst of feeling.

Figure P.6   The Sentence Diagram. "As a means of discipline nothing can compare with a training in the logical analysis of the sentence." From Alonzo Reed and Brainerd Kellog. *Higher Lessons in English*, 1909, first edition, 1877.

essential to using language well, but was a prerequisite to its use. You may also see a pedagogical connection between traditions in the teaching of reading (from alphabet to whole word) and the teaching of grammar (from parts of speech to sentences). This tradition, the assumption that language is best taught from part to whole, runs very deep in literacy education, and as we will see, has given rise to strident controversies over the aims, purposes, and functions of teaching the English language arts in both schools and colleges.

The parts-versus-whole controversy could also be seen in the teaching of written composition, which followed grammar into the school program. By the mid-nineteenth century, teachers were coming to realize that mastery of grammar *per se* not only did not guarantee correctness in writing, it certainly didn't offer guarantees that students would write coherently and effectively. In the introduction to his *First Lessons in Composition* (1841), George Pyn Quackenbos quoted a county superintendent of schools:

> For a long time I have noticed with regret the almost entire neglect of the art of original composition in our common schools, and the want of a proper textbook upon this essential branch of education. Hundreds graduate from our common schools with no well-defined ideas of the construction of our language.

Richard Green Parker began his book, *Aids to English Composition* (1845) by noting:

> It would be presumptuous in any author to attempt to give rules, or to lay down laws to which all the departments of English Composition should be subjected. Genius cannot be fettered, and an original and thinking mind, replete with its own exuberance, will often burst out in spontaneous gushings, and open to itself new channels through which the treasures of thought will flow in rich and rapid currents.

Despite such apparently modern sentiments, which are solidly in the tradition that led to American progressive education a half century later, the actual implementation of writing instruction was far less libertarian and utilitarian than one might suppose. Many nineteenth-century texts emphasized analysis of structure—including discourse forms (*narration, description, exposition,* and *argumentation*), paragraph structure, and theme organization, including outlining skills. In her *Elements of English Composition* (1884), a text "for the lower grades of the High School," Miss L. A. Chittenden of the Ann Arbor, Michigan, High School reveals a mildly patronizing tone toward the young writer:

> The object has been to furnish, with as little theory as possible, such a set of directions and exercises as, even before the pupil has attained the maturity of mind necessary for the formal study of rhetoric, will enable him to become a tolerably correct composer; at least to avoid the blunders, if not to acquire the graces of composition.

Her book alternated chapters in grammar and punctuation with "exercises in composition," the latter featuring exercises called "reproductions," in which the student was to take a narrative poem—e.g. "The Leak in the Dyke," "The Sad Little Lass"—and reproduce or translate it into prose. Another kind of exercise was the "development," where students were given the bare bones of a story—"The Mouse and the Elephant," "Found Dead in the Street"—and asked to elaborate on it. Neither of these exercises actually called upon the students to develop material of their own, and both convey the notion that the young mind was simply too young, too empty for original composition. Both exercises, incidentally, are firmly rooted in classical traditions of teaching Latin and Greek, essentially *foreign* language exercises adapted for the mother tongue.

Chittenden's book also clearly reveals the interest of the nineteenth century teacher in correctness. The red pen as a way of marking errors, thoroughly discredited in our own time, was first advocated during this period, and a book like Copeland and Rideout's *Freshman English and Theme Correction at Harvard College* graphically illustrated a kind of error-intensive correcting of errors that was advocated for all levels of instruction.

The teaching of literature was a relative latecomer to the English language arts curriculum, added only during the final quarter of the nineteenth century. Although

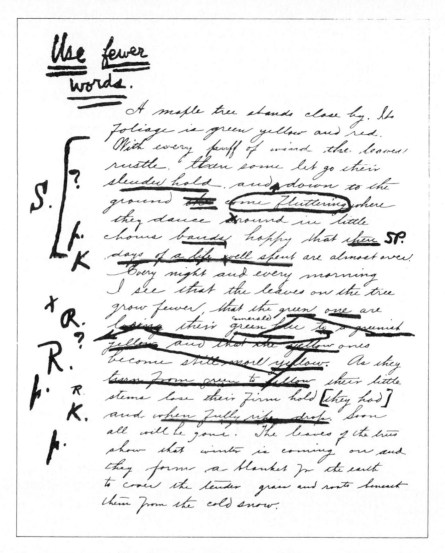

Figure P.7 C. T. Copeland and H. M. Ridout, *Freshman English and Theme Correction at Harvard College*, 1901.

reading had been central to schooling since Colonial times, the study of literature had been largely limited to the Greek and Roman classics, read in the academies and colleges in the original Greek and Latin. However, growing interest in American writing as having merits of its own—promoted in no small measure by the literary successes of people like Cooper, Irving, Hawthorne, Emerson, and Thoreau, the canonical guys of American lit classes today—and an increasing interest in practical subjects led to the introduction of selected works in English in the 1870s and 1880s.

Teachers were initially more concerned with literary history, biography, criticism, and even vocabulary (Anglo-Saxon versus Latinized words) than with the content of the literature. The last quarter of the nineteenth century saw the development of the literature "compendium," a handbook of information on authors and their works. Although the youngsters who studied Jennie Ellis Keysor's *Sketches of American Authors* might never have *read* anything by James Fenimore Cooper, they would know that Cooper's literary style was "pure, simple, strong, breathing of untrammeled outdoor existence; weakest in portrayal of character and strong in description of scenes and narration of events." They would learn and recite that Cooper himself was "truthful, fearless, uncompromising, sensitive, impulsive, pure-minded, partisan, aristocratic, [and] ingenuous."

The emphasis on knowledge about literature was promoted both directly and indirectly by the colleges, particularly through the medium of the entrance examination. Concerned about the preparation of entering students, many colleges created their own exams, requiring students to demonstrate their knowledge of grammar, literature, and composition. Classics of British and American literature provided "set" readings for the exams, and these books, in turn, found their way into the schools. By 1880, *Silas Marner* was a staple in the school curriculum, to remain as a curricular mainstay for ninety years. A standard set of Shakespearean plays—*Julius Caesar, As You Like It, Macbeth, Hamlet,* and *The Merchant of Venice*—became established as a standard repertory for study by precollegiate high school students. Those titles, augmented by *Romeo and Juliet,* and minus *The Merchant of Venice* (censored in recent years for its alleged anti-Semitic content), have remained as the Shakespearean canon ever since.

By the end of the nineteenth century, examinations had proliferated to the point that many school teachers demanded a unified examination and a single list of books. Regional groups such as the North Central and Middle States associations of school and college teachers were formed to help solve the problem, and these led to the founding of the College Entrance Examination Board in 1900. The resulting common book lists and exams had a standardizing effect, and tended to reduce literary study to biographical, philological, or narrowly analytic drudgery. Writing from a vantage point a quarter of a century later in 1931, Oscar McPherson wrote in *Library Journal:*

> About twenty-five years ago, . . . adolescents in general stopped reading the classics of [the nineteenth century] for their own entertainment. I was and am convinced that the demise of those classics, so far as the average boy or girl en route to college was concerned, is traceable directly to the college entrance examination boards. Those boards, then made up largely of members of college faculties, composed their own restricted lists of thus formally decreed classics" (Cited in *The English Journal,* October 1985, p. 72).

Well before the twentieth century, then, a tradition had been established. English (the term "language arts" was still a half-century away) consisted of three major components: language, composition, and literature. *Language* meant grammar, including parts of speech, the nature of the sentence, parsing, diagramming, and sentence correction. *Composition* was principally the study of the structure of essays (from paragraph to theme), followed by the writing of practice themes, that followed by error correction. *Literature* centered on examining selected great works from a historical/critical perspective. As Arthur Applebee has shown in his history of English teaching, *Tradition and Reform*, that structure has been challenged throughout the twentieth century, but its roots run deep and strong. Although the influence of the nineteenth century is less strong at the elementary and middle school levels, a look at the curriculum of a great many high schools today (and the textbook displays at conventions and conferences) clearly show the residual power of that program. In addition, readers will also recognize its influence over the college English curriculum and in the courses taken by prospective English language arts teachers.

BREAKING WITH TRADITION

So what's wrong with that tradition? If it worked for the nineteenth century and for the medievalists and for the Romans and the Greeks, why challenge it? Beginning in 1917, several national committees objected to the overly academic nature of the curriculum, in many respects, a college curriculum in miniature. Further, under the influence of John Dewey and the progressive education movement, educators were beginning to consider the imaginative powers of young people and to focus on engaging them in rich and relevant experiences. This approach to teaching was probably best demonstrated in the writings of Hughes Mearns in the 1920s. Describing his teaching at the Lincoln School in New York City (and dedicating his book *Creative Youth* to those students), Mearns attacked the conventional approach to literature. The foreword to that book, written by Otis Caldwell, observed:

> We have drilled, memorized, analyzed, dissected, and philosophized up and within the 'world's best literature.' At the end we have often found our students examinable regarding certain standard selections, but mechanically unsympathetic with them; and there was no burning fire within driving them toward endeavors to shape their own reflections and buoyant visions into forms worthy of record in print.

Mearns's book described a program of "supervised" and "unsupervised" reading, the latter—free reading—a radical concept—a mix of teacher-guided and student-selected books that would include "juveniles of distinction" (meaning excellent or established books for young people, e.g., *Little Women*), "juveniles purely" (strictly entertainment reading, *The Rover Boys, The Campfire Girls*), "standard authors" (e.g., Kipling, Conrad, Stevenson, Frost, in increasing quantities as students moved through the school), and "commonplace adult fiction" (popular reading, *The Lone Horseman of the Pampas, The Middlemarch Mystery*). Although there was a touch of snobbery in his categories (and a presumption that the distinctions between quality and commonplace literature were clear), one can see in Mearns's work a genuine effort to bridge the gap between students' immediate interests and concerns and their long-range growth toward adulthood.

Mearns was emphatic in declaring that student writing deserved publication, display, and praise, that young people were capable of creative writing of quality. He published his students' work in literary magazines, and over one-third of the material in his books consisted of examples of student's imaginative writing, prose and poetry,

104   CREATIVE YOUTH

BOOKS OF INTEREST PRIMARILY TO ADULTS

GRADES	VII	VIII	IX	X	XI	XII
Standard authors: to Kipling	.15	.10	.25	.37	.30	.19
Standard authors: from Kipling on (Kipling, Masefield, Conrad, Shaw, Barrie, Synge, Stevenson, Moody, O'Neill, Frost, for example)	.14	.20	.17	.25	.36	.32
Contemporary writers of consequence (Poole, Merrick, Cather, Train, Walpole, Morley, Stevens, for example)	.06	.29	.23	.28	.27	.46
Commonplace adult fiction (*The Lone Horseman of the Pampas*, *The Middlemarsh Mystery*, *The Purple Fan* are type titles)	.09	.12	.07	.06	.05	.03

UNSUPERVISED READING

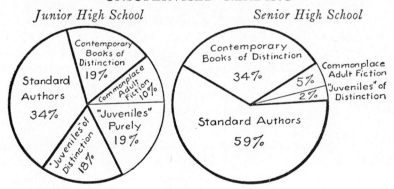

A random selection of eight hundred titles of books read outside of class discloses a high standard of reading-for-interest: in the Junior High School 71% and in the Senior High School 95% may be classified as books of distinction.

Figure P.8   *Creative Youth* by Hughes Mearns (1925).

far removed from the sterility of the college preparatory examination writing. Above all, Mearns (and others who shared his views) was uncompromising in his positivism toward children. Concluding the foreword, Caldwell echoed Mearns's belief in children. Children may "try some dangerous experiments," Caldwell observed (adding "Our generation did so."), but:

. . . so long as young people really desire the good of one another as they do, even more I believe, than ever before, they are to be trusted in their thinking and in their writing. This trust must not be a half-hearted trust, but must be an actively sympathetic confidence. . . . Reading the writings which follow will surely give a large measure of new hope to all those older folk who have retained plasticity and educability."

The traditional literature curriculum remained in place, the kind of writing students did and the kind of grammatical instruction and correction they received changed little in a great many schools.

A major attempt at breaking with the tradition took place in the middle 1930s, documented by a book titled *An Experience Curriculum in English* (NCTE, 1935). The report presented the work of a committee chaired by W. Wilbur Hatfield, longtime editor of both *The English Journal* and its college edition, which eventually became *College English*. The report once again emphasized the students' own experience, knowledge, and creativity in language learning and stressed the social value of English. Perhaps its two most important developments were its emphasis on teaching literature by patterns, themes, and ideas and its focus on teaching socially useful skills such as letter writing and conversation. Later the Experience Curriculum was to be criticized for its clearly middle-class values—writing invitations and thank you notes, always writing with "tact" and good manners—but it also clearly shows the interest of the profession in combining concern for the traditional elements with a practical and social focus.

Published just three years later, another NCTE committee report, *A Correlated Curriculum in English* (1939), explored ways of fusing or correlating elementary, secondary, and college English with work in other fields. This document reflects one of the first expressions of interest in interdisciplinarity, a public statement showing that language (unlike many other fields and disciplines) was concerned with materials beyond its own, immediate traditions. It anticipated current interest in "language across the curriculum" and offered teachers an opportunity to make language study something more than literary history, *belles lettres,* and syntactic correctness.

However, the potential of the *Experience Curriculum* and the *Correlated Curriculum* was never realized. Some educational historians felt that the outbreak of World War II and an ensuing interest in English as part of the war effort blunted the effects of the new programs. Others believe that these experience-based curricula were perceived as too permissive, too "progressive," too exclusively focused on social skills while ignoring traditional academic interests. Some critics and teachers of the era also felt that the *Correlated Curriculum* would mean the death of English, which would become fragmented among other disciplines (a worry that has resurfaced as part of the language-across-the-curriculum movement).

In the early 1950s, a Commission on the English Curriculum of the National Council of Teachers of English published an extraordinarily ambitious five-volume series on the k-college curriculum. It introduced the term "English language arts" (a term we will use throughout this book) to emphasize that this field was more than traditional "English" studies and to reflect the progressive interest in language as an imaginative or creative "art." In launching the first volume in 1952, *The English Language Arts*, the Committee acknowledged that "the goals of teaching the language arts are as old as the ideals of Western civilization," including clear thinking, effective

LITERATURE, GRADES 7—12

5. PRIMARY OBJECTIVE: To observe man's industrial expansion.
   ENABLING OBJECTIVES: To compare industry as it was before our time with our own industrial age; to participate
   vicariously with men and women who worked and are
   working under conditions both good and bad; to analyze
   our present economic system, and to compare it with
   systems of other days.
   Typical Materials: Silas Marner (Eliot); David Copperfield
   (Dickens); The Last of the Mohicans (Cooper); The Slave Ship
   (Johnston); The Luck of Roaring Camp (Harte); Roughing It
   (Twain); Two Years Before the Mast (Dana); A Son of the
   Middle Border (Garland); The Oregon Trail (Parkman); The
   Crossing (Churchill); Seven Iron Men (de Kruif).

6. PRIMARY OBJECTIVE: To observe the effects of widening
   trade horizons on our daily lives.
   ENABLING OBJECTIVES: To see how new frontiers and new
   customs were the direct result of the desire of man to
   increase his trading area; to catch some idea of the need
   for invention, investigation, and discovery; to note the
   organization of big business and the resulting efficiency
   and economy which it implies.
   Typical Materials: I Hear America Singing (Whitman); Modern
   Pioneers (Cohen and Scarlett); Pete of the Steel Mills (Hall);
   Making of an American (Riis); Our Foreign Born Citizens
   (Beard); "The Thinker" (Braley); Andrew Carnegie's Own
   Story (Brochhausen); At School in the Promised Land (Antin);
   Greatness Passing By (Neibuhr); The Pit and The Octopus
   (Norris); The Harbor (Poole); I Went to Pit College (Gil-
   fillan).

Figure P.9 Teaching literature by patterns, themes, and ideas. From *An Experience Curriculum in English* (1935). Note that in addition to expanding literary study into social domains, the Experience Curriculum also drew on a widening range of literature, including contemporary works. At the same time, the tradition—here represented by *Silas Marner* and *David Copperfield*—continued as a strong component in the program.

communication, thoughtful reading, and intelligent listening in support of "democratic ways of living." Moreover, the Committee reemphasized the power of literature "to quicken the understanding and to sensitize the feelings." But times change, and the Committee argued that the traditional goals had to be reinterpreted in terms of modern society. Reflecting the progressive movement of the first half of the century, it linked the language arts closely to "the growth of young people" and continued to

WHAT'S YOUR TELEPHONE SCORE?

Do you?

	YES	SOME-TIMES	NO
1. Answer promptly			
2. Greet the caller pleasantly			
3. Identify yourself properly			
4. Explain waits			
5. Leave word where you're going			
6. Ask questions tactfully			
7. Take the message			
8. Signal the operator slowly			
9. Know the number			
10. Allow time to answer			
11. Ask if convenient to talk			
12. Speak in a natural tone			
13. Visualize the person			
14. Say "Thank you" and "You're welcome"			
15. Listen attentively			
16. Use the customer's name			
17. Speak directly into transmitter			
18. Apologize for mistakes			
19. End the call properly			
20. Replace receiver gently			
Total			

Figure P.10   Answering the telephone, from *Building Better English 9* by Mellie John, Paulene M. Yates, and Edward N. DeLaney. Copyright © 1951 by Harper & Row Publishers. Reprinted by permission.

PRINCIPAL PARTS   PARTICIPLES AND INFINITIVES

Present Tense: *see* ⟶ Present Participle: *see*ing
            ⟶ Present Infinitive: to *see*

Past Participle: *seen* ⟶ Perfect Participle: having *seen*
            ⟶ Perfect Infinitive: to have *seen*

Practice 3 Using the Principal Parts

For each of the verbs below make two charts like those above. Use *I* as the subject of the verb when you write the tenses. Several pupils may each write the charts for one verb on the board.

1. go	5. come	9. bring	13. shrink
2. lie	6. hear	10. sever	14. acquire
3. sell	7. swim	11. write	15. discuss
4. walk	8. take	12. choose	16. flutter

Practice 4 A Verb's Progress in Outline

Write the forms of any six of the irregular verbs listed on page 173. Follow the model below.

Example: PRINCIPAL PARTS

    Present tense: Today I *take*
    Past tense: Yesterday I *took*
    Past Participle: For a long time I have *taken*

Present tense: I *take*	Present perfect tense: I *have taken*
Past tense: I *took*	Past perfect tense: I *had taken*
Future tense: I *shall take*	Future perfect tense: I *shall have taken*

Figure P.11 Graphics and grammar. From Don M. Wolfe and Josie Lewis, *Enjoying English 10*, 1964. Copyright © 1964 by L. W. Singer Company. Reprinted by permission of Random House, Inc.

stress the role of "experiences in the Language Arts program." It exhibited a concern for the "Challenge of Individual Differences. " It articulated a need for a "Modern View of Grammar and Linguistics," including recognition of the naturalness of language change and a call for teachers to be tolerant and understanding of dialect differences and for grammar to be taught "functionally," directly linked to clear writing. The Committee called for a "student-centered" approach to teaching literature, with considerable emphasis on wide and individualized reading, and at the college level, it suggested the need for broad general, liberal education and offered alternatives to the traditional chronological/historical approach.

Despite the depth and thoughtfulness of these five volumes, like so many committee reports, the work of the Commission on English was slow to be adopted. A few elements of the experience approach filtered into the schools, most notably the concern for teaching social graces such as answering the telephone. Yet the familiar chronological-historical approach to literature remained in place, and the thematic emphasis of the 1930s appeared in modified form in a few junior high school texts with themes such as "Animals," "Friends," and "Family." The new look of the fifties was often graphic, not pedagogical. Texts were printed in multiple colors, with "amusing" drawings to illustrate rules and principles. Textbooks tried to stress the *fun* in English, as illustrated by such series titles as *Enjoying English* and *Enjoying Life Through Literature.*

Interestingly, possibly the most influential textbook of the 1950s emphasized neither fun nor graphics; it was a stern little volume called *Handbook of English,* written by a high school teacher, John Warriner. Just as Lindley Murray's books became synonymous with "grammar" in the nineteenth century, "Warriner's" came to mean grammar for generations of mid-twentieth century teachers and students. Equally interesting are the similarities in content between Murray's and Warriner's books. Both men taught the basic structure of English through traditional grammar, and each succeeded with his book because he told about this structure more clearly than anyone else in his time.

SCHOOLING, SOCIETY, AND THE "NEW ENGLISH"

Perhaps the strongest challenge yet to the tradition grew from events outside education: the launching of the Soviet Union's "Sputnik" satellite in 1957. This event opened the space era and shocked the United States, which had assumed they would be first in space and that the Russians were far behind in rocket technology. No one had imagined that the Russians possessed such technological skills, which, incidentally, could also be used to launch nuclear warheads at an enemy. Suddenly, American education found itself blamed for the "missile gap." If the schools had not been so "soft," so "progressive," it was argued, our students would have learned more and American technological supremacy would have been preserved.

Initially, this concern, and even anger, was directed toward teachers of the sciences and mathematics. In 1958 Congress funded the National Defense Education Act, which provided funds for curriculum development and teacher in-service training in mathematics and science. The NDEA completely ignored English. However, the National Council of Teachers of English argued for the centrality of literacy

Handbook of English

JOHN E. WARRINER
Head of the English Department,
Garden City High School, Garden
City, Long Island, New York

The English Workshop Series

HARCOURT, BRACE AND COMPANY

NEW YORK   CHICAGO

Figure P.12 Cover from *Handbook of English* by John E. Warriner, copyright © 1951 by Harcourt, Brace & Company, reprinted by permission of the publisher.

studies in the schools and published a monograph with the propagandistic title, *The National Defense and the Teaching of English* (1961). NCTE's effort was rewarded when, in 1962, Congress provided for a series of English summer institutes and "Project English" curriculum study centers in the English language arts, part of an expanded NDEA.

A variety of "new English" programs emerged. At one extreme, educators looked toward the emerging "transformational generative" grammar of Noam Chomsky to provide a structure for English. This, in turn, led to publication of a number of "linguistic" textbooks for the high schools, most short-lived because of their complexity and their remoteness from actual language use. Other teachers, drawing on the roots of progressivism in America, looked to students' growth and development for the organizing principles of curriculum. For instance, at the Hunter College (New York) project, Marjorie Smiley and her team produced a series of high-interest, thematically-organized, graphically interesting textbooks designed for use by a heterogeneous school population. At Northwestern University, Wallace Douglas (to whom this book is dedicated) wrote pioneering materials that described "the process of composition," based on the notion that students needed to learn, not rhetorical forms, but ways of planning, organizing, revising, and polishing their work.

The "new English" revolution was also linked to several other movements in teaching:

- In the mid–1960s, a group of "romantic" critics of education—John Holt, Jonathan Kozol, Herbert Kohl, and George Leonard—to name a few—wrote indictments of the schools for being oppressive and static. Learning, the critics argued, must be student-directed, natural, positive, and pleasurable. Their writings led to an "open classroom" movement to reflect these principles, and some schools were even architecturally planned as "open space" institutions, where students and teachers could move freely about in essentially interdisciplinary, student-centered, individualized ways.

- Paperback books became common in the schools. Formerly perceived as "blue" literature sold mostly at drugstores (and hidden by pubescents under their laundry), paperbacks came of age, making a wide range of classic and contemporary literature available to English language arts teachers at low cost. Daniel Fader's 1966 *Hooked on Books* argued persuasively for the sort of free reading program that had originally been proposed as early as the 1920s, now made more practical with the use of paperbacks. Scholastic publishers offered an innovative series of thematic literature units, boxes of books that could be toted into the classroom, containing core paperback anthologies and a half dozen copies each of a dozen free-reading books on the theme.

- An "Anglo-American" Seminar on the Teaching of English, held at Dartmouth College in 1966, brought together British and American educators to discuss new directions. This "Dartmouth Seminar" was highly critical of traditional approaches, in his book, *Growth Through English,* John Dixon described the historical evolution of English language arts instruction through three "models":

> The first centered on *skills*: it fitted an era when *initial* literacy was the prime demand. The second stressed the *cultural heritage*, the need for a civilizing and socially unifying content. The third (and current) model focuses on *personal growth*: on the need to re-examine the learning processes and the meaning to the individual. . . " (Dixon, 1968, 1975).

- At the high school level, elective courses came into vogue, replacing the traditional high school courses—English I, II, III, IV—with a range of courses, from "mini-courses" of a few weeks to semester-long courses. Many of these courses were based around paperback books, displacing the hard-bound anthologies. There were courses in "Sports Literature," "For Girls Only," "Humor," and "Supernatural Literature" along with conventional literature such as "Shakespeare" and even electives in "Transformational Grammar."

Underlying all of this change was America's military engagement in Viet Nam, an event whose effect on the values and politics of this country is still being assessed. The national debate, the national shift of consciousness was very much in keeping with the tenets of a "personal growth" approach to education.

As the 1970s dawned, then, a revolution from the tradition seemed, if not complete, at least solidly under way. The traditional "tripod" of literature, language, and composition, with more or less common course content for all students, seemed to have been replaced by student-centered programs based on a wider range of reading materials than had ever been seen in the schools.

But the revolution was by no means complete. Nor, as it turned out, had the schools entirely discarded tradition.

For one thing, much revolutionary activity took place only in the pages of professional journals and in conference meeting rooms. Teachers "in the know" kept up with and experimented with the latest in professional ideas. Some teachers picked up the trappings of the new education, but did not totally synthesize the theory; thus they might place their students' desks in a circle and replace their red pencils with gray, but they kept on teaching their Warriner's and the traditional chronological literature. And vast numbers of teachers were either opposed to the new directions (for we teachers do tend to teach as we were taught), thought them excessive, or simply didn't think very much about them.

Further, beneath the glitter, the "new English" had some obvious weaknesses. Elective courses at the high school level energized faculty and were popular with students, but sometimes the concept of "curriculum" disappeared under a blanket of choices. In their eagerness to replace the traditions of *skills* and *cultural heritage*, teachers may have startled the public with themes and courses such as "Who Am I?" or "Rebels with a Cause," and the movement certainly bred suspicion in the general public that teachers were ignoring basics and fundamentals, that they had "thrown correctness out the window," that nobody cared about the values of previous generations.

STASIS AND CHANGE

The recent history of English language arts instruction lies, for the most part, within the lifetimes and experiences of readers of this book. Whether you are preparing to become a teacher or have been in the classroom for a while, you will recognize the trends, issues, problems, and debates that we will describe next, and you can test our description against your own understanding and appreciation of the English language arts.

For us, this relatively recent history was catalyzed by an event in 1974. In that year, the College Entrance Examination Board announced that scores on the Scholastic Aptitude Test of verbal ability had been dropping for over a decade. The announcement immediately focused attention on public education, and although the SAT could not be properly regarded as an accurate measure of the quality of schools (it is, after all, administered only to a fraction of college-bound students and tests a limited range of skills), the media were quick to indict the schools for perceived failures. In particular *Newsweek* magazine devoted an entire issue to the "crisis" in literacy, declaring:

> If your children are attending college, the chances are that when they graduate they will be unable to write ordinary, expository English with any real degree of lucidity. If they are in high school and planning to attend college, the chances are less than even that they will be able to write English at the minimal college level when they get there. If they are not planning to attend college, their skills in writing English may not even qualify them for secretarial or clerical work. And if they are attending elementary school, they are almost certainly not being given the kind of required reading material, much less writing instruction, that might make it possible for them eventually to write comprehensible English. Willy-nilly, the educational system is spawning a generation of semiliterates. (December 8, 1975, p. 58, Copyright © 1975 by Newsweek, Inc. All rights reserved. Reprinted by permission.)

Much of the *Newsweek* article could have been dismissed as journalistic hyperbole. Looking at that passage alone the reader might observe a combination of gross over generalizations, coupled with waffle words, "almost certainly," "might make it possible," "may not even qualify." Nevertheless, the impact of this article and dozens of similar ones appearing in newspapers and magazines nationwide, led to what became called "the back-to-basics" movement. Under public and administrative pressure, and often of their own volition, a great many English language arts teachers returned to the traditional approaches to literature, language, and composition. Within just a couple of years, a great many high schools replaced their elective programs with the older English I, II, III, IV approach, and the literature and grammar textbooks returned, replacing the paperbacks and high interest, accessible reading books of the previous decade or so. Despite a considerable body of research generated by Project English to suggest that the traditional approach itself was failing youngsters, classrooms returned to methods that had been challenged and frequently discredited throughout the century. In 1976, for example, in conjunction with celebration of the American Bicentennial, the publisher brought out a new edition of Warriner's *Handbook,* wrapped in red, white, and blue covers and called the "Heritage Edition." The publisher's vague claim that the book had "passed the test of time for millions" was apparently believed, and the book enjoyed its best sales ever.

Indeed, even as the New English was emerging in the 1970s, some new terms began to crop up in the professional literature: "behavioral objectives, "accountability," "mandated goals." While educators in many disciplines were moving in the direction of broad concept- or inquiry-based learning, others had been calling for more assessment and quantification as a means of creating more efficient, effective school curricula. In 1962, Robert Mager's influential *Preparing Instructional Objectives* called for increasing specificity in stating learning goals. Mager's interest was not in something as apparently vague as "personal growth"; his book was intended for anyone "interested in *transmitting skills and knowledge* to others" (emphasis added). The book presented the "behavioral" objective, a goal that would state the specific "behavioral" outcomes to be observed, the conditions under which they would be observed, and the criteria for successful performance. The links between this approach and Skinnerian behavioral psychology were obvious, for Mager, like Skinner, wasn't particularly interested in knowing what was inside a person's (or animal's) head, merely on how that critter performed a set task. While some skills (e.g., mastery of a spelling list) and knowledge (e.g., the date of the *Lyrical Ballads*) in the English language arts could be measured in this way, clearly such multifaceted skills as writing a successful letter to the editor or relating the concept of "romanticism" to contemporary literature could be fit into the behavioral mode only with difficulty.

Nevertheless, the behavioral objective appealed to a public convinced the schools were failing, and Mager's work became part of a much larger movement toward local, state, and national assessment of minimum objectives. So-called accountability models spread so rapidly that by the mid–1970s, state departments of education and local school districts all over the country were industriously engaged in writing objectives and developing assessment programs. The conflict between such programs and student-centered or progressive English language arts was dramatically shown by artist David Kirkpatrick on the cover of *The English Journal* .

Not all teachers responded by retreating into traditional approaches. Indeed, groups such as the National Council of Teachers of English, the National Writing Project (formed in part in response to the writing "crisis"), and the International Reading Association continued to explore and advocate New English models. Many argued that the new approaches could not possibly be responsible for the test score decline, if only because the New English was by no means the dominant school model. They noted that concern for the decay of literacy was an ongoing phenomenon (Jonathan Swift once declared that he was the last writer alive who would use the English language well!), and that test scores needed to be factored into a much broader picture, including the fact that in the 1960s and 1970s, American education had made enormous strides in keeping more kids in school and expanding higher education opportunities for an increasingly diverse student body. Yet the attacks persisted, and even as we write, the broadly-based public perception is that schools have failed (not only in literacy, we might add, but in other areas as well). Since 1974, virtually every major professional effort to expand and improve understanding and methodology in the English language arts has been met with counter-movements. As teachers have expanded the range of reading in their classes, for example, censorship cases have increased through a movement to restrict reading to safe and conventional books. Efforts toward teaching writing as a process to be learned rather than a set of forms to be imitated have been counteracted by calls for increased teaching of basics in the form of spelling lists and grammar books. Attempts to improve the liberal arts nature of English language arts instruction have been countered by an increasing call for teaching fundamental job skills.

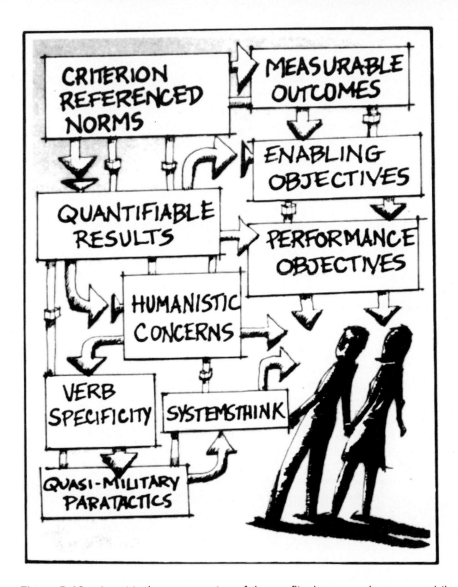

Figure P.13   A satirical representation of the conflict between the accountability movement and the student-centered approach to English. David Kirkpatrick's cover for *The English Journal* copyright © 1975 by the National Council of Teachers of English, reprinted by permission.

We cannot in this chapter go into the full complexity of these issues and debates, the charges and responses, the committee and commission meetings, the resolutions passed at professional meetings. We will close, however, with a problem and struggle that has dominated the recent history of the English language arts: that of standards for the profession.

In 1989, with nearly universal support, U.S. President George Bush launched an educational reform initiative called "Goals 2000," including a broad set of aims for the schools from decreasing school dropout rates to a mandate that is particularly relevant to this book: that national standards of "what every young person should know and be able to do" be written for every major subject area. Taking office in 1992, President Bill Clinton, supported by the nation's governors and with bipartisan support, continued the initiative; as recently as 1997, Clinton threatened to veto any education bills that were not directly related to national testing. No tests, no money. Such a mandate, as the reader can probably sense, is slanted toward a very traditional view of learning. Where many educators were calling for integrated, interdisciplinary instruction, especially for younger students, Goals 2000 essentially mandated the isolation of the traditional "big four" of schooling: math, science, social studies, and English. For the English language arts, the call for standards of what students should be able to "know" hearkens back to the cultural heritage model, and what they "should be able to do" sounds dangerously like a basic skills model. A number of English educators argued that the concept of "standards" comes from science and technology, where one can in fact create agreed-upon measures for, say the length of a meter or the duration of a second, but that the English language arts are poorly suited to develop such rigid markers.

The National Council of Teachers of English and the International Reading Association weighed issues in this debate and determined that it was in the best interests of both organizations and teachers in general if they, rather than other agencies or organizations, were to prepare a set of standards for English and reading. In 1992 they formed a partnership with the Center for the Study of Reading at the University of Illinois with the support of federal funds to write a set of standards. The project found itself walking a tightrope: On the one hand—let's say the left—it needed to prepare standards consistent with the best teaching and research on English language arts; on the other—the right—it had to write "standards" that would satisfy the federal and public demands for a tidy package of skills and knowledges.

At one point, the project lost its balance toward the left; and the Department of Education ended its funding in 1994, essentially saying that the standards being written were too vague, not measurable, not meeting the mandate of Goals 2000. After considerable debate, NCTE and IRA determined to continue the project using their own funding, and *Standards for the English Language Arts* was published in 1996. The book presented a dozen statements broadly describing the aims of the English language arts. (These standards are reprinted in Chapter 1.)

Perhaps most important, the NCTE/IRA standards were subtitled, "For the Profession, By the Profession: A Guide for Discussion," suggesting, first, that they represent teachers' views, not necessarily those of the federal government or the critical public and, second, that they are not seen as a Procrustean approach to the English language arts, but as a starting point for initial discussion.

It is at that point in history that we'll bring this necessarily brief history to a close. As we've shown, the twentieth century history of the English language arts has been essentially a struggle between two opposing views and theories of how language is learned and should be taught: the traditional model (represented by the basic skills and cultural heritage approaches) and the progressive (from Hughes Mearns to the

NCTE standards). The continuing question that the profession must face in the early twenty-first century is quite simply this: Can those two positions be reconciled? And by reconciled, we do not mean some sort of hollow compromise, where, say English language arts teachers offer a state-mandated curriculum of spelling, grammar, and great books on Mondays, Wednesdays, and Fridays while pursuing a student-centered curriculum on Tuesdays and Thursdays.

We—Diana Mitchell and Stephen Tchudi—are convinced that such an accommodation can be reached. In the pages of this book we will outline a research- and theory-based approach to the English language arts that we think can provide synthesis. Not that this is an easy task. In our home states of Michigan and Nevada, for instance, good-faith efforts of teachers to create such models have been rebuffed by state legislatures and state departments of education for roughly the same reasons that the NCTE/IRA standards were rejected by the federal government. Our faith, in the end, rests with individual teachers, the readers of this book, to be precise. We think synthesis can probably never be achieved by governmental mandate; it won't be brought about by standardized tests; it cannot be achieved by national reports; it cannot be accomplished by a textbook on methods of teaching the English language arts.

It *can,* we believe, be accomplished by exploring, inquiring teachers, teachers who study the research and mandates but are committed to finding a philosophy and methodology for instruction that will meet the needs of the particular students. The remainder of this book is dedicated to that purpose, inviting the readers of this book to write the next chapter of the history of English language arts instruction in America.

◆ EXPLORATIONS

◆ Throughout the history of English teaching, a number of central issues and questions have been debated. Why do we teach English? How can we teach students to write? What is good literature? Where does language study fit in? Answers have been offered, tested, modified, accepted, and rejected—sometimes following repetitious cycles.

What follows is a collection of statements made over the past two thousand years. It constitutes a brief overview of the kinds of questions this book will explore. Write down your reactions. Discuss them with colleagues. Do you agree or disagree? In what ways? You might also discuss how each of these statements reflects differing historical values about English language arts instruction, in particular Dixon's division into *basic skills, cultural heritage,* and *personal growth* models. Save your notes (perhaps using them as a bookmark). When you have finished reading *Exploring and Teaching the English Language Arts,* reread the statements to see how your thoughts on the teaching of English have changed. (Warning: Don't let the vintage of these statements shape your opinions. Not all good ideas are new, and not all of our contemporaries have profited from the mistakes of history.)

Hateful to me as the gates of Hades is that man who hides one thing in his heart and speaks another.

Homer, *The Iliad*

Many [words] which have now dropped out of favor will be revived, and those that are at present respectable will drop out, if usage so choose, with whom lies the decision, the judgment, and the rule of speech.

Horace, *Ars Poetica*

Reading maketh a full man; conference [conversation] a ready man; and writing an exact man.

Francis Bacon, "Of Studies" (1625)

It is no matter what you teach [children] first any more than what leg you shall put into your breeches first.

Samuel Johnson in Boswell's *Life of Johnson* (1763)

Purity of language expresses and aids clearness of thought: vulgarity, profanity, coarseness, carelessness in language, deepen the characteristics they express.

J. M. Blodgett, *Journal of the Proceedings of the American Education Association*, 1870.

"When I use a word," Humpty Dumpty said in a rather scornful tone, "it means just what I choose it to mean, neither more or less."

"The question is," said Alice, "whether you *can* make words mean so many different things."

"The question is," said Humpty Dumpty, "which is to be Master—that is all."

Lewis Carroll, *Through the Looking Glass* (1872)

The province of the preparatory schools is to train the scholar, boy or girl, and train him or her thoroughly in what can only be described as the elements and rudiments of written expression—they should teach facile, clear penmanship, correct spelling, simple grammatical construction, and neat, workmanlike mechanical execution. And this is no slight or simple task. . . . It demands steady, daily drill, and drudgery of a kind most wearisome. Its purpose and aim are not ambitious—its work is not inspiring.

Committee on Composition and Rhetoric of the Harvard College Board of Overseers (1898)

Language is acquired only by absorption from contact with an environment in which language is in perpetual use. Utterly futile is the attempt to give a child or youth language by making him learn something about language. No language is learned except as it performs the function of all speech—to convey thought—and this thought must be welcome, interesting and clear. There is no time. . . when language will be learned in any other way.

Samuel Thurber, teacher
Girls' Latin School, Boston (1898)

He who can, does. He who cannot, teaches.

George Bernard Shaw, *Man and Superman* (1893)

[In literature] the pupil should be given experiences that have intrinsic worth for *him*, now. No matter how much the story may thrill us sophisticated adults who make and teach the courses, no matter how much the play may inspire us or the poem charm us, if it is beyond the intellectual and emotional range of our pupils, we are worse than wasting time to attempt to impose it on them.

An Experience Curriculum in English (1935)

Ideally the teacher should not only read every paper and mark its formal errors, but should write detailed comments. . . . In the course of the year, the comments should make as coherent a progress as the classroom teaching, directing each writer to examine and correct his worst faults, one by one, so that at the end of the year he can look back on measurable improvement.

The Commission on English of the College Entrance Examination Board (1965)

[The student] should be familiar with the "reservoir" literature that forms a common background for our culture (classical mythology, European folk and fairy tales, Arthurian legends, the Bible, etc.), with a range of selections from English and American literature and with some from other literatures in good translation. So far as possible, he should have some "time sense"—not a detailed, lifeless knowledge of names and dates, but an imaginative sense of the past.

Study group on "Response to Literature,"
Anglo-American Seminar on the Teaching of English (1966)

Standard English is not just a bourgeois dialect, after all, but the most common and widespread form of English, and no education for life in a democracy can be complete without it. . . . Refusing to teach it to poor children would automatically condemn most of them to remaining poor and underprivileged, seal the division into sheep and goats.

Herbert Muller, *The Uses of English* (1968)

We affirm the students' right to their own patterns and varieties of language—the dialects of their nurture or whatever dialects in which they find their identity and style. Language scholars long ago denied that the myth of a standard American dialect has any validity.

Conference on College Composition and Communication (1974)

The history of American Education is the triumph of hope over experience.

Fred and Grace Hechinger, *Growing Up in America* (1975)

Everyone has the right to be literate.

Study Group on Language, Politics, and Public Affairs;
Conference of the International Federation for the Teaching of English (1984)

> Literacy expectations are likely to accelerate in the coming decades. To participate fully in society and the workplace in 2020, citizens will need powerful literacy abilities that until now have been achieved by only a small percentage of the population.

Standards for English Language Arts (1996)

We leave you, dear reader, with a final thought to consider, a thought on the profession of teaching the English language arts that may cause you to look deeply into your pedagogical soul:

> The teacher who has not a passion and an aptitude for imparting instruction in English, who does not feel it is a great thing to live for, and a thing, if necessary, to die for, who does not realize at every moment that he is performing the special function for which he was foreordained from the foundation of the world—such a teacher cannot profit greatly by any course of training. . . he lacks the one thing needful.

G. R. Carpenter, F. T. Baker, and F. N. Scott,
The Teaching of English, 1909

RELATED READINGS

Given the pressures of classroom teaching, it may be that books about the history of your profession are not high on your list of leisure-time reading. Nevertheless we suggest that reading in the history of the English language arts from time to time can help give you perspective on your work. Arthur Applebee's *Tradition and Reform in the Teaching of English* is a standard reference, especially when coupled with J. N. Hook's *A Long Way Together,* a history of the National Council of Teachers of English. If you have access to a university library, you may enjoy looking at some of the historical documents mentioned in the text, including *An Experience Curriculum in English, A Correlated Curriculum,* and the five-volume NCTE series *The English Language Arts.* John Dixon's *Growth Through English* is a "paradigm breaking" book that was instrumental in launching the New English movement and deserves reading. We also recommend the NCTE *Standards for the English Language Arts* for its perspective on the recent standards movement.

Beyond that, a number of specialized histories may be of interest. *The Story of English* is the book spin-off of an outstanding PBS series on the history of the English language (a series that is a bit dated but nevertheless quite interesting and accessible for older students). David Russell has prepared a useful history of college writing across the curriculum in *Writing in the Academic Disciplines, 1870–1990,* and James Berlin's history is accurate in its title, *Writing Instruction in Nineteenth Century American Colleges.* Gerald Graff's *Beyond the Culture Wars* provides important insights into current debates over the "enculturation" model, while *The New Literacy* by Paul Morris and Stephen Tchudi places the call for basic skills and a return to the 3Rs in the context of emerging literacy's for the twenty-first century.

Finally, our interpretation of the history of English language arts education has been shaped by the following histories, some recent, some dating back to the nineteenth century, all worth a thorough skimming or a detailed reading:

W. H. G. Armytage. Four Hundred Years of English Education. Cambridge, UK: Cambridge University Press, 1970.

Gillian Avery. *Behold the Child: American Children and Their Books*. Baltimore: Johns Hopkins, 1994.

Thomas Davidson. *The Education of the Greek People and Its Influence on Civilization*. New York: D. Appleton, 1903.

Louise Field. *The Child and His Book*. London: Wells Gardner, 1892.

Arthur Francis Leach. *English Schools at the Reformation*. New York: Russell & Russell, 1968. (Reprint of the 1896 edition.)

Nicholas Orme. *English Schools in the Middle Ages*. London: Methuen, 1973.

Hastings Rashdall. *The Universities of Europe in the Middle Ages*. Oxford, UK: Clarendon, 1987.

Jeffrey Richards. *Happiest Days: The Public Schools in English Fiction*. New York: St. Martin's, 1988.

Patrick Scott and Colleen Fletcher, eds. *Culture and Education in Victorian England*. Lewisburg, Pa.: Bucknell University Press, 1990.

John C. Sommerville. *The Discovery of Childhood in Puritan England*. Athens, Ga.: University of Georgia, 1992.

CHAPTER 1

EXPLORING AND TEACHING THE ENGLISH LANGUAGE ARTS

Whence comes [the mind] by that vast store which the busy and boundless fancy of man has painted on it? Whence has it all the materials of reason and know-ledge? . . . In one word, experience. . . Words, in their primary or immediate signifi-cation, stand for nothing but the ideas in the mind of him that uses them, however imperfectly soever or carelessly those ideas are collected from the things they are supposed to represent.

—John Locke
An Essay Concerning Human Understanding, 1690

Every person is born a learner. From the moment of birth (and even earlier), the human organism engages in this process we call "learning": sifting through ex-periences, organizing them, rearranging them, and acting upon them. It was the British philosopher, John Locke, who helped humankind see and struggle with the implications of the fact that the mind does not come preprinted with "innate" ideas (as Plato taught), but that each human being starts anew constructing his or her own uni-verse of understandings, beliefs, conceptions, generalizations, plans of action, ways of living. Locke's "sensationalist" psychology—named that because of its emphasis on sensory experience—was itself a *sensational* idea, one that changed the world and, even four hundred years later, influences what we think about how people learn.

For all its interesting features, Locke's psychology *didn't* deal particularly well with the concepts of *insight* and *creativity*. John Locke saw ideas as being created from sensory information rather as piles of bricks or building blocks, with small ideas stacked together to create larger and larger ideas in a cumulative fashion. By

> . . . I am waiting
> to get some intimations
> of immortality
> by recollecting my early childhood
> and I am waiting
> for the green mornings to come again
> youth's dumb green fields
> come back again
> and I am waiting
> for some strains of unpremeditated art
> to shake my typewriter
> and I am waiting to write
> the great indelible poem
> and I am waiting
> for the last long careless rapture
> and I am perpetually waiting
> for the fleeing lovers
> on the Grecian Urn
> to catch each other up at last
> and embrace
> and I am awaiting
> Perpetually and forever
> a renaissance of wonder
>
> From "I Am Waiting" (last stanza), by Lawrence Ferlinghetti, *A Coney Island of the Mind.* Copyright © 1958 by Lawrence Ferlinghetti. Reprinted by permission of New Directions.

Figure 1.1

contrast, Lawrence Ferlinghetti's poem, "I Am Waiting," strikes closer to describing what we now see as the nature of human imagination, especially in the young. Ferlinghetti seeks a "renaissance" of wonder, the sort of wonder that allows children to make imaginative and poetic leaps in their thinking, to be delighted by the new and unfamiliar, and, on the negative side, to be frightened by the unknown. Ferlinghetti would like to get back to the natural, romantic state of childhood in his writing (and many would argue that in writing this particular poem, he did so successfully!).

Both Locke and Ferlinghetti saw the connection between *language* and experience. Ferlinghetti is waiting for the inspiration that will "shake my typewriter" and let him write "the great indelible poem." Locke realized that words are "mere representations or symbols of things," that is, that words are not identical to the objects and actions they stand for. The French philosopher, Rene Descartes, wrote, "I think, therefore, I am," as evidence of the way in which the mind creates the individual. We presume to think that Descartes' statement would have been even stronger if he'd say, "I think, *I speak,* therefore I am." Johnny Hart's caveman Grog seems to have figured that out a few millennia ahead of even Descartes!

Figure 1.2   "B.C." by Johnny Hart. 11/22/96. Copyright © 1996 by Creator's Syndicate. Reprinted by permission.

Ideas are inextricably bound to the words we use to express them, and life can be seen as a kind of "wondering" process, where we grope through our experience and put it into words. Steve recalls that when one of his children was about three years old, the boy was out on an apartment balcony, resting his chin on the railing and staring off into the sunset. His mother, concerned about paint and lead poisoning, called out to him, "Are you chewing on that railing?" The boy thought about that for a moment, then turned and said, "No, I'm *wondering* on it."

Such uses of language by the young continue to amaze and delight us as teachers. With Ferlinghetti, we'd like to get back to the imaginative stages of childhood ourselves. Most adults recognize that the ability to wonder tends to diminish with age, and we know that the loss comes about, in part, as a natural result of refining language skills. As children learn more and think more, they employ language with more precision and at the same time lose some of their ability to make broad, poetic jumps. This increase in the precision of children's language is an important part of growing, and thus it is natural for some of children's "wondering" capacity to disappear.

When Steve's son was eight, his language growth had taken on new dimensions. While father and son were pedaling their bikes down a back street, they paused to watch a mangy, battle-scarred tomcat sniff the contents of a garbage can. The boy thought, then asked, "Is this an alley?" In that case he was using language in a very different way, not so metaphorically, but in an effort to link an experience to words he had previously heard. He wanted to pin down a definition and to learn the right kind of label for the cat. As both semanticists and logicians have observed, the more mature and sophisticated our labeling systems, the less easy it is for us to jump beyond the limits of our own language.

We declared at the beginning of this chapter that "Every person is born a learner," of life, of language. The language learning part is incredibly complex and sophisticated; learning how to use a language is far more than mastery of a few nouns and verbs or learning how to say "am not" instead of "ain't." At a surprisingly early age, children come to master tens of thousands of words and multiple thousands of linguistic operations that allow them to participate fully and successfully in the larger community of language.

Now we want to add that "Every person is born a teacher." By that we do *not* mean that teachers are "born not made," or that there are just some folks who have a gift of teaching from birth. Rather, we observe that *every* person spends a great deal of his or her life teaching, instructing, coaching, and responding to other people, sharing information as well as receiving it. Although each of us is faced with the daunting task of constructing a life and constructing a language from the ground up, we get and give an enormous amount of help along the way. (The lion's share of that is done through the medium of *language*.) Although parents are primarily engaged in teaching their babies, most parents will also admit that their baby taught them enormous amounts: fundamentals (such as, "I am hungry") and even greater fundamentals (such as, "I need love and affection"). Parents coach their babies into language, but are amazed by and learn from the original things children do with language, creating and wondering in ways undreamt of by the parents—wisdom out of the mouths of babes.

Once we humans have even the most preliminary grasp of language, we talk about our experience. "Look at that, will you?" "Here's what I think!" "In my experience...," "You know?" And we question: "What's that?" "What next?" "What do you think?" "What's going on?" As psychologists and linguists from John Locke to the present have helped us see, we learn and we teach about the world through language.

If you are ever challenged about the importance of teaching the English language arts, repeating the last phrase above is a pretty good mantra, "We learn and we teach about the world through language." English language arts teachers, more than any other group in the schools, are linked in fundamental ways to the world out there and the world "in here"—the world each one of us creates. This view of learning and teaching through and in language is what contemporary educators call a "naturalist" and "constructivist" position. It holds that human beings learn "automatically" (try to stop a child from thinking and talking), sharing ideas with others, and through interaction with others to becoming part of the various communities. We construct and create worlds for ourselves, but also worlds that connect us with others. Walt Whitman helps us see this connection clearly.

Now, some might take this naturalistic, constructivist view of language learning to what the rhetoricians call a *reductio ad absurdum* and claim that it simply proves that there is no need for "teaching" the English language arts, since people do a pretty good job of learning language on their own. Predictably, we find *that* reduction absurd. Although it is clear that many people *do* learn a great deal on their own,

---

> There was a child went forth every day.
> And the first object he look'd upon, that object he became.
> And that object became part of him for the day
> or a certain part of the day.
> Or for many years of stretching cycles of years.
>
> —Walt Whitman,
> "There Was a Child Went Forth"

Figure 1.3

including language, that doesn't mean that language cannot be learned better, more satisfactorily, and more richly and fully with the guidance, assistance, and coaching of a teacher.

We do feel, candidly, that English language arts teachers have not always played a productive role in the process of language learning. Steve's son, the wonderer and alley-cat definer later was flunked on a research report because he didn't follow footnoting conventions. In our own work, we have encountered dozens if not hundreds of people who have a hard time writing because an English teacher told them they were no good at it, that their "grammar" was weak or that their ideas weren't "coherent." We have met hundreds, possibly thousands of people who don't particularly like to read because they link reading with the English language arts where "you always had to come up with the meaning that the teacher had in mind and remember all those names and dates."

The learning of English *is* natural and constructive, and if English language arts teachers were vaporized from the planet tomorrow, people would still learn language and construct meanings and lives in words. But, we repeat, that learning process ought to be a good deal more satisfactory, even sensational, because of the role of English language arts teachers.

LANGUAGE, EXPERIENCE, AND THE TEACHING OF ENGLISH

To explain our view of the role of English language arts *teachers* in the process, we need next to articulate the core philosophy of this book, what we call the *experiential model* for English language arts learning and teaching.

The dictionary definition of "experience" stresses three main meanings:

1. "direct observation of or participation in events as the basis of knowledge"
2. "the fact or state of having been affected by or gained knowledge through direct observation or participation"
3. "practical knowledge, skill, or practice derived from direct observation or participation"

(Merriam-Webster's Collegiate Dictionary, 10th Ed.
Springfield, Mass.: Merriam-Webster, 1993)

These three meanings may be roughly translated as *perception, reflection,* and *application.* In this book we argue that the learning of language is essentially *experiential,* catalyzed and enhanced by teachers who understand the language learning process and can maximize its benefits in the classroom. This view, we argue, is firmly supported by the vast and growing body of research on the English language arts, research that we will discuss elsewhere in this chapter and throughout the book.

There are two central tenets to our *experiential* philosophy:

1. *Language is learned through the "experience" of using it in the widest possible range of situations.* We're obviously not the first to articulate this notion. You'll recall from the historical Prologue that as early as 1898 Samuel Thurber recognized

that "Language is acquired only by absorption from contact with an environment in which language is in perpetual use." Thurber's word "absorption" is a bit vague here, implying almost a magical process. Actually learning language is hard work, although people do it largely automatically by making generalizations based on the myriad examples of language that are perpetually available to them. The powerful implication for English language arts teachers, then, is that *the language classroom must focus on language in use.* If we want to teach reading, writing, listening, speaking, media, and critical thinking through language, we've just gotta get the kids engaged in doing those things, not talking about them. While young people can and obviously do learn vast amounts of language on the street, in their homes, through perpetual contact with friends, English language arts teachers have an opportunity to extend that range through the materials they bring into the classroom and by the ways they engage students in productive use of language, productive *experiences* with language.

   2. *Experience with the world drives experiences with language.* To create language, you must have ideas, experiences, thoughts, responses. People don't build their linguistic houses out of twigs or straw, but out of the solid bricks of their experience. For the classroom, this suggests that *the language classroom should also be a forum for enlarging experience.* It should be a place where students bring their outside experiences—with friends, parents, family, other adults, the world at large—for discussion and review. Of course, some of that experience can be vicarious. Books and other language experiences (including TV and film) provide the English language arts teachers with unique opportunities to expand young peoples' worlds through literature about life and death, boys and girls, men and women, truth, justice, betrayal, travel, science, art, music, and math.

   We have sketched out this model in Figure 1.4, "The Language/Experience Cycle." It consists of four parts:

   1. *The World Out There* (represented by a globe)
   2. *Experiencing and Perceiving*
   3. *Thinking*
   4. *Communicating* or *"Languaging"*

There is a fifth component, shown at the center of the model: *the child.* We present that child as a single individual to emphasize that although one can talk about the cycle in general terms (we could have put dozens, hundreds, thousands, millions of people, children and adults, in the center of the diagram), *the language cycle is unique for every person.* You could paste a photograph of yourself over the drawing of the kid in Figure 1.4, or a photo of a son, daughter, parent, niece or nephew. You can place a picture of students you know, whether grade four or English IV at the center (be sure the photo shows each *unique* youngster clearly).

   1. *The World Out There.* We have spoken of the world out there as the "real" world, yet each of us perceives that world somewhat differently. After John Locke's work, philosophers amused themselves and got themselves into something of a paradox by questioning how we could know that reality is "real" if, in fact, our only

Figure 1.4   The Language/Experience Cycle

knowledge of it comes through the senses. Children often play a variation of this philosophical game: "How do I know that 'blue' is 'really' *blue*?" "How do we know that the color I see and call 'blue' is, in fact, the same as the color you see and call *blue*?" "How do I even know that *you* are *out there*? Perhaps I just made you up!" We won't go into the arguments and counter arguments that were offered on this topic, but we will note a famous rebuttal to the non-existence problem by the British essayist Samuel Johnson three hundred years ago. Dr. Johnson simply kicked a stone and felt pain to show that reality is out there, as any fool could plainly see. For the moment, let's just assume that the universe exists, with its stars and space-time continua, with its planets and black holes, with *our* planet and its people. Furthermore, it's a reality that can be established by language, as we'll show next.

  2. *Experiencing and Perceiving.* In our time, social construction theorists deal with the perceptual problem by linking it to language: Neither "blue" nor "stone" is an absolute, they would say, but over time we've reached agreement in our language about correspondences between what we and other people see and experience. We may not have total agreement on our words (I may see "powder blue" when you are thinking "royal" blue), but, hey, this naming system *works*—we form consensus about reality through our language.

Two anthropologists/linguists in the early twentieth century, Edward Sapir and Benjamin Whorf, struggled with this problem and came up with a famous hypothesis, now discredited, to the effect that language systems actually place *limits* on perception. That is, they claimed that once people master their native language, with its words describing *blue* and *stone* and *weather* and *love* and *hate,* they become conditioned by that language to think only in those terms. At an extreme, the Sapir-Whorf hypothesis suggested that people who spoke "simple" or "primitive" languages had created those languages because of the rudimentary nature of their "primitive" thinking and that it would be extraordinarily difficult for them to move out of those "simple" modes of thinking and speaking. Linguistics has since shown that (contrary to the racist portrayal of "savages" in the movies) there are no "simple" or "primitive" languages, and that language systems expand to accommodate people's experience, culture, and need to communicate. We humans are remarkably adept at reinventing our language. We constantly create new words, new expressions, new metaphors. Our language is bursting at the seams, because as we gain in experience, we gain in language as well.

Why, then, all this talk about antique philosophers and anthropologists? Why worry about whether the sky is *blue*?

Our important point for the English language arts teacher is to show that language is vastly more than a mere tool for communication. In older philosophies, "ideas" were seen as having a reality quite independent from language, and communication was seen as a kind of act of translation, of finding the right words to express these transcendent ideas. Contemporary philosophy and psychology hotly dispute those assumptions. Rather, they say, perceptions, concepts, and ideas are inseparable, indivisibly linked together. Granted, language can shape our perceptions (look at our knee-jerk response to political labels: *scoundrel, carpet-bagger, liberal, fascist*), but our language also grows to accommodate what we are seeing, thinking, and feeling.

3. *Thinking.* In a great many school systems in recent years, a "critical thinking" movement has been popular. One hears of teaching "right brain" or intuitive thinking as opposed to "left brain" or logical ratiocination; one sees workbooks and exercise sheets showing students patterns of logical thinking such as cause and effect, small to large, and even "reasons." We are suspicious of that movement, not because we are opposed to clear thinking, but, to the contrary, because we see thinking as firmly rooted in *language.* English language arts teachers are already centrally concerned with "critical thinking" every time a student opens a book or a mouth, every time we ask students to write a paper or poem, or whenever we put kids into discussion groups.

The precise relationship between the mysteries of thinking and the equally interesting mysteries of language is beyond the scope of this discussion, but we invite you to consider the role of language in your own thinking. Do you "talk to yourself"? Do you ever "think aloud"? Do you rehearse conversations before you have them or revisit them afterwards? Have you ever been caught, say while stopped at a traffic light, muttering to yourself about some problem or other (and then possibly turned up the radio to pretend that you're singing along with a top forty tune)? Philosopher Susanne Langer once remarked that although not all thought is verbal—in words—it's pretty difficult to reveal thought without words. That is, even if pure "thoughts" exist, language is required to get them out of the brain. "I gotta use words when I talk to you," said a character in T.S. Eliot's poem, "Sweeney Agonistes."

Just as with perception, language both simplifies and endangers clear thinking. Linguists concerned with meaning or "semantics" remind us that the more abstract a word becomes, the less direct its connections with reality. Compare the specificity of "animal" (abstract) to "dog" (more specific) to "poodle" (more specific still) to "Fifi" (a particular pet). Abstraction allows us to manipulate large chunks of meaning in our heads, but it also results in a blurring of distinctions and differences. Consider the amount of abstracting involved in a term like "freedom" or "equality" or "professionalism" or "justice." Think about the problems involved in making statements about poodles or dogs in general on the basis of Fifi's tendency to bite people with red hair. It is quite easy for thinking to go astray because of inaccuracies induced by the abstracting process.

Now, we don't want to seem guilty of a kind of "mentalism" here, implying that people think in whole words and complete sentences, like a cartoon character whose thoughts are revealed in a balloon, or, for that matter, like Hamlet conducting a soliloquy on "to be or not to be." That view would be as naïve, say, as supposing that one can teach critical thinking by passing out worksheets on preferred thought patterns. The deep structures of mind and language are vastly more complicated than that. Our point, again, is that this richly textured set of brain activities we simplistically label "thinking" (consider briefly the details lost when the activities of millions of brain cells are reduced to that one ubiquitous word, "thinking") is linked to language in complex and vital ways. The English language arts teacher is not a brain specialist or psychologist or logician and does not need to be; but our experiential approach does involve messing with people's minds in complex and vital ways. We don't think the English language arts teachers should be out to program kids into "right" ways of thinking, but we do argue that in the process of teaching well, the English language arts teacher can catalyze and encourage thinking and powerfully influence how young people go about shaping their world through language. *Literacy,* then, is more than word processing; it includes and relies upon thinking.

4. *Communicating* or *"Languaging."* Other words subsumed in this part of the language/experience cycle that one might include are *talking, chatting, writing, jotting, hollering, painting, singing, dancing,* and, who knows, running around naked in a spring rainstorm to celebrate love or a high mark in a test or plain old *joie de vivre.* "Communicating" just doesn't sum it up fully, but it is here that schools have traditionally spent the most time: focusing on the sending and receiving of messages. Indeed, too often the schools have spent most of that time correcting what is judged to be errors in faulty communication. The experiential approach rejects that sort of emphasis on error correction (although we hasten to add that this does *not* mean we *don't* want our students to speak and write "correctly" when the time comes). An error correction approach, though perhaps intuitively appealing, fails to deal with fundamentals of perception and thinking. The error-correction model is rather like giving an old clunker a nice new paint job while the engine, brakes, and suspension are where work needs to be done.

Underlying any communications act, the surface utterance, is a wealth of linguistic and other activity. Through perception and thinking and sub-vocal languaging, people structure a view of reality and a view of themselves. When it comes to generating language, they formulate that experience, sometimes for their own scrutiny (as in a journal or talking to oneself), sometimes for others to respond to (as in a phone call, speech, poem, or novel). It is important to recall, too, that each "consumer " of language has a structure of words and experience in his or her mind, so that communication is not quite as simple as just pasting words on a page and sending them out; it is a complex psychic act for both communicator and communicatee. The fit between the two is often rough and ragged—what I think I say and what you think I said are seldom a perfect match.

To see these functions more clearly, it is useful to draw on the work of several teachers and language researchers who allow us to see language on three scales or continua as shown in Figure 1.5.

James Moffett distinguishes between *personal* or *private* language and *public* language depending on the audience(s) that one selects. *Personal* language may be composed for oneself, for a circle of close friends and acquaintances, or people who know us and recognize our values and interests. Public language, obviously, is directed toward broader audiences, often strangers. Moffett urges a naturalistic evolution of teaching emphasis in the schools. He argues that the youngest students need mostly personal audiences and sees older students moving toward increasingly far-flung audiences as their powers of abstraction and conceptualization expand or, as Moffett describes it, as their egocentricity diminishes (not that it is ever lost, even in a fully functioning adult). Thus the kindergartner will focus on oral "show 'n tell" for friends, while the high schooler will reach wider audiences through, say, publishing a letter to the editor of the local newspaper. Moffett worries (as do we) that the schools have traditionally done too much work on public language, ignoring the vital foundation that personal/private expression provides.

Louise Rosenblatt agrees. Her argument is that the schools place too much stress on *efferent* language (from the Latin, *effere*, to carry away) rather than expressive or

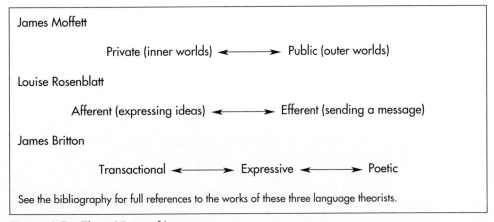

Figure 1.5   Three Views of Language

afferent language (from the Latin root of "affect"). All discourse, she explains, contains both efferent and afferent language (a good example being the one word message, "Help!", which is both a cry of alarm and a message asking for assistance). In literature, Rosenblatt explains, teachers have been too concerned with the efferent message being sent by an author rather than on the afferent meaning that a child creates as he or she interprets a text. In teaching writing, she says, we have spent far too much time on expository or explanatory writing and should maintain high levels of imaginative or afferent writing.

James Britton presents us with a continuum that goes in two directions. At the center is what he calls *expressive* language (which is close to Moffett's *private* and Rosenblatt's *afferent*). A scholar of the works of Russian psycholinguist Lev Vygotsky, Britton feels that expressive language is at the heart of literacy; it is where we conduct the business of life, on the cusp between our inner and outer worlds. In public, Britton sees language leading off in two directions: It becomes *transactional* if it is principally concerned with sending a message or "transacting" communication; while it is *poetic* if it is concerned with aesthetics as well as message and if (as does most literature) it invites contemplation that goes beyond the content of the words themselves. Britton laments that transactional language has been overemphasized in the schools, in particular, language that is addressed only to a teacher and principally to prove that one has mastered certain schoolhouse material. There is nothing "wrong" with transactional language—that's what you're reading right now—but Britton argues that students must develop skill in expressing things for themselves as well as for transactional purposes with teachers or employers. Moreover, like Rosenblatt, Britton recognizes that all discourse modes are mixed, that poetic and imaginative language can also be a part of the transactional.

The ways of classifying language are myriad. One could theoretically create as many scales, dichotomies, and distinctions as there are utterances in the universe. The point of our discussion of Moffett, Rosenblatt, and Britton is not to argue that theirs are the only ways in which one can think about this act called communication, but to emphasize its complexity and its tight links to perception and thinking. Once again, we hope that the discussion provides English language arts teachers with a heightened sense of the importance of their profession.

Completing the Cycle

With the generation of language, the experience cycle is complete; the speaker/writer establishes contact with the real world. When a person creates language, he or she asks a fundamental question of an audience: "Is my sense of the world an accurate one?" People may not always agree with our views—they may radically disagree—but even in obtaining disagreement the language user gets a kind of confirmation of his/her perceptions, thoughts, and expression.

There's one more wrinkle to add to our discussion, and that concerns the relationship of communication to that real world. Although we have stressed the importance of first-hand experience in driving expression, most of us use language heavily as a substitute for real-world experience. If you want to fix your car, you don't just open the hood and start pulling wires. Rather, you read a book or talk to a knowledgeable friend or find a mechanic by reading the Yellow Pages. In history, that "Columbus discovered America" is not something we can experience for ourselves, but most of us believe it, based on lectures from knowledgeable people and from books. (Those same people and books will also help us think critically by telling us that Columbus was not the first European explorer to arrive, that he didn't originally land on the American continent, that his discovery was something of an accident since he was trying to find India, and that, in any case, there were people living on this side of the Atlantic long before Columbus who had "discovered" this homeland for themselves.) Much of learning, then, is a matter of working with language through information, expression of ideas and emotions, dialectic, dialogue, argument, and debate, often combined with practical experimentation; e.g., we work on the car with a wrench in one hand and a repair manual in the other.

Figure 1.6 summarizes our discussion by showing the processes of language overlaid on Figure 1.4. Of particular interest is the dotted line that shows how language provides a "short cut" that alleviates the need for each of us to reinvent every wheel for ourselves. Also important to note is that although we have stressed reading,

Figure 1.6   The Functions of Language

writing, listening, and speaking in this discussion—these are generally seen as the four cornerstones of the English language arts—communication in our age uses language in a host of other ways. These English language arts don't just cover books and school themes, they're concerned with the quality of thinking and communication in film, television, recordings, the fine arts, the business world, other fields and disciplines. If it has to do with words, it has to do with the English language arts.

Steve and Paul Morris, his coauthor on a book called *The New Literacy*, got to thinking about the limits of the phrase, the "3 Rs," synonymous with basic learning. Although they were pleased that literacy is at the heart of two of the three Rs, they felt that thinking of literacy solely in terms of reading and 'riting is very limiting. They started brainstorming and came up with a list 39 Rs, traits or characteristics of human behavior that they think the schools ought to be promoting. We offer that list for your contemplation in Figure 1.7, emphasizing that every one of those Rs is tied to language, experience, and the teaching of English language arts.

THE EXPERIENTIAL MODEL

To recap, in the experiential approach, we argue that language learning is *naturalistic* and *constructivist,* which is to say that people acquire language as they employ it to construct or create meaning for themselves. Moreover, we argue that language learn-

---

The 39 Rs

Reflection	Relevance	Rationalism
Reliability	Responsibility	Ratiocination
Realization	Rhetoric	Resourcefulness
Resolution	Resonance	Revolution
Renovation	Reconstruction	Romance
Radicalism	Range	Razzmatazz
Reach	Reaction	Readiness
Recognition	Reciprocity	Reconnaissance
Redemption	Refinement	Renewal
Refreshment	Regeneration	Rejoicing
Relationships	Reformation	Remembrance
Repertory	Representation	Responsiveness
Revelation	Reverence	Rootedness

From Paul Morris and Stephen Tchudi, *The New Literacy*. San Francisco: Jossey Bass, 1996. Copyright © 1996 by Jossey Bass, Inc. Reprinted by permission.

Figure 1.7

ing is also a *learn-by-doing* skill. That latter idea may seem to imply that language learning somehow happens by magic, but we need to look more deeply.

Research in language acquisition helps to reduce the mystery by revealing that the human mind is an extraordinarily powerful analytic engine with incredible powers to see patterns and understand underlying generalities and regularities. For example, most readers of this book can probably do some language imitations or impressions; you can "do" the president of the United States or a film star or you can talk "just like" your mother or father or some member of your family. Kids, too, have this power—just ask them to imitate a cartoon character or the star of their favorite TV program. Nobody taught us how to do these imitations; in fact, nobody even taught us a set of procedures to learn how to imitate. Yet we do it. After being exposed to a large enough sample of language, people come to understand the rules and principles by which it is generated.

Just in case you are *not* able to do imitations, we'll offer another example, what linguists call *registers,* which are variations in how people speak in different contexts. You are undoubtedly in control of a rich variety of registers: You speak one way to a boss and another way to a friend, one way to a lover and quite a different way to a stranger, one way when asking instructions at a gas station and quite another when complaining that you've been overcharged at the auto repair shop. Registers turn out to be extraordinarily complex. They involve changes in lexicon (vocabulary), tone of voice, sentence structure, and even body language and gestures. Few of us are even aware of how often we change registers or what we are doing when we shift. Indeed, on those occasions where we start to become aware of register—say being introduced to a powerful person, not wanting to offend a boss, or trying to get on the good side of a judge in a court of law—if we become conscious, we may even become tongue-tied. Again, nobody taught us the traits of particular registers, and nobody taught us how to analyze language situations and create a "grammar" appropriate to the setting.

The linguistic research (which we admittedly will oversimplify here) suggests three principal ways in which people master language skills:

1. *We imitate and generalize.* People absorb language from their surroundings, imitating what they hear. In this way people begin and continue to master the systems and conventions of language. Sometimes imitation is direct—as when a child starts using the four-letter words a parent just used, without having a clue as to what those words mean or why they are "bad." More often imitation is less direct: After being immersed in a language environment for any period of time, people begin to pick up its traits. You've probably experienced this if you have ever found yourself in a different dialect community; after a day or two you start to use some of the speech traits of those community members.

But there's more to it than slavish imitation. Through imitation, the child (or adult) comes to generalize a complex network of rules or principles. If one can say "Bye-bye, daddy," one can also probably say "Bye-bye, mummy." And we come to learn that "so long" fits the bye-bye slot and so does "hello." The child who is reprimanded for using a parent's four-letter vocabulary picks up a notion of appropriateness and factors that into a growing and increasingly complex "grammar."

In this way, language grows. By the time children are four or five, they have mastered thousands of linguistic rules and tens of thousands of vocabulary words. Beyond that, they have a considerable knowledge of language customs and conventions, a broader, and in some ways more important, collection of rules and linguistic generalizations. Adults maintain this ability to understand new languages and linguistic elements, and we will all of us be continuing to acquire language until virtually the day we die. And all this is done mostly without lessons in grammar, without textbooks or school teachers, without exercise sheets and drill. For the system to work, people need to have abundant examples of language and opportunities to practice. It is thus axiomatic and automatic for parents to talk to their babies, and it is equally important for young people and adults to be in environments where they will be exposed to fresh language and given an opportunity to figure out its rules.

We are stressing oral language in this discussion, for the spoken language is the primary form that humans use. But exposure to language also includes outside sources such as radio, television, and especially *reading,* all of which provide people with models and examples outside their immediate spoken language community.

2. *Invention and creativity.* Closely bound to imitation and generalization is experimentation: testing out new language structures to see how they work. The baby experiments with one- and two-word utterances, babbling and cooing and shifting sounds until something works. Young people and adults experiment as well. In using oral language, for example, we watch for cues in body language and quiz our listeners—"You know what I mean?"—to make certain our message is coming across. In writing, people draft and revise, trying to find the words they want, and they seek feedback from peers and potential audience members—"How is this coming? Can you understand it?"

Creativity in language is also deeply linked to creativity and originality in responses to experience. We don't just try out new language forms for fun or self-education, we do so because we are stretching to explore and understand and communicate our experiences. Invention in language provides an important connection between expressive and other kinds of language (Britton), private and public (Moffett), and efferent and afferent language (Rosenblatt). "Creativity" is not something that is limited to the gifted few or to poets and novelists. Every human being has the power to be inventive with language and inventive with experience, and an inarticulate but spontaneous cry of joy or anger can be seen as being at the other end of a continuum that leads to literature, with most of our conversation and writing falling somewhere in between.

Inventing with language involves some risk taking, and some failure. We wave our hands wildly when words fail us; we state and restate our ideas until people catch on. Learning to expand language is a process of trial and error.

Unfortunately, from the Egyptians and Greeks to the present (see the Prologue), schooling has often been based more on a philosophy of error correction than on helping students succeed with original trials, on correcting grammar faults rather than praising students for fresh and original ideas and expression. Actually, the naturalistic nature of language learning pretty much takes care of the "error" part, provided people are using language for their own, real purposes, rather than, say, completing school themes and worksheets. That is, in face-to-face situations, language is often self-correcting—we *know* when we've said something that isn't quite right and set about correcting it. Teachers would be a good deal more effective in language instruction, we believe, if they concentrated on helping students arrange for some realistic trials with words, with opportunities to respond imaginatively to experience through language, rather than pointing out errors.

3. *Information and instruction.* Of course, there are times when language cannot be learned entirely by imitation or by trial and error. In reading, in particular, it seems evident that students need to be told something about the print code in order to be able to crack it. And it's very difficult to pick up the distinction between *who* and *whom* just by listening to people talk. Although young children seem to do remarkably well with something called "invented spelling," where they take a guess at the phonetic representations of words, it's also unlikely that they will figure out odd spellings (say, the sound of "sh" spelled "ti" as in "nation" or the sound of "t" spelled "pt" as in "ptarmigan.")

As we implied above, reading is a powerful source of information about language, perhaps the most powerful aside from speech. Readers pick up vocabulary, ideas, syntax, registers, and all sorts of other linguistic goodies by studying the printed page. And they do so largely in spite of, not because of, study questions and vocabulary lists in their language arts textbook.

Too, there are times when a teacher may want to present some rules or facts about usage and spelling to the students. One popular feature in many language arts classes is the "mini-lesson" where the teacher pauses briefly to give a short lesson about language, say a punctuation item or an interesting spelling possibility. We believe firmly that teachers ought to offer students that kind of help when it is needed. We also encourage our students to ask for help. When students request assistance or identify a problem, they need prompt, useful assistance, not a lecture on adverbs. It is important to recall, too, that not all students will master information about language at the same pace. The teacher needs to be very cautious about supplying information or giving overt instruction, while being equally cautious about not denying youngsters access to information they will need for jobs or higher education.

The experiential model, through the research that supports it, places far and away the greatest emphasis on language learning elements of imitation, generalization, creativity, and trial and error, all growing from and supported by the students' rapidly expanding range of experience. Direct instruction about language is often of relatively minor importance.

INTO THE CLASSROOM

Despite the knowledge we have of how young people and adults acquire their language experientially, that knowledge is sometimes left behind when teachers begin to work with young people in the classroom. Partly because of parental and administrative pressure, there seems to be a great rush to propel young people through their linguistic childhood. Spelling errors are attacked in the earliest grades, even as children are first learning to write, even learning to hold a writing tool. Kids are pushed to write in complete sentences, even though their natural oral language is quite flexible in this regard. In general, throughout the history of teaching the English language arts, there has been an overwhelming concern for what we call "adult language standards"—what adults, say, do, read, and write—with the schools requiring young people to meet these standards as early in the game as possible.

The adult standards model is visualized in Figure 1.8. It shows the adult standing at the top of the stairway of learning, the child at the bottom. Since adults perceive adulthood as a generally desirable end product, adult knowledge is parceled out along the K–12 stairs. In this model, children pause at each level to learn the required material—this year nouns and topic sentences, next year the three-paragraph theme. Sometimes children get stuck and must spend an extra year on a step; occasionally a bright child comes along who can take the steps two at a time. In terms of the school system, the diploma symbolizes the attainment of adulthood.

In English language arts classes, this approach has created an obsession with "good English," grammar and vocabulary lessons, spelling drills, phonics approaches to reading, and an undue interest in the monitoring of grade and achievement levels in reading and writing. It too often kills off imaginative writing after the grade school years and conveys an overdone concern for the business letter, report writing, and the "term" paper at the high school.

Figure 1.8   The Adult Standards Model

A prospective teacher in one of our classes wrote:

I feel sad that we can't capture the "wondering" part of language in childhood and adolescence, and I keep seeing the image of us pushing kids so hard into adulthood that like caterpillars becoming butterflies, we lose part of the metamorphosis and end up with older caterpillars that have sprouted wings but can't fly.

Now, we don't want to be overly dramatic about the effects of the adult standards approach; nor do we want to be among those who get their kicks "teacher bashing," complaining about the alleged inadequacies of the schools and the incompetence of teachers. Nevertheless, the evidence is clear that in a great many schools, the adult standards approach is the dominant mode of instruction, despite the fact that it is pretty well discredited by research.

Unfortunately, the adult standards approach has an intuitive or common sense appeal. Why not just identify the end product and direct instruction to it? Let's take adult standards, break them up into their components, and teach those one at a time until the student has the whole adult package.

But as we have shown, that view makes several false assumptions about the nature of language, thought, and experience. It separates language skills from the experiences that power them and thus places undue emphasis on mastery of skills in isolation from meaning. It implies that every child should and can be on the same step of the stairway to adulthood at the same time, and it grossly oversimplifies the language learning process by perceiving it as a few simple steps rather than a complex and infinitely diverse web of linguistic and experiential relationships. Most damning, we think, is that the adult standards model denies the language competence of young people. The child is shown at the bottom of the stairway, far removed from the ideal of adulthood. In effect, every child is seen, from the start, as a remedial adult; this is what educationists call a *deficit* model, rather than a *positivist* or *constructivist* model.

POSITIVISM AND CONSTRUCTIVISM

Figure 1.9 represents how the experiential model looks at growth in language from a constructivist or positivist viewpoint. The adult world of language is here shown as a series of arrows at the edge of the figure; this implies that adulthood is not static, that it is constantly expanding its boundaries of language and experience. The child is shown as a free-form shape within those boundaries, with growth arrows of its own. Over time, the child will grow to fill the boundaries—it will become an adult. But the experiential model holds that the child will necessarily have to seek out its own pattern of growth based on its own experiences.

In the previous paragraph we spoke of "the child" in the singular. Imagine now what the diagram would look like if we pluralized to speak of "children," several children each with his or her own shape, his or her own directional arrows of growth. Now imagine thirty or thirty-five kids and you'll get a sense of our view of the English language arts classroom. It's much too complex to draw in a diagram because although each of those classroom critters has its own shape, there is also a good deal of overlap as in a mathematical Venn Diagram or the middle of a three-ring pretzel.

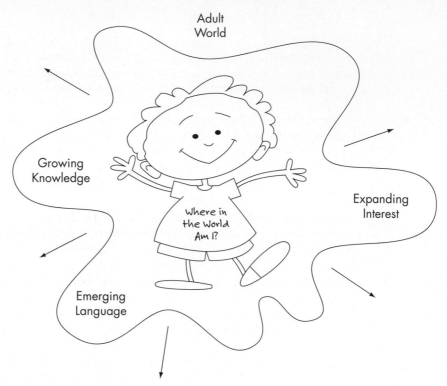

Figure 1.9 The Developmental Alternative

THE COMMUNITY OF LANGUAGE

We visualize the young person as a growing, inquiring member of a community—of all humankind—linked together by its use of language. The range of participation varies from one person to another, from one age level to another. The baby in the cradle participates in its own way, making contact with one or two people, sharing with them to the best of its ability and learning from them. As young people mature, as they meet new people and probe new ideas, their participation in the community of language naturally broadens until it becomes full and "adult." In coming of age, young people learn the language that supports their needs.

The English language arts class, at its best, offers a particularly rich language community, a place where students can explore their ideas and experiences through language. The teacher is anything but passive in this classroom, as subsequent chapters will show. The teacher will balance individual, even idiosyncratic needs and common interests. She will engage her students in using a common language, even as she recognizes the individuality and creativity of each person's language. He will provide students with common experiences while allowing and encouraging them to develop and think about their individual interests and needs. A central aim for the English language arts teacher is to help students participate in the community of language to the fullest possible extent by providing situations and experiences that allow them to use language naturally and with increasing competence. This is no small task.

THE QUESTION OF "STANDARDS"

Our Experiential Model, then, relies on the concept of *developmentalism,* which holds that each learner will have unique skills and knowledge, individual interests and concerns, but that one can see developmental patterns of growth as well. First graders, as a group, will be far more interested in puppy dogs than in nuclear theory. Twelfth graders will be concerned with moral and ethical issues far beyond the basic ethics of the typical first grader. Second graders will use invented spellings, write in short sentences, and read children's books; eleventh graders will use (mostly) standard spellings, write in longer sentences, and read the full adult range of literature. Yet any statement that attempts to describe what *all* children in any grade will do must necessarily fail, the weakness of the adult standards approach with its monistic view of literacy.

This brings us to the dilemma of "standards" for the English language arts. As we noted in the Prologue, in the early 1990s it became evident that by and large the public and legislators were unhappy with the performance of American public schools and considered "standards" as the route to unifying the schools and improving pupil learning. The English teaching profession struggled with this mandate. Obviously, what the politicians wanted was a list of adult standards: spelling and grammar lists by grade or school level, lists of books that every child should read, a lock-step and testable set of aims and goals for every child. As a state superintendent of schools, an advocate of "standards," once explained, "I want to know exactly when we can expect every child to *read.*" We won't even bother to analyze the absurdity of that statement, although we can comprehend the administrative impulse that would find such standardization appealing.

The National Council of Teachers of English combined forces with the International Reading Association to respond to this mandate and to create an alliance of two of the most powerful subject-matter organizations for teachers in the country.

The two organizations, argued that only standards produced by teachers themselves would be valid and acceptable to the profession, and in 1996, they published *Standards for the English Language Arts.* The writers recognized the "worry" of many teachers about "standards," teachers "fearing that the result will be to restrict the creativity and flexibility that characterize good teaching and learning" (p. 68). They urged "a more positive view of standard-setting," feeling that "guidelines for English language arts education are necessary because they provide a clear map of the goals of schooling." We have reprinted the NCTE/IRA standards in Figure 1.10.

As you read that list, you can perhaps sense why the federal government and some media have been highly critical of the NCTE/IRA "standards." They don't specify lists of books to read, hierarchies of skills to master. They don't say when all children should read or dot their "i"s or cross their "t"s. Those who wanted a prescribed national curriculum for English language arts were naturally disappointed, as were those who wanted guidelines that could easily be translated into national standardized tests.

What the standards do represent, we think, are coherent statements that sum up the best current thinking about teaching the English language arts to date. They are a bit general, to be sure, and subject to interpretation. Take, for example, standard six,

1. Students read a wide range of print and nonprint texts to build an understanding of texts, of themselves, and the cultures of the United States and the world; to acquire new information; to respond to the needs and demands of society and the workplace; and for personal fulfillment. Among these texts are fiction and nonfiction, classic and contemporary works.

2. Students read a wide range of literature from many periods in many genres to build an understanding of the many dimensions (e.g., philosophical, ethical, aesthetic) of human experience.

3. Students apply a wide range of strategies to comprehend, interpret, evaluate, and appreciate texts. They draw on their prior experience, their interactions with other readers and writers, their knowledge of word meaning and of other texts, their word identification strategies, and their understanding of textual features (e.g., sound-letter correspondence, sentence structure, context, graphics).

4. Students adjust their use of spoken, written, and visual language (e.g., conventions, style, vocabulary) to communicate effectively with a variety of audiences and for different purposes.

5. Students employ a wide range of strategies as they write and use different writing process elements appropriately to communicate with different audiences for a variety of purposes.

6. Students apply knowledge of language structure, language conventions (e.g., spelling and punctuation), media techniques, figurative language, and genre to create, critique, and discuss print and nonprint texts.

7. Students conduct research on issues and interests by generating ideas and questions, and by posing problems. They gather, evaluate, and synthesize data from a variety of sources (e.g., print and nonprint texts, artifacts, people) to communicate their discoveries in ways that suit their purpose and audience.

8. Students use a variety of technological and informational resources (e.g., libraries, databases, computer networks, video) to gather and synthesize information and to create and communicate knowledge.

9. Students develop an understanding of and respect for diversity in language use, patterns, and dialects across cultures, ethnic groups, geographic regions, and social roles.

10. Students whose first language is not English make use of their first language to develop competency in the English language arts and to develop understanding of content across the curriculum.

11. Students participate as knowledgeable, reflective, creative, and critical members of a variety of literacy communities.

12. Students use spoken, written, and visual language to accomplish their own purposes (e.g., for learning, enjoyment, persuasion, and the exchange of information).

From *Standards for the English Language Arts*. Copyright © 1996 by the International Reading Association and the National Council of Teachers of English. Reprinted by permission.

Figure 1.10   Standards for the English Language Arts

that "students apply knowledge of language structure, language conventions . . . to create, critique, and discuss print and nonprint texts" (p. 3). Such a statement could be taken to justify an in-depth study of traditional grammar (or even sentence diagraming!) if a teacher felt that such study could somehow help students create and critique language more successfully. Such an approach could not be justified by current research, and we rather suspect the NCTE/IRA framers may have included such a vague statement partly to satisfy a diverse range of teachers in the profession and possibly even to provide evidence to doubting parents, media writers, and legislators that yes, NCTE/IRA *do* care about more than effusive "self expression."

We urge you to read those standards carefully, and as we suggest at chapter end, to obtain a copy of the whole standards document, which contains a series of "vignettes" showing the standards in action in elementary and secondary school classrooms (vignettes that clearly do *not* include sentence diagraming as a route to linguistic excellence).

Quibbles aside, the NCTE/IRA standards are very much consistent with the experiential model on which this book is based. In very brief paraphrase, the standards stress *growth and expansion* of language for *personal, social, and academic/vocational purposes.* The students extend the range of literature they read (including strong emphasis on multicultural literature); they expand the range for forms and genres in which they can write; they read for pleasure and information; they become increasingly competent in the use of electronic media. The standards do not attempt to specify attainments at particular grade levels; rather, they suggest that the same standards or guidelines for growth in language apply K–12 (even cradle to grave) and obviously leave it to the teacher to figure out what sorts of activities are appropriate for his or her own students.

THE EXPERIENTIAL MODEL IN ACTION

The NCTE/IRA standards are illustrated by numerous *vignettes,* short descriptions that illustrate the sort of teaching implied by an experiential model. There are descriptions of:

- an elementary school teacher reading a story to youngsters and helping them figure out meaning based on their own experience and context clues supplied in the text.
- two children in a multi-age (6–8 years) rural classroom who collaborate on writing an animal fable.
- fourth graders engaged in an individualized reading program that allows them to choose books themselves and to challenge themselves to read more and more widely.
- middle schoolers in an ethnically mixed classroom reading international folk tales, keeping journal responses, and telling stories to one another.
- a middle school teacher who engages students in a collaborative discussion of just what classroom rules are needed for the class to function successfully.

- high school students developing confidence in their own responses to literature by maintaining reading logs.
- a high school class that gets into the study of Shakespeare's *Hamlet* through careful use of contemporary film and media.

In such vignettes (and other examples of good teaching we'll offer in this volume, and you can collect on your own), one sees the breadth and imagination involved in "experiential" teaching. Clearly there is no set "right" way of getting students to expand in their use of language, to explore diverse experiences. Yet, the principles we have described in this chapter do lead to a consistency in approach. You'll note that the vignettes do not include spelling lists, vocabulary drill, paragraph practice, memorizing classic poetry, memorizing names and dates of classic authors, or intense dwelling on figures of speech or literary structures. At the same time, the vignettes do show kids in action: spelling words, using vocabulary, writing paragraphs (and more), responding to a rich variety of literary works, authors, and structures.

OBSERVING GROWTH AND DEVELOPMENT

A nagging question remains concerning these sorts of developmental or evolving standards and the experiential model: Just how do we *know* whether students are becoming more skilled as language learners? If we reject uniform levels of achievement and standardized tests, how can we as teachers know whether our students are getting any better at their use of language? Perhaps more important, how are we going to be able to report growth and learning in satisfactory ways to students themselves, parents, and others?

We'll begin with a slightly digressive observation: For years we've asked teachers to tell us about how well their general classroom observations of students match up with student performance on standardized tests. Although teachers report a fair number of surprises—students who score higher than one might expect or, more often, students whose scores are lower than expected—usually teachers have a pretty good sense of how their students are going to *scan* in a testing environment. One conclusion that could be drawn from this admittedly unscientific poll is that on the whole, the standardized tests don't do too bad a job of measuring what students learn in the classroom. A more interesting conclusion, we think, is that since teachers have an accurate idea of how students will do, the tests may be superfluous. Why test if tests don't add significantly to the teacher's knowledge of students? In fact, as part of this same poll, we've asked teachers how they are able to *use* standardized test data in the classroom. Almost invariably, the answer comes back, "Well, the tests aren't that directly useful." Even when test scores are broken down by categories—e.g., vocabulary, usage, writing—a numerical score doesn't give the teacher much assistance in planning instruction. What does a high, low, or middle score mean in terms of the specifics of teaching? The tests just don't say. And so we reiterate our concern that standardized tests don't add much to the teacher's information storehouse. More important, the tests cannot explain the surprises, especially those kids who do pretty well in class but perform poorly on tests. Is this because the students don't really know the information? Or, perhaps, do they simply take tests badly? Again, the tests don't say.

An even *more* interesting conclusion to be drawn from this is that teachers are instinctively and consciously *data gathering machines,* and the data they collect are vastly more complex and sophisticated than that gathered by a test. Youngsters walk into your class at 9 A.M. You look them over and immediately get some first impressions about who's happy and sad, who's having a good or bad day. You look at their writing and gather vast amounts of information about their language skills to go on top of your perceptions based on how and when and why they talk in class. You listen to their responses to literature and make assessments about what they've read and how they've read it and what sorts of experiences they are bringing to bear on it. You know which kids in your class have high computer skills, which ones have a good grasp of standard spellings, which ones struggle with standard edited usage. If asked, you could probably talk about each student in your class for a half hour or more—you have near-encyclopedic knowledge of your students.

What needs to be done to demonstrate growth and to show students and the public what is happening in the English language arts is for teachers to get some of that data from their heads down on paper. We suggest that at the more mundane end of things that the teacher simply be a good record keeper. More interesting and imaginative, we think, is that the teacher should be an explorer and inquirer, always hypothesizing, trying new ideas and collecting data to test out new and experimental directions.

Noting down students' growth and development goes far beyond the teacher's grade book or even some of those slick computer programs that will keep all the teacher's test score data and compute a grade at the end of the term. Figure 1.11 is a list of approaches to assessment developed by Nevada teachers who were involved in developing a set of state curriculum materials. As one teacher remarked, "The trouble with assessment is that it always comes *after* everything is *over*." She went on to argue that assessment in English language arts should be a constant process; we assess before we teach, during teaching, and afterward. And we use every kind of assessment tool we can think of to see whether we're getting the job done.

For example, the Nevada teachers believed in the value of surveys and interest inventories, done orally or on paper, as a way of assessing young people's interests and ideas before a unit of work begins. They relied heavily on their students' writing at all phases of instruction, not principally as a means of finding out "what's wrong" with literacy, but as one of the best ways of seeing their students' interests and experiences described in detail. Yet, lest writing be overemphasized, they advocated conferences: short mini-conferences of a minute or less, regular longer conferences to discuss work with students, conferences with groups of kids, conferences with individuals. They discussed the need for parental advisement and input and recommended regular communication with parents, possibly through the school parents' night, perhaps more satisfactorily through notes home and scheduled conferences, where teachers and parents can pick up vital information about the young people in their classes. You'll note that standardized tests appear on the list as well. Although we have voiced criticism of those tests, the teachers pointed out that placed in the larger context of a variety of sources, tests, too, have a part to play; those tests become dangerous primarily when they are the sole measure of student achievement or used inappropriately as a measure of success for a school or a teacher. The Nevada teachers found lists helpful: lists of books and magazines read by the student, lists of writings completed, lists of the student's participation in small-group projects. The teachers put reliance on assessment and evaluation of student work, in particular, through the concept of *portfolio* assessment, looking at a variety of pieces of student work, permitting discussion of concrete achievement, growth and development, needed work, and so on. (Portfolios will be discussed in more detail at several points in this book.)

Many teachers in this project also put strong emphasis on journals and diaries, not only materials written by students as a record of their learning, but as *documents carefully maintained by the teacher*. Now, after you've put in a long day of teach-

---

Eye contact

Morning greetings

Interest inventories

Diaries and journals

Learning logs

Student writing of all kinds (expository as well as imaginative)

Oral discussions

Small-group projects

Mini-conferences

Longer conferences

Student self-assessment (oral or written)

Peer response

Real audience response

Parental response

Public response

Student portfolios

Published writing (class, school, beyond)

Letters and notes (to teachers, to peers)

Reading reactions

Book reports (use with caution)

Teacher-made tests (essay or short answer)

Commercial tests

Authentic assessment (on-the-job)

Standardized tests

Figure 1.11   Some Means of Assessing Language Arts

ing, writing a diary might seem to be the last thing you'd want to do. But we strongly recommend cultivating this habit, a habit of reflecting on what you've done, how it went, how you would do things differently. Your journal can also prove to be an extraordinarily valuable assessment tool as you write down observations about particular young people, what they are doing, how they are growing, what you see happening for them next.

THE TEACHER AS RESEARCHER

All of this data collecting positions any teacher to participate in one of the most exciting movements in recent years, that of *teacher-as-researcher.* "Research" does not always have positive connotations for a good many teachers. Often, college level courses in research deal with abstractions only dimly related to classroom experiences. Many teachers—math haters in particular—have had to struggle through basic statistics courses, puzzling over and never quite comprehending the value of T-tests, chi-squares, and significant differences.

But research in its more general sense simply means *systematic inquiry.* Those language-learning babies we talked about earlier are, in fact, language researchers, very systematically testing out the language to discover its underlying truths. And teachers engage in research every day they walk into the classroom. The teacher/researcher movement does two interesting things: First, it encourages teachers to make that research somewhat more conscious and formal, and, second, it validates the findings of classroom teachers, making them the authorities in their own classrooms. When teachers *don't* operate with an experimental attitude, teaching on the basis of intuition, hunch, teacher lore, and gut-level reaction, administrators and parents rightfully complain that teachers don't seem to know what they are doing and look for standardized tests and accountability programs as a measure of protection.

We believe that when teachers do systematic evaluation and informal research in their own programs, they are not only better teachers, but they satisfy outsiders as well.

In teacher research, one usually begins with a question or a nagging problem. Just as a lab scientist would stake out a problem for investigation, so too the teacher needs to be clear and explicit. So step one is *describe a question or problem or hypothesis.* A social scientist once remarked that a great deal of research seems, inappropriately, to be a test of which is the worst of two bad ways of doing things. He implied that researchers often fail to ask *significant questions.* For example, "Which of these two grammars is better?" is a question often asked, but one that is limited in its value. A much better, more comprehensive question might be, "Does grammar—any grammar—produce change in students' language use?" A still better, or, at least more practical question for the classroom researcher might be, "What strategies can I use to help my students edit their work better?" (for, after all, what we're concerned with is the bottom line of a finished product, regardless of whether or not "grammar" is involved).

A second step is to *teach in experimental ways.* Traditional research would call for the teacher to isolate variables and to put students into experimental and control groups, say, one group practicing small-group or peer editing while the other group received only feedback from the teacher. Or one group would receive formal grammar instruction while the other would not. Teacher research doesn't require that kind of artificial separation. Instead, it suggests that because classrooms are so complex, there really is no way to isolate variables and kids neatly and cleanly. So the teacher concerned with editing skills might try a number of ideas, perhaps different approaches in different classrooms, perhaps several alternatives in the same class. The teacher might try small groups or paired partner editing for a while—long enough to be satisfied that the trial is a fair one. The teacher might try one-to-one conferencing with students or some combination of conferencing and teacher editing, again, a long enough trial that in the researcher's mind, the test has been a fair one.

Throughout this teaching, the teacher will engage in step three, *collecting data.* Review once again all the assessment tools listed in Figure 1.11. How many of them could be used to collect information on this project? This data gathering should not be an *add on* to the teacher's workload, but a normal part of classroom management and assessment. We're really just suggesting that teacher research takes a couple of small steps further, in particular, step four, *synthesizing and reflecting.* Although there is danger of bias in teacher research, of the teacher seeing only what he/she wants to see or going with a forgone conclusion, it has been our experience that teachers are honest and self critical and deeply committed to finding answers, so their reflection on their teaching is robust, critical (often too self-critical), and above board. Thus when teachers arrive at step five, *form conclusions,* whatever they have to say has strong validity, especially in the context of their own classroom. That is, we must be very cautious about generalizing results beyond the group of students in a classroom research project. It *may* be that peer editing is the world's best method for helping students with editing, but the results of teacher research cannot be generalized to that level. It's enough that a teacher figures out what works best in his or her classroom and possibly shares those findings with some colleagues (that's not to exclude the distinct possibility that sharing may include writing up one's ideas for a local, state, or national English education journal).

Although we've used the word *conclusions* here, it might be better to call them *tentative conclusions* or even *refined hypotheses,* for it's rare that teacher research leads to broad and universally fixed conclusions. Indeed, as often as not, the research may just lead to the next level of questions, "Well, if peer groups seem to work well, how can I make them work better?" "What size groups work best?" "How can I most successfully introduce peer response in my classes?" At that point, the teacher/researcher returns to the beginning of the cycle: With new questions or problems, the cycle begins anew, and in this way, we grow as teachers.

Those experienced with the teacher-as-researcher idea will realize that our description here is somewhat less formal than many research projects, particularly those done, say, as part of a graduate degree program. Without seeming to reduce standards or to encourage sloppy research, we want to argue for a middle ground between casual observation and strictly disciplined research. By proposing that you be a serious and regular data collector, we hope to encourage you to be what we call the *exploring teacher,* for whom this book is written. The exploring teacher has a clear and articulate philosophy of learning and teaching, yet sees this as tentative and fights the tendency that resides in most of us to become settled into our own orthodoxy and routines. This teacher can celebrate his or her successes and honestly and accurately discuss perceived failures, while constantly pushing forward to explore new dimensions and possibilities in the English language arts. The "explorations" that we suggest at the close of each chapter encourage you to operate in this exploratory mode. You'll note that we provide open-ended questions for discussion and observation; there is no answer key at the back of the book. We hope that you'll engage in exploratory teaching that will let you write your own answer key, but in pencil, subject to revision as you probe more and more deeply into this complex and fascinating field of the English language arts.

◆ EXPLORATIONS

◆ Make a list of your principal encounters with language during a busy hour of your life, say, the first hour of the day or the last or one in between. Actually, you may find it difficult to even list *all* of the language you send and receive during that time, but get down the essentials, e.g., talk with friends, listening to the radio, writing a note, reading shopping lists, reading a novel. . . . Develop a consciousness of your uses of language. How do you use it to gain control over your environment? to influence other people? to entertain yourself and others?

◆ Have students keep a list of their own uses of language—just as you did in the previous exploration—for a period of time, a day or part of a day. Elicit their opinions on the functions of language in their lives. In doing so, you may well help them raise their own awareness of language.

◆ Analyze a skill that you have developed outside of school—fly casting, Thai cookery, woodworking, participating in a family, community leadership. What are the subskills that make up this art, craft, or talent? Think about how you learned, perhaps writing a page or two of reminiscence. What drew you to this area in the first place? What were your first efforts like? How did you gradually gain skills? Were there peaks and valleys? When did you reach the point that you felt competent or adequate? What are your weaker points now? Compare your learning to the experiential model we have described for language in this chapter. What similarities do you see?

◆ In Figure 1.6 we included a little slogan, "Literacy is beyond words." What are some possible meanings of that expression? When you think of a literate person, what kinds of skills and knowledge does that include? What do you see as the connection between a liberally educated person and his or her literacy? What do you make of a term like "scientific literacy"? "mathematical literacy"? "visual literacy"? What connections do you see between these sorts of literacies and what goes on in an English language arts class?

◆ In the previous chapter, we suggested that you respond to various historical statements about the English language arts and save those for review when you reach the end of the book. Now do the same for the NCTE/IRA standards in Figure 1.10.

Rate each on a scale of 1 = strongly agree to 5 = strongly disagree. More important, perhaps, write a brief interpretive statement for each, describing in more detail what you think it means. For *you*, what would it mean to say that students "participate as knowledgeable, reflective, creative, and critical members of a variety of literacy communities"? And do you think this is a good idea? Save this bit of writing as well for review when you reach the end of this book. In addition, consider what seem to be the major obstacles to implementing these standards in the kinds of classrooms with which you are familiar.

◆ Figure 1.5 presented three "scales" of language:

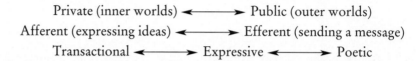

Private (inner worlds) ←——→ Public (outer worlds)

Afferent (expressing ideas) ←——→ Efferent (sending a message)

Transactional ←——→ Expressive ←——→ Poetic

Look at some words in print, from the newspaper, from a literary text, from your own journals and correspondence. Where does the writing fall on each of these scales? Capture some oral speech (either in memory or on tape) and do the same sort of classification. Listen to a talk radio show and see how people's speech is functioning. How often do callers (or for that matter, writers of letters to the editor) exhibit what is primarily expressive or afferent speech (sounding off!) versus transmitting a message to a wider public?

◆ Observe a class for a twenty minute period and make a list of the language skills exhibited and learned—question asking, discussion, teacher lecture, even student sass. If this seems to be a successful class, describe one or several of the language components that make this community work. If it is unsuccessful, think about some of the changes that seem to be required.

◆ Based on your understanding of the experiential model and/or on the basis of your own, emerging philosophy of language learning, respond to the following statements. In what ways does each of them correspond to or deviate from what you take to be the best practice in English language arts instruction?

"Young people nowadays just aren't literate the way we were in my day."

"Those literature textbooks are killing off reading interest."

"Kids nowadays just don't know their cultural heritage."

"There are certain great books that everybody just ought to know."

"Teach the basics first; then let students go on and 'express themselves'."

"If students' errors aren't corrected quickly, they'll just keep on making them."

"The language arts are probably unnecessary, since everybody learns to talk."

◆ Finally, here are some questions that many teachers (including ourselves) ask about their teaching. For each of these, brainstorm about the idea of teacher-as-researcher.

What sorts of trials or experiments might you conduct to seek answers? What sorts of data would you collect?

"What can I do about kids who just don't or can't read the assigned text?"

"Can students fruitfully respond to each others' writing?"

"How can I get better discussion in my classes?"

"Does literature matter anymore to the TV generation?"

"What language skills will my students need for the future?"

"How can I best inform parents of what their children are doing in my class?"

"Is grammar dead?"

RELATED READINGS

We've already mentioned *Standards for the English Language Arts* (NCTE/IRA) and recommend that you obtain a copy, not only for the standards themselves, but for the vignettes and supporting material included in the publication. The two organizations have also published a series of monographs on particular topics treated by the standards and are listed in their publications catalogs, which are a rich source of up-to-date publications for teachers. Membership in those professional organizations is also highly desirable. We're partial to the National Council of Teachers of English (1111 Kenyon Road, Urbana, Illinois 61801) because of its comprehensive concern for all aspects of the English language arts; but in recent years, the International Reading Association (800 Barksdale Road, P.O. Box 8139, Newark Delaware 19711) has considerably expanded its interests beyond reading into other areas of English language arts instruction. The NCTE journals *Language Arts* (elementary), *Voices From the Middle* (middle school), and *The English Journal* (secondary) are particularly useful in keeping up to date on new practices and research as well as being informed about new books and upcoming professional conferences and workshops.

The research supporting the standards (and other contemporary models for English language arts) is well-documented in the encyclopedic, *Handbook of Research on Teaching the English Language Arts,* edited by James Flood and others. Although not all teachers would want to own a copy, it certainly should be a well-thumbed part of any professional library in English teaching. Its chapters cover a comprehensive array of topics, from the history of the profession to political issues, with special focus on the research on language learners as well as the particular features of instruction in language, literature, oral language, reading, writing, and curriculum.

There are, of course, innumerable books about language and learning that one "ought" to have read. In the Bibliography we list not only the books we refer to in various chapters, but basic reference books on theory and practice that we think deserve a place in professional libraries.

Among books on the teaching of English language arts, we especially like Leila Christenbury's *Making the Journey: Being and Becoming a Teacher of English Language Arts.* Nancie Atwell's *In the Middle: Writing, Reading, and Learning with*

Adolescents is mentioned frequently in our classes and workshops as being an especially helpful text, as is Moffett and Wagner's *Student-Centered English Language Arts, K–13.* Alan Purves' book with the intriguing title, *How Porcupines Make Love II* is an especially good book on teaching literature, and we must also shamelessly plug two other "methods" type books, *The English Teacher's Handbook* by Susan and Stephen Tchudi and *The Interdisciplinary Teacher's Handbook* by Stephen Tchudi and Stephen Lafer.

To look further into what research in the classroom involves, read Cathy Fleischer's *Composing Teacher-Research: A Prosaic History of the Teacher Research Movement.* Brenda Power Millers shows teachers how to do research in their classrooms in *Taking Note*, in particular, helping teachers find ways to productively record observations from their classrooms.

For basic reading, John Dixon's *Growth Through English* remains central to our list, describing the "Dartmouth Seminar" that prompted a paradigm shift in English teaching from traditional to experiential models. More recent conference reports that provide broad summary statements of aims and goals in the English language arts include Tchudi's *Language, Schooling, and Society,* as well as Richard Lloyd Jones and others', *Democracy in Education,* and Peter Elbow's *What is English?* Finally, we want to acknowledge the influence on our thinking of a number of theorists whose books are listed in the bibliography. These include J. W. Patrick Creber, John Dixon, John Dewey, Jean Piaget, Lev Vygotsky, Susanne Langer, James Britton, James Moffett, John Mayher, Frank Smith, Louise Rosenblatt, Connie Weaver, and Peter Abbs.

CHAPTER 2

THE INTEGRATED CURRICULUM

The heretic spoke at an faculty meeting: "Curriculum? Integration? The only thing holding most educational institutions together is the brickwork and the heating and plumbing. Schools find it convenient to centralize the purchasing of books, fuel oil, and hamburger meat and, as economical, to gather children in blocks of five hundred or two thousand for the purpose of educating them. But aside from these considerations (and perhaps a winning football team), most schools are

---

Students move from teacher to teacher and subject to subject along a curriculum continuum that may or may not exhibit planned articulation. The most carefully designed curriculums are often fragmented into various subjects or disciplines. Teachers supply some coherence in terms of how they transform an intended curriculum into an experienced curriculum. Students provide the last measure of coherence, based on mastery of previous material and their ability to relate learnings to other life occurrences. Real coherence in a curriculum is an elusive theme and may not be possible, at least in the philosophical sense. The pursuit, however, must not slow its pace.

—Arthur W. Steller, President
Association for Supervision and Curriculum Development

Humpty Dumpty sat on a wall.
Humpty Dumpty had a great fall.
All the king's horses and all the king's men
couldn't put Humpty together again.

—Children's nursery rhyme

Figure 2.1

simply physical conveniences—like bathrooms—with no spiritual or intellectual relationship to draw people or to hold them there."

"Not so fast, heretic," admonished the assistant principal for instruction, who, with difficulty, lifted a heavy volume and let it fall dramatically on the table, raising a small cloud of dust. He thumped it with his fist. "This book provides our unity here. It is the curriculum guide for our school."

The book was some three hundred pages long, held together by a spiral comb binding. The preface included a letter from the school board, thanking members of the curriculum committee for their dedication and long hours of work, along with a note from the principal adding some comments about the tradition of excellence that the school had long enjoyed. Inside the guide could be found a pie diagram showing the disciplines of a liberal education, long lists of goals and standards for the various disciplines, the approved textbooks and supplemental reading, and a map of the school. As it turned out, the assistant principal was the only person in the room who actually knew where a copy of the guide could be found, as the rest of the faculty had long since put it aside to follow their own interests.

We don't intend to be harsh or unduly gloomy in offering that imaginary scenario, but it helps us emphasize our belief (reinforced by Arthur Steller and metaphorically by Humpty Dumpty) that this thing called "curriculum," the weaving together of instruction, is one of the weakest areas in the schools (and colleges) for most fields and disciplines, in general, and for the English language arts, in particular.

Imagine a "concert" played by musicians reared under the sort of "curriculum" most of us have experienced in our school and college days. To begin with, you're learning four or five instruments at once, say clarinet, violin, snare drums, piano, and banjo. Once an hour, you change instruments and teachers. Your clarinet teacher insists on the basics and you spend most of your hour playing scales; your violin teacher is an advocate of the Suzuki method and has you playing no scales at all in preference to learning songs by ear; the piano teacher favors a "balanced" method so you spend a half hour on the scales and then try to play a concerto. And about the time you start to master any one of those instruments, they are all taken away and you are given new ones: oboe, bass fiddle, bass drum, accordion, and lute.

It's quite possible that one could learn a good deal of music in that sort of orchestral madhouse—one would learn that an oboe is a lot like a clarinet, that the principles of the piano work for the accordion and that a xylophone draws on one's skills as a drummer *and* as a piano player. It's quite conceivable that some incredibly powerful and versatile musicians might be produced. But, we think, there are better ways of going about producing full and accomplished musicians, that something more than eclectic instruction by diverse methods on an array of instruments would work better. In short there needs to be a *curriculum.*

The common dictionary definition of curriculum "as a set of courses or subjects offered by an institution" simply doesn't go far enough. To teach students effectively, a curriculum or program of study ought to have what Arthur Steller calls "coherence," and sad to say, that trait is largely missing from school and college curricula. Now, we don't propose to take on the whole of the school curriculum, every subject and discipline, in this chapter. We'll limit ourselves to the English language arts, although before we are through, we will suggest how our field of language can, in fact, offer coherence in other fields and disciplines. Moreover, we'll argue that the concepts of coherence and integration do not apply just to the large structures of the school—the orchestration of courses—but to one's individual teaching as well. That is, many readers of this book will not be in a position to direct the orchestra and help it play with unity and integration. Many of us will play second fiddle or be exceptionally good oboists somewhere in the middle of the orchestra, hidden from the floodlights. But that should never prevent us from finding a kind of curricular coherence in our own day-to-day playing, our classroom teaching of flute or cymbals.

COHERENCE IN ENGLISH/LANGUAGE ARTS

Examining a typical English language arts curriculum guide often reveals an incredible amount of inconsistency and disarray, carefully masked by a good typing or printing job. In preparing this chapter, we reviewed over fifty curriculum guides from elementary, middle, and high schools around the country (and over a dozen from other countries). Some of them were collected during our travels to school districts and national meetings; many of them were described as "exemplary" by the National Council of Teachers of English, and a number of them were a part of the (inter)national movement to develop frameworks and standards for the English language arts. We also examined most of the major English language arts textbooks now on the market, for these, rather than the dusty curriculum guide or standards list, often describe what's "really" going on in the schools. While there is no obvious national curriculum or prototypical school, we think it will be useful to present some generalizations about the common characteristics of these materials in order to create a view of the current state of the K–12 English language arts curriculum.

The Elementary Years

"English," as such, does not exist for the elementary teacher. It is called "language arts" but is often broken down into its various components: reading, writing, spelling, vocabulary, etc. Here is perhaps the greatest weakness of the elementary curriculum, for despite the opportunity for integrated studies presented by the self-contained classroom, a great many elementary teachers tend to fragment language, presenting it to children in small bits and pieces. "Spelling" becomes a component all to itself. "Writing" becomes penmanship, often separated from "writing workshop." Elementary school children even pick up on these distinctions. We were talking to a third grader who was careful to distinguish "reading" (which meant going to the library) from "reading workbook" (which involved learning to alphabetize and to find "story grammars"), and to distinguish both from "story hour" (where the teacher read to the kids) and "literature" (where the youngsters read and discussed children's books). Is this a bassoon or a French horn we see before us?

In recent years, the "whole language movement" (See Weaver, *Understanding Whole Language*) has made great strides toward ending this fragmentation—to develop a natural flow from talk to writing to reading back to talk by centering instruction on "workshop" methods, where kids are essentially free to write on self-selected topics and to read and respond to either self-selected or clearly relevant books. If you're not familiar with "whole language," you'll learn a good deal about it in this book; it is complimentary to the experiential model we've described in the previous chapter. Yet even within this movement, the cracks sometimes show. We've been surprised to attend a number of meetings where, perhaps pressured to go "back to basics" or to produce high test scores, teachers have given mixed-message presentations on such topics as "Teaching Spelling: A Whole Language Approach" or "Phonics and Whole Language: Partners in Education." (We would have titled both those sessions "Strange Bedfellows"!) In short, though whole language offers the potential for truly integrated curricula, there is still a long way to go.

The Middle Schools

We also think that middle schools have done some very interesting things with efforts at curriculum integration in the past several decades. Rarely are these places called "junior high school" any longer; the "middle school approach" calls for centering instruction on adolescent needs and interests rather than mere preparation for high school, and middle school teachers have been particularly innovative in developing teamed, interdisciplinary instruction. Look at the list of units in Figure 2.2, a list that constitutes the English language arts curriculum in a middle school that we regard as doing a pretty good job of educating kids. There are many clever and engaging units here, many of them interdisciplinary: "Aquanauts and Astronauts" was a science/English unit, while "People in Conflict" involved social studies/language arts, and "Curtain Up!" was a team-wide effort at having kids write and produce one-act plays. Nevertheless, we invite you to consider the tacit definition of "language arts" that emerges from this list. Why must "Creative Composition" be isolated from literature units such as "Encounters and Insights"? Why must instruction in language basics always be isolated in "Building Blocks" units? If mass media are important, why are they set apart in a unit of their own rather than integrated with either literature or composition work? Children characteristically take many good and energetic units in these middle school years, many units inspired by both whole language and interdisciplinary intentions, yet often the work is not well orchestrated, leaping from jazz to country western to classical with no real bridge, no theoretical underpinning.

The Senior High Years

Now, at the risk of alienating the English staffs of some top-notch high schools, we'll argue that in contrast to both the elementary and middle school programs, senior high English comes off as a hodgepodge, that in the past several decades, far too little progress has been made in the thoughtful development of high school English programs. Indeed, our survey found that the dominating organization pattern remains as it was in the 1950s, with the dreary English I, II, III, and IV as course titles. The pattern we see most frequently in our review of curriculum guides (reinforced by the content of major senior high textbook series) is that of using the first two years of the high school as a general course in the core elements of reading and writing, followed by the too familiar pattern of literature approached chronologically and nationally at the upper levels: British, American, and possibly world literatures. There are some explanations for this conservatism. For one, high school teachers tend to see themselves as teachers of disciplines (in contrast to the lower levels where the focus is

Building Blocks of Communication
Curtain Up! (drama)
Focus on Life
People in Conflict
Power of the Paragraph
Western Sampler
Reinforcing Language Skills
Aquanauts and Astronauts
Communications Through Mass Media
Encounters and Insights
Creative Composition

Figure 2.2   Middle School Curriculum Units

more centered on children). Further, there is pressure to cover the elements of the field, whether English or science or math. College looms ahead for many students, and thus high school teachers are seriously committed to coverage of preparatory materials: college prep writing, the "canon" in literature, etc.

There has, in recent years, been enough interest in thematic teaching that many of the major textbooks offer alternative tables of contents, showing how national and world literatures can be broken down into a variety of themes or topics. Like the middle school topics previously cited, these seem to us interesting ways to engage with language (although the very tone of some of these units, e.g., "Critics of Society," imply a seriousness of purpose on the part of high school teachers that may take some of the spontaneity and laughter out of schoolwork). Further, many of the texts we examined offer a second alternative table of contents, divided by genre: poetry, drama, fiction, and nonfiction. This also suggests the academic or "coverage" nature of much high school English, with a focus, not so much on the experience of literature as on its formal traits and characteristics (topics which assuredly will be taken up all over again in students' "intro to lit" courses as English majors). A few high school programs continue to offer elective courses (often a holdover from totally elective curricula that were explored in the 1970s), but even these tend to be specialized or academic ("Shakespeare," "Advanced Creative Writing," "Journalism").

CURRICULUM: NOUN OR VERB?

Well, enough negativism. We fully recognize that the schools have, in recent years, been under enormous pressure to satisfy conflicting forces: parents and administrators interested in "basics," communities demanding job preparation skills rather than liberal arts training, colleges exerting pressure for "enculturated" entering students, the perennial complaints over graduates' "bad grammar" or "slovenly spelling." We also see strong evidence that English language arts teachers would like to push for curricula or programs that encompass the best of current thinking about language,

Critics of Society
Choice and Consequences
The Struggle for Justice
Search for Values
Freedom and Responsibility
Media and Modern Man
Inner Struggles
Hopes and Aspirations
Freedom and Responsibility
Popular Heroes
Family Courage and Challenges

Figure 2.3   Some Themes for High School Units

that they would like to get away from some of the old and conservative models and move toward genuinely experience-centered programs where students do, in fact, find and create coherence in their study. With that very positive assumption, then, we will proceed to suggest some of the ways in which we think English language arts teachers can not only find curricular coherence, but even serve as instructional leaders for finding coherence in other disciplines as well.

The word "curriculum" is a noun, "the name of a person, place, or thing." We'd like to see it transformed into a *verb:* something dynamic and changing, something that happens to and with persons in places called school where "things"—ideas, books, concepts—come alive. In the end, curriculum is not the dusty tome listing goals and objectives, but a set of flexible relationships and activities that evolve from a group of adults (the teachers) and a larger number of young people (the students) interacting with a set of resources: bricks and mortar, books, desks, pencils, paper, and language. When these parts function well together, they produce a community of language, a place where students read, write, and talk about concerns of their own, steadily and coherently increasing the range and complexity of their language skills. The English language arts curriculum, in short, is a process—somethin' happenin'—rather than a product or object, and its dimensions grow and shift just as surely as the needs and interests of the students change.

In order to be a verb rather than a noun, we think an English language arts curriculum (or any curriculum) needs to have four traits: For the first three, it must be *collaborative, experimental,* and *constructivist.* That is, it must involve negotiation between students and teachers; it must not be fixed in its content or form; and it must center itself on constructing or creating meanings. Forthly, it must be based on an *integrative* theory of instruction, created by teachers who are willing to take on the task of putting Humpty back together again, taking the scattered and fragmented elements of our field—spelling, vocabulary, expository writing, creative writing, learning to read, reading, speaking, play making, media reception, media production—and putting them back into a whole.

Figure 2.4 shows the product of teachers who do just that. It was compiled by groups of teachers across Nevada who were making an effort to create a coherent outline of English language arts instructions K–12. (The fruits of their efforts will be presented, in skeletal form, further along in this chapter). You might not agree with all the points in that outline, and you might find some of its points phrased a bit euphemistically; it is a product of a committee effort and involved a good deal of debate (often heated) and effort to articulate consensus. But it is a clear start toward a coherent curriculum, laying out the principles of an integrated theory of instruction that acknowledges the "parts" of the field but relates them to one another.

In our experience with curriculum development groups, we have found that many teachers balk at the task of writing down a philosophy of instruction. They often want to "skip the philosophical stuff," and move the discussion to brass tacks: What books do we want to teach? Why don't eighth graders know their parts of speech? Should we put *Romeo and Juliet* in grade nine or ten? Tempting as it may be to get down to the fine details of curriculum, we argue that without a coherent statement of philosophy, curriculum projects are pretty much doomed to regluing Humpty Dumpty. Curriculum needs to start with the whole egg. We always urge—fight with—curriculum groups to articulate their principles. Statements like Figure 2.4, like the statements of National Standards and various state standards, should be seen as both the starting point and an important end point of curriculum discussion, providing a touchstone for the more concrete matters that follow. (We also argue that individual teachers need such a *credo* of their own. Indeed, a major purpose of this book is to assist you in developing yours.)

THE DEVELOPMENTAL APPROACH TO CURRICULUM

Our own work on English language arts curriculum has been powerfully influenced by the work of a British educator, J. W. Patrick Creber, formerly of the University of Exeter (*Sense and Sensitivity; Thinking Through English*). He argues that for too long, the demands of disciplinary learning (the "content" of the disciplines) has taken precedence over the needs and interests of children. "We cannot," he says, "accept any such sacrifice—any dichotomy between the interests of the pupil and the interests of the subject. Such a distinction seems based on the false premise that the two are mutually exclusive or radically opposed." In English language arts, this means that, for Creber, what kids need to know about this thing called "English" must synchronize with what they need to know about language as they employ it for their own purposes. And this alliance is natural, he claims: "That method which is of greatest benefit to the child seems to be precisely the method which makes for the greatest vitality and sensitivity of language" (*Sense and Sensitivity*, p. 84).

This view leads Creber to a simple but ingenious approach to developing a course of instruction. First, the teacher must study the students in terms of their psychological, emotional, cognitive, and linguistic development. Only then can the teacher intelligently select experiences that mesh with both the students' needs and the content of the disciplines of English. We have come to call this a "developmental" approach to curriculum, meaning, simply, that as young people grow and *develop* as

"Our greatest human task is to make sense of the world. Even the youngest students come to school with years of experience at attempting to make sense of the events of their everyday lives. As educators, we become facilitators in helping children to continue to make sense of new forms of communication in the literate world."

Valerie Truce
Rita Cannan Elementary School, Reno

The overarching aim of the Nevada English/Language Arts Framework is for students to graduate from our schools able to communicate skillfully, both orally and in writing, to read and gather information for informed decisions and for pleasure, to use language successfully in modern communications media, to employ reading and writing across the curriculum, and to use their literacy successfully in their community. Research shows that language learning occurs best in a classroom environment where young people use and experiment with language in ways that provide meaningful and purposeful opportunities to think and communicate. Students should also have opportunities to assess their own experiences and to formulate problems and solutions both orally and in writing. Teachers should value and model the links among oral language, reading, writing, and other forms of discourse. The long-range aim of a literacy program is for students to become lifelong readers, writers, and learners.

The following principles of English/Language Arts learning are drawn from the experiences of Nevada teachers and from the professional literature . They provide the philosophical center for the Nevada Framework:

- Literacy should not be taught in fragments, but as a whole. Although teachers will necessarily discuss discrete activities of reading, writing, and oral language, our aim is to unify language arts instruction through a curriculum that draws on all elements of language in coordination.

- Students should increasingly develop consciousness of the nature of language and of their own processes for communicating successfully and solving new language problems.

- Schools must respect, appreciate, and build upon the diversity of languages students bring with them to school, while acting on the need for students to expand their uses of language into a variety of social, academic, and economic settings.

- Oral language skills such as storytelling, listening, and classroom talk form the basis of the language arts program, particularly in the primary grades but continuing throughout the K–12 program.

- A successful reading/literature program is based on frequent encounters with books, reading, and writing, with the broadest possible range of reading materials available: classic and contemporary, literary and workaday, teacher-, librarian-, and student-selected.

- Reading is best taught by helping readers extend the range of strategies they apply in order to comprehend and interpret texts.   *(continued)*

Figure 2.4   Nevada English/Language Arts Framework Rationale and Philosophy

- A successful reading program leads students to see reading not only as a utilitarian pursuit, but also as a pleasurable, aesthetic, and intellectual activity that can be continued outside the classroom for the rest of their lives.

- Writing is best taught as a process that leads to composing in an increasingly broad range of discourse forms that communicate successfully to a variety of audiences for a range of purposes.

- Students will increasingly develop control of the conventions of standard oral and written language through the processes of speaking and writing for real audiences.

- Mass media and electronic technologies are forms of receiving and producing language and, as such, are a vital part of the English classroom, the library, the school, and the community.

- Language arts are basic to learning in all disciplines, for language is a tool for learning, a medium of communication, and the basis of all thinking; thus, English/Language Arts activities must be practiced across the curriculum.

- Teachers of English/Language Arts should model involvement with the literacy program by reading, writing, and engaging in substantive discussion with their students.

From the *Nevada English Language Arts Framework* (August 1, 1995). Principal authors: Bill Abrams, Shirley Altick, Mary Beth Cody, Juliana Gabica, Launie Gardner, Elaine Healy, Anne Marie Kinne, Karen McGee, Bob McGinty, Diane Olds, Marsha Rogers, Anita Schlatter, Elaine Sherman, Stephen Tchudi, and Joanne Walen. By permission of the authors. All rights reserved.

Figure 2.4

people and as language learners, the task of the teacher is to find materials and activities that maximally support that development. Where does *Romeo and Juliet* belong? Before one assigns it to the ninth grade or the tenth, one should ask, "How well does it mesh with young people's growth, development, and interests?" An answer might be that because of its adolescent love interest, it might be quite appropriate for the ninth grade. Another, intriguing, challenging answer might be that because of the difficulty of Shakespeare's language, perhaps *Romeo and Juliet* (at least as a reading rather than viewing experience) isn't appropriate for the high school years at all! Creber challenges us and challenges the discipline. Gone are the days when one can simply teach books "because they're there," when one teaches *Moby Dick* or *The Scarlet Letter* because they're classics or because "these are great books that everybody should know." The classics must pay their way anew with every generation, every reader, with the support, of course, of a knowledgeable teacher. So does one or doesn't one put parts of speech in grade eight? First the teacher must ask, "Why is it that parts of speech don't stick in the minds of eighth graders? (Or for that matter, for fifth graders or twelfth graders?) What's the connection between parts of speech and student performance?" Taking a developmental approach, one might say, "Perhaps formal grammar just doesn't relate directly to the eighth grade students' writing. Perhaps instead of worrying quite so much about parts of speech, we should focus our work on helping students to learn to edit their work by other means." Under a developmental plan, the image of a restored Humpty Dumpty begins to emerge, like the reverse of the fading smile of a Cheshire Cat.

Our approach to curriculum, then focuses heavily on teacher observation and data gathering about students. Some of the questions teachers need to ask are shown in Figure 2.5. We think one must begin by creating a profile of students at various grade levels. To some extent, this involves a kind of stereotyping—this is what fourth graders or tenth graders are like—a stereotyping forced upon us by the nature of the school structure and the fact that it's *fourth* or *tenth* graders who show up in September and are clustered into classes by age levels. A good profile, then, also needs to discuss a range of behaviors.

In Nevada, a number of teachers statewide looking at student writing and other work, discussed their experiences teaching, talked over "what works" and what doesn't at particular levels. After a great deal of kid watching and talk, the teachers were able to describe broad developmental stages for their youngsters. They discovered "clusters" of developmental interests and characteristics, and they grouped these roughly by grade levels 1–3, 4–6, 7–8, 9–10, 11–12 (with plenty of room for overlap). The broad developmental clusters or "stages" they discovered are shown in Figure 2.6.

Excerpts from the profiles—we called them "benchmarks" following the terminology of David Jackson—are provided in Figure 2.5. Readers acquainted with the work of James Moffett and G. Robert Carlsen (as well as that of Creber) will recognize that the pattern identified here is one of "inner worlds to outer worlds," based on the observation that literacy begins with a small and personal community of parents and friends for the youngest children and moves to encompass the whole world, while literacy forms themselves begin with the oral and move to more and more sophisticated and "adult" kinds of reading and writing. Note, too, that as we discussed in Chapter 1,

- What are the principal common interests of students at this age: animals and pets? other boys and girls? the world outside? careers? college?
- What are the principal concerns that the students feel? What do they worry about most: themselves? their relationships with peers? their relationships with adults?
- Where are they in the process of becoming adults? In what ways are they adult like? In what ways are they operating under different patterns?
- How do these youngsters differ from one another? What are the ranges of interests, concerns, even physical and emotional traits?
- Which books, poems, stories have proven "sure fire" with this group?
- Which books appeal to their special interests?
- What kinds of writing and speaking topics work well for the students? Which prove less successful?
- What is the range of writing and reading interests in the group?
- Given free choice of language activities, which ones will students choose? What does this tell us about our students?
- What general range of language skills have students mastered to date? What can they *do* with language? What are they learning to do?

Figure 2.5   Profiling Students

this model sees adult competence as emerging naturally from children's growth and development, rather than imposing adult standards from the very beginning.

What can one do with such profiles? We argue (with Creber) that the profiles—constantly subject to revision—provide the rationale for teachers to make selections of materials and activities. Working with eleven- to fourteen-year-old students in British schools (the equivalent of U.S. grades seven through ten), Creber chose to focus on emerging adolescent sense and sensibility. Rather than giving students an "adult" diet of college preparatory literature, he emphasized such themes as "rediscovery of the familiar" (where students sharpen their memories and visual awareness), "growth of consciousness" (as they explore relations among themselves, their peers, and their community), and "imagination and morality" (as students move beyond "adolescent self consciousness" to explore wider and broader issues). Reading and writing activities of appropriate maturity were then selected (*Sense and Sensitivity*). (Again, the influence of Creber on the Nevada curriculum should be apparent.)

The Nevada teachers used the profiles or "benchmarks" in a variety of ways:

• to describe broad aims for English/language arts teaching at each level. For example, given the profile of kindergartners, the curriculum emphasized giving students initial awareness of the nature of print (but not compelling students to "read" or "write"), intensive oral language and dramatic activities, and considerable development of and languaging about personal experience. At the other end of the scale, the upper high school profiles suggest that instruction should emphasize independence of reading and writing, a wide range of canonical and noncanonical literature, research and investigative writing, and a focus on broad national and global languages and literatures.

• to describe appropriate books and readings for the various levels, developing a rationale for the selection and use of children's, young adult, and adult literature.

• to develop a set of model classroom teaching activities appropriate for the various grade levels, e.g., dramatically retelling stories for kindergartners, using invented spelling and language experience in the primary grades, moving into elementary "language across the curriculum" activities for the upper elementary, creating autobiographical journals and books in the middle school, developing group editing skills in the lower high school, and exhibiting success in a senior inquiry project at the upper levels.

Grade Level	Developmental Stage
Pre-K (before formal schooling)	Pre-emergent Literacy
Kindergarten	Preparations for Literacy
Early Primary: 1—2—3	Emergent Literacy
Upper Elementary: 3—4—5—6	Exploring Literacy
Middle School: 6—7—8	Personal Literacy
Early High School: 8—9—10	Community Literacy
Late High School: 10—11—12	Extended Literacy

Figure 2.6

• to describe the kinds of language skills that can be expected to emerge at various levels. Under pressure from the legislature and the state department of education to develop lists of minimum skills, the Nevada teachers found that the benchmarks or profiles provided a sensible rationale for describing expectations. One can explain why, for example, total mastery of standard spellings is quite unrealistic for primary graders, while reasonably full mastery might be expected of high school seniors, or why *Moby Dick* should assuredly not be required reading for high school sophomores, but might be placed on an individualized reading program for the seniors.

• to orchestrate the selection of themes and topics for instruction. Refer again to figures 2.2 and 2.3. We noted the apparently eclectic nature of that list. Profiles or benchmarks provide a rationale that allows one to sequence and structure topics to create a natural or developmental flow.

• to integrate the curriculum by showing how reading, writing, listening, speaking and media activities flow into one another.

• to integrate the curriculum by finding and offering a rationale for interdisciplinary work. As the "benchmarks" suggest, each developmental level or stage in kid development is matched by an expanded view of the world. Creber has claimed that there should be no mismatch between the demands of English, the discipline, and English, the language used by kids; therefore, the benchmarks allow us to extend this concept to other disciplines as well, in particular, by showing how students can use their emerging language skills for an increasingly wide range of knowledges in other fields.

• to describe appropriate ways of assessing student work. The profiles point the way toward classroom activities, which in turn suggest means of assessment: How will we know whether students are, in fact, achieving what we think is appropriate (or, for that matter, whether our original profiles were accurate)? The Nevada teachers observed that too often, assessment is seen as something emerging at the end of teaching—as after you teach a unit, you give a test. They argued that to the contrary, assessment is an essential feature of curriculum development from beginning to end, from the initial profiling of students, through assessment that guides the teacher in understanding the skills and interests of the students, through classroom activities that produce visible, tangible results. A list of the kinds of assessment strategies useful in this sort of work is given in Figure 2.7.

To recap: The "developmental" approach to curriculum we're describing here calls for:

1. Articulation of a rationale or theory of instruction.
2. Profiles of students' intellectual, emotional, and linguistic growth, development, needs and interests.
3. Selection of aims, materials, activities, themes, topics, etc. based on the profile.
4. Constant and multivariate assessment as a means of not only measuring or documenting student achievement, but of the focus of the curriculum and program itself.

A good curriculum is "assessment based"; we need to assess our students constantly for their strengths, levels of development, and indications of readiness as well as problem areas. Thus teachers should design assessments that inform the curriculum process from the outset. Assessment should precede instruction and continue through curriculum development. It must be carried out using a variety of measures, including those developed by the teachers who create the program. We call this an "assessment base" for the English/Language Arts curriculum. Many different forms of assessment will be employed by the teacher seeking a comprehensive understanding of students' work.

Within the school system, Nevada teachers use the following methods of assessment, arrayed here from lower to higher grade levels:

- Children's oral story reading
- Discussion of children's literature
- Performing tasks, following instructions
- Drawing pictures in response to reading
- "Make believe" writing and reading (reading and writing readiness)
- Oral retelling of stories
- Children selecting and handling books
- Voluntary reading
- Teacher-created attitude surveys
- Observation records of strategies used in oral reading
- Student self-assessment
- Teacher/student conferences
- Teacher/parent conferences
- Interaction with other children
- Show and tell presentations
- Children's bulletin board displays
- Computer work (writing and reading)
- Video or audio tapes of class performances
- Teacher-made examinations—short answer, multiple choice, essay
- A specific project that requires reading and writing
- Activities that reflect reading and writing for pleasure
- Oral presentations
- Participation in discussions
- Books selected from a variety of genres
- Students' written reflection on their work
- Displays as a reflection and a source of pride in learning
- Public presentations of school work
- Publication of student writing in newsletters and/or magazines
- Reports of independent study across the curriculum   *(continued)*

Figure 2.7   Assessment Strategies Nevada English Language Arts Framework

- Library use
- Media use
- Observation of student response to literature (written and oral)
- Expressions of interest, enjoyment, curiosity
- Student involvement and interaction in class
- Standardized testing
- Reading and writing beyond the classroom
- Peer group discussion, panels, debates
- Large-scale student projects
- Reading as making choices
- Reading beyond school materials
- Writing for public occasions
- Samples of work from other classes: science, mathematics, history, art, health, and physical recreation
- Report card grades

We encourage teachers and schools to have students create *portfolios* or collections of their work—demonstrations of what they can do with language. As students complete and continue their work, it is placed in a folder. From time to time, the teacher asks the students to order the folder and to select their work to be placed in the portfolio. Teachers may also specify that a portfolio needs to include evidence of a variety of kinds of writing and reading. A portfolio can also contain other kinds of evidence of performance, e.g., an audio or video tape, artwork, photography, letters sent and received. In addition, portfolios include student self-assessment as young people describe what they feel their work demonstrates. Students also reflect on their growth as language learners and even on their development as learners.The broad array of assessment strategies outlined in this document, coupled with portfolios of student work, and aligned with various standardized tests, will provide a rich and detailed portrait of the ways in which students are growing as language learners.

From the *Nevada English Language Arts Framework* (August 1, 1995). Principal authors: Bill Abrams, Shirley Altick, Mary Beth Cody, Juliana Gabica, Launie Gardner, Elaine Healy, Anne Marie Kinne, Karen McGee, Bob McGinty, Diane Olds, Marsha Rogers, Anita Schlatter, Elaine Sherman, Stephen Tchudi, and Joanne Walen. By permission of the authors. All rights reserved.

Figure 2.7

We don't by any means imagine that this is the only way to go about creating a coherent program; it is the best one we can come up with that is consistent with what we see as state-of-the-art thinking about the relationships among individual development, the need to instruct students in "classes," the demands of the public for accountability and assessment, and, above all, teachers' intuitive sense of what is right, what "works" in instruction. In contrast to many curriculum approaches, the developmental model expands and rationalizes opportunities rather than limiting them.

DEVELOPMENTAL CURRICULUM AND INDIVIDUAL CLASSROOMS

And limits there are in most school systems. Comprehensive school-, district-, or state-wide curriculum efforts are all too rare in the schools, in no small measure because of the amount of time and energy required. All too often, we've found, curriculum design centers around adoption of a textbook, which, in turn, dictates the pattern of instruction. State and district mandated tests place other limits on the teacher, as do the expectations of teachers at the next level as well as parental concerns. What is the teacher to do?

We suggest, quite simply: *Know the limits.* Then *teach within and through* and, if necessary, *around, over,* and *under* them. Creber's program, which inspired our developmental approach, was actually created for an individual classroom, not a massive curriculum project. Even in the most limiting and restrictive of schools, there remains an enormous amount of freedom and initiative open to teachers. For example, if the district or state has some sort of writing proficiency test, the teacher can prepare students for it most successfully by having them write *at their appropriate developmental level* on self-selected topics, rather than, say drilling them on grammar or having them write abstract papers on arid topics. If a school district has stated expectations for literature and reading achievement, the wise teacher will meet those expectations by teaching texts appropriate to students' abilities and needs. If the district has adopted and mandated a textbook, a good teacher will use it flexibly, picking and choosing among literary selections that are appropriate to the students, certainly not following the text slavishly from beginning to end. If the school requires and tests on *Moby Dick* (heaven forbid), well, that's just one of those things, but even in that absurd situation, we think a developmental framework gives one a rationale for approaching the task, knowing, for example, that students will be much more interested in the adventure story of the whale hunt than in Melville's literary theory or his expository passages about the nature of whales and the whaling industry.

INTEGRATING AND EXPANDING THE CURRICULUM

We'll make one last claim on behalf of the developmental model: Not only does it provide a way of integrating the curriculum, it offers directions for extending and expanding it as well, to create what we call the *multi-curriculum* based on its core value of seeing and searching out multiples: disciplines, communities, media, intelligences, and languages.

The Multidisciplinary Curriculum

To us, one of the most exciting areas in curriculum these days is that of the multidisciplinary or interdisciplinary curriculum. Although definitions and descriptions vary (see Tchudi and Lafer, *The Interdisciplinary Teacher's Handbook;* Jacobs, *Interdisciplinary Curriculum*) this approach assumes that formal "disciplines" serve much better as scholarly organizers than as ways of packaging instruction for novices. To learn the disciplines, one needs not isolate them; to learn a field, one needs to learn it in context. Language, of course, is the most natural of inter-disciplinary topics, for no iota of information, no fact or concept, no principle or law in *any* field is void of language. Where English language arts teachers have often limited their reading and writing activities to more or less classic children's, young adult, and adult literature, the multi-disciplinarians propose opening the whole library, the whole universe of inquiry to students. This can often happen in team-taught classes or through block scheduling or linked and fused classes—social studies and English teachers, science and language, math/science/language. But the fact is that the English language arts teacher is in an ideal position to go it alone if necessary. All you have to do is open up the boundaries and possibilities for your students.

Let's briefly explore two of the themes suggested in figures 2.2 and 2.3, "Aqua-nauts and Astronauts" (middle school) and "Critics of Society" (senior high). For the former, the interdisciplinary connections between math, science, and English are pretty clear. We imagine that this unit would include a good deal of reading of young adult nonfiction (books for adolescents on sea exploration and outer space), but we could also imagine it moving nicely into social studies, with questions ranging from society's needs to explore beyond *terra firma* to political and ethical questions: Will it be necessary for us to farm the sea because of overpopulation? Is it possible that we will have to send our trash and nuclear wastes into outer space, and is this a responsi-ble thing to do? "Critics of Society" already sounds rather like a social studies unit, so we could imagine team-teaching this with a history teacher who could help us ex-amine major social critics of then and now. Equally valuable, we think, would be to help students see the connection between literature, art, and social criticism. After all, artists seldom do "pretty pictures" just to be amusing—they have messages, often powerful and resonating ones—to communicate through their art. Science would certainly come into play as we examine technological advancements—the motor car, the television set, nuclear power—and the unintended side effects those have had on society. And it almost goes without saying that virtually *any* work of literature, from short poem to *magnum opus* novel, can be successfully interpreted as an act of civic criticism. Such a multidisciplinary unit would quickly move beyond classroom walls to involve investigation of "our town."

Perhaps the most important contribution English language arts teachers can make to the multidisciplinary movement is through the idea of a "rhetoric of in-quiry" (Simons). In this "post modern" age, people have come to realize that the idea of "truth" is elusive, that knowledge does not exist so much "out there" waiting to be "found," as it does "in here"—in the individual and collective mind—where it is cre-ated out of perceptions, values, and intentions. Although "the rhetoric of inquiry" is an abstract concept, it cuts at the heart of any multidisciplinary unit. The aim of mul-tidisciplinarity is not just to expand knowledge (though it does so very effectively and, we think, more efficiently than isolated disciplinary classrooms), but coming to see the processes by which knowledge is constructed, and that process involves argu-ment, judgment, and persuasion. The English language arts teacher, whether teaching alone or as part of a team, serves as more than one who can locate good books and design engaging writing assignments; he or she is also a "rhetorical inquisitor," help-ing kids look critically at the making of knowledge: Why do you think the author said that? Why do authors disagree with one another? Define your terms! What does that statement really mean? How do scientists write differently from historians? How do historians write differently from one another? How is a painting like a poem? like a newspaper editorial? Whom do you believe and why? Can you restate that in your own words? Can you move beyond restatement and add new ideas? Convince us!

The Multiple Community Curriculum

We use this term to refer to several related areas of curriculum interest, the push toward *multicultural* and *multiethnic* studies, the interest in recognizing underrepresented communities (women, special interest groups and others), linked to the concept of the *classroom as community* and the need for schools to encourage *community involvement,* even to the extent of regarding the world itself as a *global community.* The developmental curriculum invites such expansion, for kids at all levels are almost insatiably curious about communities, the ones of which they are a member, and the ones of which they are not.

Chapter 6 of this book goes into considerable detail on reading resources for young adults, in particular, multicultural and multiethnic literature, as well as literature about other previously neglected communities. We hasten to add that the interest in such literature should not be mere tokenism, as it is in so many commercial textbooks with their sprinkling among the traditional canonical literature of works by minorities, writers from other cultures, literature by and about women. As we've implied, in a developmental curriculum, the standard literary works will have to prove their value anew, *as will literature from other communities.* That is, the test is not whether a work is great *or* representative of another community, but whether it sings to the students, makes connections with them and their lives. The interesting thing about multicommunity literature, we find, is that it *does* sing to our students, at least on a par and often eclipsing traditional literature from the traditionally privileged classes. Finding these literatures is more work than teaching out of a text but is infinitely more rewarding, and we hope our work in Chapter 6 will give you a start and some enthusiasm for the search.

Though not immediately apparent, perhaps, we see community involvement as closely and excitingly related to the introduction of a wider range of cultural literatures in the classroom. In recent years, schools have made great progress in getting kids out of the classroom and into the community. Many schools, particularly secondary schools but not excluding the elementary grades, have developed a range of internship, public service, and community involvement programs. Kids work in day care and senior citizen centers, they make physical improvements to their community, they interview all manner of citizens and community leaders, they bring guest speakers to class, they write letters to editors and politicians, and they develop and present plans for urban and suburban renewal, both physical and spiritual. In the process, they come to see that the concerns they read about and discuss in their multicultural literature are not simply "out there" in exotic and foreign lands and cultures. Those same concerns are reflected in "our town," and one can find local examples and illustrations of all the great questions that are explored by literature and the humanities: How do I get along and survive? What makes for a good life? What are valid aims and ambitions? What's the right thing to do? Where am I going as an individual? What is my "family"? Who are my "neighbors"? What do I owe to my community? How do we—the community—express our concerns? What is our music and art? our politics? our communal culture?

Such questions about one's immediate community lead inexorably to concerns about the global community. Multicultural exploration should lead to more than a collection of postage stamps, an international "food fair," or the conventional unit on "mythologies from other lands" (although each of those may play its part). In our experience, many social studies and history units turn global cultures into museum pieces for study and exposition. We argue that the English language arts teacher is in a strong and powerful position to make cultures *live,* through literature, through writing and discussion, through community connections.

In addition to filling the classroom with multicultural literatures (a task made much easier, by the way, with an Internet connection that lets one browse the world for cultural information), making the community connection for a class is literally no further away than the telephone book. As teachers plan units—aquanauts, critics of society, justice, humor and laughter—they merely need to browse the yellow pages to find resources: the local dive shop or SCUBA center, a community housing authority, judges and attorneys, comedians and comediennes. Moreover, most community libraries have extensive lists of resources, including public service agencies that can both supply speakers and benefit from your students' involvement, lists of hundreds of volunteer organizations, even sources of funding for school-based projects in the arts and humanities. Fax, phone, and particularly electronic mail extend the dimensions of the community at low cost, making it quite possible for the English language arts classroom to become a microcosm of the global village.

The Multimedia Classroom

We will make the case for English as a mass medium in Chapter 12, arguing that all media are, in one way or another, language based and therefore not only appropriate, but vital as sources of information and expression in the English language arts classroom.

To that we'll simply add two points:

1. The "multimedia" classroom can and should also include the "media" of the brother and sister fine arts: painting and graphics, photography, dance, music, design, and so forth. The fine arts have traditionally been given short shrift by the schools: Witness the fact that in most elementary schools the music and art teacher come in as outsiders once a week or once a month and that in the high schools these topics are almost invariably electives, often limited to a select few students who are seen as talented. In his book, *English Within the Arts,* Peter Abbs makes the case that artistic production can be a unifying theme in the English language arts, with students' written work being treated as and enhanced by expressions in the fine arts. While just a few English teachers have the qualifications to teach fine arts, and we're not recommending that you turn your class into a painting workshop or music lab, you can certainly

encourage and offer options for your students to explore these areas as part of their work. Too, we highly recommend that as a break from your hectic life as a teacher, you sign up for the occasional community fine arts class: Take a course in water colors and compare what you learn to the writing process; sign up for a workshop on computer graphics; sing in the community choir. Bring what you learn back into your classroom.

[handwritten margin note: we as Eng-teachers should take fine arts class & bring back]

2. Study the cultural and community implications of media. The media—film, television, photography, music, sculpture, art—are both tools or technologies of expression (as are the pencil and brush), and definers of culture. In a wonderful book, *City as Classroom,* the late Canadian media critic, Marshall McLuhan argued, that any tool or technology is an extension of a human faculty and thus can be examined as a "medium." For McLuhan, the car is an extension of the human foot, and can be examined for its cultural effects, just as we would study how computers have revolutionized communication and the hammer revolutionized construction. What "messages" do cars send by way of design? Why do people pay more attention to the shape of a car than its engine? How do cars effect the way we design and lay out our cities? Other media explored by McLuhan include *money* (which saves us carrying barter items around on our backs), *light bulbs* (which have extended our days to twenty-four hours), and *airplanes* (which, along with electronics, have turned our world into a global village). The links to cultural studies and our emphasis on multiple *communities* should be apparent, and we urge you to include the study of media effects as part of your expanded English language arts classroom. What tools and media of communication do different cultures employ? How do urban oral art forms—street art, rap—differ from and influence what's heard on the radio and hung in museums? Why do some cultures value music more than literature? Why do we put literature in heavy anthologies (tools) for students to carry around? How is television reshaping global cultures? How do media—particularly TV—reshape and influence our culture? In this way media become more than novelty items in the classroom. Not only do they help us extend the curriculum, they can provide a means for integrating our study as well.

The Multiple Intelligences Curriculum

[handwritten margin note: Gardner = multiple intelligences]

The work of Harvard psychologist Howard Gardner in promoting the concept of "multiple intelligences" is widely known. In his words, "the essence of the theory is to respect the many differences among people, the multiple variations in the ways that they learn, the several modes by which they can be assessed, and the almost infinite number of ways in which they can leave a mark on the world" (in Armstrong vi–vii). Gardner's research suggests seven major modes or ways in which people can go about learning and expressing themselves in the world. Two of these—*linguistic* and *logical-mathematical*—have been the mainstays of education. The domination of those two is evidenced by our traditional interest in the 3 Rs of reading, 'riting, and 'rithmetic. He argues that at least five more intelligences need to be explored:

spatial or artistic: the ability to visualize imaginatively, to see relationships, to represent one's ideas graphically

bodily-kinesthetic or physical: the ability to act, dance, play a sport, sculpt, perform surgery, change the oil

musical: both understanding through music and the ability to create it

interpersonal: the characteristics of "people persons," those who get along best in the world face to face, chatting rather than writing

intrapersonal: the characteristics of the independent person, one who knows and can operate from a reservoir of self knowledge and understanding. (See also Armstrong.)

Predictably, we find much to admire in Gardner's work and find its implications quite consistent with the developmental, multicurriculum. We do wonder about his limiting of intelligences to *seven;* if seven, we say, why not seventeen or seventy or seven hundred? In verbal behavior alone one can see a rich variety of intelligences at work: kids who excel at poetic intelligence or expository intelligence; youngsters who are best at interpretive responses to literature and those who do better at affective response. To pigeon hole all skill at language in one category seems to us to be a self contradiction in the theory. Moreover, we need to point out (as we do throughout this book), that verbal intelligence is a necessary part of the other six. We have a hard time imagining a sculptor or painter who does not, at one level or another, talk about his or her work, if not publicly, at least internally. The linguistic base of the interpersonal intelligence is obvious, and the person with intrapersonal self-knowledge develops this through *language* as we have shown in Chapter 1.

Drawing on those concerns while fundamentally agreeing with Gardner, we suggest that an English language arts program may be the best place in the school to develop multiple intelligences. Gardner and his colleagues include a considerable amount of thematic, interdisciplinary teaching in their work. By encouraging students to read, write, listen, speak, and create in as many media, forms, and genres as possible, English teachers, rather than limiting their teaching to one intelligence, are automatically helping students extend the range of their verbal *and other* intelligences. Moreover, as we have clearly suggested, we think the English language arts classroom ought to be a friendly haven for the fine arts, so that we claim the languages of art, music, dance, and even physical recreation as part of "our" program.

Gardner's list of intelligences can, in fact, serve as a kind of checklist for planning an English curriculum or unit.

- Are we relying too much on traditional verbal intelligence—readin' and 'riting—in our classes? In particular, are we limiting our use of print forms to traditional canonical literature and schoolhouse essays? Are we making the most of our potential to help students make their mark on the world by exploiting the full creativity of language?

- Have we made links with other arts? Do our units include music and art? Are students allowed to compose in these forms as well as in words?

- Is there a physical, hands-on element in our program? Do kids *perform* their writing? Can they create plays and dramas? Do they get out of the classroom and meet with real people who do things other than write books?

- Is our classroom a true community where kids can maximally develop their interpersonal skills?

- Does our classroom provide multiple opportunities for personal reflection and the development of (linguistic) and other kinds of self reliance?

The concept of multiple intelligences, then, offers yet another way in which we can expand the curriculum while finding ways to integrate it, in this case, putting Humpty back together again by carefully linking our instruction to an understanding of the multiple ways in which the human mind functions.

The Multilingual Classroom

Under this concept we will link several curricular concerns. First, as we've implied in the previous section, we think the English language arts curriculum must take responsibility for developing multiple intelligences, multiple *languages.* The aim of the developmental curriculum is to help students become fluent in myriad languages, the languages of interpersonal relations, the languages of other disciplines, the language of poetry, the language of exposition, the language of independence and self reliance. We aim for multiple oral literacies: the ability to converse, to speak in public, to negotiate with others, to listen intelligently to others. And we aim for literacies beyond print: the ability to view and respond to television, skill at using the Internet, the capability to use the full range of electronic tools that are available.

However, the concept of multilingualism is important in another, more restricted sense, and that includes a "literacy" that appreciates and has the ability to function in a variety of discourse communities, an understanding of what Patrick Courts calls "dialect, discourse, and community." In his book, *Multicultural Literacies,* Courts deals powerfully and candidly with the question that worries both educators and the general public, "What do we do for people who don't talk and write the way 'we' do?" He carefully explores the concept of discourse communities and argues for a constructivist approach that expands language use and can honor the voices of such minorities as African Americans, Native Americans, Asian Americans, and Latino Americans while offering them opportunities to grow as language users.

As we will discuss in more detail in future chapters, an English language arts program ought to be *expansionist;* that is, we believe that every child, regardless of language variety, should be given the fullest and richest opportunity to expand the range of discourses he/she can employ and appreciate. In this respect, we strongly favor what is sometimes called "mainstreaming" of second language students. Although kids who are new to English obviously need some introductions to the language, separate from the other native speakers, as quickly as possible they should be put into classes where they will experience the full and natural range of English language. However, this does not mean mainstreaming them into classes where the reading is *Moby Dick* or *The Scarlet Letter.* Rather, we would have them mainstreamed into classes built on the principles of the developmental curriculum, including mentoring

relate)
to the
imp. of
Mainste-
aming
ESC

by a teacher who is willing to help students find the right materials to read, to allow them to engage as full members in the classroom community. We would have them mainstreamed, then, into highly individualized English language arts classes that feature self-selected reading and writing, a great deal of lively interaction, and the opportunity to push one's literacy to the next level. Despite the conservatism of school curricula, we find increasing numbers of classrooms where those conditions exist, and we hope that the readers of this book will be among those whose classrooms are both havens and opportunities for the kids who don't talk the way "we" do, where, no matter what a child's previous background may be, he or she leaves the class confident in saying, "I speak a lot more languages than I used to."

CURRICULUM PLANNING: TOP DOWN—BOTTOM UP

We began this chapter talking about curriculum guides, mandated objectives, required textbooks, and the like. For some very good and sometimes not-so-good reasons, top-down curriculum planning is a built-in part of the educational system. Top-down planning and mandating is a bad thing when it comes about from a distrust of teachers, often reflected in an obsession with "standards" and testing. We've heard a number of administrators argue that unless skills and knowledges are placed on an exam, teachers won't teach them. This sort of Procrustean approach to curriculum may appear to provide unity and integration, but in fact leads to further isolation as teachers find themselves covering fragmented knowledge that is likely to be tested, rather than being free to integrate their discipline.

On the other hand, we don't particularly favor the kind of license that de-unifies curriculum by leaving it all up to the individual teacher. Despite or because of external mandates, that's the way it is in a large number of schools today, with teachers working in isolation.

We favor what's called bottom-up curriculum reform. In the first place, this notion respects the skills and abilities of individual teachers, even the idiosyncratic ones who may be off "doing their own thing." Bottom-up curriculum theory also acknowledges that, in the end, the curriculum is what happens in individual classrooms, not what is written in the guide or textbook. But it also calls for the English language arts faculty (and the larger faculty) to function as a true community of teacher/learners, with openness to discussion and debate about what is happening and what needs to be happening. In the many workshops that took place during formation of the Nevada Framework cited earlier, the most exciting and important components were not the production of lists and caveats, but the interaction between teachers. Time and again we've seen that when teachers are given a chance to talk—especially time away from the hurly-burly and confusion of everyday teaching—they come up with imaginative and often integrative solutions to curriculum issues.

Our closing bit of advice in this chapter, then, centers not on the design of curriculum or even the principles of the developmental curriculum, but on the need for teachers to cultivate their own communities of discourse. Sometimes the schools will supply that opportunity through in-service days, common planning periods, and the like, but our experience suggests that too often school-sanctioned curriculum planning is concerned with top-down rather than bottom-up efforts. Teachers need to find ways of creating these communities for themselves: regular lunches with colleagues (in school if necessary, sometimes on Saturdays), active participation in professional organizations, seeking out summer education opportunities such as college classes or educational travel, getting on the Internet to converse with colleagues on common issues and problems, forming a writing group, forming a reading group, lobbying with the principal for a new program or structure, talking with kids about what's going on in their lives and classrooms . . . the list of possibilities is endless.

The integrated curriculum, in the end, is a matter of community.

◆ EXPLORATION

◆ What is *your* theory of instruction for the English language arts? That's too broad a question! Look at Figure 2.4, the set of assumptions Nevada teachers have made about the curriculum. Where do you stand on these questions and issues? What do you think is missing from the list? How would you revise or challenge these statements? As a step toward building a collegial community, hash over this list with a group of colleagues, including, if you're bold, people whose point of view may differ sharply from your own.

◆ Review the Nevada profiles or benchmarks in Figure 2.6. Based on *your* own experiences, critique these profiles. Do they ring true to you? How would you expand or extend or modify each profile? Remember, the purpose of this work is *not* to pigeon-hole or limit students, but to try to get a handle on curriculum from the perspective of the student, rather than letting the disciplinary materials, *Moby Dick* or *Wind in the Willows,* parts of speech or parts of poems, dictate the structure.

◆ The administrative structures of a school both simplify instruction and make it more complex. Given your responses to the two previous items, consider whether the following structures would help or hinder your curriculum. Which of the following are worthy of being preserved or saved? Which would, with some modification, be useful? To whom?

	Preserve	Discard	Modify
Schools	[ ]	[ ]	[ ]
Classes	[ ]	[ ]	[ ]
Courses	[ ]	[ ]	[ ]
Grades	[ ]	[ ]	[ ]
Teachers	[ ]	[ ]	[ ]
Textbooks	[ ]	[ ]	[ ]
Disciplines	[ ]	[ ]	[ ]
Semesters or terms	[ ]	[ ]	[ ]
Administrators	[ ]	[ ]	[ ]
Counselors	[ ]	[ ]	[ ]
Class periods	[ ]	[ ]	[ ]
Recess	[ ]	[ ]	[ ]

Alton P. Grandstaff,
Superintendent

NEW INSTRUCTIONAL PROGRAM IN ENGLISH

Deeply concerned about the quality of literacy education, the Board of Education of Canterbury is encouraging the development of three alternative or charter schools: Chaucer Senior High School, Pardoner Middle School, and Pilgrim Elementary. The Board seeks proposals from groups of citizens and educators for the language arts curriculum for these schools.

Proposals must be broad in scope and reflect the range and diversity of Canterbury young people. We have won an "Everytown USA" award and see ourselves as being representative of small cities everywhere in the U.S. We have a reliable but aging manufacturing base and a growing service sector of the economy. Our minority populations have grown considerably in recent years, and the Board is committed to equal educational opportunity and to preserving and celebrating diversity. Our schools need to prepare some students to enter the job market after high school graduation, but a number will go on to higher education; the needs of both groups must be met.

The Board of Education has no particular pattern or model involved and invites groups to develop highly imaginative, but sound innovative programs.

Proposals will be discussed at a public hearing.

Figure 2.8   The Canterbury Public Schools, Canterbury, U.S.A.

◆ Explore "The Canterbury Schools Simulation." This activity roleplays the development of an English language arts program for an alternative or charter school for the public schools of Canterbury, U.S.A. The superintendent of schools, Alton Grandstaff, has invited educators and parents to submit designs for three new experimental schools: a high school, a middle school, and an elementary school. Read Grandstaff's letter (Figure 2.8). Working with a small group of peers and colleagues, draw up a plan for the school of your choice. How would it be structured? What would it aim to accomplish? How would you go about creating the school? In short, this activity invites you to brainstorm for your ideal school, presumably putting into practice some of the ideas proposed in this chapter.

To add to the simulation:

1. Make sure members of your planning group role play school constituents: parents, students, business people.
2. Hold the public hearing mentioned in Grandstaff's letter. While planning teams present, other members of your professional community can role-play board members, school administrators, parents, other teachers, etc. What are the obstacles and objections to implementing your plan?

◆ Explore the implications of the multicurriculum concept for a course or unit that you are interested in teaching. Consider:

• What provisions have you/can you include to make the project truly multidisciplinary?

• In what ways does it involve and reflect multiple communities of language learners, including involvement in the local community as well as multiethnic, multicultural, and global concerns?

• Does it provide opportunities for students to explore ideas and express themselves in multiple media, in particular, the fine arts?

• How does it offer students of different learning styles to expand the repertoire of their intelligences? (Is language a solid component in the exploration of any intelligence?)

• How can your unit or course expand students' grasp of languages? In particular, how does the project integrate the needs and interests of youngsters whose native language may not be English and/or who speak a variety of English not usually regarded as "prestige."

• Looking at the assessment strategies described in Figure 2.7, what sorts of assessment and evaluation instruments and strategies can you build into the unit to ensure that you are meeting your multiple aims and objectives?

RELATED READINGS

In addition to the works by Creber, Moffett, Abbs, and Carlsen mentioned earlier, we strongly encourage a reading of David Jackson's *Continuity in Secondary English,* which, while written in the 1980s, remains the best and most detailed exemplar of the ideas of the developmental curriculum in action. Steve's book for the Association for Supervision and Curriculum Development, *Planning and Assessing the English Language Arts* expands on some of the ideas discussed in this chapter. It includes four strong narratives written by English language arts teachers who have been through a variety of top-down and bottom-up curriculum development projects, and their experiences are usefully studied. The National Council of Teachers of English publishes an annual volume of exemplary English curriculum guides which can help you keep in touch with schools all across the country. The NCTE journals also include frequent discussion, if not of broad curriculum issues, at least of specific curricula in action. The best source for up-to-date discussion of school curriculum issues, in particular, interdisciplinary approaches, is *Educational Leadership,* the journal of the Association for Supervision and Curriculum Development.

CHAPTER 3

CREATING INSTRUCTIONAL UNITS

The term "units" is one that teachers use loosely. "I've just finished a unit on writing poetry," says Teacher A, who has spent a week having students read and write poetry in many different forms. "I'm about to start my popular culture unit," says Teacher B, who will spend the next eight weeks having her students explore mass media. "I'm falling behind in my unit on intolerance," says Teacher C, who is halfway through reading *The Diary of Anne Frank*.

An instructional unit can range from a few days of concentrated study to an entire course. Some teachers may have several units going at once: a Fridays-only writing unit, taught along with a Monday-Wednesday literature unit, while a Thursdays-only free reading unit is in progress.

In this chapter we use the term "unit" to mean all of the above, consistent with popular usage. A unit, then, is simply an organized block of instruction. However, we place particular emphasis on units that extend over a period of time—from a few weeks to a month or more. In general, it is fairly easy to put together short units where the end is in sight right from the beginning. By contrast, teachers often have difficulty planning and sustaining experiences for their students working over a period of many weeks or several months. If a unit is not carefully structured, it can degenerate into a string of loosely related activities, and, to borrow from Shakespeare, "Tomorrow, and tomorrow and tomorrow, creeps in this petty pace from day to day."

Of course, there are some very good reasons for keeping a unit flexible, not planning it so tightly that there is no opportunity to change course or direction. If teachers are responsive to the needs, interests, and abilities of the students, some of the outcomes of an instructional unit will emerge as students react to the material. In the course of reading a novel such as Peter Dickinson's *A Bone from Dry Sea,* students may become fascinated by scientific ideas such as the sea-ape theory or the beginnings of human reason, in which case the teacher may want to schedule library time so that students can find information they will share orally or in writing. Still, it is one thing to individualize by providing options for students *within* a well-designed unit framework and quite another to teach from day to day with no real sense of direction. This chapter presents a pattern for planning units—whether a ten-day "mini-unit" or a full-term course—that allows for careful, comprehensive design, yet still allows room for meeting individual needs. Much of unit building depends on the teacher and his or her individual style and values. You must discover patterns of organization and activity that are comfortable for you while still being productive for your students.

It is also important to state two axioms about unit building:

1. A good instructional unit will be based on careful assessment of students' needs and interests. This may seem self-evident to the reader, but we have witnessed (alas, sometimes in our own classes) students plodding through ingeniously designed units that simply do not make connections. In some cases the failure grows from inappropriate content (e.g., a unit on eighteenth-century British poetry for a class of general ability juniors); in others it may simply be a result of expecting too much (e.g., the formal, footnoted research paper for seventh graders).

2. A good instructional unit will be consistent with the teacher's articulated philosophy of the discipline and of instruction and be in line with what is considered to be best practice. That is, a unit should reflect the teacher's absolute conviction that this work is something valuable for students to know, and it should further reflect his or her understanding of how young people go about learning in and through language. It is with this second axiom that prepackaged units, whether in textbook or school curriculum guide, may cause problems, and the teacher needs to make some careful decisions before teaching from or adapting such materials.

TOPICS AND STRUCTURES FOR UNITS

An instructional unit can be created on almost any topic in the known, or for that matter *unknown* universe. In secondary English programs, units have traditionally been centered on the following;

Literary history—covering periods in British, American, and world literature.

Literary genre—focusing on a particular kind of literature: poetry, short story, the novel, or a subgenre such as science fiction.

Literary theme—with an emphasis on driving ideas that are common to a number of works.

Elements of language and composition—ranging from "grammar" to "personal writing" to "analyzing public doublespeak."

While it is possible that very good units could be built using any of these organizing principles, each kind places some limitations on the concepts and materials that a teacher can naturally introduce, and it is useful to consider these limitations. For example, in a literary history unit, matters that go outside historical interest are often ignored or introduced accidentally, and literature is presented from a single point of view: its location in a chronological parade. Similarly, genre units run the risk of becoming "self-centered," dealing only with the elements of a single genre: the rhyme and meter of the poem, for example, or plot and character in the short story. Language and composition units may be taught in isolation from literature (or language in use) and sometimes treat language fragmentarily rather than as an organic whole.

Of the four organizing patterns, we prefer the *thematic* or *topical* unit more commonly used in elementary and middle schools, but quite viable in senior high as well. This pattern, like the other three, can foster its own kind of blindness to some aspects of teaching. For example, "theme" may be taken to mean exclusively literary themes or recurring motifs: "courage," "identity," the "westward movement." If literary theme is the sole concern, the thematic unit, like a genre unit, may become self-centered, with the theme providing the central quest and teachers and students looking for little beyond it. Thus, once the students find a reference to "innocence" or "experience" or "love and hate," they conclude they have correctly solved the puzzle of a particular piece of literature.

We like to treat the concept of theme or topic very broadly, so thematic units take on a wide range of issues. Perhaps most important, a broadly selected theme invites integration of students' personal experiences and interests, their oral language, their reading, their knowledge of disciplines beyond English, their writing, and even their understanding of literary history and genre. A good thematic unit will offer a variety of writing, reading, research, and speaking activities without unduly limiting kinds of materials or methods of response.

As Figure 3.1 shows, units can center on topics as diverse as Growing Up and Fairy Tales and Fables. They can include authors (R.L. Stine Meets Stephen King), literary topics (Narrative as a Way of Knowing), and social issues (Separation and Loss).

We are particularly convinced of their usefulness because of three advantageous characteristics of thematic/topical units.

1. *They accommodate a wide range of literary and other linguistic materials.* Not limited to any genre or in many cases to any era or national literature, a thematic unit can contain poetry, prose, drama, and nonfiction that ranges over a spectrum of literature from classic to contemporary, from all areas of the globe, from highly accessible reading to that which challenges the most able. Further, thematic units invite the use of language in various forms, including films, videotapes, television programs, talk, conversation, speech, and drama. In a unit on "Violence In America" students would certainly explore the theme of violence in literature, but they could just as easily make a study of contemporary television programming and what's happening on the Internet. They might look at violence in literature reflecting various cultures, or they might compare some of the eyeball-spearing classics to violent books from their own time to reflect on similarities and differences.

2. *They are naturally interdisciplinary.* A unit on "Independence—Why is This Drive so Strong and What Gets In Its Way?" can easily include: psychology (how do humans become independent psychologically and developmentally?); history (what

Loneliness and Alienation	Self-improvement
American Folklore	Afterlife
Science Fact/Fiction	Accepting Oneself
Education	Duty
Families	Fairy Tales and Fables
Relationships	Mythology
Growing Up	Creating Communities
Neighborhoods	Freedom
Brothers and Sisters	Independence
Bonding	Maturity and Mortality
Worry and Anxiety	The Voice of the People
Separation and Loss	Differences
Emotions	Successes
Violence and/or War	Work
Inner Conflicts	People in Crisis
Friends	Getting It Together
Beliefs	Discovery
Survival	Learning from Nature
The Environment	Intolerance
Addictions	Importance of Animals
Sports	Understanding Others
Thoreau and Gary Paulsen	R.L. Stine Meets Stephen King
Chris Crutcher and Emily Dickinson	Narrative as a Way of Knowing
Dreams and Goals	Rites of Passage
Disillusionment	Finding Love

Figure 3.1 Topics for Thematic Units

have people been willing to put on the line for independence?); economics (how does the economy and resource base of a country affect its ability to be independent?); science (compare humans' and mammals' drive to be independent and self-sufficient. What can we learn from the animal kingdom?); art (when did American art come into its own, independent of Europe? How is the theme of independence represented in art?); vocational education (what people skills are needed to be independent enough to get and keep a job?); futuristics ("Is it possible to create a society which could produce everything it needs?").

3. *They allow a natural integration of reading, writing, listening, and speaking.* The traditional unit often isolates the components of the English language arts: literature is studied alone; language is treated by itself; writing is separated from both. Thematic and topical units, by contrast, invite students to apply all the language arts to the topic at hand. One day they write or talk about it; the next day they read or listen.

It should be noted, too, that thematic/topical units can often be worked into courses or curricula that have been structured along other lines. For example, within a chronological American literature course, a teacher may subdivide to create topical clusters of readings: " American Identity," "Dreams and Goals," "Rites of Passage." Recognizing this flexibility, some textbook publishers provide alternative tables of contents for their books, showing how an anthology can be used to teach by theme, genre, or chronology. If your textbook lacks such helpful apparatus, you can do the same thing by looking for literature that flows together in a thematic pattern. Even composition courses can be structured by themes, often beginning with units on personal experience and moving toward social or academic issues and problems.

We do not wish to oversell the thematic/topical approach, for there are drawbacks and abuses. If a thematic approach is used simply to teach in a top-down manner with the teacher positioned as the giver of all "answers," then rearranging the material into themes will not utilize the strengths of the approach. The point is to find ways to organize and use material that give you the broadest options of approaches and assignments. By removing the restrictions the other kinds of unit organizations imply, you can bring in more material that will interest students and create a wide variety of ways for students to become engaged in the unit and to respond to the material. Thematic units are meant to open the door to possibilities, to nudge both teachers and students in new directions in their reaction and response, not to narrow the ways they can write or respond.

We acknowledge that misuses are possible with thematic units but there are, of course, solutions to each of those problems (we invite you to consider the Explorations that conclude this chapter). However, it is important to distinguish between practical or applied abuses and the theoretical power of an approach. No method— genre, chronology, language, or themes—should be rejected solely because some teachers abuse it; probably any style of teaching can be turned into a parody of itself through excess. The critical question is which approach (or combination of approaches) can offer students the greatest access to language; for us, the answer to that question is largely by teaching in a thematic way.

What follows, however, applies to any approach to unit development and should help teachers who value a variety of patterns of organization in creating well-organized units. We'll discuss this in five stages as shown in Figure 3.2.

SELECTING A FOCUS AND SETTING OBJECTIVES

We all like things to come in neat little packages. We don't like loose ends sticking out. We want order and harmony. But unit creating cannot start from the premise that everything is linear and that we all go from point A to point B. The purpose of constructing a unit is to find ways students can connect to the material and to find ways to help students make sense of their world as they grow in levels of literacy. Permeating this ideology is the belief in the importance of student input, student discovery, and student response. A unit is not a prepackaged set of materials. It is not meant as a structure that puts students "through their paces."

We have found it helpful when imagining a unit to begin with a "big question" or idea and to state in writing for ourselves what we would like our students to try to

---

SELECTING A FOCUS AND SETTING OBJECTIVES

> What do you envision your students exploring or finding out? What do you want your students to learn or accomplish?

CHOOSING MATERIALS

> What can you build the unit around? What other materials and resources can you include?

STRUCTURING THE UNIT

> How will you start the unit? What activities will you include? What kind of management structures will you use?

ORCHESTRATING ACTIVITIES

> How will you organize classroom activities?

EVALUATING AND ASSESSING

> How will students demonstrate their learning?
> How will you know the unit has been effective?

Figure 3.2   Creating a Unit

discover or answer or explore. We follow this by working to articulate why this unit is important and what it has to do with our students. If we don't know why a unit can be important and how it can be connected to student lives and interests, students certainly won't see the point of what we're doing. The next step involves brainstorming and writing down any ideas that come to you, any writing connections, questions, material, or issues that can be built on. If you find through brainstorming that this "overriding question" has lots and lots of pieces and parts, then it will probably be rich enough to engage the class. If you run into blocks and dead ends, then you'll probably want to rethink your idea for a unit.

Next, make a list of possible activities that will involve students. If you see ways to incorporate such things as interviews and small group work and projects and writing assignments, then you can see that this unit is full of possibilities and will likely involve students.

Write down the language arts skills that will be emphasized through work on this unit. Will you focus on having students understand memoir and learn to write descriptively in that genre? Will you ask students to understand the elements in a fable and be able to write one? Will you work with students on improving their ability to use dialogue in their stories?

The setting of goals or objectives has been a subject of considerable debate ever since the publication of Robert F. Mager's *Preparing Instructional Objectives* in 1962. Mager objected, rightly, that many teachers phrase their goals fuzzily, and valid criticism has been directed toward English teachers because of their failure to make objectives explicit.

"I want my students to appreciate literature," says the English teacher.

"What do you mean appreciate?" asks a skeptic. "How will I know that your students 'appreciate?'"

Although some English language arts teachers may hide behind the vagueness of a word like "appreciate," part of the problem may be in terms of language; it's not that teachers don't know what they're doing, it's simply that it is difficult to get it into words.

What can students who appreciate literature do? Here are some possibilities:

- They might be able to choose from among many works some that they find particularly satisfying.
- They will certainly be able to express their reactions to literature orally or in writing.
- They will probably do some reading on their own beyond that required in school.
- They may even become frequent library users or book buyers

So even something as seemingly vague as "appreciation" can be broken down into observable processes and skills. There is a danger, of course, of fragmenting a global skill—appreciation—by trying to specify its component behaviors too tightly; many of Mager's followers made that error when they tried to apply the behavioral objective in English. Although one can identify a number of discrete skills mastered by a good reader—who may, for example, respond to metaphors in a text—it is not necessarily appropriate for the teacher to turn around and teach that skill directly: "The student will be able to identify eight of ten metaphors in a passage from literature."

A way out of the dilemma of specificity may be to worry less about the exact form of the objectives than about their rationale and their theoretical underpinning. The lack of focus that concerns many critics of education results not from lack of a proper statement but from failure to develop a rationale for teaching. Perhaps the question should not be "What is appreciation?" A better one might be "Why are you teaching something called 'literary appreciation' in the first place?" That seems to us a valid and important question, especially in an age dominated by media and a powerful national will to succeed in the "practical" domains of business and industry.

Any objective needs to be clearly justifiable in terms of the following questions:

Is this objective consistent with what we know about the nature of the learning process and the aims of schooling?

Is there any evidence from research or critically examined experience that having students do this will actually help them use language more successfully?

Keep in mind when setting objectives

Is this goal consistent with the developmental levels of the learner?

Is it based on real expectations (i.e. what we know students do) rather than on wishful expectations (what we think students "ought" to do)?

If these criteria are met, the objective can be described in a number of ways:

As skills or processes that the students will master during the unit.

As course activities: what the students will read, talk about, write on, or experience.

As a set of "exit skills": activities the students will be able to perform after the course is over.

Objectives can be phrased as infinitives ("to learn," "to read," "to write") or imperatives ("you will _____"). They can also be written as aims for teachers, sketching out what is to be accomplished in a course. Some teachers we know write a "scenario" instead of a list of objectives, describing what they want to have happen in the "drama" of the forthcoming class. Others put their aims in epistolary mode, writing a plain English letter to parents and students outlining what will be happening in the course and why that's a good thing.

In themselves, objectives are a dime a dozen. Most of us can generate long lists of trivial to significant goals on any topic in English. Clearly stated objectives that mesh with current research and understanding of teaching are not so easily produced, because one is constantly thrust back to the real question, "Is this objective a worthy one?" See Figure 3.3 for samples of solid objectives.

CHOOSING MATERIALS

When we envision a unit, we like to start with a centerpiece, something to build the unit around. It may be a video, a short story, an audio tape, a piece of non-fiction, a novel, a TV show. The centerpiece is used as the focus and as a way to kick off the unit and get students involved.

Our second step is to make a mental inventory of what other materials can be used. Will children's picture books work? How about myths? Can you think of a movie or video that would work with the theme and contribute to the unit? How can poetry be worked in? non-fiction? music? art? The newer teacher does not have to figure this out alone but can ask other department members for possible resources. Once underway, students can also become sleuths, hunting for material that would work with the unit.

Too often the adopted textbook, rather than the teacher's own philosophy, sets the curriculum. Of course, the adoption of texts allows schools to believe that there is a degree of consistency in courses that are taught by a number of different teachers, that there is some continuity between grade levels. It also simplifies the selection of materials for teachers, and it cuts down on paper work in ordering books. Unfortunately, adopting textbooks creates a great many pedagogical problems.

For one thing, educational publishers see that the largest sums of money are to be made through getting series of books adopted by large systems. The effects of

Students will:

- Demonstrate their understanding of a genre by writing in that form (memoir, fairy tale, poem)
- Demonstrate their ability to use literary devices (such as foreshadowing and flashbacks) in their writing
- Demonstrate their ability to change a piece of writing from one format (such as a newspaper story) to another (such as a poem)
- Be able to explain how differing writing formats affect a piece of writing and its impact on the reader
- Demonstrate their ability to write effective, interesting pieces that engage their readers
- Demonstrate their ability to gather information on one topic from varied sources (interviews, Internet, non-fiction books, movies)
- Demonstrate in their writing the use of several strategies to develop character (use of dialogue, inner thoughts of character, emotional responses to a situation and so on)
- Demonstrate their ability to articulate ideas in small group settings
- Demonstrate their ability to gather information through interviewing others
- Demonstrate their ability to use spoken language to discuss, clarify, describe, evaluate and justify ideas
- Demonstrate their ability to hold the attention of their listeners when they are presenting orally
- Be able to compare their own views to an author's views and explain similarities and differences
- Be able to evaluate the effectiveness of a short story in terms of how believable characters are, how compelling the plot is and so on
- Demonstrate through writing, art, or drama how literature connects to their lives
- Demonstrate their ability to enter a story world by writing or drawing the scenes they "see"
- Be able to describe the differences in the styles of authors read
- Demonstrate their ability to shift perspectives in responding to literature by writing from a character's point of view

Figure 3.3   Sample Objectives

large-system adoptions—particularly the state adoptions in Texas and California—are notorious in educational circles. The massively adopted series are designed to satisfy large numbers of teachers and to be as inoffensive to as many people as possible. Thus they are often conservative in tone, reflecting not the best of current practice, but simply the practices of a majority.

Closer to home, adoption can be time consuming for a school staff and, once completed, it locks a school or district into a fixed curriculum for the period of time it takes the books to wear out. Nevertheless, most teachers do work from an adopted text, and in many schools it is the only resource provided to the teacher. We'll suggest two stages in working with the text in Figure 3.4.

1. Choose the best of a text. In most school districts, teachers have broad flexibility to select portions of the adopted text for teaching. The truly "lockstep" curriculum where everybody covers "Mending Wall" on the third Thursday of October is an anachronism or a myth. Your first step, then, in working with the adopted text is to survey it as you have the time, listing its resources that meet with your goals.

2. Supplement the text. Except for occasional problems with censorship, we've never seen a school district that objected to teachers using supplemental or enrichment materials. In selecting materials for your instructional unit, then, you will probably want to consider, in addition to the adopted texts:

- Community resources: speakers, consultants, guests
- Nonprint materials: films, filmstrips, videos, audio tapes
- Poetry that will complement the unit
- Children's picture books that look at the theme of the unit from a different point of view
- Fables, fairy tales, myths that might contribute to the unit
- Short stories from collections especially for young adults
- Non-fiction titles from the library that speak to the theme
- Clusters of four or five titles for small-group reading

Before putting something on a book list or a resource list, a teacher should ask:

- Does the material support the course or unit objectives?
- Do I have a rationale for its selection?
- Could some material required of all students be objectionable to special interest groups?
- Has the material been approved or recommended by a professional organization or listed on an established bibliography for young readers?

Figure 3.4   Working with and Supplementing the Text

We are believers in presenting students with a richness and variety of resources and materials, not to dazzle or confuse them, but to make the most of our possibilities as teachers for engaging students with language. As we'll show in this and subsequent chapters, the strict one-book, one-assignment approach in English need not be the norm any longer. For example, in a thematic unit on Family in which students look at what makes a family a family, poems, fairy tales, and picture books that show various kinds of families and different aspects of family life can be brought in. In collaborative groups students can look for views of family that appeal to them and talk and write about the positive or negative aspects of family that they find in those readings. They could read young adult novels like *Maniac Magee* by Jerry Spinelli, *The Watson's Go To Birmingham—1963* by Christopher Paul Curtis, *Deliver Us from Evie* by M.E. Kerr, *Spite Fences* by Trudy Krisher, or *Drummers of Jericho* by Carolyn Meyer. They could discuss their novels in literature circles (see Chapter 7 for more information) focusing on strengths and weaknesses of the families portrayed. Students could listen to a school or family counselor talk about what children need from a family. The Internet or the non-fiction section of the library could garner more information on healthy and dysfunctional families, different family configurations, functioning in a stepfamily and so on. Collaborative group projects such as conducting a talk show on families can be one of the end-of-unit options.

STRUCTURING THE UNIT

In our unit creation we need to construct introductory activities and possible end-projects and assignments. In this bare-bones plan we also consider how we'll use different class groupings and on what we'll assess students. Although we like to have a long-range plan we realize the necessity of adapting or changing plans after we see the direction students want to go with the "big question." We also need to figure out what kind of modeling or instruction we need to include so all the students have the skills necessary to do what we would like them to do. Sometimes we might need to draft a script on the overhead together so students know the necessary conventions. Other times while working on effective beginnings of stories, we might construct multiple introductions on the overhead and discuss the impact of each type.

Once we have a sense of what we'll be doing, we look at the following kinds of management structures to see which will work best when.

Whole-class

Meeting the class as a whole is the time-honored mode of teaching. It allows the teacher to convey common content efficiently and to involve students in whole-class discussions. If handled well, this approach can create a sense of community. The obvious disadvantages of whole-class teaching are that it tends to force the teacher into a dominant role, it allows for relatively little student interaction, and it permits little time for students to work on their own. Steve seldom uses whole-class sessions for presentation of material, but Diana likes to use whole-class time to introduce core material and to pique the students' interest and to get them involved. Both of us use class meetings as show-and-tell sessions for presentation of students' work or to organize along the several patterns that follow.

Small Groups

A student in one of Steve's classes once remarked, "This is the 'groupinest' class I've ever been in." Both of us like to use groups, and we find them an effective middle ground between whole-class instruction and a totally individualized program. Groups usually involve a high degree of interaction among students, yet control is still maintained. The major disadvantages of small groups are that the teacher cannot always tell what is happening within them and that students don't always know how to work well in groups (a problem we will take up in another chapter).

Situating Workshops in a Unit Format

Increasingly, educators are combining these various ways of teaching under the rubric of the "workshop" approach which has students working in a variety of ways all at once. We have found that when you want to organize such structures as an extended writing workshop in your classroom, it works best to begin with a focus and with objectives.

Writing workshops can be focused around such things as point of view, voice, effective beginnings and endings, learning to write memoir, writing persuasively, learning a form such as satire or a stylistic device such as foreshadowing, writing about one's experiences in several different ways, creating an effective piece of writing that keeps reader interest. Objectives can include student demonstration of the ability to write from another point of view making diction and details effective. Another goal or objective could be to ask students to manage different forms of writing. This could be broken down into using logical sequencing in story writing, writing an original story within the framework of another story, using knowledge of one medium to develop a text in another medium, writing factual accounts in both first and third person, writing a narrative using dialogue, or writing a news story and a feature on the same topic. The students' objective could be to create a portfolio in which the writing is about themselves, but with at least three pieces written in different genres.

Whole units or mini-lessons can be constructed around the above focuses. Structuring a writing workshop unit need not be intimidating. You can begin by asking students to:

1. Read and examine works that illustrate the topic (for point of view you can have them read Paul Fleishman's *Seedfolks* (HarperCollins 1997), a collection of thirteen brief stories of people in New York and their relation to a vacant lot that they turned into a garden; for good beginnings, students can examine an array of picture books; for writing persuasively, editorials and letters to the editor can be used.)

2. Make generalizations based on the readings about the common elements in this kind of writing or naming the variations shown through the readings. (In *Seedfolks* students can list the similarities between the sections to see what kind of information the author chooses to represent a point of view).

3. Generate lists of what students learned about writing in this form or with this element. (From *Seedfolks* students have probably noticed that each person uses different kinds of words that reflect their backgrounds, that some use dialect, that vivid images of their lives are shared, that the author starts in different places in the slices of life he shares, that the characters' connection to the vacant lot is always the focus of the piece, etc.)

4. Brainstorm topics or events students can write about with some authenticity, using the unit focus. (For point of view, students might brainstorm all the points of view from which an account of the death of a teen by a drunk driver could be written.)

5. Students select a topic using prewriting strategies such as clustering or listing and then write.

6. Papers are shared in small groups for reaction and response. Students also discuss whether the conventions or elements of this topic are present in the writing. (Does the word choice seem appropriate for this person, are the details concrete enough so the reader learns about the character?)

7. As a class, create rubrics which will be used to assess the pieces.

8. Revise papers.

9. Present to a broader audience.

10. Encourage metacognition by asking students to reflect on strategies used to write the piece, what worked, what didn't, and so on.

The major difference between the writing workshop unit and any other is that there is generally less emphasis on selecting materials, since they are often only used to kick the unit off and as the basis of mini-lessons to teach a specific concept or skill.

When organizing an experiential or inquiry-based approach it also works well to begin with objectives and with what you want your students to do or demonstrate, since many of them will be working with different materials. Some objectives might include: to research a topic or some aspect of a topic that the student is interested in; to have students broaden their view of research and see that information can be gained through interviews, the Internet, and surveys as well as through observation and reading books, magazines, and newspapers. Another objective is to have students describe the "process" of the journey to find information, explaining what avenues of research were fruitful and which were not. With their research students can "publish" by videotaping some aspect of it, writing a pamphlet, or making an oral report to the class. Each of those end-products contain many, many sub skills which may also be used.

Individual or Independent Work

Involving individual students in their schooling in a meaningful way has long been a goal in education, one complicated by the economic necessity of clustering students in groups of thirty or more for efficiency. It's difficult to find ways to meet all students at their interest and need levels when English teachers have at least 5 classes and 150 students. However, if students have some choice about selections and also have a variety of appealing writing assignments, the teacher has made a good start toward individualizing. Time can be set aside in class for students to work individually on such tasks as composing, researching, and reading.

Individualization can, of course, be taken too far if students work in isolation and never come together to share and discuss what they have done. Some schools in the 1970s developed programs based so heavily on individualized study that both students and teachers became downright lonely. Although individual study may be important, education seems to require the sharing of ideas and information as well.

Peer Learning and Tutoring

Jean Jacques Rousseau's educational ideal was an adult working one-to-one with a child. Contemporary educators have discovered that face-to-face learning need not always involve an adult, that young people of almost any age have much to learn from one another. Babies who have older brothers and sisters learn to talk more rapidly than those who don't. Why? Because the older siblings interact with the baby and help the infant to learn to talk. In elementary school classes, peer learning can be used in everything from spelling to reading. In the secondary schools peers can edit each other's papers, pair up to generate ideas related to literature, and work through more difficult assignments together. We are just beginning to understand how peer learning works; it is an area that deserves exploration and experimentation in English classes.

for one on one

Contracts

This form of organizing individualized classes, contracts, require that the teacher and student agree on an amount of work to be done by the student to receive a certain grade. Quality controls are built into the contract so that students must do more than produce rote work on assignments or breeze through the reading and writing work mindlessly. In some schools, projects have point values assigned—e.g. 10 points for a book report, 15 points for an essay—with grades depending on point accumulation. Contracting sometimes has the effect of generating work simply for its own sake— the more students do, the higher their grade—but handled cautiously, it allows teachers to control individualized work and manage it effectively in rather large classrooms. Further, contracting offers clearly defined structures and expectations for students who may get lost in a totally individualized classroom.

Resource Areas

English teachers often have students working on several activities and projects at one time. The classroom can have resource areas where students can find a wide selection of poetry; materials to complete projects; tape recorders so that student work can be shared; reference materials including dictionaries, thesauruses, and books on editing; shelves of books for browsing; and a table where students who need to plan a project can discuss their ideas. As teachers collect more resources on particular units such as science fiction they can also create resource areas that include supplementary readings, suggestions for writing, pictures and photographs as well as lists of recordings or videos available in the library.

ORCHESTRATING ACTIVITIES

Another area to consider as we plan a unit is classroom organization and the structure of the class. How much of this unit is teacher-directed and how much is student-centered? Can you see lots of opportunities for students to work in small groups on issues that will concern them? How will you organize class time? What will you expect your students to do each day? Orchestrating is creating a sequence both in the order of materials and the order of class structures you will use daily.

How objectives, materials, and structures are woven together to create a class is as much a matter of art and intuition as it is of science and rationality. As we orchestrate activities, we create a sequence that allows the course objectives to be met while providing a variable mix of activities for the students.

Wolfgang Amadeus Mozart claimed that there was a moment of inspiration when a symphony came to him all of one piece, where he could hear it from beginning to end. Few teachers will be fortunate enough to be able to visualize the orchestrations of a unit all at one moment (much less find the model students who will play that masterfully composed symphony precisely as written). Nevertheless, we often have an "aha" moment when the grand plan comes into mind:

"Yes, if I begin with poem X, then introduce short story Y, then send the kids off to the library for free reading, that will get the flow started so I can play the video of novel Z on Tuesday and Thursday and have their first writing due on Friday the umpteenth."

At other times orchestrating moves more slowly, and our desks and briefcases are filled with scraps of paper showing charts and diagrams and possibilities. In general, however, the patterns of orchestration for our teaching run along several sequences:

1. From large to small group. Initial class sessions describe the course or unit, stake out the class ground rules, clarify objectives, and provide some common experiences such as reading several stories or writing on a central or introductory topic.

2. From assigned work to individualized projects. We want our students to work toward exploring topics on their own terms and generating their own assignments for response and writing, so we move toward that goal by offering them lots of choices in assignments and encouraging them to create their own activities.

3. From small group or solo work back to large. At the conclusion of group or individualized work, students have ideas, projects, and writing to share. This sharing helps the class to operate as a cohesive group rather than as a collection of individuals or subgroups.

There are many other sequences that we recognize as part of our teaching, and perhaps you will find some of these familiar from your own teaching or learning:

From writing that draws directly on personal experience toward writing about acquired experience (either from the world or from reading).

From private response to public display or demonstration.

From contemporary literature, often very accessible, to older, more difficult pieces.

From shorter works to longer (the latter often read individually, with support from the teacher).

However, we can find examples of contrary movements in our teaching as well. There are times, for example, when we may begin with a complex work, one which requires our sponsorship or leadership, then move to "simpler" works (are any literary works truly "simple"?) which the students can handle on their own.

An example of one kind of orchestration is one Diana often used in her classes. The whole class reads a short story together. Then students write responses individually to the story mentioning the things that stand out for them in the story, the characters they relate to or dislike and so on. These responses are shared in a small group which then collaboratively generates a list of themes they believe are present in the story or a list of values they think are present in the story. This work is shared with one other small group then each group reports to the whole class the themes and values they feel are most strongly present in the story. Class discussion/reaction follows. Based on the group work, writing/drawing/drama options are discussed and students individually or collaboratively choose an option to complete.

As a teacher/artist, you will certainly want to develop your own patterns, techniques, and strategies. It is important to note, however, that good art is seldom improvisational, random, or chance. There is science to our discipline, some widely accepted principles of good teaching, and they must underlie our artistry. Further, good teaching happens when we plan rather than improvise.

EVALUATION AND ASSESSMENT

Our students only seem to take seriously what we assess or "count." Therefore it is important in your unit planning to decide how you will access or evaluate student work. Will you develop a rubric for projects both oral and written? Will you have students write and reflect on what they have learned? Will you construct essay-like questions on skills you want to emphasize? Will you ask students to evaluate group work using such sentence starters as "My major contribution to the group was . . ." and "In our group, here's what we accomplished on our tasks . . ." How much will you access through observation? More information will be given on evaluation and assessment in Chapter 13. Additionally we think it is helpful as you're planning a unit to reflect on whether or not the unit is in line with best practice in the field and whether or not it is consistent with your philosophy on the teaching of language arts. Does the plan for a unit integrate reading, viewing, writing, speaking, and listening? Are students expected to make meaning and relate this material to themselves or does the teacher control all the outcomes? Are the students being given a chance to raise real issues and answer questions that the teacher does not have the predetermined answers to?

EVALUATING UNIT PLANS

When we speak of best practice we are referring to strategies, plans, and assignments based on principles of active learning and what we know theoretically and practically about learning and involving students in their own learning. The list in Figure 3.5 includes a focus on best practice as well as on use of the language arts content standards. This check list is intended to help you, the practitioner, look at your own units and curriculum and find your areas of strength as well as those areas in which you would like to do more work.

We would like to end this chapter by presenting several detailed unit plans that illustrate the wide range of possibilities that exist for conceptualizing and creating units, including a unit that is built around student inquiry. We start with a unit built around a single short story (Figure 3.6) to demonstrate one way to build a unit around pieces in anthologies. Next we move to an experiential or inquiry-based unit (Figure 3.7) to illustrate how teachers can start with what students are interested in

To what extent does your current language arts curriculum and/or unit provide opportunities for students:

1. to actively construct meaning through their reading, writing, speaking, and viewing?
2. to work in small groups?
3. to have their thinking expanded or challenged?
4. to develop rubrics and criteria to apply to their own and others' work?
5. to have some choice in materials or formats of assignments?
6. to have their contributions viewed as an important part of the class?
7. to build on what they already know?
8. to read and work independently?
9. to look closely at and reflect on their own written work?
10. to engage in research and other projects that are authentic and can be presented publicly?
11. to read about a topic in several genres and construct a response to the reading?
12. to engage in authentic, real-life learning?
13. to be involved in activities that ask them to synthesize and/or apply what they have read about?
14. to be involved in a classroom that integrates speaking, listening, reading, and writing and puts all skills instruction back in context?
15. to receive writing instruction that is embedded in authentic activities and assignments and that focuses on the content of the writing?
16. to read widely both classic and contemporary works?
17. to learn vocabulary, including literary terms, in the context of the reading they are doing in class?
18. to read works by and about the diverse peoples who are part of this country?
19. to do daily writing in support of reading?
20. to think about the literature they are reading and make connections among the pieces they have read?

Figure 3.5   Evaluating Unit Plans

and how they can draw on the broad array of resources available outside the class. We end our unit plans with a thematic unit based on a typical author in American Literature and his work (Figure 3.8).

Our purpose in presenting this mix of units is to show the variety that exists in unit building and in unit topics. Although newer teachers often will not have an abundance of resources at their fingertips, our intention in illustrating how units can be built is to help you see unit possibilities in everything you hear or read or view. Thinking of unit building in this way makes it an exciting and provocative endeavor which can be a very satisfying and creative part of teaching.

Starting Small—Creating a Unit Around a Single Short Story

Instead of feeling overwhelmed by tackling a lengthy unit, one way to start out is by creating a thematic unit around a single short story. By "exploding" the story you can see how units can be created. This example is built around "Charles" by Shirley Jackson, which appears in many anthologies.

SELECTING A FOCUS AND SETTING OBJECTIVES.

This unit, "The Way We Were," is intended for freshman at the beginning of the year so they have an opportunity to dig back into their memories of childhood and look at the way childhood is portrayed in literature. Objectives include involving students in responding to literature to show them how literature can be connected to their lives; involving students in writing narratives and at least one other genre; familiarizing students with how a different point of view could change a story; having students compare how childhood is viewed and portrayed in different kinds of literature; having students measure the "reality" or accuracy of the way childhood is portrayed by comparing it with their own life and experiences.

SELECTING MATERIALS.

The short story "Charles" by Shirley Jackson was chosen from the anthology because it quickly engages students in the antics of a kindergartner. The kindergarten years are a time in students' lives they can remember, relate to, and talk about without feeling threatened by the topic. Children's stories like "Little Red Riding Hood," "Goldilocks," and "Hansel and Gretel" will also be used. Stories in the newspaper about kids, TV shows that feature small children, and students' stories of their own kindergarten experiences would also be shared and used.

STRUCTURING THE UNIT.

As an introductory activity we planned for students to do quick-writes on what they remembered about kindergarten. For individual student work we could envision students writing reactions and questions, developing writing options, choosing poems the main character would like, and bringing in and sharing newspaper stories about children or summaries of TV programs which featured young children. In groups, students would respond to each other's work, share reactions and questions to the stories, and serve as peer editors for each other. In whole group we planned on reading the stories aloud, sharing memories, reporting what was talked about in groups, and sharing our end projects. For end projects we could imagine students adding additional scenes to the original story, writing pamphlets for parents on how to raise children, and role-playing how Laurie's parents could have better responded to him.

(continued)

Figure 3.6   Short Story Unit

ORCHESTRATING ACTIVITIES.

After the quick-write and sharing in groups, "Charles" is read aloud. Students write about their own kindergarten memories, talk about what little kids are afraid of, how they got away with things like "Charles" did in the story, and how a story changes when told from a different point of view. Children's stories like "Little Red Riding Hood," "Goldilocks," and "Hansel and Gretel" were brought in and discussed in terms of what behavior and actions were attributed to children. Students talk about their favorite TV programs when they were small, toys they cherished, the way they dressed, and the games they played. Students look at themselves as children and also looked at how childhood is portrayed. The writing connections pop up everywhere. Students write letters to the main character's parents to tell them to be firmer and not believe everything that Laurie told them, they write to the parents from the teacher's point of view, and they do interior monologues from Laurie's point of view as he was making up the "stories" he told his parents.

Students compare the rather pampered way the kindergartner was treated by his parents in "Charles" to the way they see children characterized in other texts. They talk about lessons young children learn from the stories they read, the movies they see, and the way their parents treat them. Projects at the end of the unit include scripts of scenes students add to the story, pamphlets advising parents on how best to deal with kindergartners, presentations on what fairy tales teach children, and videos of children playing games with a voice-over of what lessons and values each game teaches children. Once the unit starts and students get involved, the activities flow from one to the other, going from large group to small group to individual work to group work and then back again to the whole-class.

EVALUATING AND ASSESSING.

Since students have an aversion to anything they feel they won't get credit for, assessment is discussed with them. It is important that they understand that group work is an essential part of class since much of the material of the class is generated from groups. Students learn that they would either write a response to each group they participated in or the teacher would give them credit through her observation of the group. Since the talk they share in the large group is also a big part of their meaning-making, the teacher rotates the responsibility each day for keeping track of who made contributions so students can get credit for all the discussions. This can be varied by asking students to complete a few sentence-starters at the end of class such as: I did/did not participate today because. . . ; I wished I had said. . . ; I learned from the discussion today that. . .

Of course, written pieces are workshopped, responded to, revised, and put in a classroom booklet entitled Kindergarten Memories. After reading many of these stories from other classes, students create rubrics which guide the evaluation. Final presentations also are evaluated through the use of rubrics. All presentations are videotaped and students have input into which ones become part of the classroom video library.

Figure 3.6

Developing an Experiential or Inquiry-Based Unit Around Classroom Concerns

Inquiry-based and experiential approaches have as their foundation student interest and input as well as students acting in the role of expert—measuring what they are learning against their own experience.

SELECTING A FOCUS AND SETTING OBJECTIVES.

When we saw too many of our urban ninth graders get in fights or verbal shouting matches over perceived signs of "disrespect," we decided to confront the problem head-on by developing a unit on respect. Our question was: "What does respect really mean and how do people handle it when they don't get the respect they think they should?" Through this short unit we hoped that students would at least begin to think about their actions and what they meant and perhaps develop other ways to handle people they felt disrespected them.

After brainstorming with students we could see that this topic was chockfull of issues. Students wondered: Why do some kids see respect as so much more important than other kids? How do we get true respect? Does our drive for respect cause us to do things that we don't want to do? Is this true respect? Who do we respect? What did that person do to gain our respect? What's going on beneath these incidents of "calling someone out of their name"? Are there other ways to handle incidents of perceived disrespect? What can we learn from others about settling disagreements?

When we considered the language arts skills students would use in this unit, many jumped to mind. In literature we would do such things as compare the structures of the genres used looking for similarities and differences between them, compare our views of respect to the authors, and evaluate the short stories in terms of how realistic the characterization was and how believable the actions were in terms of students' own experience.

SELECTING MATERIALS.

We could see that we had plenty of material to start with. We selected a chapter from Nathan McCall's *Makes Me Want to Holler* (Random House, 1994) called "Respect" as the centerpiece. As a kid growing up, the author felt the way many of our students felt, that all they had was their name and that they became less if others disrespected them. McCall's chapter is tough and tells it like it is. Since the chapter stops without much reflection on the author's part, we skipped ahead in the book to find passages we could read that would show how he had reconsidered his position on respect as he got older. We also brought in Aretha Franklin's recording "R-E-S-P-E-C-T" to look at how she viewed respect, and two short stories "On the Bridge" by Todd Strasser in *Visions*, edited by Don Gallo, and "Fourth of July" by Robin G. Brancato in *Sixteen*, edited by Don Gallo.   *(continued)*

Figure 3.7   Inquiry-based Unit

STRUCTURING THE UNIT.

Activities that seemed to fit the theme were interviews of older people and peers, skits, talk show dramas, writing a narrative on the topic, finding poems on the issues, writing an expository piece on getting respect, writing an editorial on why this issue is so important to teens and how adults can help, options to verbal and physical battles, small group discussions on getting respect, having the assistant principal for discipline share her insights on kids who fight for respect, having a member of Peer Assisted Listening (PAL) talk about and demonstrate approaches to mediation, and writing up class activities into a newspaper on the topic.

Besides the materials already mentioned, we also thought we could work discussions of TV shows into the unit to see what models TV offered for getting respect. We would also invite students to go on a children's picture book hunt for books that give younger children advice on the topic of settling disputes. We knew we could count on our students to give us titles of movie or video possibilities and to suggest songs that dealt with disrespect.

When we looked at what we were expecting of our students we decided that work would have to be done on using dialogue, what vivid details look like in writing, why word pictures are important to readers, how to construct interview questions, how to conduct an interview, how to effectively write an expository piece, and what goes into writing an editorial. This modeling or instructional part of the unit could be done with the whole class, using the overhead projector and having students contribute their ideas. For instance, we could construct dialogues on the overhead, paying attention not only to the format, but to what makes a dialogue interesting. When we looked for vivid details, we could put up several sentences from past student writing and have students identify which sentences create pictures in their minds. We would learn to construct interview questions by first generating questions that would give the interviewer little information and then move to learning to construct more open-ended questions.

We decided that the short stories and the chapter from Nathan McCall's book would be read aloud. Small groups could focus on specific tasks from topics in the stories, be used to create a survey to give to fellow students, and to generate questions for interviews on the topic of respect. We wanted to leave lots of room for whole-class discussions.

ORCHESTRATING ACTIVITIES.

To begin the unit, we would start in a very simple way by having students write on a large note card their definition of what respect means, how to get respect, how you know you aren't being respected, and possible ways to handle a show of disrespect. Students would not put their names on the cards, so we could collect them, shuffle them, hand out the cards to small groups. The groups would read the cards they received and then write a list of what they learned from the cards. This introductory activity would give us lots of information and raise even more interest in the topic. When we considered end projects we looked at some of the activities and decided to create end-products around them. We wanted to give

(continued)

Figure 3.7

students the opportunity to construct a pamphlet on what the older generation has to say about respect and one on what their peers have to say about it. Others could do a newspaper whose articles focused on what we found out about the topic as well as stories on guest speakers. We also envisioned a talk show presentation in which students role-played specific points of view on the topic. We knew other projects would emerge as we became involved in the unit.

EVALUATING AND ASSESSING.

As we thought about assessment we knew we would do much of it as we worked our way through the unit. We would ask students to explain and compare Nathan McCall's definition of respect to the definitions the main characters in the short stories had and to their own. We would grade these on how well each definition was explained and whether or not examples were used, looking for evidence that students understood how to compare the different definitions.

For group work we would give out a sheet of paper that had a circle on it, telling students to divide the circle or pie into pieces according to who contributed the most to the group that day. They would have to explain their reasons for dividing the pic the way they did.

We also wanted to be sure students measured their experiences with respect against what they were researching and learning. We asked them to write reflective papers or incorporate their "expertness" into their projects.

Since all of the end products were to be presented in public ways (the pamphlet, the newspaper, the talk show) we would create a rubric that would include the presentation as well as the content. For instance, we would include an item (to be responded to by: 1] not at all; 2] a little; 3] a lot; or 4] a great deal) such as "It was obvious from the way the (newspaper, pamphlet, the talk show) was put together that a large amount of time was spent on this project." Another item would be "The project was composed in such a way that readers or viewers gained new insights or information."

EVALUATING THE UNIT.

In reflecting on what elements of best practice were embedded in the unit, we could immediately see that the language arts were integrated, that students would be actively constructing meaning through their work, that the skills were being taught in the larger context of the unit, and that students were engaged in authentic, real-life learning. Students would also have a choice about which aspect of respect they worked on.

Students would be writing in many formats and genres and focus on such things as the use of dialogue, the selection of details to make an impact on the reader, use of persuasion, and how each piece was organized. Thinking, writing, speaking, and listening skills would be combined through creating interview questions and interviewing an older person, sharing responses, and drawing conclusions about what the younger generation can learn from the older generation about respect. Speaking and problem solving would be emphasized when we role-played after hearing the PAL demonstrations on conflict mediation.

Figure 3.7

Creating a Thematic Unit in American Literature

Although most teachers have some kind of anthology they can or should use, this use need not stop them from creating units using only some of the material from the anthology. Plodding through a textbook, moving from story to story, doesn't usually give students the idea that the work in the language arts class is in anyway related to them. Once you know what is in the American Literature anthology, you can feel free to develop units that focus on involving your students instead of focusing so much on the history and characteristics of different literary movements. Diana developed and used the following unit in her American Literature classes. Here are some of her first-person notes written after the unit.

SELECTING A FOCUS AND SETTING OBJECTIVES.

Henry David Thoreau has always interested me because I constantly learn from his writings. To really get my kids involved with Thoreau, I wanted them to see why he valued individualism. I wanted them to look deeper into the world and recognize the part nature can play in our learning and in our nourishment. Since high school is such a stressful time for students I wanted them to get some perspective on what else might be important in life. Thus, this unit was framed around the question: "Does Thoreau Have Anything to Teach Modern Humankind?"

SELECTING MATERIALS.

I started with the play *The Night Thoreau Spent in Jail* by Robert Lee. The class also read selections from his journals which I felt free to shorten. I brought in a newspaper article which told of a superintendent who fired a teacher because he refused to conform to the faculty dress code. The last text we used was Gary Paulsen's *Woodsong* (Scholastic 1990), the story of his relationships with his sled dogs and his running of the Iditarod in Alaska.

STRUCTURING THE UNIT AND ORCHESTRATING ACTIVITIES.

As we got close to beginning the unit, I asked my students to spend five to ten minutes under the stars by themselves, trying to clear their minds. When they came in they were to write what they experienced by focusing on the stars. The students who did the solitary viewing were very philosophical. This assignment led us to a discussion of what, if anything, we can learn from nature. Then they were ready to meet Henry David himself. We read the play aloud in class. Through this play they saw Thoreau in action, saw what a rebel he was and how he questioned everything in his search for the "essentials" of life.

After reacting to the play and to Thoreau's actions, students were ready to read excerpts from *Walden*. In their response journals I asked my students to find ten sentences or concepts in the selections from *Walden* that they either strongly agreed with or vehemently disagreed with and to explain why. I typed up a list of lines from parts of his work that weren't part of the reading assigned, and asked students to explain what the quotes meant and whether or not they agreed with them. Then I asked them to rank the fifteen quotes from most important to them personally, to least important. In small group discussions they shared their views, trying to persuade others to share their rankings. *(continued)*

Figure 3.8   American Literature Thematic Unit

My students believed the action of the superintendent in the newspaper article was ludicrous and so wrote letters to the superintendent from Thoreau's point of view. We posted the letters on the bulletin board and it was obvious that my students were beginning to understand Thoreau's values and beliefs. My students gobbled up *Woodsong.* They loved it and enjoyed thinking about what Paulsen learned from his dogs and from nature. I asked them to respond to the book by writing about what they thought Paulsen learned from nature, what Thoreau and Paulsen had in common, and what parts of the book had the biggest impact on them.

EVALUATION AND ASSESSMENT.

Later I asked the students to write a reflective paper about whether or not they could be a Thoreau in their own time, and in what ways they could connect Thoreau's values or beliefs to their own.

The last project we did in our Thoreau unit evolved from an idea I got from Tom Romano's *Clearing the Way.* I had my students write short stories or plays about Thoreau appearing in our time with his values intact. They were to include what Thoreau would bring with him from his time period and how he would react to the world today. Some students set the plays in the school and had Thoreau enroll as a student. They shared what he said as he went from class to class and how he reacted to the whole school culture. One creative student even had Thoreau fall into Walden Pond and enter into this time period through a locker at our school! This assignment captured the imagination of my students and because they poured so much energy into the project, we ended up with many memorable scripts and stories. On the day the writing was due, students met in small groups in class to share their pieces with each other. Then each group begged to have at least one or two pieces read to the whole-class. We spent the whole next day enacting scripts and reading short stories. To make students aware of how much they had learned about Thoreau and about writing, I had each small group write up a short report on two or three stories or scripts detailing all the ways the writer showed his or her understanding of Thoreau. I also asked them to comment on the aspects of the writing that were especially strong.

This unit ended on a high note because students had so much ownership in their plays and scripts and enjoyed the chance to use the knowledge they had gained in creative ways.

Figure 3.8

◆ EXPLORATIONS

◆ Learn about common goals that have been prescribed for a school or district. Do common skills lists exist? Is there a set of goals that every teacher is expected to cover? How is mastery of these goals measured or monitored? Evaluate the list in terms of your own knowledge and beliefs about the teaching and learning of language. How can you mesh the mandated goals with your own as a teacher?

◆ Review the adopted textbooks for a school or district. Read the preface to see what the authors have stated as the aims or goals of the text. Read some of the study questions or exercises to see how those goals are actually put into practice, in fact or by implication. Are there inconsistencies? How well do the goals of the text mesh with your own aims and beliefs? Consider strategies for drawing on the adopted textbook in your own teaching.

◆ Make a list for yourself of the potential uses and abuses of the various kinds of units we have described: genre, language, historical/national, thematic/topical. Also list what you see as the strengths and weaknesses of each from a theoretical perspective (i.e., how well the unit style meshes with your understanding of basic principles in English teaching). On the basis of your lists, consider which kinds of unit structures work best for you.

◆ Create a list of units that you would like to teach some day. (This is a list that will grow over the years as you teach.) How can your particular areas of interest and expertise be focused for students (without, of course, imposing your own literary hobbyhorses on your students)?

◆ Learn about textbook adoption procedures in a school district or your state. How often are books adopted? For what kinds of courses? Who decides which books are chosen? Is there a written policy? Also investigate the ground rules for use of supplemental materials. How free are teachers to supplement the required texts with books of their own choosing?

◆ Develop plans for a unit along the lines suggested in this chapter.

RELATED READINGS

The professional literature is surprisingly sparse when it comes to course and unit planning. It is almost as if it is assumed that through experience, teachers will somehow know how to put together a well-organized, coherent plan. The *English Journal* publishes outlines of courses and units from time to time. In addition, the National Council of Teachers of English published a series focusing on the National Standards. Two books in this series provide several examples of full-blown units for secondary teachers. One is *Standards in Practice Grades 6–8* by Jeffrey D. Wilhelm and the other is *Standards in Practice Grades 9–12* by Peter Smagorinsky.

Perhaps the best source of ideas for units, however, is fellow teachers. "Idea exchanges" are popular at professional meetings, and conference organizers will frequently invite teachers to bring one hundred or so copies of a unit plan, course design, or teaching idea to share. Join these exchanges to enhance your collection of good unit plans. If such exchanges don't exist in your area, you might even want to organize one for the school district where you teach.

CHAPTER 4

CREATING CLASSROOM COMMUNITY

We like to borrow from the great thinker and futurist Buckminster Fuller and think of the English class as a potential synergistic structure. Fuller's geodesic domes illustrate the principles of synergy: a number of separate parts act in concert to create a structure that is stronger than any of the individual parts. As Fuller pointed out, the human body is also a synergistic unit, with separate organs—each one incapable of surviving alone—all working on different tasks for a common purpose.

Teaching language arts class can be perceived as the task of creating a synergistic structure using people. On the opening day of class, the teacher is faced with students of widely divergent interests and expectations. Each of these students has special strengths and individual weaknesses; the teacher's task is to figure out how to design a class to maximize strengths and help every student succeed, thus creating a strong unit, a community of learners who are willing to work together. If the class comes together and works well, it will become self-supporting—like a geodesic dome. Unfortunately, unlike dome builders, teachers don't know quite what the final structure will look like, and there are no clear-cut engineering principles or mathematical formulas to guide them. As much as they would like to produce a smooth, geometric unit, the English class will probably be more like the human body: subject to malfunctions and disease, with parts that need glasses, or braces, or occasional shots to keep operating. But, like the body, a class is capable of doing some marvelous, unanticipated things.

Eng. Class ≠ perfect

WHAT IS A CLASSROOM COMMUNITY?

In classrooms where community has developed, students experience a sense of being a part of something bigger than they are, of having the freedom to work with others without being accused of "cheating," of feeling that they have something to contribute to the class. In such classrooms collaborative work is valued and the teacher believes that every student can learn from every other student. In these classrooms students feel validated by both the teacher and other students since students' experiences, interests, and knowledge help form the work of the class. Although there are many, many aspects to the classroom community, we think that Kohn's explanation gives a good overview.

In saying that a classroom or school is a "community," then, I mean that it is a place in which students feel cared about and are encouraged to care about each other. They experience a sense of being valued and respected; the children matter to one another and to the teacher. They have come to think in the plural: they feel connected to each other; they are part of an "us." And as a result of all this, they feel safe in their classes, not only physically but emotionally.

From Alfie Kohn, *Beyond Discipline* (Alexandria, Va.: Association for Supervision and Curriculum Development, 1996), p. 101. Reprinted by permission of the author.

The Impact of the Affective

Teachers who work to connect to their students and to make their classes safe places realize the importance of the affective in their classrooms. Too often the affective domain in secondary classrooms is pooh-poohed and dismissed as nonessential. Little is written about this affective realm in the content area materials that secondary teachers most frequently read. But the bottom line is—if kids don't feel safe psychologically, emotionally, and physically, they can't grow and learn and write and respond to literature. This kind of safety often comes through building community.

In her work co-directing a Writing Project site, Diana sees this principle in action each summer of the project. Teachers come from diverse school districts, have a wide range of teaching experiences and a wide range of writing experiences. The first week of the project people begin rather tenuously, not sure if their writing and their views will be accepted by the group. In sharing their writing, participants feel the need for long prefaces, disclaiming this or that because they don't feel safe yet. However, once a community has been established and trust has been built, these teachers blossom. They are willing to share not only their writing, but their struggles with teaching. But before they will do this, they have to feel safe. Too often as teachers we forget that our own students need to feel this way too. Everything we say and do as teachers either builds this sense of safety or shows students our classrooms are places of dangerous risks. And it does start with us. Everything in our classroom from the arrangement of desks to the way we respond to children speaks loudly about who we are and how safe students can be in our class.

(handwritten margin note: being part of something)

(handwritten margin note: Everything we do or say & everything in the room)

Mike Rose in his *Possible Lives* said that the excellent classrooms he visited across the country did exude a sense of safety. Not only was there physical safety but also safety from insult and diminishment. He found that this in turn leads to the safety to take risks, to push beyond what students can comfortably do at present.

Another seemingly invisible element in the affective environment in the classroom has to do with authority and with where a teacher's authority comes from. Rose tells us that in the effective classrooms he visited a teachers authority "comes from multiple sources—knowledge, care, the construction of safe and respectful space, solidarity with students' background—rather than solely from age or role" (p. 414). He also noticed that authority was distributed. Students contributed to the way events unfolded, shaped the direction of discussion, became authorities on their own experience and on the work they were doing.

But to build real community takes time. The students and teacher must feel they have a common purpose and must come to know and trust each other. Since the time factor is so vital, we acknowledge it is more difficult to build community in classes that meet only forty-five minutes each day. Still, in our estimation it is worth the effort, because the values undergirding this notion of community are values that provide a solid base for an education worthwhile for students.

Strategies to build community center around fostering relationships with the adults, helping students connect to each other, and providing opportunities for the whole class to collaborate on common projects.

Fostering Relationships with Adults

Before our students even want a relationship with us they have to get the sense that we respect them. Mike Rose says respect can mean fair treatment, decency, an absence of intimidation, and beyond the realm of individual civility, a respect for the history, the language and culture of the peoples represented in the class (p. 416).

Students are masters at reading body language to figure out what teachers really believe. They will know immediately if you like young people or merely tolerate them. They will know if you are deeply afraid of them. Even from what you say to them the first few minutes of the first day of class, they will get a pretty accurate sense of the kind of person you are and if you see teaching as "just a job" or as an important commitment.

So where to begin? Given all the pieces and parts, how does the teacher start the class-building process? One of the first things a teacher can do is discover the human resources of the class and take a brief glimpse at the attitudes and ideas the students bring with them.

An introductory letter from the students to the teacher can serve this purpose and let the teacher begin to get a sense of the students in the class. Students like the chance to show a bit of their uniqueness to the teacher, and they usually respond enthusiastically to this type of letter. See Figure 4.1, which suggests questions the teacher may use to help students compose the letter. The teacher's questions can be varied for different kinds of classes and levels of students.

These letters are responded to (not graded) and given back to the student within a day or two. The immediate response, including comments on what the students

Purpose: So that we may have the best experience possible this year and so that I can plan instruction by taking into account your interests, your literacy needs, and your past experiences in language arts classes, please write a letter to me including as many of the following topics as possible:

Tell me about yourself. What are you like as a student? How do you usually behave in class? How would you describe your personality?

How do you like to be treated? How is it easiest to get along with you? What behavior in a teacher really bothers you?

Explain how you feel about reading aloud in class or doing a presentation in front of others. Tell me about yourself as a reader. Describe any experiences you have had reporting on books.

Describe your writing/composing abilities. Do you consider yourself a good writer? What kinds of things do you like/ hate to write about? What are your strongest and weakest skills in English? In what areas would you like to improve?

Think back to the last few years in English classes. Describe assignments or activities that you loved and those that you hated.

What would you like to accomplish in this class? What do you like/hate to be evaluated on in an English classroom? On what do you like to be graded?

What are your interests/talents/skills/hobbies? What are you proudest of that you have accomplished in school or outside of school?

What can I do that will be most interesting or helpful to you? Is there any other advice you'd like to give me or any questions you'd like to ask me? Is there anything else you feel I should know about you?

Don't forget to sign your name.

Figure 4.1   Letter of Introduction

have said or even questions for them to answer in a further interchange, builds rapport between the student and the teacher. Students often feel they have received personal attention from the teacher and thus have a personal connection to him or her as a result. Thus, letters can help establish the tone and atmosphere of the class, since students feel from the start that what they think does matter. This letter can also help to defuse any antagonism or hostility from some students. Diana encourages the students to state right away what bothers them about the required English class and about teachers. Not all hostile students will answer—some preferring to wait to see if the teacher can be trusted—but the fact that the option of responding negatively exists will have been duly noted.

Before having students write their introductory letter, we usually explain each question and emphasize that any question can be skipped. This is the place for the teacher to explain that when they describe their personality, students may just be stating that they're talkative and friendly or quiet and thoughtful. We also emphasize that this letter is a guide to help us know how best to treat each student so that they can do well in the class. We invite students to tell us if they respond to prodding or do best when left alone. Or if they like to be called on or cringe at the thought of it. Or if they appreciate a literal pat on the back or recoil from any kind of physical touch. These letters give the teacher more information about each student than can be digested at one time, so it's a good idea after students have read the responses for the teacher to collect the letters and reread them. (We also find that the letter has the practical consequence of helping us learn students' names early in the game.)

Throughout the school year, teachers can continue to work to connect with students by letting students know they are aware of some of the things students do outside of class or school. Responding to student learning logs and journals with questions and leaving the door open for further contact if the student desires it, also helps students see that the teacher does care.

i keep open door

Helping Students Connect With Each Other

Just as adults are often uncomfortable when they are in a new situation and don't have any sense of who the rest of the people are, so too do students feel uncomfortable in a new class. If we expect our students to build trust with others in the class and work collaboratively, it is essential that we recognize how much hard work it takes on the part of the students to create this community that we think will be so beneficial to them. One way we can help is to provide opportunities for students to get a sense of each other, to work with others in non-threatening ways. The following activities can be used the first few days of the school year to illustrate the importance you place on students getting to know each other.

Imp of students getting to know one another

Getting to Know You Although some students may have friends in your class, in large schools many of the students will be strangers. The teacher may also be a stranger to the students. Students generally respond positively to teacher attempts to get to know them. However, as important as that teacher-student relationship is, student-student awareness of each other is even more important. Before the class will function as a community, the students and teacher will need to get to know one another—not only by name but also as personalities.

If teachers explain why it is so vital that students know each other before beginning any getting-to-know-you activities, students will tend to see the activities as more than beginning-of-the-year time fillers. The teacher can explain that they will be working together in groups frequently and that to develop as a community, a group of students that will work together helping each other, it is necessary and an act of common courtesy to know each others' names.

The payoff for students is that they are more comfortable with each other. Working hard at the beginning of the year to learn each others' names can save them the embarrassment of having to ask someone his or her name after they have been in the class two or three months. It can also save them from feeling unimportant or not valued when no one knows their name.

do it at the beginning

There are many ways in which students can get to know each other. The most common one is "going around the circle," with members of the class—including the teacher—talking a bit about themselves and their interests. Diana often asks students to use alliterative words to describe themselves. She begins by telling them that she is Mrs. Mitchell and can be both Marvelous and Mouthy. Though this sort of "round the circle" device is useful, it is usually not enough to bring about solid acquaintances. To become partners and functioning peers, people have to work and talk together, exchanging ideas and information. The next several activities supply opportunities for the students to work together on cooperative ventures while eliciting expressions of interest, abilities, and problems.

Silhouettes   Have students pair off with other students in the class whom they haven't met. Using contrasting colors of construction paper, each partner makes a cutout profile of the other, using a source of light (an overhead projector works well) to cast a shadow on the paper.

After the silhouettes have been completed, have each person interview the partner about interests, beliefs, ideas, and background and then write a thumbnail sketch of the person directly on the silhouette. It often works well to have students generate these questions in groups so that the burden of creating them doesn't fall on each pair of students.

Hang the completed silhouettes with written commentary around the room for a week or two. This display provides an interesting and colorful "rogues' gallery" but in addition, proves to be a help in learning names.

Although this activity may seem complicated to the teacher in terms of the students taking turns using the overhead and elementary in its use of construction paper, scissors, and glue, we've used it very successfully in grades seven through graduate school. Without overselling, the teacher should show that this assignment includes a number of language arts skills that are part of the overall curriculum, thus encouraging students to take the assignment seriously even while enjoying it.

Personal Surveys   Another good way to get students to work together and learn more about one another is to have them work in groups, sharing the results of a class survey they have made. Possible items to include in the survey are number of brothers and sisters; hours spent watching TV per week; hours helping out at home; hours talking on the phone; work; or favorite foods, books, colors, animals, music, movies, TV programs, comic strips, sports; and hobbies. For older students, surveys can move into local, state, and world affairs; careers; thoughts on marriage and family; and plans for further education. Encourage students to keep the questions light and not too personal so that everyone will be willing to share the responses with others. After students have completed the survey, have them work in groups to compile results. Each group can report to the class on its findings, and results can be posted on the board. From these survey results, have students write up news articles describing the profile of the class or have them create a radio bulletin or essay describing teenagers today. By integrating group work with getting-to-know you activities and with writing activities, students will know what the teacher means by saying that thinking, reading, writing, and talking are all part of the language arts class and are all related to each other.

CLASS COLLABORATIONS

Working together in meaningful ways builds community. But since very little real cooperation is taught or required in the classroom students will need help, need encouragement, and need affirmation to work against the norm of competitive individualism.

examples of getting to know one another

Figure 4.2 Silhouettes

(margin note, handwritten) great group poem activity

(margin note, handwritten) to decrease / minimize competition

Middle-class America seems to accept the "common sense" embedded in the idea of a hierarchy created by competition. In this view someone ends up at the top and someone at the bottom.

It will usually take a lot of self-monitoring on the part of the teacher to become aware of how he or she inadvertently encourages competition which in effect pits one child against another. To get students to work collaboratively we have to help our students see that everyone can benefit from the contributions of everyone else and that by working together we can go farther than working alone.

Only recently this point was brought home to Diana during a demonstration in the Writing Project. Up to that point she thought collaboration was a nice idea but she didn't understand how powerful it can be. The high school teacher who was doing his demonstration asked the participants to cut out words and phrases that appealed to them from magazines, then work with two other people to create a poem out of the material they had gathered. Deep discussion of language followed as each group worked towards constructing the poem. With three people working together the results were surprising and amazing even to the participants. Group members saw unusual and interesting ways words could work together to create powerful images. Participants saw that each poem was richer because it had been constructed collaboratively. Throughout the summer other opportunities for collaboration proved as fruitful and Diana internalized the underlying principles of collaboration—it yields more for everybody, not less, and higher-level thinking skills are brought into play as each person provided explanations for their choices and suggestions.

Mike Rose reached a similar conclusion in his work in *Possible Lives.* He found that to a significant degree, "the occasion and energy for intellectual growth came from engagement with others, often over a common problem" (p. 416).

One way to work towards collaboration is to begin the school year by asking students to help set the rules in the classroom. Diana, on the first day of school, has often asked students to individually write up a list of five to ten rules of behavior that the student thinks is important. She then compiles the lists, types them up, and passes them out to students the next day. In small groups students read over all the concerns of the class, then rank the five or ten rules they think are most important to feeling secure in a classroom. All the top choices from each group are shared and students can see what the major things other students worry about or don't like to see happen. Not getting picked on or put down is usually at the top of the list, followed by being able to work without classmate's disruptions. By going through this procedure, students begin to take ownership of class rules, see that they have a voice in the classroom, and have a positive experience working together.

Another activity to involve students early in the year is called "inkshedding" a term Russell Hunt of the English Department at St. Thomas University in Fredericton, New Brunswick, shared with the Red Cedar Writing Project at Michigan State. This strategy is used to respond to written work when dealing with meaning. For instance, if students have been asked to write their reading autobiography discussing what they remember about reading in their home, how they remember learning to read, and positive and negative experiences with reading in school, this piece of writ-

peer editing method (of sorts) w/ groups

ing can be used for inkshedding. In this case, we would want students to share their reading experiences with others, figure out positive and negative ways schools reinforce reading, and come to conclusions. Generally, Hunt does not have groups read papers written by group members. To begin, the teacher collects the papers that group members have written and passes out the papers to different groups. The group task is to read each paper individually and make marks like a short, straight line next to any lines they feel really say a lot, or that they find strike a chord with them, or that they think are powerfully written. As the papers go around the group all members will have a chance to make marks in response to each paper.

Then the next phase of the work begins. The group takes notes on what was marked most frequently and then categorizes those points. They begin by making columns labeled positive, negative, and other and listing the frequently noted points under each heading. These lists are then shared with the whole class. Discussion follows on what has been learned about students' experiences with reading in the classroom.

This kind of strategy can be used with many, many kinds of assignments. Students generally respond positively to it because their paper is not one that is under discussion in their group and because they can see that the material generated by the students through the assignment is being used and is part of the material of the classroom. This is a real task that doesn't have right or wrong answers and the teacher is genuinely inviting student response and thought. When students see that all of their writing will not just be read by the teacher but could be part of the work of the class, they feel their work is more important, since it is being used in authentic ways.

These kinds of activities set the stage for even more collaboration when students actually work together on projects. Of course, before any such work can be done it is important to make sure students understand the process and what is expected of them. It is also important that the collaborative effort be followed by reflection on the process. Students need to think about their own learning, become aware of the processes they use, and begin to recognize that they can learn from classmates. Spending time on this kind of reflective work also shows the students that the teacher considers the work important and values what they are doing, an important step if students are to take this kind of work seriously.

Diana always worked to have at least one whole-class collaborative project each semester in her classes. For instance, students in her ninth grade English classes would pick one or two issues that they thought were so important that others should be aware of them. Issues included dealing with the death of a friend or loved one, divorce, a suicidal friend, or alienation from school. Groups poured their energy into finding information on the topic and then decided how to present their information and advice to others. Some worked on skits that could be presented, others constructed pamphlets, worked on a series of public address announcements, or created posters. Some ambitious groups even produced talk shows and video tapes that were shown to other classes. On projects like this students work together and come to understand that the more viewpoints and information and ideas they have, the better their project will be. They also realize that because these projects reach a broader audience than just the class, they should be their best work.

- having research papers connect w/ the real world

1. Form groups of 3 to 5 people. (This is often the most difficult part of the collaborative process since a balance between students who want to work together and students who will actually work together must be achieved.)

2. Discuss the task or choose a task if you have options. List all the parts of the task—everything that must be done.

3. Decide how you will complete the work—which parts can be done together and which need to be done individually?

4. Discuss, negotiate, and then decide who will do what parts of the task.

5. Talk about how your group made this decision and how satisfied group members are with this process.

6. Begin work on the tasks, giving each other frequent feedback.

7. Upon completion, write about and discuss the hardest parts of working together and what you each learned from the experience about yourself and from others.

8. Upon completion, evaluate your own part of the work in writing, explaining what you contributed to the effort. Write comments about what others in your group contributed.

Figure 4.3   The Process of Collaboration

KNOWING WHO OUR STUDENTS ARE

[handwritten margin note: must acknowledge the cultural stuff of the student]

We often choose the field of teaching because we loved school, we did well in school, and we felt validated and appreciated in school. We assume most students feel this way or if they don't, we think we can help them have positive experiences in education. Many of us have never examined our own cultural backgrounds, have never questioned what makes up what we call "knowledge," have never asked why some things are taught and others not, have never looked closely at how economic, racial, and social differences can privilege some children at the expense of others. While this section can obviously not deal with these "heavy issues" in any comprehensive way, we hope we can illustrate that these are issues that every teacher needs to give thought to. Not being aware of who our students are, how they are culturally situated, what knowledge is privileged, and what our own cultural background predisposes us to view as right or good could work to deprive some of our students of educational opportunities in our classrooms.

What It Takes On the Part of the Teacher

Through education courses most teachers are aware that the student population today continues to change and that children of color constitute an increasing proportion of our students. While students of color represent 30 percent of our public school population, teachers of color make up less than 5 percent of the public school teaching population, according to Gloria Ladson-Billings (p. x).

These statistics make clear that teachers increasingly come from backgrounds different from their students. Thus, teachers can no longer assume their students are like them, and now must work toward becoming what Ladson-Billings calls a culturally relevant teacher.

Teachers who practice culturally relevant methods can be identified by the way they see themselves and others. They see their teaching as an art rather than as a technical skill. They believe that all of their students can succeed rather than that failure is inevitable for some. They see themselves as a part of the community and they see teaching as giving back to the community. They help students make connections between their local, national, racial, cultural, and global identities. Such teachers can also be identified by the ways in which they structure their social interactions: Their relationships with students are fluid and equitable and extend beyond the classroom. They demonstrate a connectedness with all of their students and encourage that same connectedness between the students. They encourage a community of learners; they encourage their students to learn collaboratively. Finally, such teachers are identified by their notions of knowledge: They believe that knowledge is continuously recreated, recycled, and shared by teachers and students alike. They view the content of the curriculum critically and are passionate about it. Rather than expecting students to demonstrate prior knowledge and skills they help students develop that knowledge by building bridges and scaffolding for learning.

From Gloria Ladson-Billings, *The Dreamkeepers,* p. 25. Copyright © 1994 by Jossey-Bass Inc., Publishers. Reprinted by permission.

Validating Our Students' Cultures and Life Experiences

Teachers can begin to validate students' cultures by creating assignments that let students share some of their background and give them ways to showcase the strengths of their culture. For instance, if your class was reading the widely anthologized short story "Charles" by Shirley Jackson, in which a kindergartner misbehaves, you could ask students how they think this child should be treated. Students then would talk about how their parents would have dealt with "Charles." Discussion may then turn to child-rearing practices and how they differ culturally.

Mike Rose emphasizes the importance of learning about students' backgrounds and cultures. The effective teachers he studied educated themselves about the communities and cultures of the students before them, connected with parents and involved parents in schooling, saw students as resources, and learned from them. Lisa Delpit in *Other People's Children* also stresses the importance of helping students make connections with their local, racial, and cultural identities. She believes the teacher can reduce the sense of students having to choose between a school self and a home self if the learning is embedded in culturally or racially familiar contexts.

So how can the English language arts teacher begin to connect to students' lives? One avenue is to tap into the students' home life for assignments. For example, Diana once had her ninth grade students interview parents or other relatives about how the student was given his or her name. After students talked to the adults they came back to class with the short stories of how they had been named. Students shared these in small groups, and other students asked mostly clarification questions. Stories were revised to include the details classmates had asked for. Because students were so excited about the stories, each student read his or hers aloud. These classes were made up of students of Latino, African-American, and

[handwritten margin notes: can use books to incorporate/create cultural diff.]

[handwritten margin note: through exploration of names]

European-American backgrounds. Students were fascinated by how each group seemed to have different traditions. In Latino families the majority of children were named after someone special in the family. In African-American families, many parents created a name especially for the child. In European-American families no one tradition stood out. Often the children were named because the parent "just liked the name." All the traditions were talked about and valued and students wanted to further the discussion about how they would like to name their own children.

Another kind of assignment that taps into family history is the intergenerational interview. Students chose an older relative or friend and interview the person on tape or write down the answers. Students create the questions to ask. The ones who decide to tape record the interview often come to class with tape in hand begging to have it played for the whole class. While the tapes play, students usually hang on every word. Parents' feedback is very positive on projects like this. They love that what they or the child's grandparents know is being validated and that a connection is being made between the home and the school. (See Chapter 7 for information on inquiry-based learning that builds on student experience and interest.)

[handwritten margin note: interview an older family relative]

Working with Students with Limited English Proficiency   Many of the students who come to us from other cultures also have limited proficiency in English. Providing the atmosphere and structure in which these students can grow as language learners takes teacher awareness, planning, and thought. Norma Mota Altman and Carol Younglove, who work extensively with language-minority students in California, gave this advice, in a presentation Diana attended, about creating a sensitive multicultural classroom where students with limited English proficiency could feel comfortable and grow:

- Emphasize cooperation, not competition.
- Use cooperative groups.
- Tap into students' home stories.
- Share information on the cultures of the students, not just the cultures of majority students.
- Discuss vocabulary. If you have some support systems, have key concepts written in the language of the students and posted in the room.
- Start with student questions on materials such as literature and validate different perspectives.
- Encourage students to question the text so they will see that texts aren't the holders of truth.
- Broaden sources of knowledge drawn on in the classroom—use videos, audio tapes, as well as books.
- If a child responds in one word—expand on it instead of correcting it.
- Use visual aids as much as possible.
- Deal head-on with discrimination, labeling, and name calling.

- Ask open-ended questions: model, expand, restate and enrich student language.

Some things not to do include:

- Constant and insensitive "correcting" of student verbal responses.
- Having everything in English with no visual aids.
- Using worksheets that focus on piecemeal, out-of-context work.
- Having occasional token celebrations (signs, food, hats) not woven into the curriculum.
- Using materials only from the majority culture.
- Writing in cursive on the board. Students struggling with English would be unable to read it.
- Speaking loudly to students who don't appear to understand you.
- Making students repeat words when they have no visual clues about what the word might mean.

Many excellent books have been written that can give helpful information to teachers who are suddenly thrust into the role of working with many students who are just beginning to acquire English. We list several of these sources at the end of the chapter.

Differences in Learning Styles, Behavior, and Culture   When a significant difference exists between the students' culture and the school's culture, teachers can easily misread students' aptitudes, intent, or abilities as a result of the difference in styles of language use and interactional patterns. When such cultural differences exist, teachers may utilize styles of instruction and/or discipline that are at odds with community norms. Lisa Delpit gives an example of the differences in the way directives are likely to be given to unruly students. An African-American teacher would be direct and in an explicit fashion would say, "I don't want to hear it. Sit down, be quiet, and finish your work NOW!" A middle-class European-American teacher is likely to say something like, "Would you like to sit down now and finish your paper?" This indirect command downplays the display of power but can easily be interpreted to be the words of someone who is fearful. Thus students often ignore a command given this way (p. 168).

Delpit also says that African-American boys, as a result of cultural influences, often exhibit a high degree of physicality and desire for interaction. This can take

[handwritten margin note: — their culture effects the way they act]

> If we are to successfully educate all of our children, we must work to remove the blinders built of stereotypes, monocultural instructional methodologies, ignorance, social distance, biased research, and racism. We must work to destroy those blinders so that it is possible to really see, to really know the students we must teach.
>
> From Lisa Delpit, *Other People's Children* (New York: The New Press, 1995), p.182.

positive forms like hugging and other shows of affection or negative forms like hitting and other displays of displeasure. Because students are usually expected to remain in seats and these boys are used to interaction, it is apparent why many African-American boys do not do as well in school.

Delpit also shares an example from Native American culture. Many Native American communities have a prohibition against speaking for someone else. In one situation students appeared unable to write summaries, and even when explicitly told not to, continued to write their opinions of various works rather than summaries of the author's words. A researcher concluded that the prohibition against speaking for others may have caused these students considerable difficulty in trying to capture in their own words the ideas of another. Because they had been taught to always speak for themselves, they found doing so much more comfortable and culturally compatible (p. 170).

Gloria Ladson-Billings shows that cultural strengths that African-American children bring with them to the class room are rarely capitalized on by teachers. She tells us that teachers see "nonstandard English" without seeing that the language is rich and diverse, that students understand subtleties in language and the importance of tone and inflection in speaking. Teachers see the frankness of African-American children and think their authority is being challenged instead of recognizing that these children don't try to deceive by pretending that something is all right when deep down inside they don't think it is.

Although the above examples show only the tip of the iceberg as far as cultural differences in behavior, we hope these will sufficiently motivate readers to do research on the culture of the children they teach. An often overlooked resource, though, is the parent. If a child seems to waste time in class or doesn't seem to be responding to the teacher's style, parents may be able to give sound advice. The teacher can explain the problem to the parent and ask the parent what he would say to the child in that circumstance. Using this strategy also gives the teacher more information about the culture of the community and the expectations they have for their students.

DEALING WITH DIFFERENCES

Our students know that differences exist among them. They know who's rich and who's poor, who's popular and who's not. They have inklings about which students have supportive families and which students are struggling to survive in their families

It's we adults who often have trouble acknowledging differences. It makes us uncomfortable. Because we haven't always found ways to deal with differences without seeming to draw attention to specific groups or without making someone seem less fortunate than others, we just avoid dealing with difference. In our attempts to make students feel comfortable then, we often unwittingly silence voices in our own classrooms or simply don't acknowledge the multitude of voices that exist.

Students sense this hesitancy in us. They hear the silence about issues of difference that include race and gender and sexual orientation and economic and social class. How do they interpret the silence? What do students learn from us when we teach such books as *The Adventures of Huckleberry Finn* and never mention the racial implications? Perhaps students view this absence of talk on these issues the same way they view the absence of talk about sex in their homes—as something forbidden or too shameful to talk about. Lisa Delpit believes this to be the case.

Many well-intentioned teachers say "I don't see color, I only see children." What message does this statement send? That there is something wrong with being black or brown, that it should NOT be noticed? I would like to suggest that if one does not see color, then one does not really see children. Children made "invisible" in this manner become hard-pressed to see themselves worthy of notice.

From Lisa Delpit, *Other People's Children* (New York: The New Press, 1995), p.177.

[handwritten margin note: must embrace diff.]

So where do teachers start? How can we go about talking about differences? Some ways to open the discussion include asking students to write ten sentences beginning with such starters as: Being European-American means. . . , Being African-American means. . . , Being Latino means. . . , Being Native American means. . . , Being Asian-American means. . . . Students turn in the completed work but need not include their name. The student responses are typed up and brought in the next day. If students who have a European background have trouble thinking of sentence completers, that is an excellent point of departure since it helps these students become aware that people in the majority don't often think about race. Students can be prompted to use these completed sentence starters to go deeper into the issues. They can write in response to how other students perceive race; they can turn these completed sentence starters into scripts that can be performed for their own or others' classes.

Another good way to make students aware of gender or racial issues is to have each student write a narrative based on a time he or she was treated a certain way simply because he or she was a male or a female or a black, white, or brown person. Before students are asked to write about their race, a very high level of trust has to be established in the class. In Diana's experience at a racially mixed school, students were very willing to write about these racial experiences and share them with class members, since it provided them with a vehicle to make other students aware of some of their concerns. Students bring these kinds of stories to class without names on them and share them in small groups where students mark the parts they think are especially powerful. Pieces of these stories that the students considered powerful can be excerpted and used in a script that is read to the whole class. Through this kind of sharing students are made aware that racism and sexism are far from dead.

Children's books can also be used to get students to look at how males and females or people of different races are portrayed. Bring in lots of picture books from the library and have students analyze them in terms of who is the main character, who is shown doing what, how frequently people of color are in the picture books, etc. Students can draw conclusions about whether they think these picture books contribute to or refute gender and racial stereotypes and how much these books seem to mirror society.

During literature discussions, as students talk about characterization, ask them to look at how gender, race, and socioeconomic status are portrayed through the characters. Integrating this kind of response with other talk of characterization keeps these issues alive throughout the year.

If we are to deal with differences in our classrooms in honest ways we also have to allow discussions of oppression as part of our language and literature instruction. Looking at words used to describe races, genders, and socioeconomic levels can tell our students much about how society views these groups in terms of what they should and should not do and what is expected of them. For instance, one way females are "kept in their place" is through the language we use to describe them and their actions. A man who is forthright and honest would be called "confident" while a woman exhibiting those characteristics would be called aggressive or worse. In dealing with differences we can help students become aware of the power of language to control as well as discern patterns of oppression by looking closely at our language.

DEALING WITH CONTROVERSIAL ISSUES

Needless to say, being willing to deal with differences can lead to being involved with controversial issues. We have the opportunity to open new windows on the world to our students and help them see things in new ways through honest discussions. In classrooms such as these, students can often see a connection to their own lives and the world they live in. They don't feel that school is merely a series of hoops to jump through. They begin to trust the teacher because the teacher does not ignore important issues. And they may bring up issues the teacher isn't ready to deal with.

But how far should the new or inexperienced teacher go? We suggest that teachers stay within their own comfort zone and that as they become more knowledgeable and confident about dealing with tough issues, they confront them. However, such things as name calling ("fag" is one such name that often goes unchallenged in the classroom) can never be allowed even if the teacher feels uncomfortable confronting this behavior. If questions come up that put the teacher on the spot such as "Do you believe marijuana should be legalized?" teachers should feel free to sidestep the issue. Comments such as "I think it's less important what I think than sorting out how you think about the issue" can often be enough to let students know this is not an issue you will discuss. Other times simply saying, "I'm not comfortable dealing with this issue in a public school setting" will tell students where you stand. Students can also be made aware of the precarious position they are putting the teacher in when they try to engage the teacher in issues sensitive to the community.

Thus a second recommendation we would make is that teachers need to know their own communities. If the topic of abortion is raging in the community, novels or short stories that deal with this issue must be selected with great care or avoided. There is so much excellent literature available, especially young adult literature, that wonderful novels can be found that don't hit the hot buttons of the community, even while fostering the discussion of crucial issues.

New and inexperienced teachers need to be aware that oftentimes as they become known and trusted by the community, they will be freer to raise more sensitive issues. In Diana's experience as a long-time teacher in a large urban district she was free to choose the materials she thought best and to confront any kind of controversial issue in her classroom. But she had been in the district more than twenty years and was trusted as a teacher by administrators and parents. In this time only one parent challenged a novel she was using—*Of Mice and Men.* This set of parents did not want their son reading what they considered to be a "godless" book which had "nothing but swearing in it." The discussion revealed that the parents had not read the book but had only looked at samplings of the language. Diana, of course, bowed to the parents wishes and provided a different book for their son.

As far as district or school censorship goes, the district she taught in followed the National Council of Teachers of English suggested guidelines. The parent had to show evidence of reading the whole book. The concern had to be presented to the Curricula Council and go through several layers of administrative bureaucracy. So in Diana's years in that district not one book was ever censored district wide although teachers knew that individual parents had the right to veto specific books for their own children.

Teachers in other districts are not always as fortunate. For those who do need advice on censorship issues the National Council of Teachers of English and SLATE (Support for the Learning and Teaching of English) can provide it. SLATE has materials that can be used when dealing with censorship. This organization can be reached through NCTE. Another place to get help is *Preserving Intellectual Freedom* edited by Jean E. Brown (NCTE 1994), a wonderful collection of articles on just about every aspect of censorship.

there are outlets for helping teachers incorporate issues into curriculum

DEFINING WORK

Another way we display our views of how learning takes place and how students fit into the picture is through what we "count" as work. These views come from our own cultural and educational background and our ideological and philosophical beliefs, areas which may be outside of our awareness. What we actually deem as "work" in our classrooms and what we chose to assess bespeaks our views on what education really is and what parts of our students' skills and experiences we choose to value (see Chapter 13 on evaluation for further discussion).

First of all we have to figure out how we think learning takes place. Do we think children come to us with empty heads that we are to fill? Or do we believe that learning takes place through the interaction of the learner and new information?

We believe in the constructivist theory of learning that the Wells' quotation articulates. What this theory implies is that students need time to talk and interact with

Constructive Theory of learning

Knowledge has to be constructed by individual students through the progressive extending and modifying of their existing knowledge that occurs when they attempt to make sense of new information and experience.

From Gordon Wells and Gen Ling Chang-Wells, *Constructing Knowledge Together* (Portsmouth, N.H.: Heinemann, 1992), p. 99. Reprinted by permission.

others so they have time to reformulate knowledge. Students are part of the process of learning, not simply the subject of the learning. This stance also serves the culturally relevant teacher well, too, for it allows her to acknowledge, value, and incorporate student knowledge into the classroom.

If teachers don't view students as bringing anything to the learning process than student talk in the class will simply be seen as extraneous and won't be counted. Role-playing activities meant to help students understand such things as characterization would be seen as frivolous and not counted. Reading silently and then drawing a response to the chapters read would be seen as fluff. The actual ways that students come to make meaning in the class would not be seen as the "work" of the class. Only written products count in this view.

Another example might help to make this clearer: Students are asked to write in a learning notebook daily about the connections they see among the activities that are going on in the class and to reflect on what they are personally learning. In these notebooks a lot of higher level thinking skills could be demonstrated with students making creative leaps and offering connections that are original. But because these notebooks are not viewed by some teachers as "formal learning" they would tend to count them as very little towards a student's grade. Thus as teachers we make decisions all the time on what counts in class and what does not count. The scary part is that we often think our decisions are "common sense" when they actually go against what is known about learning theory and what is known about the differences in the way students learn. Toni Morrison addressed this concern.

> "It is a disservice to hobble the young, cut them off at the knees, and not give them the widest education just because you have your own agenda."
>
> From a speech on the campus of Michigan State University by Toni Morrison April 2, 1997.

Janet Hale-Benson's landmark book *Black Children: Their Roots, Culture, and Learning Styles* discusses the differences in the analytical and the relational approaches to the methods individuals use to select and classify information. From the work of Rosalie Cohen and Asa Hilliard she explains how some students "lump" things together looking for commonalities, while others "split" things up, noticing the unique. Interestingly enough, schools only require the analytic approach, and reward the development of the analytic style of processing information and the "lumpers" are the ones who benefit. The overall educational ideology and environment only reinforces behavior associated with that style. So if children respond more affectively, usually personify the inanimate, identify the unique, not the commonalities, don't use linear notions, have a poor response to timed, scheduled, preplanned activities that interfere with the immediacy of the environment, these children's style of learning will not be validated by the school.

> Pupils who have not developed these [analytic] skills and those who function with a different cognitive style will not only be poor achievers early in school, but they will also become worse as they move to higher grade levels.
>
> From Janice E. Hale-Benson, *Black Children—Their Roots, Culture, and Learning Styles* (Baltimore, Md.: The Johns Hopkins University Press, 1986), p. 31. Reprinted by permission.

To contrast the two cognitive styles, Asa Hilliard created a table. He found that *—analytical -vs- relational organization* analytical organization includes, among other things: standardization, conformity, memory for specific facts, regularity, rigid order, "normality," differences equal deficits , precision, logic, and meanings are universal. In contrast, relational organization emphasizes freedom, variation, creativity, memory for essence, novelty, flexibility, uniqueness, sameness equals oppression, and meanings are contextual.

Children who function with relational styles are unlikely to be rewarded socially with grades regardless of native ability, the depth of this information, or background of experience. In fact, this child will probably be considered deviant and disruptive in the analytically oriented learning environment of the school

We bring this research up to show teachers that there is a cause for concern. When we are working with students we have to understand that we are not always *must try to acknowledge* providing them with ways to show their learning, because we are not capitalizing on their cognitive strengths.

Current work on multiple intelligences, a term made famous by Howard Gardner as he tried to broaden our narrow definition of intelligence, also suggests that students learn and make meaning in very different ways. This information encourages us to stretch our own conceptions of what we consider "work" in the classroom. For instance in most English language arts classrooms, writing is the only form of showing knowledge that we privilege. If students know things and can demonstrate what they know through talk, drama, art, or music, we don't validate those forms of showing meaning which could be used for such things as responding to a piece of literature.

Gloria Ladson-Billings points out that perceptions of deficiency and competence are socially and culturally constructed; in other words, we learn from our own social and cultural background. So without greater exposure to the students' culture, teachers lack the tools with which to make sense of much that transpires in the classroom.

DEFINING RESOURCES

If we are to build a strong classroom community and students are to feel that they bring important information and experiences into the classroom with them, then we must also be aware of the affect that defining resources has on our students. If a textbook is used as the only valid source of information, then other possibilities are closed off to students and they learn that all information and perhaps "truth" comes from books. In language arts classrooms, because we are dealing with such a broad array of content and so many processes, we can bring into the classroom many kinds of resources. We can use audio tapes of radio shows, TV shows, picture books, the Internet, videos, young adult literature, interviews, surveys, and student-generated responses as the content of our classes. By bringing in other sources of information we let students know that knowledge can come from places besides books. We can affirm that the interviews they do of family members can be part of the information base of the classroom. We can weave in student's experiences with other kinds of resources.

For instance, when a short story or novel is read, students can come to class with two or three questions on paper. These can be pooled and used as the basis of small-group work in which the groups answer the questions other students have brought to class. When Diana used this as the basis of instruction for Stephen Crane's "Open Boat," students asked such questions as: What was the significance of the oiler dying? Why was he the only one with a name? Why does the story start in the middle? Why is there so little dialogue? It seems if you were stranded you'd have a lot to discuss. Why did Crane concentrate so much on detail? Do the waves and sea gulls and sharks have any symbolism?

Students can also be asked to list recurring themes and motifs in a novel and then work to make generalizations about the novel from those themes and motifs. The point of this kind of work is that students are working from their own questions and thus are more interested in thinking about the material; students are constructing meaning by using higher level thinking skills; students are being shown that what they bring to the class is valuable since the teacher is not just teaching from his or her own agenda and imposing his or her questions on the students; and that student learning and constructing meaning is at the heart of the class.

Of course, another consideration we must make when we select and thus define resources, is whether we will use traditionally taught material commonly known as the "canon" or whether we will bring in newer, more contemporary texts. If we are working to create a classroom community in which all students can feel a part, it seems obvious that we must use resources that represent the many faces of the cultures inhabiting our classes and our country. Lisa Delpit clearly states what can happen if we narrowly define the material we use.

> In part, the problems we see exhibited in school by African-American children and children of other oppressed minorities can be traced to this lack of a curriculum in which they can find represented the intellectual achievements of people who look like themselves.
>
> From Lisa Delpit, *Other People's Children* (New York: The New Press, 1995), p.177.

If students are part of the ethnic minorities we don't acknowledge, or part of a kind of family they have never seen in literature, or part of the less-well-to-do segments of our society that they never read about, they are like invisible members of our class. When students see themselves represented in the literature we teach they no longer feel that they are invisible, because an author has recognized that people of their race or economic level or family background are worthy of writing about.

THE TEXT BOOK AS RESOURCE

While we hope new teachers will eventually be able to expand beyond the textbook, we do acknowledge that the major teaching resource for any classroom is likely to be the required textbook. Since the new teacher may not have the resources to begin with materials besides the text, careful review of the textbook as resource is in order. *[read thoroughly]*

Some texts provide helpful teachers' manuals; sometimes teachers either find the manual missing or discover that its philosophy and organization do not mesh with their own. Since the textbook alone or with a guide should not be allowed to dictate the structure of your course, you will need to figure out how to make the material useful. Hopping from one section of the text to another is confusing to students who need reasons to read a text and need to see patterns and organization. If you keep these ideas in mind, using a standard or adopted textbook need not be deadly. In the magical world where everyone wants to dwell (the world where everybody wins the lottery), there would be time before school begins for the teacher to read the book cover to cover, picking out the most teachable materials and leaving out the rest. Unfortunately, most teachers have far less time available. A good way to prepare, therefore, is simply to skim the contents and look at the organization of the text. If it's a literature book, does it use a genre approach or does it operate by chronology, themes, or some combination? Where is the poetry placed? Is it integrated throughout the book or is it in clusters? Which old literary favorites are there? Which classics that are readable by your students? Which new pieces that you'll want to read yourself? If it's a composition text you can sense its philosophy from the table of contents: Is this book dedicated to writing-as-process, structural rhetoric, grammar/correctness? How well does the books' table of contents coincide with your own philosophy? Glance at some of the exercises and rate them on an imaginativeness scale of 1 to 10 or A through F. *[try not to hop = too confusing]*

From these skimmings you can begin to work out the details of a course, even to plan for the first week or more. Do you want to begin with literature or composition (or neither—perhaps oral discussion or drama)? Which stories in the literature text might be reasonably sure-fire for the first days of teaching? Which topics in the composition book will most directly make contact with the students and help them see that English really can be of some help to them in school? *[when to use & which not to]*

At some point, you'll probably want to draw a map or chart of your teaching journey, tentatively identifying textbook chapters you want to use, in what sequence, and for what purposes. That, in turn, helps you begin to think about other resource needs for your class. Conclude the text survey by writing down what isn't there. How will you have to supplement the book to enrich your class? Will you need to find a wide range of novels related to a theme? Will you have to develop your own writing topics to substitute for dry-as-dust topics in the textbook? Make a shopping list and then start looking for more resources.

How to decipher decipher a textbook!

1. What is the title of the textbook?
2. What is the copyright date? What might this mean about the kind of stories that will be included or excluded from the text?
3. Look in the Table of Contents and together write down unit headings that seem interesting to you.
4. List the names of authors you have heard of before. Did either of you like those author's work?
5. Skim the Table of Contents for titles of selections that sound interesting to you. Write down two or three.
6. Turn to the text. Pick a story and look at what you are asked to do with the story after you have read it. List the names of the sections after each selection (For Discussion, Language, and Vocabulary). Discuss with your partner how you feel about the way the authors ask you to respond to selections. Record your reactions.
7. Look at the pictures in the text. Discuss whether you think they add interest to the text or not. Record your reaction.
8. Spend a few minutes looking through the poetry sections. Find a poem each of you likes or hates, explain your reactions to each other, and record titles of poems, and your reaction.
9. Find the glossary and write down two or three words that you each know the meaning of already.
10. Find the index and write down the kinds of information you can find there.
11. Are there any other sections or parts of the book? Write down the names of those sections and explain what can be found there.
12. Briefly explain your general impressions of this textbook.

Figure 4.4   Assessing the Anthology

To again demonstrate to students that their evaluations and opinions are important in your classroom and that books are meant to be questioned, ask students in pairs to assess the anthology.

BUT WHAT ABOUT DISCIPLINE?

In our years of teaching school and college students, we have found that a well-managed class is based on principles that go deeper than the issues of control and discipline, important as they may be. Classroom management requires a strong theoretical framework of what English is as a discipline and as a set of processes, and it demands an evolving understanding of what produces growth in students as well as a clear set of personal values, sound teaching ideas, and good classroom organization. This section, then, is a summary of the organizing strategies and other bits of practical information we have gleaned from our years in the classroom that will help build towards classroom community. These can help blend content and teaching methodology into a workable whole so that learning can take place in the classroom and disruption is minimized. We also intend to offer suggestions to teachers, both new and experienced, who, sufficiently overwhelmed by the annoying details of classroom life such as attendance taking, paperwork, hall passes, and pencil handouts, simply have little energy or patience to even think about group work or classroom drama or a publication of student writing. We'd like to remove some of the managerial roadblocks so the teacher can focus on effective strategies to involve students more deeply in their learning. We are also certainly aware that order does come before community building and that well-planned, interesting lessons are not always the antidote to disorder so we also summarize some of the methods we have used to work towards achieving an orderly classroom.

Teaching Strategies and Practices

Knowing content is only one piece of the teaching puzzle. The other half is learning how to involve students in the subject matter in meaningful ways. Everything done in a classroom is based on a strategy—a plan of action—or a practice—what you believe should happen in the classroom on a regular basis. How and what you do in the classroom is where the hard work of preparation should be focused. Good material by itself is not enough, it's the strategies you use and practices you embed in the classroom that breathe life into the material you select.

Motivating students is essential to a well-run classroom, because the more fully students are involved in their work, the less desire they will have to be disruptive. When students are difficult to manage and are not responding to anything planned, a teacher's immediate instinct may be to crack down and show them who's boss. Fantasies of the military dictator bloom in your mind, and you see yourself marching down aisles, swagger stick in hand, giving orders, and watching students obey unquestioningly, doing assignments with care, watching you with awe mixed with respect and fear. Unfortunately, punitive measures seldom get the desired results; indeed, cracking down often leads to more and more rebellion. (Who ever said school isn't like "real life"?) Under the generalissimo system, teachers (and dictators) spend all their time controlling the class and monitoring every little piece of inattentive or annoying behavior.

[handwritten margin note: —punitive measures seldom get result]

One productive solution to the difficult class is to focus on ways of involving the very students who most irritate us. Since we believe that content, in the best sense of language and living, is at the heart of the matter of discipline, we try to involve students—all students, not just disruptive ones—by drawing on their own experiences and the language skills they have in hand, rather than dwelling on deficiencies.

Capturing and Maintaining Student Interest

[handwritten note: try to involve the most irritating student]

Some ideas and strategies that have worked for us:

Use group work.   Aside from being a sound way to operate instructionally, grouping helps with classroom management because you can "divide and conquer." Many behavior problems occur when students are expected to quietly listen to the teacher; that's when many students try to show off for their peers, and that's when it's easy to make a teacher look inept or foolish. When students are involved in groups, their focus is on others in the groups and on the work and they get fewer chances to show off to the whole class. (Of course, group work invites other kinds of behavior problems, and we'll offer more on how to make group work productive elsewhere in this chapter.)

Change activities frequently.   Especially in middle school and junior high, kids need a change of pace. We reject the notion that kids of that age are incapable of maintaining interest for sustained periods of time, but we know only too well that lively, growing youngsters need to be up and about, physically and intellectually. So instead of expending energy on keeping students doing one single task the whole hour, we plan two or three shorter activities. The class might start off with a written response to what has been read, then move to discussion groups, and conclude the hour with a whole-class discussion on what was brought out in the groups. Or a class period might begin with a listing on the board of possible writing topics, move into writing time, and then wrap up with shared writing with the whole class or with a partner or small group.

Interest students in what they are being asked to do.   Student curiosity and engagement can be piqued by telling them something about a reading that will raise their interest quotient or by brainstorming and discussing possible topics. Stories can be left hanging at the end of the hour, "to be continued." The teacher can discuss his or her responses to a book under discussion or challenge students to refute the teacher's "accepted" or conventional view of a plot, character, or theme. Literature, language, and life are, for all but the Living Dead, filled with excitement; the teacher needs to work on helping students become more curious about all three.

Find a range of materials for students to explore.   Bring in magazines, newspapers, comic books, new paperbacks, brochures, videos, cassettes, or a set of moose antlers. Encourage the students to bring materials to share as well. Link these materials to the topic under discussion; find connections between the themes explored in literature and the stuff that people find interesting in their daily lives (the two often converge).

Do projects that have a genuine payoff.   Exchanging projects with other grades or classes for reaction and response works well, providing an honest audience and a visible end point to a class unit. Diana had particular success with a poetry project in which eighth graders selected ten to fifteen poems that they thought third graders would like. At first the older students were skeptical, but by the second day they were gleefully reading poems aloud to one another from poetry books borrowed from the library. The students then copied the selected poems, made a cover, and sent the books to the third grade classroom. The third graders replied with letters commenting on selections and even on neatness and handwriting!

Demonstrate that student work is important and valued.   Refer to it often and display some of it in the classroom. If students are asked to list all the ideas Mrs. Joe had on child rearing in *Great Expectations,* then compile the best ideas and post or announce the results in class. Sharing work done by the students will usually get good results in the English classroom because students perceive that they are doing something for more than the teacher.

[handwritten: sharing work good, be could they feel like they're doing something good]

Promoting Student Success

It is axiomatic that nothing succeeds like success. More important and more subtle is that success demonstrates a growing body of skills and knowledge and is thus a direct indication of learning. We don't believe in piling on vague or half-felt praise, and we certainly don't advocate giving students a false impression of their own skills and abilities. Rather, we like to build on what students concretely accomplish in our classrooms.

Start with what they know. Students already feel that they have a lot to learn without the teacher telling them so all the time. To get positive results, begin with as-signments the students can respond to successfully, then gradually move to areas that are less familiar. If the teacher is interested in teaching a specific form of writing, for instance, lead students into the assignment by letting them explore some writing they can do already. The formal persuasive paper, for example, can more easily be taught if students are first asked to write a letter to their parents persuading them to let them have, do, be into, or get out of something.

[handwritten: or relating to their life]

Make assignments at which students can succeed. After reading a student's first writing assignment, the teacher will often recognize the student's strengths and weaknesses. If we are truly interested in the learning of students, it becomes obvious that asking them to do something that is far beyond their skill level is self-defeating for student and teacher. For instance, assigning a research paper to a student who has no idea of how to search for and gather information is frustrating for the student and discouraging for the teacher. Instead, ask the novices to put together a dictionary on topics which interest them: hunting, music, UFOs, dreams, astrology, or cock-roaches. Next the student creates appropriate definitions for each term. As they put together the dictionary, they will naturally interview one another on word meanings and do some elementary research in the library. This project, then, builds their confi-dence in research skills and prepares the students for further research projects. It is also much easier to teach students the skills they will need if they are taught in the context of an interesting assignment to which students can build commitment.

[handwritten: assignment for those who struggle w/ research]

Give good directions, model what you want, and give concrete assignments. Be-fore asking students to write a "response" to a story, tell them what a response is and what kind you expect. Tell them you want them to react to or summarize the story, to detail what they didn't understand, to describe what made a strong impression on them, to explain what they would like to say to the author or a character in the story. Or, better yet, model how to do one by doing one yourself on the overhead and then having the class create one together. Vague assignments will elect vague and often bor-ing work.

Help students make sense of what they are doing in class.   The ever-present "Why are we doing this?" should be answered. If you can't answer this convincingly (to yourself as well as the students) you may need to think more about your goals. Teachers who understand the links between reading, writing, thinking, and speaking and can convey information about purpose to students will usually get a better response from them. Students also need to be shown how plans fit in or expand on what they've already done. Presenting material without providing a context not only confuses students, but often makes them angry because they can't see the point. They resent "busy work," not only because it is usually boring but also because they don't see what they will gain from it. Another way to help students make sense of what is going on in class is to ask them daily to reflect on their own learning in the course and write about the connections they are making between the reading, writing, and talking that is part of the class.

just help

Help students know what kinds of resources are available in the library.   But don't just take them on one more grand tour of the card catalog and the Reader's Guide. Help students identify a topic they're excited about, then explore the resources. Show them vertical files, reference books, the catalog, bibliographies, how to use the Internet, how to access computer banks of information. Use your expertise as a library user to help them find what they need. Then ask them to report back, not only on what they found, but on where and how they found it.

diff. learning

Encourage artwork and drawing to embellish stories and projects.   This can build commitment on the part of the student to completing the project. Many students enjoy art as a change of pace, and even the least talented can do scissors-and-paste work with colored paper or magazine photographs. Work done by Karen Ernst in *Picturing Learning* and *New Entries* has shown that pictures and words work together to create meaning, thus expanding literacy potential. Such projects also help build pride in class work and add to audience impact.

Teacher Attitudes and Behavior

Teachers set the tone of a class not only through management procedures and instructional strategies but also through their own attitudes and behavior. Our experience suggests the following general guidelines for English teachers to follow.

Consistency   Students like to know where they stand. If gum chewing or failing to put their names in the upper left-hand corner of their papers doesn't bother the teacher on most days, students will not understand when the teacher suddenly becomes enraged by these acts.

Fairness   Students like to feel that they are being judged on their own merits and are upset if a teacher assumes that because a sibling was a troublemaker or a good writer, the present student will be like that too.

Interest and involvement   Teachers who seem genuinely interested in their work will generally receive positive responses from students, who like teachers who interact with them and show their willingness to help them. It is helpful if teachers remember that they are not simply servers who dish out assignments and then sit at the table until the meal is over.

Sense of humor   Humor in the classroom can save the day for both the teacher and the students. The ability to see the humor in a situation says something about the teacher's willingness to be human, and students respond positively to that trait.

Willingness to listen   Everyone likes to be listened to and have their ideas and opinions count for something. Students are no exception. They have little tolerance for teachers who exhibit a know-it-all attitude and refuse to listen to them.

Liking students   Teachers who view adolescents as subhumans will not get far with them. Successful teachers appreciate adolescents for their uniqueness and vitality.

Willingness to be the adult   Although we have written of the ideal of student-centeredness, this concept does not imply that one refuses to take on authority. As the adult, the teacher makes the classroom a place where students can work without being bothered by excessive noise or by teasing. Students need to feel that someone will set guidelines in the classroom and they look to the teacher to do this. They often do not feel they can set limits on themselves, and they rely on the teacher to help them do this.

— they need structure/ rules

Taking actions to match   *what's being said* When Diana first began teaching junior high she would tell students in a very pleasant voice that she was angry at their behavior. They simply didn't believe her and continued with their disruptive behavior. As she learned to show through her voice and facial expressions that she was unhappy with their behavior, they would listen.

Showing students what kind of behavior is appropriate   If students are getting a little too noisy, the teacher reminds them to keep the noise level down before it gets out of hand. If a student walks in front of the teacher while she is talking, the teacher reminds the student that that is not appropriate. A willingness to deal with seemingly minor issues goes a long way in maintaining a classroom where students respect each other's right to learn.

When Misbehavior Occurs

Well-planned, engaging, relevant, student-centered materials and plans are deterrents to misbehaving students; however, for some students this will not be enough. Misbehavior occurs for a wide variety of reasons. Misbehavior can be the only way a student gets feedback and response from other students; it can be caused by a student acting out his or her problems at home in the classroom; it can be a display of boredom; it can signal that the student doesn't have the necessary skills to do what has been asked, it may occur because the child feels emotionally safe in the class and can try to get extra attention from the teacher; or it can be a cry for help from seriously hurting or disturbed students.

Reasons for misbehavior are complex and varied. The point here is that what is going on in the class is not always the trigger or the reason a student misbehaves. If large numbers of students are unruly and uncooperative, the teacher has to look closely not only at what she is asking students to do but also what messages she is sending to students.

Often new teachers who are emotionally stable and caring people cannot understand why the students in their classes are so hard on them—why they can appear to like them and the work but still act in inappropriate ways. Many of these students are pushing as hard as they can to find what the boundaries are in the classroom as they think of countless ways to test the teacher. The majority of these students want to know that they are emotionally safe in a class and that poor behavior will be dealt with. They want the teacher to tell and show them through her actions that this will be a no-nonsense kind of class when it comes to not allowing hurtful words or actions.

Teachers also need to learn not to overreact to student comments or to minor infractions. If students know they can get on the teacher's nerves they will continue their irritating behavior. This is where it helps if you allow your sense of humor to kick in since a show of humor often deflects student attempts to be annoying.

It's also important to evaluate the level of control you want in the class and your reasons for it. Diana learned that even though collaborative work groups can be noisy, the noise level can be kept to a manageable level through reminders of "use your inside voice, it's getting too loud in here." She also could enforce total silence on quiet reading days. Students are much more willing to be cooperative if they see a reason for being asked to be quiet. In this case it made sense to them that on reading days other students couldn't become engaged in a book if there was distracting talk.

Just as the teacher knows which students will present the biggest challenges behavior-wise from their body language and expressions, so too do students know if the teacher has the inner strength and stability to believe she has the right to make demands on them and the good sense to know what simply should not be tolerated in a class. No long-time teacher would allow students to call him (or other students) a name. Threats are not tolerated. Physical aggression is not tolerated. Shouting matches of the "your mama" variety cannot be allowed in the classroom. The above kind of behavior is different than the stray social talk that students engage in or the purposeful dawdling over work.

So what is a young teacher supposed to do? First, know the school rules and the district rules. They will give you an indication of what are considered serious infractions. Also talk to a teacher who seems to like teaching and ask him or her how teachers handle minor misbehavior, and what the administration will really deal with. If obscene language is used in a class would the administration deal with that or is it a case where the teacher is expected to call the parent? A mentor in the building can help the new teacher figure out ways to deal with behavior issues and let the new teacher know how others handle the same situations in their classes.

One of the best ways to curb poor behavior is to call the parents of misbehaving students. Students do not want their parents to know about their inappropriate behavior at school. They have a school persona which is very different than their home persona and they prefer not to have parents involved in the school part of their life. Word gets around quickly when you do phone home, so it is a very effective tool. If students do not have a phone in the home, let the administrators know that you have tried to deal with the student and solicit suggestions from them.

If behavior is occurring in class that is physically or verbally aggressive and potentially explosive, remove the offending students from the room at once. Call the office or security people and have them escort the students to the office. As sometimes happens students will leave the class in a fit of anger, cursing, and slamming the door as they leave. In such cases, Diana has always alerted the office that that student is in the halls and explained the emotional state the child was in. This kind of outburst is very upsetting to students in the classroom and they need to know the student will not be allowed back in class the next day as if nothing has happened. Usually a parent conference is necessary before the child can be readmitted to school. Most of the students who have this serious kind of blow-ups have emotional problems and are often getting special education services. If this is the case and the teacher senses an incident is brewing, it is appropriate to call the special education resource room and then send the student there. The important thing to remember when dealing with serious misbehavior is to get help in figuring out how to handle it. Don't isolate yourself and assume you have the resources to know what to do. Don't lock all your anguish and emotional turmoil from these situations inside. Also know that very, very experienced teachers are still shaken by extreme student behavior and that it helps to have a mentor or friend in the building with whom you can sort out your actions and feelings.

ESTABLISHING PROCEDURES IN THE ENGLISH CLASS

We've stressed that helping students achieve a strong sense of purpose and involving them in the content of a course is crucial to their (and your) success, but this will not happen unless the English classroom is well organized, so that students know what they can expect and see that the teacher has procedures to follow. Without careful organization, chaos often erupts, especially at the beginning and end of the class period. When this happens at the start of class, the teacher has to use much energy to get the class settled down and on task, and much valuable time is wasted.

Beginnings and Endings

Although seating charts can be extremely helpful to the teacher in taking roll quickly and efficiently, another important reason to have them is to insure that students have their own space when they come to class. Seating charts guarantee that students will not have to negotiate or bicker with others about where they sit and are another way — _benefits of a seating charts_ the teacher constructs a safe emotional environment. If the teacher is dealing with mature groups of eleventh and twelfth graders or very small groups, seating charts may not be necessary. However, a seating chart is invaluable especially to teachers who have 150 students a day. Seating charts allow the teacher to learn names quickly and to identity noisy cliques from the first day of class. One useful technique Diana has developed is to make a miniature copy of the seating chart, which is then taped into the attendance book—the chart folds out for attendance taking and saves the teacher a lot of time that would other wise be spend flipping back to the seating chart or hunting for it on the desk. Steve now uses a computer data processing program to record students' names and sundry kinds of relevant information; this list can be reformatted in various ways without retyping, so the master list can produce a seating chart, attendance log, phone and address list, and even individual summaries of course progress.

bellwork —

In peppier classes it is important to structure activities for the early moments when attendance is being taken or other class business is being transacted. Students can routinely

- Write in their journals or learning logs.
- Copy assignments from the board into their notebooks.
- Write a mini-essay on the quotation of the day.
- Take turns to be responsible for telling a suitable joke or story.
- Take turns reading favorite poems.
- Offer brief reviews of last night's TV shows.

Sometimes, however, with classes that can handle it, it is good to let kids chitchat while roll is being taken so that their social needs will be met and they'll be more willing to get on task as soon as they are asked to.

The end of the class hour is another sticky time. If closing details are not handled smoothly, students can become an instant mob, racing to the door and jockeying for position. We'll sometimes offer such quickie activities as filling in Mad Libs, reading humorous poetry, or asking students to figure out two or three limericks.

Distributing Materials

Even passing out books or assignment sheets and collecting student work need to be handled carefully or the room can quickly erupt into pandemonium. These cautions are not necessary for the more mature classes, but organization makes distribution easier in any case. If books in the room are to be passed out to everyone (a common practice in schools with a text shortage or in classes where teachers use supplemental works), a good plan is to have one student from each row or table or section of the room come to the front to get enough books for their entire row or table or section. Rotate this responsibility and have other students collect books so that no student feels overburdened.

Passing back papers can be a nightmare that begins with calling out student names, continues with students jumping up to get their papers, and ends with the whole room in an uproar because student attention has been diverted. It's inviting for kids to watch all the action—the moans and exclamations—as their cronies respond to the evaluation. Whispers of "whad ja get?" soon turn into the infamous dull roar. A simple procedural matter is to have students put their row or group number on their papers, along with their name and class hours. You can even set up routines where students know to place their papers on the bottom or top of the stack as papers are passed up the row or around their section of the room, so you can keep them in order and pass them back without sorting. It works especially well to have these stacks of papers on the students' desks as they enter the class so that the usual before-class activity and paper-passing-back activity are combined into one.

For especially high energy classes you can even place books and materials on front desks before students arrive. This way there is no reason to move around the room and poking and pushing and shouting are minimized.

combine passing back + whatever activities at once

MISCELLANEOUS BOTHERS AND PROCEDURES

One teacher we know had to develop guidelines for the use of the pencil sharpener, which became a place of impromptu conferencing among the students. Friskier students loved to frequent the pencil sharpener so they could either bop other students on their way or meet their friends for a bit of quick but often loud gossip. The English teacher of our acquaintance was so harried by pencil-sharpening issues that she removed the pencil sharpener from her room. However, now she often has to deal with almost unreadable papers written with very dull pencils! We suggest allowing students to use the pencil sharpener only before class or allowing only one person at the sharpener at a time.

Now, pencil sharpeners may seem far removed from the glories of Wordsworth and Shakespeare, but given the nature of the captive audience, it is amazing how much teacher time these seemingly minor issues require unless teachers very quickly come up with procedures they can live with. You don't want a classroom that is bogged down in rules and regulations, either. The key decision each teacher must make centers on which procedures are necessary to make classroom management smooth and efficient.

Order in the classroom is enhanced if materials, books, and supplies are organized in such a way that students know where things are without asking the teacher. Markers, tape, scissors, and pencils can be kept in coffee cans on the teacher's desk or on a table nearby. Dictionaries and other reference materials are accessible if they're clearly labeled and on reachable shelves.

Student journals or notebooks, which many teachers have their students leave in the classroom, are stored on shelves or in boxes by hour and by row. That way students can easily pick up their journals on the way into the classroom. Keeping a small box on the teacher's desk clearly marked for incoming work encourages students to put their drafts in an identified place rather than in the middle of the teacher's desk or in his or her hands. If student writing is to be collected in a portfolio throughout the year, a file drawer or collection of cardboard boxes set aside for this purpose will ensure that students can easily find the work they need.

Some teachers shy away from individualized reading programs because of fears about record keeping. This need not be as complicated as it might seem if the teacher utilizes the student people-power available in the classroom. Diana has found it effective to appoint one student to be in charge of counting any library books in the class at the end of the hour and making sure all students have returned the books to the front of the room. To keep in-room free reading books organized, have students make a file card for each book, writing the title and author's name on the card. These cards are put in a small file box, alphabetized by the author's last name, and kept near the front of the room. When new books arrive, they can be distributed for student perusal while the students write book cards.

A student can also be in charge of the in-class paperback library checkout system: Students simply sign the card of the book they choose and place the card in another small file box for books in circulation. When books are returned, the student in charge finds the card, crosses out the borrower's name, and refiles the book on the shelves.

To alphabetize books or not? Diana has collected at least five hundred books in her classroom, and she has students shelve them by the author's last name. Bookshelves are organized by portions of the alphabet, A-E, F-M, etc. If your in-class library is small, or if you know it well, you many prefer random shelving, since you can spot books quickly. Still, some students love to help keep the room organized, and using them as librarians pleases them and eases the burden on the teacher.

Steve always thought the problem of "pencil thieves" was limited to the elementary and secondary schools until his university department chair sent 'round a somber note saying that so many pencils had disappeared that the department could no longer supply them for students to use in completing course evaluations. The supply of pencils is precisely the sort of problem that can drive the English teacher into early retirement or an early grave. Many students simply do not bring pencils to class. Teachers rant, rave, and gnash their teeth, but the problem persists. Elaborate systems have been devised, ranging from securing collateral for borrowed writing implements (a method that leaves the teacher with a drawer full of lunch cards, broken watches, bracelets, sunglasses, but no pencils) to the obviously self-destructive system of forbidding pencil-less students to do any work in the class. One teacher used a sign-out system and soon found the class hour shot with thirty-three students signing out and checking in pencils every day. Diana always has eight to ten loaner pens and pencils available and puts a student in charge of collecting and distributing them. Steve suspects that system might even work at the college level since students also can borrow from classmates and seem more committed to returning the pencils to their peers than to the teacher.

Managing English Activities

For teachers who have resource areas in their rooms, it also takes forethought to figure out how to move students to these different areas in the room without having traffic jams or bickering over resources. On days when students will be working on different activities, the easiest way to handle movement is to call groups of students alphabetically or by rows to select materials. Some may be choosing poetry books which you have brought in from the library; others will retrieve a piece of their own writing from their writing folders for further work; while still others may be getting supplies to put the finishing touches on a project that will be displayed in the library.

Group Work   To a teacher who has never had students work in groups, the whole process may seem potentially chaotic: desks being pushed willy-nilly around the room, loud students' voices, the irritating sounds of scraping furniture, books being flung to earth. Our commitment to group work is based on the experience that careful planning can not only eliminate these problems but also involve students more deeply than if they were working alone. Initially, small group discussion and projects take a great deal of careful planning by the teacher to figure out how to move students around the class and how to keep them involved in the group work. When students are used to groups, they can move to them quickly—but training *is* required. Sometimes the teacher can arrange the desks in circles before the students arrive, perhaps listing group assignments on the board. It's also a good idea initially for the teacher to choose group membership until the students have built skill in the group process and can see the positive outcomes.

Once seated, students need specific directions about what they are to accomplish and how they should go about it. Asking them to do anything as general as "discuss the story" will not usually work. Task-oriented groups work best, and this can often be enhanced by a handout or summary sheet for the students to prepare. Limit group work at first by giving groups ten or fifteen minutes to solve a problem; then extend the amount of time in groups. It's better at the beginning to stop before everyone is done than to wait until each group has finished and run the risk of having students sitting and not quite knowing what to do. Always follow up with group reports so that students know they are accountable for the assigned work.

Although it's difficult to acknowledge that it is a part of group work, the first stage generally involves what we have always thought of as aimless chitchat. However, every time groups get together, including adult groups we've been part of, they talk casually until they get a sense of the other people and feel safe expressing their ideas with them. Thus what might seem like stray talk is actually students testing the waters for where they stand socially in the group and whether or not they can talk honestly. This is not to say that off-task behavior will not occur, because it does. If the teacher circulates around the room this can be minimized through a word or a glance from the teacher. However, once students believe in the importance of group work and see it is valued by the teacher and included in evaluation, they are more willing to participate fully and stay on task more and more of the time.

When group work is completed, students can help put desks back where they belong if your next class needs a different room arrangement. Giving students this responsibility frees the teacher from one more detail of group organization. After several sessions of small group work, the teacher will probably find that students prefer this kind of classroom organization because they get a chance to be involved and can voice their opinions and ideas.

Writing Conferences   Books on writing instruction frequently make conferencing sound effortless and glitch-free. The experienced teacher, however, quickly raises an obvious question: "What do I do with the other twenty-nine students?" Steve likes to use silent reading days for conferences, though Diana prefers to maintain the silence and even read along with the students. A good time to conference is when students are working in pairs or alone, perhaps on an assignment or a piece of writing. A conference may involve calling students up to the teacher's desk for five or ten minutes, but we also like to do "mini conferencing," where we float about the room and engage in thirty-second discussions on particular points while students work .

Organization and planning are essential to a smoothly run class, which then allows for community building.

Silent Reading   English teachers are told to give students time to read in class, but often they have little idea about how to actually get kids to read. Given a choice, most students would rather socialize or do homework for other classes. Students should come to see that the reading time is connected to their classwork and is a normal and legitimate procedure for English classes. If students know they will be sharing their book with others through an informal book talk or completing a project that will "count," they are much more likely to take the silent reading seriously.

The first few times students have class time to read, the teacher needs to be very precise about the ground rules; it sometimes may even be necessary to have students clear their desks of everything but the book they are reading so they won't be tempted to do homework for other classes. It may take students a while to settle down, and the teacher should remind them that there is to be no stray talk. If the teacher reads along with the students, this modeling of behavior may help bring order to the class, since once students see that the teacher is engrossed in a book they are much more likely to settle down and get into their own book. (See Chapter 7 for more on individualized reading.)

Class Discussions   Imaginative planning is also essential for successful class discussions. The prepared teacher will ask students at the beginning of the hour to jot down a sentence or two on whatever is to be discussed. Then discussion can begin with the teacher asking a sampling of students to read their responses. After a few of these are read, other students will begin to react to fellow students' statements and lively discussions can follow. Discussions also can die or never come to life at all if the teacher asks general questions. "Do you have any questions?" or "What's your reaction to this?" always seem to produce blank stares. Begin with concrete questions: "What appealed to you or bothered you about Gene's behavior in Chapter Five?" or "Have you ever been ashamed of anyone the way Pip was ashamed of Joe?"

Individualizing   Planning for the English classroom also involves having extra material available for students who finish early or who want to do something for extra credit. At times like this, having puzzles, word searches, or other word games, as well as having books for browsing, can absorb energy and maintain the interest of those who are done with the work for the day.

It's also good to keep on hand a supply of material for the genuinely disruptive student, the kid who needs to be moved. Keep on hand the *Guinness Book of World Records,* books of sports facts, and catalogs or indexes of free materials by mail. Paging through the Guinness Book, with its many pages of pictures and amazing records, has "soothed many a savage soul."

◆ EXPLORATIONS

◆ Make the trip to your public library and inquire about the services librarians will provide. Do they have a storyteller who would meet with your class? Will they allow you to check out large quantities of books for use with your class? Do they have a librarian knowledgeable about young adult literature who would be willing to give book talks in your class?

◆ Haunt garage sales, library sales, and secondhand bookstores for inexpensive books to build your classroom library. Often secondhand bookstores are willing to take "trashy" books in exchange for those suitable for school.

◆ Brainstorm with others in your group all the best classroom organizing strategies you remember from your own days in elementary or secondary school. List these ideas and consider their potential usefulness to you.

◆ Interview students or discuss in your groups what about teacher or professor be-havior most affects their learning in a positive or negative way. Why do they want to work harder for some teachers and professors than for others? Draw conclu-sions.

◆ Brainstorm in your group a list of art activities that could be used and tied into an English classroom. If possible, ask other teachers for feedback on your list.

◆ Observe a teacher who has a reputation for good classroom management and for creating a sense of community in his or her class. Or, in a group, discuss manage-ment practices in your college classes that create a sense of community.

◆ The end of the school year is also a difficult time to plan for because summer va-cation is on everyone's mind. Construct a week's worth of high-interest activities that would work at that time of year (consider using it early in the year, too, but keep a good supply in reserve).

RELATED READINGS

For the teacher seeking information about constructivism *The Case for Construc-tivist Classrooms* by Jacqueline Grennon Brooks and Martin G. Brooks and *Con-structing Knowledge Together* by Gordon Wells and Gen Ling Chang-Wells are good places to start. Not only is theory explained in detail but examples of class-rooms where the theory is in operation are shown. Merrill Harmin's excellent book, *Inspiring Active Learning,* is very useful for teachers working on developing collabo-rative strategies and for teachers working to build a classroom community. The book is chockfull of strategies for such things as efficiently using class time, for cooperative group work, and for beginning a class.

Black Children: Their Roots, Culture, and Learning Styles by Janice E. Hale-Benson, *Other People's Children* by Lisa Delpit, *Possible Lives* by Mike Rose, and *The Dreamkeepers* by Gloria Ladson-Billings are books which help make the reader aware that the cultures of our students do make a difference and that we have to take them into account when we construct curriculum. *Voices in English Classrooms: Honoring Diversity and Change* edited by Lenora Cook and Helen C. Lodge, is an excellent collection of articles that can help teachers approach differences in very cre-ative, productive ways. *Multiple Intelligences in the Classroom* by Thomas Arm-strong is for the teacher who wants more information on multiple intelligences and also wants to see specific activities and assignments that ask for each of the seven in-telligences. *New Entries* edited by Ruth Shagoury Hubbard and Karen Ernst, and *Picturing Learning* by Karen Ernst discuss art in relation to writing and to making meaning and helps the teacher see the possibilities of extending student literacy through art.

Helpful suggestions in working with students with limited English proficiency abound in Gail Heald-Taylor's *Whole Language Strategies for ESL Students,* Sarah

Hudelson's *Write On! Children Writing in ESL,* David E Freeman and Yvonne S. Freeman's *Between Worlds: Access to Second Language Acquisition* and Joy Kreeft Peyton and Leslee Reed's *Dialogue Journal Writing with Nonnative English Speakers: A Handbook for Teachers.* For further information on the presence and impact of gender issues *Just Girls: Hidden Literacies and Life in Junior High* by Margaret J. Finders, *Gender Issues in the Teaching of English* edited by Nancy Mellin Mc-Cracken and Bruce C. Appleby, *Reviving Ophelia* by Mary Pipher, *Sounds from the Heart* by Maureen Barbieri and *School Girls* by Peggy Orenstein will give teachers an idea of the complexity of the issues and why attention needs to be paid to gender.

Ralph Peterson's *Life in a Crowded Place* discusses the *hows* of making a learning community. He explains very specific aspects of this community-creating such as establishing ceremony, rites, and rituals, having celebrations, and putting routines and jobs into place.

Beyond Discipline—from Compliance to Community by Alfie Kohn is a very thoughtful and insightful treatment of the whole issue of discipline. Kohn looks for the heart of the problem and doesn't deal with surface issues. *Secondary Classroom Management* by Carol Simon Weinstein deals with brass tacks issues like managing small groups.

CHAPTER 5

ENGAGEMENT WITH LITERATURE

Most English teachers are voracious readers. We read whatever we can get our hands on and find spaces for our own personal reading in our busy schedules. Part of our love of reading comes from the rich memories most of us have of being read to and feeling nurtured and loved by those who read to us. Because reading is associated with such positive, warm memories, we think of reading with pleasure and anticipation. Unfortunately this is not the case for many of our students. If we ask our students to write their own reading autobiography (Figure 5.1) we might be startled by their responses as we learn how they view reading.

Write about your reading history from as far back as you can remember including any of the memories that the following questions elicit:

Did people read to you when you were a child? What stories did they read? Can you recall the details of the place where someone read to you?

Who taught you to read? What can you recall from those days? What were the first books you read by yourself?

Did you ever go on reading jags when you were younger, reading book after book by the same author or books linked together in a series?

Who was your best elementary, junior high, or senior high school teacher of literature? What made that teacher good? Did you have any negative experiences with books and reading? What can you recall about them?

Do you enter into the story world when you are reading, actually seeing where the story takes place, and envisioning what the characters look like?

Do you become the characters, sometimes feeling as they feel?

Figure 5.1 Reading Autobiography

But in spite of how our students think of reading, as secondary teachers we often feel that our job has little to do with reading and everything to do with literature. We don't feel students' lack of engagement with reading or other reading problems has anything to do with us. Kathleen McCormick in her thought-provoking book *The Culture of Reading and the Teaching of English* asserts that every teacher who asks students to read is indeed a teacher of reading. "Whether or not they are conscious of it, however, teachers at all levels are always teaching their students how to read. The different ways students are asked to read imply particular values and beliefs about the nature of texts, the nature of readers as subjects of texts and as subjects in the world, and about meaning and language itself" (p. 7). Thus because each of us wants our students to read in particular ways and notice particular things, part of our responsibility is to help students learn the reading skills they need to be successful in our classes. Reading skills and literary skills are not separate and clearly distinguishable, any more than it is possible to neatly separate literature from nonliterature or even poetry from prose. In this chapter we discuss various kinds of reading/literature skills and examine a range of potential materials for use in literature/reading programs, materials that range from the daily newspaper to accepted classics. There is room for both in the schools, as there is a concern for comprehension along with literary response and analysis. However, from the outset we want to make it clear that we have a *single* purpose in mind for this chapter: helping teachers help more students engage successfully with print.

G. Robert Carlsen, an early voice in the move to engage students in literature they can understand and enjoy, reassures us, "We are literature-creating and literature-consuming animals." Even in this age of media there is evidence that people like to read and that reading satisfies some fundamental needs not met by other forms of communication and artistic expression.

Every once in a while groups of self-appointed intellectuals get themselves up tight about the status of literature and the status of reading in a culture. They feel that something must be done to defend a fragile flower against the trampling of barbaric boots. Really this seems nonsense to me. Literature is not so delicate that it needs any special protection. . . .

Man, we are told, is a tool-making animal. I suggest that equally we are story-making animals. . . . And something deep within us impels us to cherish the product of the writer. I have watched it happen over and over. Given a modicum of reading skill, some free time, and accessibility to literary materials, people read . . . not every person, but most. People read in cramped bunks under the arctic ice. They read 40,000 feet above the earth. They read as they have their hair cut or dried, and while they wait for the dentist. People read in bed, in the bath tub and occasionally, sitting upright in a chair.

We are literature-creating and literature-consuming animals.

From G. Robert Carlsen, "Literature IS!" *The English Journal*, February 1974, p. 24. Copyright © 1974, by the National Council of Teachers of English. Reprinted by permission of the publisher.

What has often gone wrong in literature instruction is that programs have consistently ignored the individual experiences and interests that young people bring to their reading. A college model of literature instruction has been pushed down into

problem= ignoring the connection students want to make

senior high school and even into junior high, with a powerful emphasis on literary surveys, reading by genres or types, and mastery of the terminology of criticism: plot, character, meter, rhyme, rising action, falling action. . . . Too often, classes focus primarily on analysis and explication, on wringing all possible meaning from a text or making "acceptable" judgments about literary works. Thus the texts chosen for analysis are those which (often deservedly) have a place in the canon of classic literature, but which speak to students in faint voices and unfamiliar languages. Thus we also deal with selection of texts in this chapter since that is an integral part of student engagement.

PURPOSES OF LITERATURE TEACHING

Before we look at instructional strategies and how to engage students in their reading, we need to think clearly about why we are teaching literature. Are we trying to teach skills through literature? Are we trying to teach the content of the literature so students can give us information that shows they know the plot line, the characters, what events happened in what order? Are we trying to make sure students get the same meaning from a text that the teacher does? Are we trying to give students experiences with literature that will encourage them to think about their own humanness? Researchers and theorists have been considering the question of the purpose of literature for years and have many provocative things to say.

> "So I cannot escape the conclusion that literature is the attempt of a sensitive person to evoke in other people those moments of significance which he himself has undergone. And the teaching of literature has a fairly simple objective: to help young people undergo the experiences considered significant by the most sensitive people that the world has produced"
>
> Reprinted in _Literature IS . . . : Collected Essays_ by G. Robert Carlsen edited by Anne Sherrill & Terry C. Ley (p. 147)
>
> "Dora V. Smith . . . first posed for me the questions about literature that have involved me all my working life. What is the function of literature in a person's life? and _What_ literature does _what_ to _what_ kinds of readers? Thus the whole consideration moved from the examination of the book as an object to the examination of what is happening in the mind of the reader as he interacts with the book."
>
> Reprinted in _Literature IS . . . : Collected Essays_ by G. Robert Carlsen edited by Anne Sherrill & Terry C. Ley (p. 86)
>
> [Literature is helping students] "outgrow their current selves " so they "will have the desire to deepen and expand their experience."
>
> From Jeff Wilhelm in _You Gotta BE the Book_ (p. 35)
>
> [Through literature] "I become a thousand [people] and yet remain myself."(p. 5)
>
> From Aiden Chambers in _Book Talk_ reporting on what C.S. Lewis felt.

"All literature—the stories we read as well as those we tell—provides us with a way to imagine human potential. In its best sense, literature is intellectually provocative as well as humanizing, allowing us to use various angles of vision to examine thoughts, beliefs, and actions."

From Judith Langer 's *Envisioning Literature* (p. 5)

Robert Probst brings the discussion back to what happens in the classroom by explaining the difference between reading literature and working on it.

When literature is *read*, rather than worked upon, it draws us into events and invites us to reflect upon our perceptions of them. It is not at that point a subject to be studied as an artifact illustrating an age or a product representing an artist; it is rather an experience to be entered into. "Entering into" literature, however, may be different from most of our other experiences. The literary work invites us in not only as participants, but also as spectators, giving us the opportunity to watch ourselves. It freezes events and holds them still for examination. Few other moments in our lives allow us that time for thought; events move too quickly and we are too deeply and thoroughly involved. Literature, however, allows us both to experience and to reflect upon experience, and thus invites the self-indulgence of those who seek to understand themselves and the world around them.

From Robert Probst, *Response and Analysis: Teaching Literature in Junior and Senior High School.* (Portsmouth, N.H.: Boynton/Cook, 1988), p. 4. Reprinted by permission of the publisher.

So what can all these ideas and opinions mean for the classroom? Hopefully, teachers will view the literature itself as important, as something to be grappled with and talked about. Literature was written to make an impact, an impression. If talking about and writing about and acting out that impact is ignored and the classroom focus is on the little pieces that make up the whole, then we often lose the interest of our students. Students begin to think of "literature" as something to be read to get the right answers. Seventh grade students of Jeffrey Wilhelm agree that literature in school is too often trivialized.

"You can read something really good and the teacher ruins it by asking you questions that you already know, that don't matter, and that you disagree with . . . "

Ron, a seventh grade engaged reader

"Most teachers must not read or they'd know how to teach reading and not ruin it for us."

Joanne, a seventh grade engaged reader

From Jeffrey Wilhelm's "You Gotta BE the Book" (New York: Teachers College Press, 1997), pp. 26 and 34. Reprinted by permission.

— don't limit
students responses, then they think you're ruining
LITERATURE AND THE READER   **157**
the reading)

If the teacher does not have a firm idea of why he or she is teaching literature, he or she may fall into the old "read the story, answer the questions" pattern. Sometimes we fail to realize that the literary theory we embrace also rests on specific views of literature and its purposes. For example, the literary theory known as New Criticism provided the background of much methodology used in literature classrooms today. Teachers who adhere (often unknowingly) to this theory focus only on the elements present in the text to try to extract the one "correct" meaning to which they are privy. Their job, therefore, is seen as either telling a student what the text means or guiding the student to the teacher's meaning. It's the old "I know the answer, now you figure out what it is" game. This theory, as exhibited in secondary classes, privileges teacher information and requires students to become passive receptacles, waiting to be filled by the teacher's wisdom. Nothing students bring to a piece of literature is seen as of any importance. Indeed, this theory does not recognize the importance of anything the reader brings to the piece. Prior knowledge is discounted and must be overcome in this view if anyone is to get the "right" meaning.

Part of our purpose for teaching literature comes either consciously or unconsciously from whatever theory we embrace. (See Chapter 7 for a fuller discussion of this issue.)

LITERATURE AND THE READER

One alternative that has emerged in the past thirty years (with historical origins much older than that) is to look toward the *engagement* of the reader with a text rather than concentrating on explication of the text by a teacher or professor. If we look at the experience of literature from the point of view of a reader, we realize that reading is a dynamic activity—no less creative than writing.

Louise Rosenblatt, whose pioneering book *Literature as Exploration* was first published in 1938, has suggested that in this respect literature is a "performing art." Not only do books "perform" for a reader, each reader "performs" on a text to create meaning as well. As readers become more experienced in responding to texts, their performances become more and more complex.

No one else can read a literary work for us. The benefits of literature can emerge only from creative activity on the part of the reader himself. He responds to the little black marks on the page, or to the sounds of words in his ear, and he makes something of them. . . . Out of his past experience, he must select appropriate responses to the individual words, he must sense their interplay among one another, he must respond to clues of tone and attitude and movement. He must focus his attention on what he is structuring through those means. . . . The amazing thing is that critics and theorists have paid so little attention to this synthesizing process itself, contenting themselves with the simpler task of classifying the verbal symbols and their various patterns in the text.

From Louise Rosenblatt's *Literature as Exploration*. 5th Edition. New York: Modern Language Association, 1996. Reprinted by permission.

The role of literary education becomes far more than filling students' heads with nuggets of literary wisdom or the chowder of cultural history. It becomes a matter of helping individuals improve their ability to engage with a wide range of books successfully.

Figure 5.2 shows the areas of reading/literature that we want to take up in this chapter:

1. Selection of literature
2. Reading skills
3. The process of engagement
4. Responding to and learning from literature
5. The place of criticism and analysis

We see the individual reader at the center of reading and literacy study and we view the areas of reading/literature study from the point of view of the reader, not from the point of view of the teacher. We place a strong emphasis on what stages or stances readers go through as they read and then try to shape instruction to build on and enhance these stages. Too often, teachers have a view of literature instruction

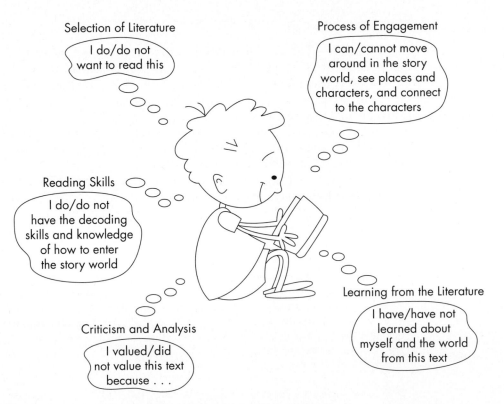

Figure 5.2   A Reader's View of Reading and Literary Study

that does not take into account the way readers read. They assume, for instance, that students are ready to talk about elements in a short story before students have had time to respond to the story, to connect with the story, to talk about what they learned from the story. Or they assume that all readers notice the same details as they read. Both assumptions get in the way of students making contact with the literature.

SELECTION OF LITERATURE

While we might love books thick with description, kids usually don't. As Lois Duncan, noted young adult author, once pointed out at a conference, "I used to be able to describe the setting in such detail on the first page that I could even talk about the curtains. Now if action doesn't begin on the first page, we lose our readers." As teachers, we have to respect where our students' literature interests are, and begin there. If we don't begin where students are, they will not be willing to go where we want them to go.

Political Aspects

Literature selection is not the innocent activity it may seem to be. All literature is written from a point of view whether we're aware of that or not. If we do not vary ~in *physical* what has been traditionally taught, then we will be mainly showing our students how *represent-* upper-middle class Anglo males view the world. To present only one point of view *ance* says to our students that other views are not worthwhile and valued. If we show representations through our literature selection of only two-parent families, of only Anglo characters, of only single family homes, of only economically secure people, of only heterosexuals, we are effectively telling our students that people in other categories don't have contributions to make—that we can ignore them. Students need to see themselves in the literature we select and see other groups who make up our society today. Some Anglo teachers have told us that since they have all Anglo students they don't need to worry about minority literature! Our response is that they need it more than anybody. How else will students learn to value the contributions of people who don't look like them? How else will students learn that they can be enriched through contact with other cultures? How else can we validate the literature written by others besides Anglo men?

At a conference in Michigan Shirley Brice Heath, noted anthropologist and educator, described an experience she had in uncovering the literature of African-Americans. She explained that she frequently haunts the archives of libraries in whatever city or university she is visiting. When she visited the archives in a library in the South, she came across the works produced by African-American literary societies whose members wrote prose and poetry, which they published locally. None of this work was ever published widely. This rich cache of African-American writing was ignored partly because it didn't portray African-Americans the way the majority culture wanted to view them. The selection of literature to be taught usually validates a specific point of view, so only African-American slave narratives and stories of overcoming odds had been selected for wider publication.

Multicultural Aspects

So today literature selection is about much more than what students will like. We need to work at bringing quality literature into our classrooms that is written by people who represent a wider view of America. Too often the argument goes that teachers hardly have time to teach what they already have in the curriculum, how can they be expected to add more? Or teachers claim that their anthology or curriculum has works of high literary merit and if others merited it they would be included in it. Both arguments fail to consider the nature of the selection process of published materials.

Reading books whose characters make visible the racial or economic or familial aspect of who students are, affirms and validates that aspect of students' lives. When students can see themselves in the literature used in school they don't feel marginalized, because they feel they are at the heart of what is being dealt with.

Interest and Accessibility

Readability and accessibility should also be taken into account when selecting literature for the class. Forcing students to leap across language barriers to get into the heart of the book will usually deter them. Where there are no language roadblocks, students will usually plunge into the story and get to its essence quickly. If students are asked to wade through the unfamiliar, swamp-like territory of vocabulary lists and explanations of what the book means, engagement may not occur.

So one way to begin to develop reading in the English classroom is to follow the old and sound advice to "match the book with the child." We suggest that a major cause of reading "malfunctions" is material that is inappropriate for the student: too tough, too distant, or too removed from experience. As John Steinbeck remarked, books must "have some points of contact with the reader." Sometimes the point of contact will be the students' own interests and problems as these are reflected in the book, but it may also be the free play the book gives to imagination or fantasy. As teachers gain experience with books and students, their sense of appropriateness grows. It is a lifelong teaching quest for many of us to read constantly in a search for materials that will make connections with our students

> A man who tells secrets or stories must think of who is hearing or reading, for a story has as many versions as it has readers. Everyone takes what he wants or can from it and thus changes it to his measure. Some pick out parts and reject the rest, some strain the story through their mesh of prejudice, some paint it with their own delight. A story must have some points of contact with the reader to make him feel at home in it.
>
> From John Steinbeck. *The Winter of Our Discontent.* (New York: Viking Press, 1961).

READING SKILLS

We want to repeat our concern that reading and literature have become separated in the professional mind. Reading even has its own organization, the International Reading Association, while literature is generally given over to teachers who belong to the National Council of Teachers of English. It is a positive sign in our profession, however, that in recent years IRA has become increasingly concerned with a whole language, reading/writing/literature model of learning, while NCTE has increasingly extended its concerns to the act of reading as well as the processes of teaching and learning literature.

Both groups are skeptical of what we might call a "skills approach" to the teaching of reading, which consists of breaking reading into a series of discrete, identifiable skills—from phonics to paragraph patterning—teaching those skills, testing for their mastery through comprehension questions, and assuming that the same skills will be transferred to students engaged in reading.

At the risk of seeming simplistic, we want to argue that many reading problems are not matters of skill deficiency at all; they result from lack of interest in the material, lack of motivation, lack of understanding about how to enter the story world, lack of confidence, lack of practice. Our "reading program," then consists of focusing on engagement by the students and providing support so students know how to do what we expect them to do. Our program is anti workbook, anti test, anti drill and pro book, pro readers.

So focus on engaging [handwritten marginal note]

Researchers and writers in the last several years have found that lack of decoding skills is not the reason students can't and don't read. Kylene Beers, Jeffrey Wilhelm, Pat Encisco, and Janet Allen have found that students who hate to read often lack the understanding of how to enter the story world. These are students who have been taught decoding skills at the expense of meaning. They know the sounds that letters represent and they can usually sound words out. What they don't understand is that all the words on the page are supposed to create pictures in their heads, that they are all supposed to add up to something. Many have been taught to read to find answers to questions, and so assumed that reading was a matter of getting the right answer, not of creating meaning. These students feel reading is something they have no part in; they do not understand that reading takes both a reader and a text to create meaning, that they are part of the process.

Jeffrey Wilhelm, building on the work of Pat Encisco, makes concrete for teachers the areas in which his reluctant readers needed help. From studying his classes, he found that the less- engaged readers needed help entering the story world since they didn't know how to get into a story or connect to what was happening in that world. They read words and didn't see characters as people doing things. They strung words together and could "sound-out" and figure out the words, but the words remained just words. Imagine trying to get the thread of a story without creating pictures in your mind. What an impossible task! To help students enter this story world researchers like Wilhelm and Allen used simulations or drama activities that connected to the events that would occur in the reading. This encouraged students to see that readers think of a story as a world with real people moving around in real spaces.

Wilhelm also recognized that students did not know how to relate to a character. He had students do such things as role play a character or enact a character by physically representing the character. Through such activities students learned to see stories as full of real people.

To help students see the story world, he asked students to do such things as draw maps of places or rooms, to draw pictures of such things as "what impressions are you forming in your mind of the people and places? What do you see in your mind's eye?"

Another area researchers have found reluctant readers need assistance in is elaborating on the story world. Students need to be able to fill in the textual gaps, to be aware that the author expects this. Students can be asked to talk or write about the episodes or information the author left out and to share how they filled in or made sense of these gaps.

By being aware of how readers read and what they have to do to make meaning, we can give our students access to the skills they need to fully engage in literature.

In today's educational world, "metacognition" is used frequently. To some it might seem like a buzz word or another trendy way of viewing education. But when it comes to helping our students become successful readers, metacognition can be extremely important. Basically, the term means thinking about our own thinking. We think it is especially important because it can empower our students by helping them recognize and articulate the strategies they use and how they do things. In the area of reading, we can help our students by making evident what readers do as they read and by helping students figure out how they enter the story world, what they do when they don't know a word, strategies they can use when meaning isn't clear.

Helping Students Surface the Strategies They Use

As readers, most English teachers aren't even aware of the way they move through a text, fill in the gaps, connect with characters, figure out what's happening. Because we see reading as so natural, it has often been difficult for us to see the strategies we use when reading. We thought that inviting students into a novel with "before reading" activities and matching students up with books of interest to them was enough. But work done in the last several years has shown us that we have to articulate and model the strategies we use and help students unearth the strategies they use so they can share strategies and broaden the ways they approach reading difficulties.

Most students have been taught to sound out words if they don't know what the word is. This can be a good start but in addition it is helpful to help students see that to understand the meaning of a word they have to learn to look at the context of the sentence, seeing what has come before and what comes after. Students who are more experienced readers know that they can often skip words they don't know and by focusing on the meaning of what they are reading they will be able to make meaning without knowing every single word.

The Question of Vocabulary as a Prereading Strategy

Many English language arts teachers have been taught to select words they think students will have trouble with in a selection, bring these words to the students' attention, and define the words so students will have an easier time with the text. Although this advice seems as if it is "common sense," recent work has brought this practice into question. One researcher, Janet Allen, realized that teaching ahead by picking out words for her students made them dependent rather than independent readers. She then devoted more of her time to helping students articulate what they did when they didn't understand a word. Her students came up with twelve strategies which included: read the sentence again, look at the beginning of the sentence, look for other key words that might tell you the meaning, think what makes sense, read around the word and then go back to it. While teaching "reluctant readers" she focused her work on helping her students become less dependent on her and more confident of themselves.

Aside from this dependency issue, picking out words ahead of time can also narrow the way students respond to and interact with the literature. They will have the tendency to think that the words the teacher picks out are the words they should pay attention to and so won't notice other things. Selecting words gives these words prominence and may skew the way a reader reads a text, since the reader might focus energy on working to see why these words are so important or why they seem most important to the teacher.

More effective ways to encourage vocabulary study and expand students' knowledge of words may be developing strategies that involve students and what they notice. Teachers may simply ask students to write down two or three words per chapter that puzzled them or interested them or that they liked. This strategy encourages students to pay attention to language and word choice as it expands their vocabulary.

instead of vocab.

Thus the evidence against continuing to teach decoding skills is powerful. Instead, we suggest that the teacher create an environment that supports the development of reading abilities and skills. The teacher can:

Present a rich variety of reading materials: classic and contemporary novels, poetry and play collections, short story anthologies, books written for young adults, newspapers, magazines, brochures, pamphlets, comics, nonfiction.

Provide time for the students to read. Young people don't have a lot of time to give to reading. By providing in-class time, the teacher not only supports reading but also creates an opportunity to offer specific help to students who need it.

Include recorded literature in a classroom library for those who find reading difficult or for those who simply enjoy listening to a good story.

Use oral presentations and classroom drama to bring literature to life. Students should not be forced to read or dramatize if they find it extremely difficult, but in most classes, many students enjoy dramatic work (see also Chapter 11).

Use guided reading, asking students to stop reading and draw or write about the pictures they are creating in their heads.

Provide reading warm-ups. Before students plunge into a new book or story, provide them with appropriate background and discuss the key issues and problems. Give students a preliminary sense of what is likely to happen, so they don't become lost.

Use television and film tie-ins. Draw on novels or television and films made from books. Look for video versions of classic and contemporary books to show the class.

Let students quit reading books they are not able to comprehend or enjoy. With hundreds of thousands of books in print, the teacher can usually help the student find acceptable alternatives.

Read aloud to students regularly, letting them follow along in a text or just listen.

Provide help with difficult textbook assignments. There are times when students will need to read materials they do not find especially appealing as part of their course work. Rather than having them struggle in silence, the teacher can offer help for both English and other assignments. Create tutorials, partnerships, or discussion groups.

Provide class time for student to get into groups to talk to other students about what they are reading.

Provide many alternative ways students can "report" on a book such as the ones offered in Figure 5.3

THE PROCESS OF ENGAGEMENT

A useful metaphor for literary study suggested itself as Steve watched a son playing with two lumps of modeling clay, one yellow and the other red. As the boy worked with the two lumps, a third color emerged—orange. In literature, the same kind of transformation occurs: a new color results from the mixing of red—the book—and yellow—the students' previous experiences. Orange then represents engagement. Too many students, especially reluctant readers, do not recognize that reading is active, that it involves meaning making, that they have to add to what the author puts down to fully understand the story. They have to fill in the gaps the author leaves, they have to create pictures in their heads about what the characters look like, where things are taking place, and actually be able to move within the story world they create.

Judith Langer, one of the country's foremost researchers into the teaching of literature, helps teachers understand what is happening to readers as they work to "get into" a book, as they are involved in it, and as they think about it. Her work moves the conceptualization of literature instruction away from how an outsider views a reader and what an outsider thinks a reader should get out of a reading to what is happening from the reader's point of view. We find her work particularly striking because it helps us rethink what we saw as a "common sense" view that we need to make sure students understand the facts before we move to other kinds of literary activities. Her work in fact demonstrates that we can often detract from students' thinking about literature by sticking to an "understanding first" line of questioning as students are developing their own "envisionments."

Langer defines envisionment as the understanding a student has about a text, whether it is being read, written, discussed, or tested. Such envisionments are subject to change at any time as ideas unfold and new ideas come to mind. It is sense-making, since meanings change and shift and grow as a mind creates its understanding of a work. Thus it is the total understanding a reader has at any point in time.

We place her first two stances in this section on engagement and the second two stances in other parts of the reading process, even though these envisionments do not happen in a linear way but are instead moved into and out of by the reader at any time.

(handwritten annotations in top margin: "– 50 ideas as to how to engage readers. various assignments" and "– range to understand the basics of reading indirectly")

1. Character astrology signs. After reading brief descriptions of the astrology or sun signs, figure out which signs you think three of the main characters from your book were born under. Write an explanation of why you think they fit the sign, drawing on their actions, attitudes, and thoughts from the book.

2. Heroes and superheros. Select two or three people your character would think of as a hero or superhero. Describe the characteristics of the heros and why those characteristics would be important to your character. Also describe which characteristics your character would most want for himself/herself that the hero or superhero possesses.

3. Create a childhood for a character. If your main character is an adult, try to figure out what he or she would have been like as a child. Write the story of his or her childhood in a way that shows why he or she is the way he or she is in the novel.

4. Critique from the point of view of a specific organization. Select an organization that might have a lot to say about the actions or portrayals of characters in the novel you read, and write a critique of the book from its point of view. For example the Society for the Prevention of Cruelty to Animals might have a lot to say about Lennie's treatment of animals in Of *Mice and Men,* The National Association for the Advancement of Colored People on the portrayal of Crooks, and the National Organization of Women on the portrayal of Curley's wife and the fact that she was never given a name.

5. Social worker's report. If the events in the novel merit it, write up a report as a social worker would on the conditions in the home and whether or not it's a good environment for a child. For example, if a social worker went to the McNab's house in *Maniac Magee* by Jerry Spinelli how would she describe the home and parenting style of Mr. McNab? What would her recommendations be?

6. College application. Create the application that a character you have just read about could write and submit to a college. Use all the information you know about the character and infer and create the rest of it. On the application include Name, Academic Rank in Class, High School Courses Taken and Grades, Extracurricular Activites and Personal Activities, and Work Experience. Choose one of the following questions to answer in a two page essay from the character's point of view: What experience, event, or person has had a significant impact on your life? Discuss a situation where you have made a difference. Describe your areas of interest, your personality, and how they relate to why you would like to attend this college.

7. School counselor's recommendation letter. Write a summary appraisal from the school counselor's point of view that assesses the character's academic and personal qualities and promise for study in college. The college is particularly interested in evidence about character, relative maturity, integrity, independence, values, special interest , and any noteworthy talents or qualities. Why do you feel this student would be well-suited to attend college?

8. Talk show invitation. Select a character, think about his or her involvements and experiences, then figure out which talk show would most want your character as a guest. What would they want the character to talk about? Who else would they invite on the show to address the issues the character is involved in? Write the correspondence between the talk show host and the character in which the host explains what the character should focus on while on the show. After the show have them exchange one more letter mentioning how they felt about what happened on the show.   *(continued)*

Figure 5.3   Fifty Alternatives to the Book Report

9. Radio exchange. Your character calls a radio show for advice. Choose which show your character would call, and then create the conversation he or she would have with the radio advice giver.

10. Movie recommendations. From all the movies you've seen in the last couple of years, pick five you would recommend that your character see. Give a brief summary of each movie and explain why you think the character should see it.

11. Create a home page. Select several characters and design a home page for each of them picking out appropriate backgrounds and pictures and then creating information that would tell a viewer about your character. Also create links to at least five sites that you think your character would be interested in. Then write up and post on the page, an explanation of how you made the decisions you did and what you believe this tells us about the character.

12. Chat room conversations. Imagine that your character has found other people to talk with while in a chat room he or she found while surfing the Internet. Describe the chat room your character was in and why your character would be drawn to the kind of group that operates the chat room. Then construct the conversation your character had with others while in the chat room.

13. E-mail directory. Create the e-mail directory of all the people you can imagine your character keeping in touch with on e-mail. Explain why you selected the people you did and what it shows about your character. Then construct several exchanges between your character and some of the people in your character's directory.

14. Title acrostic. Take a sheet of construction paper and write the title of the book down the side of the paper. For each letter in the title, construct a sentence that begins with that letter and that tells something significant about the story.

15. Cartoon squares. Create a series of six drawings in six squares that shows a significant event in the novel. Under each picture or cartoon, write a few lines of explanation.

16. Word collage. Write the title of the book in the center of a sheet of paper. Then look through magazines for words, phrases, and sentences that illustrate or tell something about your book. As you look, think in terms of the theme, setting, plotline, as well as characters. Work to get fifty such words, phrases, or sentences so the whole sheet of paper will be covered. The visual impact of the collage should tell a potential reader a lot about the book.

17. Yearbook entries. Imagine what three or four characters from your novel were like in high school. Cut out a picture of a person from a magazine to represent each character. Mount one picture per page and under each picture place the following information which you will create: Nickname of character; activities, clubs, sports they were in and what years; class mock award such as "class clown;" quotation that shows something about the person and what is important to him or her; favorites such as colors and foods; a book that has had a great impact on him or her; voted "most-likely-to" what?; plans after high school.

18. Letter exchange. Create a letter exchange between a character and the author or write a series of self-reflective letters from several characters on what the character learned about himself, others, and life.

19. Awards. Create an award for each of the main characters based on their actions in the novel. One might be awarded "most courageous" for fighting peer pressure, another might be awarded "wisest" for the guidance he or she gave other characters. For each award, write a paragraph that explains why this character deserves this award.   *(continued)*

Figure 5.3

20. Talk show on issues in novel. Create and perform a talk show around one of the major issues or themes in the novel. For example, after reading *The Crazy Horse Electric Game* by Chris Crutcher you might want to discuss the issue of running away from home. Include people to represent several points of view on the issue. You might include characters from the book, a social worker, a police officer, a gang member, etc.

21. Dream Vacation. Where do you think your character would most like to go on a vacation. Pick a spot, describe it, and explain why he or she would want to go there or download information from the Internet on the place. Then write a day by day itinerary of what the character would do each day and why you think the character would enjoy this activity.

22. Scrap Book. Think about all the kinds of mementos you would put in a scrap book if you had one. Then create a scrap book for your character, cutting out pictures from magazines or drawing the mementos he or she would have in a scrap book. Think about Willie in *The Crazy Horse Electric Game* by Chris Crutcher. He would probably have something in his scrapbook to represent his baby sister, his love of baseball, his accident, his experiences in L.A. and so on.

23. Photos or magazine pictures. Find two or three photos or magazine pictures that would have special significance to your character. Mount them on a sheet of paper and write an explanation of why they would be important to your character.

24. Music. After reading a novel, figure out how you would divide the book into sections. Then select a piece of music that you think captures the feel or tone of each section. Record the pieces and if possible do voice-overs explaining what is happening in the novel during the piece of music and why you felt this piece of music fit the section of the novel.

25. Poetry. Write three poems in response to the novel. The poems can be about the characters, where the book took place, or the themes in the book.

26. Twenty questions. Three classmates are each assigned the role of one of the characters in the book. You and your fellow classmates have to figure out which person is which character. Only 20 questions may be used. Create the questions that you and your classmates can use to figure out the identity of each of the three students.

27. File a complaint. Adapt the persona of one of the characters who you feel was portrayed in a sexist or racist manner. Write a complaint explaining what you feel was unjust in your portrayal and explain the actions you would like the author to take to remedy the biased portrayal.

28. Tangible or intangible gifts. Select a character and figure out what two or three things you believe your character most needs or wants. Draw or cut out pictures to represent these "gifts" and write to your character an explanation of why you picked these things for him or her.

29. Talk to the author. Write a letter to the author of the book explaining to him or her why you think he or she wrote the book and what he or she was trying to show through the book. Be sure to explain what you got out of the book. If the author is still alive, send the letter to the author via the publisher of the book.

30. Point of view column. Write an opinion column like those that appear on the editorial page of the newspaper. Choose a theme or topic from the novel you just read and write the column from the point of view of one of the characters. Your character might write about the importance of education or why we should accept people who are not like us.   *(continued)*

Figure 5.3

31. Character monologues. Select an event in the novel that is viewed differently by the various characters. (For instance, Willie in *Crazy Horse Electric Game,* his girl friend, his mom, dad, and friends, all had different views on his running away). Then write two or three character's opinions on the same event in the form of a monologue (one person talking to him or herself).

32. Make up a word test for the novel. Think of fifteen words that are essential to the understanding of the book. Explain why you picked the words you did and how you would define them in terms of the story.

33. Answering machine message. Answering machine messages have gotten more and more creative over the years, reflecting the interests and idiosyncrasies of the owner. Select five characters from the novel you have just read and create an answering machine message from each of them. Pay particular attention to diction and tone.

34. Found poems. Select a chapter from the novel you have just read that you consider powerful or interesting. Then select words, lines, and phrases that you think project strong images and show the impact the chapter makes. Arrange this material into a poem. The following example comes from Chapter Twenty in *Spite Fences* by Trudy Krisher:

VIOLENCE AT THE LUNCH COUNTER SIT-IN

> Fist slammed into George Hardy's face
> Glasses slid to his chin
> Shattered into a spider's web.
> River of red blood
> Running from his nose.
> It was the red color of the fence
> The red color of the earth
> on which I stood
> It was red
> The color of my life this summer
> The color of Kinship.

35. Name analysis. Select a few of the characters from the novel. Look up each of their names in a name book to see what the name means. Write all the meanings down and then write a short essay for each character explaining in what ways the name is suitable and in what ways the name does not fit the character.

36. A character's fears. One way we get to know characters is to think deeply about them and make inferences based on their actions and on what they and others say about them. Through a person's actions we can learn what they fear, what they want to avoid the most. Select several characters from your novel and write short essays on what you believe they fear the most and what evidence you used to come to this conclusion.

37. Current events. Select five current news or feature stories from television or news magazines that you think would interest your character. Then explain how your character would respond to each of the stories, and the opinions your character would have about what was happening in the story.   *(continued)*

Figure 5.3

38. Advertisements. To show your understanding of a character, go through several magazines and newspapers looking for advertisements of goods you think your character would like. Cut out the pictures, mount them on a poster board, and under each picture write a few lines about why this product would appeal to your character.

39. A pamphlet. Think of an issue that was very important to your character. Then create a pamphlet aimed at persuading others of the importance of the issue. Include factual information, testimonials, pictures or graphics etc. For instance Charlotte from *The True Confessions of Charlotte Doyle* might want to create a pamphlet explaining the reasons women should have more life choices.

40. Draw a Scene. If you are artistic, think of an important scene and draw it the way you see it. Place the characters in the scene, too, and then figure out where you were in relation to the characters when you read the book. Then write or tape your explanations of why you drew the scene the way you did and why you think you were where you were in the scene. What does it tell you about who you related to in the novel?

41. New acquaintances. Select two characters. Then think about three to five people, living or dead, that you would like your characters to meet. Write about how you selected these new acquaintances and what you'd like the character to learn from the people you introduced to him or her. For instance, after reading *The True Confessions of Charlotte Doyle* by Avi you might want Charlotte to meet Sojourner Truth so she can see other women who do important work, or Madame Curie who worked in a field not many women ever entered, and so on.

42. Book choices for character. Select a character and then choose five books for him or her, thinking about what he or she might like and need to know more about. Scan library shelves, the Internet, or use the library's computer card file. Why did you select the nonfiction books you did? What do you hope your character will like about or get out of the fiction?

43. Community resources for characters. After looking in the phone book and on the Internet, create a file of community resources that would help a character in your novel cope with an issue. If the main character has alcoholic parents, you could collect pamphlets, names of self-help groups, and any agencies that address the problem. Then create a display board so others can see what is available.

44. Family history. Create the history of the family of one of the main characters in your novel. For instance, in *Spite Fences* what would mama's life have been like? What major events affected her family? How were such things as holidays and birthdays celebrated? What is important to this family?

45. Detective work. If a detective or police officer suddenly showed up in your novel, who or what would be investigated? Write about what the detective is looking for, how he or she knew something was awry or needed investigating, and what was recommended. For instance, in *Spite Fences,* a detective could appear at Maggie's home to investigate the physical abuse or an undercover policeman could be in town investigating civil rights violations.

46. The Dating Game. Imagine that some of the characters are writing resumés so they can appear on the Dating Game Show. What would they say about themselves and what would they say they would like in a significant other?   *(continued)*

Figure 5.3

47. Create a character's room. We learn a lot about people by what they keep in their closets, what they have on their walls, what they select to put in a room. Select a character you know well and create a living room, bedroom, kitchen, or some other room that would mean a lot to the character. Draw it or write about it, making sure to include an explanation of why you designed the room as you did.

48. CD collection. Design a CD collection for a character you know well, being sure that the collection includes music that expresses as many aspects of the character as you are aware of.

49. Photo album. Think about the events that happened in your novel. Decide which scenes or pictures from the novel a character would want to remember. Then draw several of these "photos" for an album page or write about which pictures the character would want in his or her album. For instance, in *Freak the Mighty* by Rodman Philbrick (Scholastic 1993), Max would want a picture of himself opening the Christmas present Kevin made for him, a picture of Kevin on his shoulders, and a picture of Kevin bursting in to save him from his brutal father.

50. A character alphabet. Choose a character you liked and then create sentences based on the alphabet scheme that demonstrate your knowledge of the character. If after reading *Spite Fences*, you decided to write Zeke's alphabet it could start like this.

> A is for the ABUSE Zeke took at the hands of a racist mob.
>
> B is for his BENDING OVER BACKWARDS to make sure the visiting civil rights activist could work in obscurity.
>
> C is for the CAMERA he gave Maggie so she could begin to look at the world in new ways.

(This list first appeared in Diana's *English Journal* Teaching Ideas column in January 1998. Copyright © 1989 by the Natinal Council of Teachers of English. Reprinted with permission.)

Figure 5.3

Stance 1: Being Out and Stepping into an Envisionment
(Gathering Initial Ideas)

In this stance Langer says the readers begin to gather enough ideas to gain a sense of what the piece will be about. They pick up available clues. They begin to develop envisionment by using their knowledge and experience.

Readers in this stance search for starting places to rebuild an envisionment. The teacher asks questions to understand if and how the student is becoming engaged, what the student is noticing, what the student is seeing. At this point, strategies can be suggested to help students visualize the text or see images. The teacher focuses on the student sharing his/her understanding of the text. (See Figure 5.4 for sample questions in this stance.)

Stance 2: Being in and Moving Through an Envisionment
(Immersed in the Text World)

Langer tells us that from surface ideas and more experience with life or the text, readers become more immersed in developing understandings. Personal knowledge is used with the text and context to furnish ideas and spark further thinking. Readers are immersed in the text world. They take new information and use it to go beyond what they already understand. In this stance readers also fill in the gaps the author has left. (See Figure 5.4 for sample questions and activities in this stance.)

RESPONDING TO AND LEARNING FROM THE LITERATURE

One of the major reasons we read is to enjoy the ideas and people, to see what happens, to see how people handle conflict, and to learn about ourselves and others through the literature. When students are involved in a piece of literature they want time to talk about it, to make sense of it, to tell how it connects to their lives. So allowing sufficient time for response to the literature is essential. After that, students are usually more willing to move on to more teacher-centered concerns. The following stance is a big part of response but it is one often ignored by teachers, especially if they believe their job is to tell students what literature means. It seems to us that one of the major reasons we read is the essence of the next stance.

Stance 3: Stepping Out and Rethinking What One Knows

Langer explains that this stance has to do with the insights readers gain from their envisionments. In all the other stances, readers try to make sense of the text world. Here readers use the text to see how it has added to their understanding of the world. It's how it adds to the reader's knowledge and experience and what these ideas mean for their own lives. This doesn't occur as frequently as the other stances but Langer calls it a powerful stance because it contains the essence of why we read—to help us figure out our own lives.

Connecting

In this stance moral issues are dealt with. We might ask students after reading *Of Mice and Men* if killing someone like George did, is ever acceptable to them. How much would they be willing to give up for someone they loved? Would they stand by a friend until the end and be there for him/her as they moved toward death?

After reading *The Color Purple* students might wonder if they would have the strength to live life on their own terms as Shug did. Or after reading *Fallen Angels* about the Vietnam War, students might want to talk about what the novel made them realize about life or about themselves? (See Figure 5.4 for further questions and activities in this stance.)

THE PLACE OF CRITICISM AND ANALYSIS

Criticism—talk about likes and dislikes—is a natural part of making contact with literature, something that will emerge at all levels of discussion with students of all ages. Given a chance, students will talk about good stories and bad ones, poems they like and poems they don't like, and those assessments will become more sophisticated over time. Because students read, react, and articulate their responses, analysis and criticism are not in opposition to a reader-centered program. As Langer's stances illustrate, analysis is simply one part of the process.

Stance 4: Stepping out and Objectifying the Experience

In this stance Langer tells us that readers reflect on what it all means in the text and how it works and why. They distance themselves from the envisionment and reflect back on it. They objectify their understandings, reflect on, analyze, and judge them and relate them to other works and experiences. In this stance readers can focus on author's craft, text structure, and literary elements. They become critics as they analyze. (See Figure 5.4 for sample questions in this stance.)

We avoid like the plague the usual sorts of critical/analytical questions that are lined up at the close of selections in virtually any school anthology. Such questions, we find, largely ignore the readers's response (and ignore the first three stances) and plunge directly into matters of literary criticism and analysis. They fail, we think, because they don't ever encourage students to connect their own response with the writer's attempt to shape and control response.

We think using Langer's stances helps us as teachers understand what is happening in our students' minds as they read. This understanding can then help us develop strategies and approaches which will extend our students involvement with a book, not cut off their responses and discourage further interaction with the text.

In order for readers to see how Langer's stances mesh with the more familiar higher order thinking skills often related to Blooms's taxonomy, we have referred to both schemas in Figure 5.4, with references to the higher order thinking skills placed after the reference to Langer's stances.

WHAT ABOUT CULTURAL AND LITERARY BACKGROUND?

Often as readers read they naturally want more information so they can make sense of the text. For instance, while reading *Spite Fences* by Trudy Krisher students might want to know more about the history of the Civil Rights movement and the social issues of the 1960s so they can better understand why the characters behave as they do. Thus we would like to argue that cultural and literary background—knowledge of dates, periods, styles, and linguistic and literary conventions—can emerge from response to reading, especially when students are in Stance Two—immersed in the text world. Literary background does become useful and relevant as students read more and more sophisticated works. Conversely, less experienced readers fail to appreciate literary history and culture when those materials are presented for information and "enculturation" rather than for assistance in reading. In our experience, young people seem genuinely fascinated with life in, say, Shakespeare's or Twain's time and enjoy studying the historical/cultural background if that information genuinely contributes to their understanding of a work.

There is a fine line between cultural history that enlightens and that which becomes extraneous to the students' responses. One key is the length of time required to present the necessary background. If teachers must spend almost as much time providing background reading as they do discussing the work itself, it would seem that the background has gotten out of hand. In addition, teachers should recall that in-depth historical and cultural analysis is basically an adult or college-level activity. Relatively few school-age students will reach a stage where background study becomes an end in itself.

GATHERING INITIAL IDEAS (Stance One)

To help students see the process they use, we can ask such questions as:

What's the first image you see? Write about or draw it.

Where were you in the story? Were you above looking down, were you observing? Were you one of the characters?

Do you feel you are beginning to know any characters?

If you were to create a simple story board of the first chapter, how would you represent it?

Where would you put characters in relation to each other?

BEING IMMERSED IN THE TEXT WORLD (Stance Two, Interpreting)

To encourage students to continue to develop understandings and fill in the gaps, we can ask such questions as:

Think about the characters' motives. Why do you think they act as they do?

How might some of the characters be feeling?

What events or behaviors cause other things to happen?

How are the characters and events interrelated?

Why do you think one character treats another character the way he does? Whose point of view do you think you are most attuned to?

Which characters can you relate to the most?

What happens that is hard for you to understand?

Do any places in the story seem especially important?

Students can also be encouraged to respond to the following activities:

Write an autobiography for one of the characters. What was his or her life like before and after the story?

Select a character to be granted three wishes by a genie. What does the character wish for? Why? Will the character be better or worse off by getting these wishes?

Discuss what the main characters in the story would look for in a best friend.

Construct a map of the setting, showing where important events occurred.

Create a timeline of events you consider significant.

GAINING INSIGHT (Stance Three, Relating)

To encourage students to focus on what they have learned about themselves ask them to:

Discuss whether they would ever do something that a character did, such as save someone else's life or reject parental advice.

Share their ideas about how they agree/disagree with a character's view on an issue.

(continued)

Figure 5.4   Levels of Response to Literature

Write a letter to a specific character explaining what they learned from that character.

Talk about the characters they disliked the most and what they learned about themselves from these dislikes.

Pick out a specific emotion experienced by a character in the story and write about their experience with that emotion in a poem, diary entry, letter, or short story.

OBJECTIFYING THE EXPERIENCE (Stance Four, Analyzing)

Questions students are ready to look at include:

Why is this piece significant for us?

Why do we agree/disagree with other interpretations?

Were those seagulls symbolic? Of what?

Was the plot as interesting to you as in the last novel you read?

What did the author do to keep the reader involved and turning pages?

Let's look at the way characters were represented. How were minorities and women characterized? Could any of these portrayals be considered stereotypical?

What about the language? Did you notice anything about it? Was it overly descriptive? Was it so unobtrusive that you didn't notice it?

Did you think this author did as good a job with the theme as the author of a different novel?

Which novel made a strong impact on you? What did the author do to create this kind of impact?

How would you describe the author's style? How does it differ from the style of other pieces we have read this year?

EXPLORING BEYOND THE TEXT

Students can:

Look for other books on the topic.

Research an idea or issue that aroused their curiosity.

Choose an issue from the novel and create an ad campaign on it (e.g. drunkenness, cruelty to animals, cruelty to people).

Rewrite the story as a fairy tale.

Write a satire on the values or antivalues portrayed in the story.

Make a videotape on the same issue or theme.

In addition, many of the book report alternatives suggested earlier can be used.

Figure 5.4

In the course of a literature program that focuses on meaning, students will be given an opportunity to gain a great deal of cultural background. Over time, many students will read and delight in a wide range of works by the masters, and they will enjoy gaining insights into periods of history and cultures other than their own. Some students will read Dickens and Austen; some will discover James Fenimore Cooper. Other students will read Orson Scott Card and other science fiction writers and discuss contemporary and historical culture as it is reflected in intergalactic sagas. Some will read travel and geography books; others will read history and social science texts. Probably just about every student will read (or watch) a Shakespeare play. Probably everyone will read or hear some myths, legends, and folklore. Not every student will read every book in common, and not all students will know every last tidbit of cultural history. (Did they ever, we wonder?) What we can say is that students will have absorbed considerable amounts of literary and cultural history and will have done so in service of the central aim of the literature/reading program: to engage with print.

EXPLORING BEYOND THE TEXT

We believe this is part of the process of response to literature but it takes place outside the envisionment stances. In other words, sparks, which cause us to think in new directions and to think about our own experiences, have been given off by the literature. These experiences are not the ones tapped into in Stance Two, which help us understand the piece, these are memories or ideas with which the literature puts us in touch. Thus literature here is used as a jumping-off point in which the discussion is extended into new areas. The literary experience extends beyond the text as the students explore additional ideas that grow from their response. Formalist critics might throw up their hands at venturing far from the text, arguing that such discussions have nothing to do with literature. However, if the teacher has been able to get students to stretch and explore, moving into new areas of experience, the literature will have served its purpose well—the students will have grown as a result.

The explorations that grow from literature need not be limited to talk. We like to encourage students to experiment with many different ways of describing their reactions to reading. (See Figure 5.4 for sample activities.)

If the teacher supports a range of responses to literature, the students often become interested in one another's work. At this point, the traditional distinction between literature and composition vanishes. A class will flow freely from reading to creating responses to reading its own creations. The students' own work becomes part of the literature under examination.

APPROACHING A POEM

Although poetry is certainly a part of literature, we feel it deserves a special section for several reasons. First, from our work with prospective teachers we have learned that this is the area of literature where they feel particularly insecure about teaching.

Second, poetry seems more difficult to get inside since it does not have the direct avenues of characters and plot that are present in fiction—here we can give suggestions that can be applied directly to poetry. Third, even experienced teachers who seem to have no problems dealing with other genres often ask, "What do I do with a poem besides read it?" We hope to give many activities that will help deal with this problem.

Thus, since poetry does offer some separate kinds of challenges and concerns, we deal with it apart from the rest of literature. We emphasize, however, that as with other genres, the readers' engagement with the poem is still at the heart of the matter. Readers must be given time to respond to and experience the poem before they are asked to analyze it. If poetry is approached like other literature, not like a puzzle that needs to be solved, students will be more willing to interact with poetry. Give them chances to hear or read the poem several times to get the feel of it and explain that the compressed language of poetry often needs more rumination to get involved in it.

To illustrate this approach to poetry (and to all literature, for that matter), we describe an approach that we have used with three poems.

MY PARENTS KEPT ME FROM CHILDREN WHO WERE ROUGH
by Stephen Spender

My parents kept me from children who were rough
Who threw words like stones and who wore torn clothes.
Their thighs showed through rags. They ran in the street.
And climbed cliffs and stripped by the country streams.

I feared more than tigers their muscles like iron
Their jerking hands and their knees tight on my arms.
I feared the salt-coarse pointing of those boys
Who copied my lisp behind me on the road.

They were lithe, they sprang out behind hedges
Like dogs to bark at my world. They threw mud
While I looked the other way, pretending to smile.
I longed to forgive them, but they never smiled.

ERNEST MOTT by Mel Glenn

When I was younger, mothers didn't let me play with their kids.
"Billy has to come in for supper."
A lie,
Because I could see the fear in their faces.
One time I did run naked through the neighborhood.
One time I did beat up this kid who called me "retard."
One time I did smash four windows in a row.
It wasn't my fault.
Something inside of me told me to do these things.
I was always sorry afterward.
Now, after years of special classes,
Years of Thorazine and therapy,

They want to put me back into a regular class.
I don't know if I want to go back,
Back to people who still have fear in their faces.

From *Class Dismissed!* by Mel Glenn. Text copyright © 1982 by Mel Glenn. Reprinted by permission of Clarion Books/Houghton Mifflin Co. All rights reserved.

   escape by Mari Evans

   theodore R. the III
   finally
   got past aunt clelia uncle
   dan and the
   heavy glassed front
   door which
   protected
   him from the
   Other Kids
   and ran ran ran ran ran ran ran
   ran ran ran ran ran ran
   ran ran ran ran
   ran ran ran ran ran
   it
   took seven
   Other Kids
   to catch him:
   gently—for
   they greatly admired
   his defiance. . .
   aunt clelia only stood there
   damp handed
   on the
   empty front
   porch

From *I Am a Black Woman*, published by William Morrow & Company, 1970. Reprinted by permission of the author.

   We start by reading each poem at least twice. Student volunteers might be willing to do this. After each poem is read aloud, have students jot down a line or two on how the poem affected them, what it made them think about, or what they thought the poem was saying. Once all three poems have been read, ask students to write down the titles of the poems and rank the poems. The highest ranking of 1 would go to the poems they related to the most or felt they understood the best. The lowest ranking would go to the poems they didn't relate to or didn't understand. Students then share their rankings in a small group, explaining their reasons for the rankings. Each group reports to the whole class the poems they most related to and the poem they didn't feel connected to. A tally could be kept on the board of how the poems were ranked. Then each group is given one of the three poems to grapple with and eventually explain to the class— they can share phrases or lines that struck them, what the most puzzling or unclear line was, what one word seemed most important to the poem, and so on. As part of the process, students can also jot down memories or ideas the poem brings to mind.

When students get to this point of close work with a poem, this is often the time that specific terms can be given the students. The teacher might ask them to look at the form of the poem and the way it lays on the page. What can be learned from the form that could help them deal with the meaning? Does it being long and skinny mean anything? Do the number of stanzas and how they are similar or different give us clues to the meaning or intent? What about letter sounds? Are some hard and harsh, soft and stretched out? What can this tell us about the poem? Can sentence length and the way the lines are broken tell us anything? How about word choice or diction? repetition? alliteration? assonance? consonance? How do these add to the meaning? It must be noted that the purpose of reading poems is not to be able to identify terms and to find those concepts in the poems. Rather, these terms can be used as other ways into the poem, as other ways to approach the poem.

After students have presented their understandings of the poem, they could work to find out what commonalities the poems have, how they can connect and relate to each other. This will often result in a list of themes and issues. Students then reflect on the whole experience by writing about how they went about making sense of their poem, what strategies they used, how the poems connected to their lives, what they learned about people or the world from their readings.

Students are then asked to create extensions to the reading of the poems. They may suggest role-playing some of the scenes suggested by the poems but not fully developed, they may want to write to a person or group of people from the poems, they may want to draw their impressions of the poem, write a short story or play on one of the issues, conduct a panel on how children should be raised and how much they should be protected. Each student then takes one of the suggestions, develops it, and presents it to the class.

As the teacher can see, this is not a hurry-up process. If we want our students to see poetry as a genre that can touch the human spirit and capture the humanness of people, then slowing down and letting them muck around in the poems seems to be a good idea.

Responding to poetry also follows the stances Langer describes. Much of the student work described above would focus on Stance One and Two. Students would work to be able to "get into" the poem and then spend time being in it and moving through it. Students would also move out of the poem and rethink what they know as well as objectify the experience. In working with poetry, often much time is spent in Stance Four as students work to see how the author's craft affects the meaning of the poem. Poetry reading seems an excellent vehicle to inspire students to want to look at HOW an effect is created. Also, since poems are generally shorter than prose, students can more easily look at all parts of the craft, not just a few.

More Avenues into Literature

Consider some of the following strategies:

- After students have read several poems, divide the class into groups and have each group select a poem to read dramatically. Their arrangement and how they divide the poem up to be read will reflect their interpretation of the poem.

- Get students involved in the meaning of literature by having them work in groups to create a new title. Each group should agree on its new title and present justifications for its choice. It is more interesting if several groups are retitling the same work.

- Omit several words from a poem and ask groups of students to propose words that would best fit in. Compare the groups' results.

- Read more difficult poems aloud several times. Then ask students to write down a response to the poem. After giving them a few minutes to complete this, have them move into small groups of three or four and discuss their initial responses. Have one member from each group report to the class on some of the group's responses and questions. Other class members can offer possible answers to questions and discussion can continue from this point.

- After reading several works of literature on a theme, ask students to bring in a drawing, photo, or picture from a magazine that represents their response. The picture is mounted on one side of a sheet of paper; on the back the student writes an explanation of how he or she sees the picture connecting with or speaking to the theme. The teacher collects the pictures and then, while holding each picture up for the class to see, asks students to describe what work they think the picture represents.

- Make up the story behind a story, play, or poem. What has happened before, "off stage," and what will happen later?

- Have students rework a piece of literature into another genre such as a newspaper story, an essay, or a story. What has been gained and what lost?

- Give students a poem cut into stanzas or a story cut into paragraphs. They are to figure out the best arrangement of these segments. They can compare their arrangement with the way the author wrote the work and see how meanings shift when the arrangement shifts.

- Have students read a short story and a poem, and in groups, describe a relationship or a connection between the two.

- Have students read a number of poems and find those which go together. Let them explain the connection or dramatize it through an oral reading and/or panel discussion.

- Ask young readers to find a poem that could be placed at the beginning of a novel or short story as an epigraph.

- Encourage students to find literature they would be willing to read to the class.

- Have students create anthologies of favorite short literary works. They can start with the classroom anthology and then use books from the library. (Limited photocopying of literature for nonprofit classroom use of this sort is generally permitted by copyright law.) When the anthology is finished, have students share their two or three favorite works in small groups. Anthologies can be kept in the room and used as reading material at the end of the hour or as part of the classroom reading library.

From our discussions of ways to engage students in literature we hope it is clear that a response-centered approach does include elements of the more traditional approach. Indeed, done well, a response approach subsumes critical analysis, but stays with the students by emphasizing engagement and ownership.

◆ EXPLORATIONS

◆ Write out your own statement of the purpose of literature teaching. Share with others in a small group and then expand or delete parts of your statement after collaborating with others. As you design lessons and units involving literature, come back to this statement to see whether you are meeting the goals you set for yourself.

◆ Think about the ways in which you respond to literature. How do you react when you are reading a good book? How does a book affect you? What happens after you have finished reading?

◆ As you read a novel, write a journal entry after every few chapters on what you were reacting to and what you were thinking. Then go back and work to identify what stances you were in as you made the comments you did.

◆ Start a discussion with other teachers or with students: "Print is dead. Literature is dying. We ought to abandon literature classes and teach TV!" What counter arguments do people offer? Who agrees with that statement? What counter arguments (if any) can you offer? Ask students to write about or debate the same question. (Prepare yourself for a possible surprise. We've discovered that students tend to argue in favor of preservation of a literary culture.)

◆ Give a poem to a small group of students and let them discuss it with no teacher present. Tape-record the discussion. Study its ebb and flow. How do students respond to literature on their own?

◆ Choose a poem or short story that you think students will like and teach it to several groups, varying your approach each time. Try some of the response ideas suggested in this chapter. Explore the amount of historical/cultural material for reader comprehension. Write your conclusions in a journal or share them with a colleague.

◆ Examine the study questions in an anthology commonly used in the schools. Critique them. Which envisionment stances are they focused on? Try your hand at writing response questions for several selections. Develop your skill at moving beyond any perceived weaknesses in the adopted anthology.

◆ Write your own reading autobiography in which you explore and explain how you remember learning to read, what you remember about reading in your house, what you remember about reading at school. What kinds of assignments were you given to accompany your reading? Share your memories in your small group and draw some conclusions about the teaching of reading and literature.

◆ RELATED READINGS

Louise Rosenblatt's *Literature as Exploration* is a powerful book on teaching literature and deserves reading and rereading. Her more recent book, *The Reader, the Text, and the Poem,* provides a fuller theoretical view of her "transactional" approach to reading. One practical book on teaching this approach is Alan Purves's *How Porcupines Make Love II.* Richard Beach's *A Teacher's Introduction to Reader-Response Theories* helps us become aware of the wide range of attitudes that reader-response critics have about the roles of the reader, the text, and the social/cultural context that shapes the transaction between the reader and the text.

Janet Allen's *It's Never Too Late: Leading Adolescents to Lifelong Literacy* focuses on engaging reluctant readers in the process of reading. This book is packed with practical strategies that Janet used with her high school reading classes. Also especially useful in helping students learn how to be engaged in reading is Jeffrey Wilhelm's *You Gotta BE the Book.* Judith Langer's *Envisioning Literature: Literary Understanding and Literature Instruction* not only gives the reader extensive information on the stances of literary engagement but also shows what literature instruction in classrooms looks like when built upon the stances of readers.

CHAPTER 6

LITERATURE AND THE YOUNG ADULT

Although the title of this chapter is deliberately ambiguous and could be read in a number of ways, our purpose is not ambiguous. A major focus is on young adult literature ("Y.A. lit" in trade jargon), but we also emphasize that our central concern is the relationship between literature *and* the young adult, which includes selecting books that engage our student readers. Of course, much of what we say in the chapter applies to teaching any book to the young reader. Thus, in addition to finding suggestions for teaching Y.A. titles, the reader will be invited to explore ways of engaging students in familiar classics, folktales and stories, non-fiction, and even books written for children.

> Wide, voracious, *indiscriminate* reading is the base soil from which discrimination and taste eventually grow.
>
> From Aidan Chambers, *Introducing Books to Children*, Portsmouth, N.H.: Heinemann Educational Books, 1983, p.103

YOUNG ADULT LITERATURE: REASONS TO USE IT IN THE CLASSROOM

Not too many years ago teachers were wary of using books labeled as "young adult," believing that the content was light and frivolous. Many articles in *The English Journal* in the 1950s and 1960s, for example, were defenses of an emerging genre—the book about the teenager written especially for teenagers. Some academics still attack Y.A. books from time to time, arguing that they water down the cultural heritage and are used as a substitute for teaching "great books." However, the merit of using young adult books in the classroom is no longer questioned by most specialists in reading and literature. The literary richness and variety of reading that teachers desire for their students can be enhanced by contact with the young adult novel, and although good Y.A. literature can stand on its own merits, it can also serve as a bridge into adult reading. There is as much range in the quality of young adult literature as there is in any other genre. Top-notch writers such as Aidan Chambers, Chris Crutcher, Robert Cormier, Susan Cooper, Philip Pullman, and Cynthia Voigt write with skill and grace, use vivid imagery, intertwine complex plot lines, and give depth to their characters while telling engrossing stories. Skilled writers are not the exception in young adult literature, and more and more excellent writers seem to be joining the ranks.

Using young adult novels in the classroom provides the teacher with a source of reading materials that can involve students while strengthening their reading/writing/thinking/speaking skills. Contemporary language makes the books immediately accessible since students don't have to leap across language barriers to get at the heart of the book. Action in young adult novels begins immediately and teens don't have to wait around until the books get "good." The issues in these novels are often relevant to students' lives. Too often as teachers we have to do the work of uncovering themes and issues for our students and show them how these themes can relate to their lives.

By using Y.A. novels, such as Philip Pullman's *The Ruby in the Stone,* which plunges the reader into the heart of 19th century London, the books do the work for us and students can grapple with the meat of the themes, not simply figure out what they are. Young adult literature helps bridge the gap between school and what our students view as "real life." If we use literature that is removed from the interests and concerns of students, we seem to be telling them that school does not deal with real things; it is just something they have to get through. Moreover, young adult novels reflect the racial, class, and family compositions of our students. Reading books with characters that make visible the racial or economic or familial aspects of who students are, affirms and validates that aspect of students' lives. Students don't feel as marginalized when they can see themselves in the literature used in school. Young adult authors respect where their readers are coming from and work to live up to their readers' expectations. They know students want fast beginnings so they give them fast beginnings. They don't try to work against the nature of their readers or tell readers what is good for them; they work with the reader by using their skills to pique and keep student interest.

Junior high/middle school teachers have been using young adult fiction in their classes for years because it engages students and works for them in providing a positive educational experience. High school teachers in the "general" classes—the students not destined for college—seem more willing to use Y.A. literature, but as teachers of higher level literature courses become aware of the quality and the depth of much Y.A. literature, they too, seem to be more open to trying the genre, especially by pairing a Y.A. novel with one they are used to using (e.g., pairing *Staying Fat for Sarah Byrnes* by Chris Crutcher with *The Bell Jar* by Sylvia Plath [Bantam 1972]). Unfortunately, some teachers have used Y.A. lit as a starting point for lectures on symbol, theme, form, and plot, finding that it makes such aspects of literature more visible to students. We think that's a misuse of Y.A. literature, just as we have suggested that we think engagement with literature must come prior to literary analysis.

KNOWING YOUNG ADULT LITERATURE

Once teachers see ways in which young adult literature can be worked into their programs and see how positively students respond to it, they will be ready to try more and more of it. The next step for teachers is to become familiar with a broader range of Y.A. titles. We present some suggested reading lists in this chapter, but Y.A literature is a rapidly changing field. We offer some book lists and periodical sources at the chapter close, all updated frequently, that the teacher can use to discover new and established books recommended for young readers. It's also useful to find the librarian in your school or city who is interested in this area and get him or her to make suggestions. Most colleges and universities now have courses in young adult literature, but perhaps the best way is simply to locate a few titles in the bookstore or library and begin reading. Seek recommendations from your own students. Diana became an avid fan of the Y.A. genre when enthusiastic students pressed her to read such books as *The Lion, The Witch, and the Wardrobe* by C.S. Lewis as well as the works of Madeleine L'Engle, Susan Cooper, and Paula Danziger. When she saw how much it meant to students to have a teacher who could talk to them about books they were reading, she was sold on the importance of knowing the field well.

Since one can't become an expert overnight, another good way to get to know many different books is to have students read them. Diana learned about the Book Pass from the NCTE publication *Ideas for Teaching English in the Junior High and Middle School,* edited by Candy Carter and Zora Rashkis in 1980. It simply involves placing a different book on each student's desk along with a sheet on which to record reactions and information. Students list the name of the book and the author, read the book for three to five minutes, record whether or not they would like to read the book, and pass the book on to the next student. The teacher's job is to call time after the three to five minutes are up, remind students to record their reactions, pass the book, and record new book information. If this is done for a whole class hour, students can preview ten to fifteen books and will base their judgment of whether or not they want to read the book on more than just the way the cover looks.

RESPONDING TO LITERATURE

The purpose of the kind of activities that are described in this section is to get students deeper into the book, to encourage them to see through a character's eyes. We want students to take an active part in making sense of the book and getting a grasp on it. We want to immerse them in the book, get them into the story world, really engage them in the book.

Figure 6.1 lists many response activities which we developed around the following general goals which the reader will see work with Langer's four stances described in the previous chapter. The first two goals tap into Stance Two; the third one, Stance Three; the fourth one, Stance Four; and the fifth goal asks students to use what they know about the text to create something new.

1. Give students opportunities to interact with the characters and with the characters' thinking.
2. Give students opportunities to make meaning.
3. Give students opportunities to connect literature to life.
4. Give students opportunities to think critically, to analyze, and evaluate.
5. Give students opportunities to create in response to the text.

In Figure 6.1 we organize the activities around our five goals but it is easy to see that there is much overlap between categories. The major point is that activities in response to literature are not passive and are not based on recall, although recall is assumed in many of these activities. It is our hope that suggestions such as these will pull students deeper into the literature and stimulate them to think about it in new ways.

IN PRACTICE: KEEPING THE NOVEL IN FOCUS

It is important that "catchy" ideas not be applied to novels at random. It is possible to engage students in a wide range of "fun" activities without helping them become much better as readers. To this end, it is important that the teacher consider aims and purposes in teaching the novel and focus activities appropriately. To illustrate how this can be done, we will apply several of the foregoing suggestions to a young adult novel that because of its Newbery Honor status, has become somewhat of a classic with adolescent readers and with teachers: *The True Confessions of Charlotte Doyle* by Avi. It is an adventurous novel, set in 1832, of a young girl crossing the ocean to join her family, and becoming entangled in mutiny and murder. The following activities are designed to guide the students through some of their reading of the text and to help them sharpen their response to it. Along the way, students regularly refer back to the text as well as to their own experiences.

- After reading three chapters, students write out questions for Charlotte, the central character. They can ask her about her attitudes towards people, what she is most frightened of, how she has felt about her life until now, how she views her parents. One student can play the role of Charlotte and answer the questions as Charlotte would probably have answered them.
- When several chapters have been read, allow time for questioning the text. In groups, students brainstorm questions about all the events, attitudes, or people they are having trouble understanding.

Examples
of the
to do the bold
print

GIVE STUDENTS OPPORTUNITIES TO INTERACT WITH THE CHARACTERS AND WITH THE CHARACTER'S THINKING

- Create a protest campaign. When students get to a part in a novel that upsets them, let them organize a protest campaign. *The Giver* by Lois Lowry describes the futuristic "perfect" society where people are released if they don't fit in or conform. Students might have Jonas write a speech to give to the community after he discovers that the euphemistic sounding "release" really means "killed." Students could also compose the petition Jonas would have liked to compose, with reasons given for changing some of the practices in his community. Or while reading *The True Confessions of Charlotte Doyle,* students could decide on what kind of letters and information the sailors on the ship would give to officials when they disembarked so that other sailors never had to experience what they did.

- Three Words. Students write down three words that they feel best describe a character. In groups, students share their words and the reasons they selected them. Each group selects the three words they think best fit the character and share their conclusions with the class.

- Comics. Students read the comics for several weeks looking for comic strips that specific characters would like. They mount the comic strips on paper and explain in writing why each comic would appeal to or speak to the character.

- Propose characters' poetry choices. From a collection of poetry, students pick out poems they believe specific characters would like. The poems are then read to the class for discussion.

- Give advice to a character. Students choose a character and write all the advice they have to give to this character.

- Ask students to make lists of rules or moral guidelines. They begin by selecting a character who has very definite ideas on a topic such as friendship, raising children, or getting along in school. Then they make up a set of "rules" about that topic as that character might state them. Students can talk about whether or not they share these values. Powerful whole class discussions can result.

GIVE STUDENTS OPPORTUNITIES TO MAKE MEANING BY BEGINNING WITH THEIR OWN QUESTIONS.

- Question the text. Students brainstorm lists of questions they want to ask about the novel. This can be done before they begin reading, based only on the title, cover, and jacket blurbs, or it can be done throughout the novel. As Diana's students read *Ring of Endless Light* by Madeleine L'Engle they wondered why an author would start a book with death and sadness, wondered if any of their classmates could identify with Zachary's need to be destructive, wondered what the dolphins symbolized, and wanted to talk about the beginnings of the universe alluded to in the book.

- Invite students to create questions. Pass out 3 x 5 note cards. Have students write down two or three questions or issues that they want to discuss from their reading. After reading Katherine Paterson's *Jacob Have I Loved,* Diana's students asked such

(continued)

Figure 6.1   Activities in Response to Literature

questions as: Why didn't Louise try for anything she wanted until the end of the book? Why did Louise want to be like her father and accepted as if she were male? Collect the cards as the students finish them, categorize them, and begin a whole-class discussion on issues that came up. Or divide the class into groups, give each group a few cards, and ask them to respond.

GIVE STUDENTS OPPORTUNITIES TO CONNECT LITERATURE TO LIFE

- Change actions. Students choose a character in the book and look specifically at how he or she handled a specific situation. Then they discuss or write about how they would have liked to see the matter handled.
- Discuss similar situations. Students discuss a situation in the book that moved them or angered them and share situations or feelings they have experienced which were similar.
- Dramatize issues. Students list all the issues and problems they see being raised in the novel. Then they select several issues they see as critical and design roleplaying situations about them, either using the characters from the novel or creating new characters and settings. (More about classroom drama in Chapter 11.)
- Examine beliefs. Students choose a specific belief a character holds throughout the novel and discuss whether group members agree with this belief. Again, lively whole-group discussions can result as students report.
- Study language. Discussion groups go through different chapters of the novel, gathering phrases and words that are used differently than they would use them. Students list the words and phrases and explain what they mean or tell how they would express the same idea today.

GIVE STUDENTS OPPORTUNITIES TO THINK CRITICALLY, TO ANALYZE, AND EVALUATE

- Construct a time line of events. Pupils work up a representation of events in the book in the order in which they occur. They can also construct symbols or icons to represent each event.
- Prepare diagrams. Students map the actions, events, or character relationships in the novel. One group chooses an event and shows each character's relation to it, while another group might decide to show characters' relationships to each other. These diagrams can usefully be displayed on the bulletin board, with complexity emerging as the book progresses.
- Brainstorm themes. In groups, students generate the themes or recurring issues they believe are present in the book. The groups then rank their list in terms of which themes or issues are most important in the novel. When groups share their lists with the whole class, lively discussions often result.
- Create new book titles. Many book titles are not appealing to some students or don't give an accurate idea of what the book is about. Have students in groups create new titles and explain their choices.   *(continued)*

Figure 6.1

- Compare the "good old days" with the present. Many books are set in earlier time periods and show what life was like back then. Students can discuss and then list what seems to be similar or different about these "good old days." As appropriate, the teacher can introduce material of literary or historical background, but don't use this as an excuse to become a history teacher.
- Rewrite scenes. Students choose a scene that they feel didn't end satisfactorily and rewrite it. Or they create a scene they would like to have included in the book. Is this a valid form of "literary criticism"? Is it appropriate for secondary school students? We think the answer is yes, provided students and teacher go back to the text as written from time to time to discuss how it created their responses.
- Encourage students to compare gender roles portrayed by characters. Which characters' roles could be easily taken by a member of the opposite sex? Which ones would be the hardest to exchange with a member of the opposite sex? Discuss the reasoning behind the answers.
- Divide the text. In groups, students divide the novel into three to five parts, explaining the rationale for their decisions. Where does the "beginning" come to a close? Where are the pauses? If this book were on television, where would the commercials fall? In this way, students come to think about plot and structure without having the terminology imposed on them prematurely.

GIVE STUDENTS OPPORTUNITIES TO CREATE IN RESPONSE TO THE TEXT

- Design advertising posters. If the novel lends itself to this, have students design posters advertising a specific event such as the kidnapping of Maxwell in *Freak the Mighty* by Rodman Philbrick.
- Write a eulogy. If an animal or character dies, students write a eulogy for him or her.
- Design a stamp. After talking about how stamps are issued to commemorate great people or important events, students are asked to think about the book they have just finished in terms of what person or event or issue in the book would merit a commemorative stamp. After reading *The Hero and the Crown* by Robin McKinley students could create a stamp about the creation of kelar which allowed humans to fight dragons without getting burned. After reading Melba Pattillo Beals *Warriors Don't Cry* they could create a stamp commemorating the integration of Central High School in Little Rock, Arkansas. On the stamp form that Diana created, students drew a stamp design or used magazine pictures to represent the event or issue, and then wrote why they thought the person or event was worthy of a stamp.

Figure 6.1

- Rewrite scenes. Students abhor the scene where Zachariah is whipped and would like a chance to change it. Or they think Charlotte should have confronted the behavior of Mr. Grummage. After students rewrite a scene of their choice and share it in groups, discuss the rewrites in terms of whether they were true to the time in which the novel is set.

- Propose character's poetry choices. From collections of poems from the library or the classroom, have groups find poems they think Charlotte or Zachariah or Captain Jaggery might like or which describes one of them in some way.

- Identify issues. Much of the book revolves around the choices a young female had in the 1800s and what was considered proper. Invite students to write on such questions as: How much obedience do we owe to our parents? Are their activities or lines of work in which males or females shouldn't participate? What customs or manners of the 1800s would you find most difficult to live with?

- Write a eulogy for Mr. Cranick.

- Compare the "old days" to the present. Urban, suburban, and rural students can benefit from thinking and writing about the times and values portrayed in this book. Groups can develop lists of behaviors, actions, and attitudes that are the same today as they were then, while other groups develop lists of differences. Students can talk about the merits and problems of living in the time in which the novel is set and can write their own evaluation of which period is better to live in and why.

- Examine beliefs. Various views of social correctness and social class emerge in *The True Confessions of Charlotte Doyle.* Have students locate key statements in the text and then discuss their views of what is proper and whether or not they believe social classes are important and still exist.

- Study language. Several groups take two or three chapters of the novel and hunt for expressions and words that the people of this time use. Then students write down how this would be expressed today. Groups can compile their results into a Dictionary of Terms for Life in the 1800s. Students might also notice that different expressions and words are used by the working class and by the upper class.

MOVING YOUNG ADULT LITERATURE INTO THE CLASSROOM

Many teens read young adult literature on their own. Lots of kids check it out of the library, order it from book clubs, buy it at bookstores, and swap it with their friends. This is literature that speaks to them and involves them. Too often a wide gulf exists between the literature students avidly read and the literature that is taught in the schools. We encourage teachers to help foster students' literary experiences by bringing this literature into the heart of the classroom.

Since young adult literature has been written on almost any theme and issue imaginable and in many genres, there are a myriad of ways to use it in the classroom. For teachers who feel tied to using the old standbys, try pairing a young adult novel with one you usually use. Some such pairings can include *Fallen Angels* by Walter Dean Myers with Stephen Crane's *The Red Badge of Courage;* Rodman Philbrick's *Freak the Mighty* with Steinbeck's *Of Mice and Men;* Mildred D. Taylor's *The Road to Memphis* with Harper Lee's *To Kill a Mockingbird;* Philip Pullman's *Ruby in the Smoke* with Dickens' *Great Expectations;* Stephanie Tolan's *The Plague Year* with Miller's *The Crucible;* Lois Lowry's *The Giver* with Huxley's *Brave New World.*

[handwritten annotation: connect to the "classics"]

Once students have read both books they can engage in any number of the activities in Figure 6.2.

Another good way to bring young adult literature into the curriculum is to have students select a young adult novel they are interested in reading and build time into the schedule of the classroom to allow for silent reading. After a visit to the school library, a classroom book pass, or book talks by the librarian, students select a book. Once they have gotten far enough into the novels, the teacher structures a few simple interactive small-group sessions in which students talk about and compare the char-

- In small collaborative groups half the class generates lists of motifs, themes, or issues they found in one novel. The other half of the class does the same for the second novel. Students in each group keep a record of the four or five items in their list they consider the most important before exchanging their list with a group which worked on the other novel. Students then discuss the new list, adding and deleting items and then ranking which four or five items they consider the most important. Whole-class discussion follows, in which groups compare their perceptions.

- In small collaborative groups, students list all the reasons they think the two novels were paired. One spokesperson from each group shares the group's reasons with the whole class.

- Students discuss which characters in the two novels were most similar, most dissimilar, most ethical, most loyal etc. After discussing characters, students can be asked to write a conversation between characters from each novel.

- Students rank the literary elements such as plot, setting, point of view, imagery, irony, characterization, symbolism etc. from most important to least important in each novel. They then try to draw conclusions about the impact these author choices had on the reader. For instance, Diana's students noticed that figurative language and symbolism were very prominent elements in *Red Badge of Courage* while characterization and plot were more important in *Fallen Angels*. Students felt more connected to the characters in *Fallen Angels* and felt put off by the elaborate description and metaphorical language in *Red Badge of Courage*.

- Students generate award categories based on the literary elements or other noticeable features of the novels. They might come up with such categories as "Most Action-Packed Scene," "Most Courageous Act," "Most Compassionate Character," or "The Line with the Most Impact."

- Students in collaborative groups compose a time line of what they consider the major events in each of the novels. Groups compare their choices.

- Students create a word/picture collage for a character from one or both novels. Students cut out pictures, words, and phrases from magazines that they believe show something important about the character. The students completing the collage write a short paper on why the pictures and words were chosen. If time permits, students attach a sheet of paper to their collage. The collages are then passed around the class so other students can comment on the representations of characters in the collage.

- Students write a comparison/contrast between the novels, now that they have dealt in depth with many aspects of the novel.

Figure 6.2 Activities for Paired Novels

acters in their books or discuss the issues in the book. When books are finished, students give book talks to sell their book in a small group. These groups work best if they are put together around the categories of the books (mystery, science fiction, fantasy, realistic fiction, biography etc.). Each group selects one person from the group to share his or her book with the whole class. Interest in other students' books zooms! Diana used this individual approach using young adult novels with her American Literature classes before she began to integrate young adult literature into the fabric of the course. Students were enthusiastic about getting to read books in which they were really interested.

Another approach to moving more young adult literature into our classrooms is to pick common themes or concerns and to build units around them. Survival is one theme that emerges frequently in literature. When Diana has taught units based on survival she expanded the theme to include not only survival in nature, but situations people have gotten through such as trying out for a play or a sports team, getting braces, moving to a new school, coping with new stepfamilies, etc. Teens are very interested in what motivates people and why they act as they do, so the focus of the unit was on what was survived or lived through, how the persons got through the experience, what resources they drew on physically, emotionally, and through relationships, and what they learned from the experience. The class collected information on what allows people to get through these experiences, what allows them to cope, and what was learned through this survival. Sometimes Diana starts a unit with a whole-class novel like *Warriors Don't Cry* by Melba Pattillo Beals or *Woodsong* by Gary Paulsen. Beals's book examines how she was able to get through her torturous year as one of nine black students at Little Rock High School in 1957; the other book looks at what the author learned about nature and life from running his sled dogs and from completing the Alaskan dog race known as the Iditarod.

Students wrote their own survival stories and read short stories selected because of their individual merit and because they fit the theme. In selecting short stories, Diana usually begins by looking at the short story collections edited by Don Gallo because of their timeliness, quality, and high interest. Two Gallo collections that have many stories that can be related to the theme of survival are *Visions* and *Ultimate Sports*. Usually the short stories are read by the whole class and discussed. The short story is introduced by having students write or talk about an issue present in the story. For instance in using "Superboy" by Chris Crutcher (in *Ultimate Sports*), a touching story about a "mentally slow" teen who in preparing for a triathlon reveals some of his background of abuse, students first were asked to write about what they don't understand in other people's behavior. They also wrote about their hunches as to why these people acted the way they did. After reading the story, students first wrote/talked about their horror at the kind of treatment Superboy had received from his mother. Once students could pour out their feelings of incredulousness, they were then ready to look at how this boy got as far as he did in life, and what helped him cope. Another genre that is well suited for thematic units is poetry. Having students do a poetry hunt pulls in good poetry as students search for poems on the theme of survival to further their learning. We look on the reading and viewing of many pieces of literature as a collecting of information and impressions from which students can learn about the theme and about the world.

The point of creating units around a theme is to DO something with the theme. It is not an identification hunt—it's what the theme can teach us as exemplified in the story or poem. To this end, Diana has students in groups brainstorm lessons or insights they got from each piece used in class. Students might create a list of lessons, which is posted in the classroom, or do such things as create a booklet on what surviving an experience can teach us. Thematic teaching allows us to relate the literature to life.

To help the teacher create units around themes as well as to provide titles of excellent novels, we provide the lists in Figure 6.3. This list naturally reflects our reading tastes and interests, so the exclusion of a particular book title does not imply it is not of high quality or of high interest, it simply was not one that got into our hands.

Note: In some cases these books contain language or controversial issues some teachers might not find appropriate for classroom use. It's a good idea to preview books before recommending them or using them as whole-class books.

TEACHING THE CLASSICS

As English teachers, we are usually fans of the classics. We love to dig in and read and discuss and analyze such novels as *The Great Gatsby* and *Moby Dick.* However, we English teachers are adults with adult tastes and sophisticated reading skills. Our students are not adults, especially when it comes to their choices of and interest in reading material. An Advanced Placement student of our acquaintance who eventually scored high on the AP exam, was talking to another student about a classic that had been assigned in his class. He said, "I know the themes in the book are supposed to be great and important themes but why do we have to spend so much time wading through the language and antiquated sentence structures to get at the themes? Why don't we read something where the themes are more accessible so we can really get into discussions of the themes and issues instead of spending all of our time just figuring out what the themes are?"

We don't advocate teaching great books that are remote from students' young adult concerns or that contain so much archaic language that they are difficult for the teenager to read. We do encourage teachers to see classics as one more type of literature that young adults can get involved in and respond to, especially if classics are not treated differently than other kinds of novels. If activities planned for a classic are ones students can get into, they will generally have a good experience with the book. It seems that students lose interest in classics when they are told to read such books on their own and write academic essays on literary traits. The whole burden is then on the students to find their way through the novel and come up with an example of pseudo-collegiate thinking when they're often not even sure what the novel is about. Teachers need to remind themselves that there are other ways besides the essay to get students thinking, responding, analyzing, and writing. To suggest how to increase engagement between literature and the adolescent, we'll show some activities for Charles Dickens' *Great Expectations,* which is frequently taught in ninth grade classes.

ABUSIVE SITUATIONS

Chinese Handcuffs by Chris Crutcher (Dell, 1989)
Fair Game by Erika Tamar (Harcourt Brace, 1993)
Forged by Fire by Sharon M. Draper (Atheneum, 1997)—African-American
I Hadn't Meant to Tell You This by Jacqueline Woodson (Delacorte, 1994)—African-American—female protagonist
Staying Fat for Sarah Byrnes by Chris Crutcher (Greenwillow, 1993)
Uncle Vampire by Cynthia D. Grant (Atheneum, 1993)—female protagonist
The Watcher by James Howe (Atheneum, 1997)
What Jamie Saw by Caroline Coman (Front Street, 1995)
When She Hollers by Cynthia Voigt (Scholastic, 1994)—female protagonist
When She Was Good by Norma Fox Mazer (Scholastic, 1997)—female protagonist

ADVENTURE

Down River by Will Hobbs (Atheneum, 1991)
Flight #116 is Down by Caroline B. Cooney (Scholastic, 1992)
The Shark Callers by Eric Campbell (Harcourt Brace, 1994)—Pacific Islanders
The True Confessions of Charlotte Doyle by Avi (Orchard Books, 1990)—female protagonist
Woodsong by Gary Paulsen (Scholastic, 1990)

AWARENESS OF OTHER CULTURES

April and the Dragon Lady by Lensey Namioka (Harcourt Brace, 1994)—Chinese-American—female protagonist
Children of the River by Linda Crew (Delacorte, 1989)—Cambodian—female protagonist
Goodbye Vietnam by Gloria Whelan (Knopf, 1992)
Habibi by Naomi Shihab Nye (Simon & Schuster, 1997)—Arab-American—female protagonist
Haveli by Suzanne Fisher Staples (Knopf, 1993)—Pakistani—female protagonist
Heart of a Jaguar by Marc Talbert (Simon & Schuster, 1995)—Mayan
Kiss the Dust by Elizabeth Laird (Dutton, 1991)—Iraq—female protagonist
The Last Warrior by Suzanne Ellison (Northland, 1997)—Apache
Little Sister by Kara Dudley (Harcourt Brace, 1996)—Japanese—female protagonist
Morning Girl by Michael Dorris (Hyperion, 1992)—Taino Indians
One More River by Lynne Reid Banks (Morrow, 1992)—Israeli—female protagonist
Red Scarf Girl by Ji Li Jiang (HarperCollins, 1997)—Chinese—female protagonist
Rio Grande Stories by Carolyn Meyer (Harcourt Brace, 1994)
Sees Behind Trees by Michael Dorris (Hyperion, 1996)—Native American
Shadow of a Hero by Peter Dickinson (Delacorte Press, 1994)—Eastern European
Song of the Buffalo Boy by Sherry Garland (Harcourt Brace, 1992)—Vietnamese—female protagonist
The Sunita Experiment by Mitali Perkins (Little, Brown, 1993)—Indian—female protagonist
Tonight by Sea by Frances Temple (Harper, 1995)—Haitians
Twilight Boy by Timothy Green (Northland, 1998)—Navajo
Youn Hee and Me by C.S. Adler (Harcourt Brace, 1995)—Korean—female protagonist
(continued)

Figure 6.3   Themes and Titles In Young Adult Fiction

COMING OF AGE/GROWING UP

Arena Beach by Donna Staples (Houghton Mifflin, 1993)—female protagonist
Chasing Redbird by Sharon Creech (HarperCollins, 1997)—female protagonist
Dawn Rider by Jan Hudson (Scholastic, 1990)—Blackfoot Nation—female protagonist
Ella Enchanted by Gail Carson Levine (Harper Collins, 1997)—female protagonist
Facing the Music by Margaret Willey (Delacorte, 1996)—female protagonist
Fast Talk on a Slow Track by Rita Williams-Garcia (Penguin Books, 1991)—African American
Iceman by Chris Lynch (HarperCollins, 1994)
If Rock and Roll Were a Machine by Terry Davis (Delacorte, 1992)—college prep
Jacob Have I Loved by Katherine Paterson (Flare, 1980)—female protagonist
Jesse by Gary Soto (Harcourt Brace, 1994)—Mexican-American
Letters from the Mountain by Sherry Garland (Harcourt Brace, 1996)
The Melinda Zone by Margaret Willey (Bantam, 1993)—female protagonist
Out of the Dust by Karen Hesse (Scholastic, 1997)—female protagonist
Political Timber by Chris Lynch (HarperCollins, 1996)
Rhino by Sheila Solomon Klass (Scholastic, 1993)—female protagonist
Shiloh by Phyllis Reynolds Naylor (Dell, 1991)
Slave Day by Rob Thomas (Simon & Schuster, 1997)
Songs from Home by Joan Elizabeth Goodman (Harcourt Brace, 1994)—female protagonist
What Girls Learn by Karin Cook (Pantheon Books, 1997)—female protagonist
White Peak Farm by Berlie Doherty (Orchard Books, 1990)—female protagonist
Wish Your Were Here by Barbara Shoup (Hyperion, 1994)
Wringer by Jerry Spinelli (Harper Collins, 1997)

COPING WITH PROBLEMS AND/OR PARENTS WITH PROBLEMS

Baby Blues by Hope Wurnfeld (Viking, 1992)—female protagonist
Belle Prater's Boy by Ruth White (Bantam, 1996)
Bill by Chap Reaver (Delacorte, 1994)—female protagonist
Blood Relations (Blue-Eyed Son #2) by Chris Lynch (HarperCollins, 1996)
The Bones in the Cliff by James Stevenson (Dell, 1995)
Chicago Blues by Julie Reece Deever (HarperCollins, 1995)—female protagonist
Crosses by Shelley Stoehr (Delacorte, 1991)—female protagonist
David and Della by Paul Zindel (HarperCollins, 1993)
Don't You Dare Read This, Mrs. Dunphrey by Margaret Peterson Haddix (Simon & Schuster, 1996)—female protagonist
Dog Eat Dog (Blue-Eyed Son #3) by Chris Lynch (HarperCollins, 1996)
Face to Face by Marion Dane Bauer (Clarion Books, 1991)
Freak the Mighty by Rodman Philbrick (Scholastic, 1993)
The Glass House People by Kathryn Reiss (Harcourt Brace, 1992)—female protagonist
Ironman by Chris Crutcher (Greenwillow, 1995)
Kinship by Trudy Krisher (Delacorte, 1997)—female protagonist
Kool Ada by Sheila Solomon Klass (Scholastic, 1991)—female protagonist
Mary Wolf by Cynthia D. Grant (Simon & Schuster, 1995)—female protagonist
Mick (Blue-Eyed Son #1) by Chris Lynch (HarperCollins, 1996)
A Place to Call Home by Jackie French Koller (Simon & Schuster, 1997)—female protagonist
Shadow Man by Cynthia D. Grant (Atheneum, 1992)
Weird on the Outside by Shelley Stoehr (Delacorte, 1995)—female protagonist

(continued)

Figure 6.3

DEALING WITH DEATH

Acquainted with the Night by Sollace Hotze (Houghton Mifflin, 1992)—female protagonist
Missing May by Cynthia Rylant (Orchard Books, 1992)—female protagonist
My Mother's Ghost by Margaret Buffie (Kids Can Press, Ltd, 1992)—female protagonist
Rainy Season by Adele Griffin (Hyperion, 1996)—female protagonist
Say Goodnight, Gracie by Julie Reece Deaver (Harper & Row, 1988)—female protagonist
Silent Storm by Sherry Garland (Harcourt Brace, 1993)—female protagonist
The Silver Kiss by Annette Curtis Klause (Delacorte, 1990)—female protagonist
A Sunburned Prayer by Marc Talbert (Simon & Schuster, 1995)—Mexican American
Tears of a Tiger by Sharon M. Draper (Macmillan, 1994)—African-American
Tell Me Everything by Caroline Coman (Farrar, Straus and Giroux, 1993)—female protagonist
Toning the Sweep by Angela Johnson (Scholastic, 1994)—African American—female protagonist

DIVORCE, REMARRIAGE, ABANDONMENT

Dancing on the Edge by Han Nolan (Harcourt Brace, 1997)—female protagonist
The In-Between Days by Eve Bunting (Harper Trophy 1994)
Midnight Hour Encores by Bruce Brooks (HarperCollins, 1986)—female protagonist
One Bird by Kyoko Mori (Fawcett Juniper, 1996)—Japanese—female protagonist
Solitary Blue by Cynthia Voigt (Atheneum, 1983)
Witch Baby by Francesca Lia Block (HarperCollins, 1991)—female protagonist
The World of Daughter McGuire by Sharon Dennis Wyeth (Delacorte, 1994)—African-American—female protagonist
Walk Two Moons by Sharon Creech (HarperCollins, 1994)—female protagonist

FANTASY

The Golden Compass by Philip Pullman (Knopf, 1995)—female protagonist
The Hero and the Crown by Robin McKinley (Greenwillow, 1985)—female protagonist
Juniper by Monica Furlong (Random House, 1990)—female protagonist
A Knot in the Grain by Robin McKinley (Harper Trophy, 1994)
The Lion, The Witch and The Wardrobe by C.S. Lewis (Macmillan, 1950)
The Lost Years of Merlin by T.A. Barron (Philomel Books, 1996)
Sabriel by Garth Nix (HarperCollins, 1995)—female protagonist
The Subtle Knife by Philip Pullman (Knopf, 1996)
The Wings of a Falcon by Cynthia Voigt (Scholastic, 1993)
Zel by Donna Jo Napoli (Dutton, 1996)—female protagonist

HISTORICAL FICTION

Medieval

Catherine Called Birdy by Karen Cushman (Clarion, 1994)—the 1200s—female protagonist
The Midwife's Apprentice by Karen Cushman (Clarion, 1995)—the 1400s—female protagonist
The Ramsey Scallop by Frances Temple (Harper Trophy, 1994)—female protagonist

Early America

An Acquaintance with Darkness by Ann Rinaldi (Harcourt Brace, 1997)—female protagonist
Beyond the Western Sea Book One: The Escape from Home by Avi (Orchard Books, 1996)

(continued)

Figure 6.3

Beyond the Western Sea Book Two: Lord Kirkle's Money by Avi (Orchard Books, 1996)
Broken Days by Ann Rinaldi (Scholastic, 1996)—female protagonist
Bull Run by Paul Fleishman (Harper Trophy, 1993)
Lyddie by Katherine Paterson (Lodestar Books, 1991)—female protagonist
Indio by Sherry Garland (Harcourt Brace, 1993)—Native Americans—female protagonist
Mountain Valor by Gloria Houston (Philomel Books, 1994)—female protagonist
Nightjohn by Gary Paulsen (Bantam, 1993)—African-American—female protagonist
A Ride into Morning by Ann Rinaldi (Harcourt Brace, 1991)—female protagonist
Runs with Horses by Brian Burks (Harcourt Brace, 1995)—Native-American
Sarny by Gary Paulsen (Delacorte, 1997)—African-American—female protagonist
The Second Bend in the River by Ann Rinaldi (Scholastic, 1997)—Native American—Anglo female protagonist
Second Daughter: The Story of a Slave Girl by Mildred Pitts Walter (Scholastic, 1996)
A Stitch in Time by Ann Rinaldi (Scholastic, 1994)—female protagonist
Wolf by the Ears by Ann Rinaldi (Scholastic, 1991)—female protagonist

Twentieth Century America

Fallen Angels by Walter Dean Myers (Scholastic, 1988)—Vietnam War—African-American protagonist
Just Like Martin by Ossie Davis (Simon & Schuster, 1992) Civil Rights Era—African-American protagonist
Number the Stars by Lois Lowry (Dell, 1989)—female protagonist

ILLNESS/DISABILITIES

Crazy Lady by Jane Leslie Conly (Harper Trophy, 1993)
Humming Whispers by Angela Johnson (Orchard Books, 1995)—African-American—female protagonist
Izzy Willy Nilly by Cynthia Voigt (Atheneum, 1986)—female protagonist

INNER CONFLICTS/VALUE CLASHES

Baby Be-Bop by Francesca Lia Block (HarperCollins, 1995)
Come a Stranger by Cynthia Voigt (Atheneum, 1986)—African-American—female protagonist
Deliver Us From Evie by M.E. Kerr (HarperCollins, 1994)—female protagonist
Face the Dragon by Joyce Sweeney (Dell, 1990)
From the Notebooks of Melanin Sun by Jacqueline Woodson (Scholastic, 1995)—African-American
"Hello," I Lied by M.E. Kerr (HarperCollins, 1997)
On My Honor by Marion Dane Bauer (Clarion, 1986)
Memoirs of a Bookbat by Kathryn Lasky (Harcourt Brace, 1994)—female protagonist
Running Loose by Chris Crutcher (Dell, 1983)
Send Me Down a Miracle by Han Nolan (Harcourt Brace, 1996)—female protagonist
T-Backs, T-Shirts, Coat and Suit by E.L. Konigsburg (Atheneum, 1993)—female protagonist
There's a Girl in My Hammerlock by Jerry Spinelli (Simon & Schuster, 1991)—female protagonist   *(continued)*

Figure 6.3

MYSTERY/SUSPENSE

Breaking the Fall by Michael Cadnum (Viking, 1992)
Cabin 101 by Sherry Garland (Harcourt Brace, 1995)—Arawak Indian—female protagonist
Dreadful Sorry by Kathryn Reiss (Harcourt Brace, 1993)—female protagonist
Gallows Hill by Lois Duncan (Delacorte, 1997)—female protagonist
Ghost Canoe by Will Hobbs (Morrow, 1997)
The Man Who Was Poe by Avi (Avon, 1989)
Mr. Was by Pete Hautman (Simon & Schuster, 1996)
Mystery in Miami Beach by Harriet Feder (Lerner, 1992)—female protagonist
The Ruby in the Smoke by Philip Pullman (Knopf, 1985)—female protagonist
Shadow in the North by Philip Pullman (Knopf, 1986)—female protagonist
The Tiger in the Well by Philip Pullman (Knopf, 1990)—female protagonist
Skinhead by Jay Bennett (Fawcett Juniper, 1991)
Sing Me a Death Song by Jay Bennett (Fawcett Juniper, 1990)
Zoe Rising by Pam Conrad (HarperCollins, 1996)—female protagonist

PORTRAITS OF STRONG FAMILIES

The Dear One by Jacqueline Woodson (Delacorte, 1991)—African-American—female protagonist
The Fred Field by Barbara Hood Burgess (Delacorte, 1994)—African-American
Like Sisters on the Homefront by Rita Williams-Garcia (Lodestar Books,1995)—African-American—female protagonist
The Mozart Season by Virginia Euwer Wolff (Henry Holt, 1991)—female protagonist
The Rain Catchers by Jean Thesman (Houghton Mifflin, 1991)—female protagonist
Yolanda's Genius by Carol Fenner (Macmillan, 1995)—African-American—female protagonist
The Watsons Go to Birmingham—1963 by Christopher Paul Curtis (Delacorte, 1995)—African-American

PREJUDICE/DISCRIMINATION

Bat 6 by Virginia Euwer Wolff (Scholastic, 1998)—Japanese-American—female protagonist
Danger Zone by David Klass (Scholastic, 1993)—black-white
Dangerous Skies by Suzanne Fisher Staples (Farrar, 1996)—African-American
The Drowning of Stephan Jones by Bette Greene (Bantam, 1991)—gays
Drummers of Jericho by Carolyn Meyer (Harcourt Brace, 1995)—Jewish
Finding My Voice by Marie G. Lee (Houghton Mifflin, 1992)—Korean American—female protagonist
The Music of Summer by Rosa Guy (Delacorte, 1992) African-American—female protagonist
The Plague Year by Stephanie Tolan (Morrow, 1990)
The Road to Memphis by Mildred D. Taylor (Dial Books, 1990)—African American—female protagonist
Roll of Thunder, Hear My Cry by Mildred Taylor (Bantam, 1976)—African-American—female protagonist
The Shadowman's Way by Paul Pitts (Avon, 1992)—Navajo   (continued)

Figure 6.3

Spite Fences by Trudy Krisher (Delacorte, 1994)—female protagonist
Warriors Don't Cry by Melba Pattillo Beals (Pocket Books, 1995)—African-American (auto-biography)—female protagonist

RELATIONSHIPS

Moon Dancer by Margaret Rostowski (Harcourt Brace, 1995)—female protagonist
The Moves Make the Man by Bruce Brooks (Harper, 1984)—female protagonist
A Ring of Endless Light by Madeleine L'Engle (Dell, 1980)—female protagonist
Saving Lenny by Margaret Willey (Bantam, 1990)—female protagonist
Somewhere in the Darkness by Walter Dean Myers (Scholastic, 1992)—African-American
Stotan! by Chris Crutcher (Greenwillow, 1986)
Thwonk by Joan Bauer (Dell, 1995)—female protagonist
Weetzie Bat by Francesca Lia Block (Harper& Row, 1990)—female protagonist

SCIENCE AND/OR ENVIRONMENT

The Ancient One by T.A. Barron (Tor Book, 1992)—female protagonist
California Blue by David Klass (Scholastic, 1994)—college prep
Eva by Peter Dickinson (Dell, 1988)—female protagonist
Loch by Paul Zindel (HarperCollins, 1994)
The Merlin Effect by T.A. Barron (Putnam & Grosset, 1994)—female protagonist
A Bone from a Dry Sea by Peter Dickinson (Bantam 1992) college prep—female protagonist

SCIENCE FICTION

The Ear, the Eye, and the Arm by Nancy Farmer (Orchard Books, 1994)—African
The Giver by Lois Lowry (Houghton Mifflin, 1993)
Kokopelli's Flute by Will Hobbs (Atheneum, 1995)—Southwest Native Americans
Shade's Children by Garth Nix (HarperCollins, 1997)

TRAVELS TO ANOTHER TIME

Tag Against Time by Helen Hughes Vick (Harbinger House, 1996) Southwest Native Americans
A Time of Darkness by Sherryl Jordon (Scholastic, 1990)
Walker of Time by Helen Hughes Vick (Harbinger House, 1993)—Southwest Native Americans
Walker's Journey Home by Helen Hughes Vick (Harbinger House, 1995)—Southwest Native Americans

YOUNG PEOPLE SURVIVING ON THEIR OWN

Brian's Winter by Gary Paulsen (Delacorte, 1996)
The Crazy Horse Electric Game by Chris Crutcher (Dell, 1987)
Far North by Will Hobbs (Avon, 1996)
Hatchet by Gary Paulsen (Puffin, 1987)
Julie by Jean Craighead George (Harper Collins, 1994)—Innuit—female protagonist
Maniac Magee by Jerry Spinelli (Little, Brown and Co., 1990)
No Turning Back by Beverly Naidoo (HarperCollins, 1995)—black South African

Figure 6.3

Λ book like *Great Expectations* is difficult enough that we like to read portions of it aloud or in some cases to read the entire book aloud in chapters across a term. In that way Dickens' stylistic and linguistic twists don't get in the way of his great story. Some teachers see oral reading as time wasting. We do not. In our experience, every minute spent in oral reading leads to increased understanding by students, something we can't say for silent reading. Whether or not the teacher chooses to read *Great Expectations* aloud, some of the engagement activities in Figure 6.4 will prove useful.

- Have students report an incident from the book as if they were writing for a newspaper. They should remember to give the most important facts—who, when, where, what, why—in the opening sentences of their writing. They can add other details in descending order of importance.

- Have students write a letter to a character in the novel, say a letter to Pip about his frightening experience in the cemetery. Have them write letters to themselves (or to younger brothers and sisters) about terrifying experiences of their own.

- In collaborative groups, have students rewrite selected scenes as they might have been told from a different character's point of view. For example, a dinner scene might be written from the perspective of Pip's friend Joe or his wife, rather than through the eyes of Pip himself. Such a discussion of literature is especially useful when the narrator, like Pip, is blind to some of his own characteristics.

- In collaborative groups, have students write new scenes for the characters and act them out before the class. They can present events that took place before or after the story or can place a character in an entirely different situation.

- Let students write a list of rules of etiquette as Miss Havisham might have written them or a list of rules that children should obey as Pip's sister would have written them.

- After reading the opening cemetery scene, ask students what Pip might dream about that night.

- Discuss the emotions he must have felt, and possible dreams related to them. Then have each student write a dream for Pip.

- Let students discuss an authority figure who treated them as brusquely and unfeelingly as Pip's sister treated him. What would they like to say to that person?

- Discuss why Pip lied about what Miss Havisham's house was like. Discuss situations students remember where they felt they had to lie. What happened as a result of lying?

- Encourage students to create a protest campaign. If Pip were to get together with others his age, what would they have to say about how children are treated? Write the letter he and his group would compose to parents and/or care givers, explaining their reasoning and their feelings. Then have them create a petition that would go to a government official. Students could also create buttons with slogans on them and construct "bumper stickers" for carriages to get their message across.

- Explore history by having students write lists of characteristics (feelings, behavior of people, attitudes, living conditions, etc.) that are different today than they were at the time the book was written. Students can also describe the things that are the same. After sharing their lists with the class and discussing them, students can write on "Why I Prefer Living in the Twentieth Century" or "Why I Would Like to Have Lived in the Days of Dickens."

Figure 6.4   Activities for *Great Expectations*

We hope it is clear from these activities in Figure 6.4 that it is possible to engage students productively in the study of "serious literature." Steve vividly recalls from his first year of teaching, struggling with *Great Expectations,* assigning a chapter a night for silent reading, and flogging students through the discussion questions in the anthology on the following day. Teachers' options and alternatives are brighter now than they were in those shadowy times.

When a classic is used in the upper level literature courses, the teacher can assume that students are capable of reading and will read the novel at home. (That does not diminish the need for oral reading in class, we believe.) Students will often write reactions in their response log after reading each night's assignment. Another often-assigned novel by Dickens is *A Tale of Two Cities.* Here again, students are often lost in complexities of language and plot. Assuming a class of relatively independent readers, we offer the timetable in Figure 6.5 to show how the sorts of activities we have been discussing can be "orchestrated" in a classroom sequence.

Whether you use classics or young adult novels, whether students choose individual books or you choose one for the whole class, we hope it is clear that *what* you ask students to do with a novel affects their attitudes towards the book and their willingness to become engaged in it.

USING TALES IN THE CLASSROOM

Folktales, fairy tales, fables, and myths are other good choices of literature for the English classroom, and they offer yet another dimension of the relationship between literature and the adolescent. Most of the stories are short and can be read quickly. The meaning is accessible to students, so they can deal very successfully with other aspects of the stories. Since values, conflicts, and issues can usually be recognized, students can more easily discuss them, think about them, and go more deeply into the literature. These kinds of tales also provide many opportunities for research and report writing. Drama activities can spring up, as well as a myriad of writing ideas. Literary elements such as the use of figurative language, plot, stereotypical characterization, theme, setting, and point of view often arise naturally as discussion topics after students have done their reading.

Discussion of the characteristics of fairy tales, folktales, fables, and myths is often a concern of the students too. This genre provides many opportunities for the students to look at people and cultures as presented through literature and discuss the similarities and differences of such things as humans' hopes, expectations, fears, and joys. As a fringe benefit, the reading of myths and tales often provides students with a kind of cultural background that is useful in reading more traditional literature.

Many teachers are hesitant to use this literature because there is so much material in this genre that it is hard to know where to begin. Collections and anthologies are plentiful, and it is useful to enlist the aid of the librarian in finding some good resources. As in the book pass, we recommend that the teacher bring in collections of tales from the public or school library, keep them in the classroom,

Day 1. Introduce the novel by asking students in groups to respond to the following prereading questions: If your parents strongly disapproved of your choice of a boyfriend/girlfriend, would you reconsider your decision to see him/her? Do you believe the violence of killing is ever justified? Explain. If someone in your family was brutally murdered, how would you want the killer to be punished? Under what circumstances would you give up your life for another? Do you consider unquestioning devotion to a parent or spouse a positive or negative quality? Have groups report to the whole class on their responses. Then explain that each of these issues will arise in the novel.

Day 2. Read some of the text aloud. Have students read parts of their response logs from homework reading. Share questions and reactions with the whole class.

Day 3. Have students in collaborative groups of four begin to synthesize information for one of the following projects for the parts of the book read so far:

a. Have students do a visual representation of the plot, perhaps a cluster diagram, a timeline of events, a "map" or diagram of the plot.

b. Collect passages that illustrate attitudes and values of the aristocracy and of the peasants. Draw conclusions to share with the class.

c. Examine beginnings and endings of the chapters in the novel. What insights do these provide?

d. Create a "value chart" for the principal characters in the book, with quotations illustrating each value.

Day 4. Begin by having students in small groups share portions of their response log for 15 minutes. Then have each small group report to the class on questions or observations. If time permits, have students in groups make up a list of grievances the peasants had and a list of how the aristocrats would view those grievances. (These lists will be used later for a news writing assignment.)

Day 5. Read aloud or organize a readers' theater presentation, with small groups bringing portions of the novel to life through oral reading.

Day 6. Divide the class into peasants and the upper class. Each student then writes two pieces—a news story, a feature, an editorial, or a letter to the editor—focusing on the events read about so far. A good point in the novel to ask students to do this is right after the peasant child is killed by the carriage of one of the members of the upper class. The job of the members of the upper class is to assure the masses that everything is all right, while the peasants try to stir the people to revolt. If students are genuinely engaged with the novel, their feeling of moral outrage will be strong. (If the engagement isn't there, this might be a good time to pause for discussion of the barriers to comprehension.) Thanks to Rita Little's article "The Patriots vs the Aristocrats in *A Tale of Two Cities*" in *Ideas Plus*, Book Four pp. 33–34 (NCTE, 1986) for the seed of this idea.

Day 7. Have students, grouped according to whether they represent the peasants or upper class, work on putting a newspaper together. They select stories, decide on a title, work on a layout, and develop other kinds of fillers such as weather reports, horoscopes, and ads. (Be careful here that they don't let gimmickry substitute for substance; at the same time, there is opportunity here for satirical representation of some elements of the novel.)

Day 8. Read some pages of the book aloud to the students, and have them share reactions from their reading logs. Then form collaborative groups and assign each group a specific character to analyze. Students list everything they know about the character, including

(continued)

Figure 6.5   Daily Plans for *A Tale of Two Cities*

appearance, mannerisms, speech patterns, best and worst characteristics, things that bother them about the character, and behaviors that seem inconsistent or incomprehensible. During the last half of the hour, students report to the class and class members ask questions about the characters' actions, motivations, and so forth.

Day 9. For homework, have students locate a poem that exemplifies a particular theme, fits a specific character or setting, or captures the mood or events of the novel. (Keep your own anthologies available as a resource.) On the back of the poem, the students write the connections they see between the poem and novel. Collect these documents and read each poem to the class, giving students time to write down a few sentences about how they think the poem connects to the book. After two or three poems have been read, stop and ask students to share their comments with the class. Some very interesting discussions can ensue.

Day 10. Finish sharing the poems. Give time for any additional work needed on the newspaper. Read some pages aloud to the class toward the end of the hour.

Day 11. Have students in collaborative groups pick brief scenes they'd like to rewrite, quickly rewrite them, and present them to the class. Students like this activity because it allows them to have input into the novel and change parts that annoy or bother them.

Day 12. Brainstorm with the class critical issues, themes, and topics in the book. What is this novel about? Students can also suggest what makes *Tale of Two Cities* interesting as a piece of literature—its unique traits. Have the students comb their response logs for ideas which may have slipped between the cracks. This list of topics will serve as the starting point for the final writing associated with the novel. Students tentatively identify a topic they'd like to explore.

Day 13. Response logs for the whole novel are due. Spend the first part of the hour sharing responses either in groups or with the whole class. As a refresher, read some quotations from the book and play identification games with the class.

Day 14. Newspapers are completed. If the papers are duplicated or photocopied, have students assemble and distribute copies. If there is only a single copy of the newspaper, it is examined by students in small groups. Awards for best feature article, best headline, most creative papers, and the like may also be given by the class.

Day 15. For homework, have students draft an essay or choose one of the following activities:

- Write a book review. Did you think the plotline was too contrived and included too many coincidences? Were some characters cardboard-like? Were their actions believable? After reading a few book reviews from the newspaper or on the Internet, write your own review.

- You are Dr. Manette. Write a journal entry dated the first night of your imprisonment.

- Which characters did you like/loathe? Write a detailed letter to that character explaining the basis of your opinion, citing information from the novel to support your claims.

- Translate a short passage from the novel into modern prose.

- Create a talk show script. If a popular talk show host/hostess were to invite characters from this novel to the show, who would s/he choose and what would the issues be that s/he would want to explore? What kind of experts would be invited to speak to the same topic? After making these kinds of decisions, write the script of the show and perform it if that is possible.   *(continued)*

Figure 6.5

- Write "How I Came to Lead a Double Life," by Miss Pross's brother.
- Write a critique of the prison system as shown in the novel. If the topic of prisons or prisoner rights appeals to you, do a bit of research on the current theory behind the way prisons are run today. Then write a formal letter to the prison officials in the novel explaining what's wrong with their approach.
- Write on "this is `The best of times, the worst of times.'"
- Interview a character. In a group, construct a list of questions to ask that character. Then each person write up the interview, having the character answer all the questions.
- Write autobiographies for the characters in the novel. What were their lives like before and after the story? What kind of kid was Sydney Carton? What happened to his parents? How did his parents' deaths affect him? What made him loathe himself? Why did he feel stuck in the destructive cycle he was in? What was he attracted to in Lucie? Why did he fall in love with her? What made him determine to die for Charles? What did he learn about himself in the end? Try to answer as many of these questions as you can in his life story.
- As a class project, write and act out a new final chapter for the novel. Perhaps Charles Darnay is executed—would that change Sydney's relationship with Lucie? How would the doctor react to the death of his son-in-law? With Madame Defarge out of the way, will members of the doctor's family still be executed?

Figure 6.5

and have some class sessions in which students read and comment upon particular selections.

Once students have read several fairy tales and determined what makes them fairy tales, they might be ready for some fractured fairy tales. A terrific collection is *Tales from the Brothers Grimm and the Sisters Weird* by Vivian Vande Velde. Another author students would appreciate is Jon Scieszka who has fractured fairy tales with *The True Story of the Three Little Pigs, The Frog Prince Continued* and *The Stinky Cheese Man and other Fairly Stupid Tales* (Viking 1992).

Classroom Activities Using Tales

We like to read selected tales aloud to the class from time to time, but there is obviously a great deal of room for individualized reading in a "tales" unit. Have each student read several stories in a collection and then choose three or four for response. Questions and subjects which students can address in writing, in group discussion, or in whole-class discussion are included in Figure 6.6.

A folktales unit can also lead to some exciting culminating project work:

Select a tale with a theme or moral that your group liked. Then write and perform a skit that would give the same thematic message to your audience.

Research symbolic elements in the tales, such as what a hawk or a dove represents to different cultures. Present your findings to the class.

• What did you learn from reading about the characters' experiences?

• What did you learn about the culture that was associated with the tales you read?

• What were the various types of villains or heroes you found in the stories?

• Compare different virtues between cultures. What's important to each? What are the similarities? Differences?

• Do similar themes or motifs (such as questing) appear in any of the stories?

• What different things do animals represent in different cultures? For instance, are wolves always seen as sly and crafty?

• Compare the use of natural elements such as water and mountains in different stories.

• If you were going to read two stories to your four-year-old relative, which two would you pick?

• Which one would you not want to read to him or her? Explain your choices. Did the use of violence or moral lessons influence your choices?

• Television is said to be a bad influence on children, teaching them by bad examples to do bad things and form bad attitudes. Discuss violence, ugliness, and evil in the stories you have read. Would these stories be bad influences? Explain.

• Why do you believe people tell these kinds of tales? To teach? To entertain? To explain phenomena? Cite stories as evidence to support your point of view.

• Pick out three tales. List common elements such as beginnings and endings, characters, conflicts, and morals.

• Discuss the role (or lack of role) of women that you find in these tales. How are women viewed?

• How does the geographic location of the story affect its portrayal of nature and animals?

• What values seem important in the stories you have read? Can any of these values be traced to the culture? Why do you think these things are valued?

• Are there stereotypes in your tales? Are stepmothers always wicked? Old people weak or incompetent? What fears or values might these stereotypes be speaking to?

• Who is seen as being the best person or animal in these tales? What made these people or animals best? What does this tell you about what is valued in this culture?

Figure 6.6 "Tale" Activities

Make a fairy tale into a comic strip or booklet. Concentrate on the essentials in the story.

Draw illustrations for a tale. Explain why you drew them the way you did and why you chose what you did to illustrate.

Write a song or poem based on one of the tales.

Research different kinds of giants, ghosts, and witches. What traits do they have? Are these traits consistent within specific countries? For instance, are giants always evil and mean?

Of course any of the above ideas must be embedded in a context so students can see a purpose in what they are doing. It often works well to organize individual work around questions such as:

- Are the same animals (wolves, dogs, foxes) viewed the same way across cultures?
- What traits or characteristics in people or animals seem most valued across cultures?
- What is considered evil or wrong in these tales? Is it the same across cultures?
- What is considered humorous or funny in these tales? What can we learn from this?

If students are reading from many books, they can select the questions(s) they focus on. When reading and discussions have ended, students can compile the information they learned on a large chart which can be referred back to throughout the year (i.e. when doing a unit on the media, students could see if evil is portrayed in the same way on TV as it is in the tales).

As long as students understand that the purpose of what they are doing is to learn what the tales have to show them about different views of life, they will see sense in what they are doing and be more willing to become involved.

Reading Tales Aloud

Again, remember to do a good deal of oral reading of tales. In fact, tales such as these can be read aloud over and over because so many meanings emerge. Even if you cannot fit a great deal of time for using tales into the class structure, one way to expose students to this rich resource is to read the tales aloud as time permits. In those spare minutes at the end of the class, or when the schedule has been disrupted unexpectedly by such things as a fire drill, tales can often have a soothing effect. Jane Yolen's tales work especially well for this purpose, since her melodious language quiets students and draws them into her stories. Diana especially likes "Silent Bianca" in Yolen's *The Girl Who Cried Flowers and Other Tales* (Shocken Books 1974) not only because it extolled the virtues of silence but because it begins: "Once far to the North, where the world is lighted only by the softly flickering snow, a strange and beautiful child was born." For some reason language like that enthralls students and they want to hear more.

USING CHILDREN'S BOOKS IN THE SECONDARY CLASSROOM

Children's books often seem an unlikely resource to secondary teachers, who worry that students would be insulted by their use. However, Diana has used them for years in her urban high school class, so we present them as yet another way to extend the books/young adult relationship. Diana finds that if students know why children's books are in the classroom, even the oldest students find them a delight. She recalls, for example, using *Horton Hatches an Egg* by Dr. Seuss and having teenage sophisticates sitting on the edges of their seats in anticipation. Students were remembering the fun of reading and the joy of being read to, and their response to the children's books was extraordinarily positive.

Aside from helping to recapture that zest for reading and language, there are several other sound reasons for giving secondary students the chance to read and respond to children's books. As Benton and Fox point out, children's books are an excellent way to introduce or enlarge upon literary elements in the context of response. Students can much more easily grasp the idea of theme after they read or listen to a book such as Maurice Sendak's *Where the Wild Things Are.* They can find the central topics in Horton: Why does Horton stay on that egg? How do we feel about Maisie and people like her who fly off and leave their responsibilities to others?

What do picture books offer children in their reading development? Clearly those that achieve a successful integration of text and pictures in telling their stories are capable of giving their readers an aesthetic experience comparable to that gained through reading other forms of literature. Moreover, in the best of these books the narrative skills characteristic of the mature novel are to be found in simplified but effective forms. The use of juxtaposition, daydream, irony, the story within a story, climax and anti-climax. . . are present in many of the books. Such books provide not only a good, attractive introduction to more demanding literature; they are simultaneously an imaginative complement to stories that are told primarily through print alone.

From Michael Benton and Geoff Fox, *Teaching Literature: Nine to Fourteen* (London: Oxford University Press, 1985), p. 74. Reprinted by permission.

They can clearly see and explore character from the actions portrayed in a picture book such as *The Whale's Song* by Dyan Sheldon (Dial Books 1990). Through a study of children's literature, older students see more clearly why people like to read and how literature speaks to people's fears and other emotions. It is a simple transition, then, to see some of the same traits in young adult and adult literature. Diana finds it much easier for many secondary students to be objective about why children would respond to literature than to discuss elements in their own literature that are just too close for comfort.

Finally, students can learn from children's literature that it takes knowledge to write about the essentials of a topic even in a "simple" way. Children's books can also be used to model kinds of writing or as a stimulus to writing.

Activities for Children's Literature

But what can we ask students to DO with these picture books? Giving the books only a cursory reading would probably cause students to raise their eyebrows or elicit looks of puzzlement. We have to show students through the way we use the picture books that we want them to do things that will extend their literacy, like deepening their understanding of the craft of writing through an analysis of the books, or looking at the values embedded in the literature or developing criteria for evaluating the books. Some possibilities include:

- Have students use the basic plot line of a children's story and flesh it out, perhaps by adding dialogue. What kind of impact does this change have on the story?

- Pictures draw in the reader and create interest in children's books. Examine how good short story writers do this in the stories they write for young adults and adults.

- Since the text in picture books is so short, everything that is stated conveys a great deal of information. Have students take a novel or short story they have read and write it as a children's story, discussing what happens as they make changes.

- Have students turn a children's story into a radio play. They can flesh out conversations between characters, remaining true to the characterization in the story. Was this difficult to do? Did they get enough information about their characters? How did they figure out what their characters believed and felt?

- Have students read a dozen picture books and rank them from best to worst. Then list the criteria they used in judging the books, such as interest, pacing, being involved with the characters, and good use of language.

- Help the students list the themes brought out in several picture books. How do they recognize themes?

- Discuss book selection for children. Which characters in the books students have read could have a good or bad influence on children? Do you think some books should be kept from children? (And, by analogy, do the students feel they should be "protected" from some books themselves? This topic can lead to exciting explorations of book censorship cases.)

Integrating Children's Books into the Classroom Curriculum

But what about context? Just plopping children's books into the curriculum won't work since students must see how their use connects to what is going on in class. Several ideas to help teachers put children's books into a context that can fit into their already existing curriculum are shown in Figure 6.7.

TEACHING SHORT STORIES

Short pieces of fiction work well with young adults, particularly since they can be read in a single sitting and their often powerful impact can be experienced immediately. Short stories also allow a teacher to have students sample unfamiliar genres, such as fantasy or historical fiction.

We like to do a Short Story Blitz, where the teacher gathers short story collections from the library and the book room for the students to explore through browsing. The blitz exposes students to many kinds of stories at once, and almost all students will find stories they like. Keep an eye out particularly for story collections for teens such as *Sixteen: Short Stories by Outstanding Writers for Young Adults,* edited by Don Gallo (Dell 1984); *Visions: Nineteen Short Stories by Outstanding Writers for Young Adults,* edited by Don Gallo (Delacorte 1987); *Connections: Short*

• After a novel or short story has been read, bring in heaps of picture books. Ask students to think about how a specific character might respond to a specific book. Have students write and talk about their perceptions. For example, after reading *Freak the Mighty* by Rodman Philbrick, students read several picture books and pick out the three to five that Kevin would like the best or would most want to read. The same would be done for Max. One book that could be included in the selection brought into the classroom is *Goodbye Rune* by Marit Kaldhol and Wenche Oyen, which deals with death. Would Kevin, who has a fatal condition, even want to read the book? After Kevin's death, would Max feel comforted or shaken by the book? It is not essential that the teacher preselect books for this exercise. The important thing is letting kids find connections and explain why they feel the book relates to the character in some way or why it did not connect to the characters.

• After reading adult stories on a topic such as death, fear, or loneliness, find children's books on the same theme. Discuss similarities and differences and assess how each genre handles the topic.

• Before beginning a short story unit, bring in picture books and ask students to look especially for the kinds of behavior that is valued. Is perseverance something a character is rewarded for?

• Also ask students to look for connections between the picture books. Would a character from one story like a character from another story? Which characters are dealing with similar issues? As the short stories are read, students also look for connections. They then work to establish connections between the picture books and the short stories they have read.

• Study beginnings of several short stories and novels. Then study the beginnings of several children's books. How are these beginnings similar and different? What conclusions can students draw?

• Reading picture books makes the ways an author persuades a reader to like and dislike characters much more apparent. Have students work to find all the ways the author leads the reader to feel a specific way about a character. What do the drawings have to do with it? What are the characters in the pictures doing? What does the character say that causes the reader to feel a certain way? Look at the words used to describe the action. Does the author say that a character "sneered" or "whispered" or "giggled" when s/he is describing the way a character said something? Using all the evidence from the book, have students work in groups to figure out what the author is trying to show through the characterizations. Then encourage students to use some of these strategies in their own writing.

• Extend a concept. If students are learning about such things as irony or Puritanism, or are working to understand when such elements as setting and plot play a very important part in a story, have them look through picture books to find examples of these concepts.

Figure 6.7   Contexts for Using Children's Books

Stories by Outstanding Writers for Young Adults edited by Don Gallo (Dell 1989); *Join In: Multiethnic Short Stories* edited by Don Gallo (Delacorte 1993); *Ultimate Sports* edited by Don Gallo (Delacorte 1995); *Am I Blue: Coming Out from the Silence* edited by Marion Dane Bauer (HarperCollins 1994); *Going Where I'm Coming From: A Multicultural Anthology* edited by Anne Mazer (Persea Books 1995); *Mothers & Other Strangers* by Budge Wilson (Harcourt Brace 1996); *A Starfarer's Dozen* edited by Michael Stearns (Harcourt Brace 1995); *Book of Enchantments* by Patricia C.

Wrede (Harcourt Brace 1996); *Living Up the Street* by Gary Soto (Dell 1985); *American Dragons: Twenty-Five Asian American Voices* edited by Laurence Yep (HarperCollins 1993); *Tales from the Brothers Grimm and the Sisters Weird* by Vivian Vande Velde (Harcourt Brace 1995); *A Haunt of Ghosts* by Aiden Chambers & Others (Harper & Row 1987); *First Sightings: Contemporary Stories of American Youth* edited by John Loughery (Persea Books 1993); *Into the Widening World: International Coming-of-Age Stories* edited by John Loughery (Persea Books 1995); *No Easy Answers: Short Stories about Teenagers Making Tough Choices,* edited by Don Gallo (Delacorte 1997); and *From One Experience to Another* edited by Dr. M. Jerry Weiss and Helen S. Weiss (Tom Doherty Associates 1997). Teachers should make it clear that the purpose of browsing through these books is to choose stories that can be used as part of the classroom experience. Part of the students' job is to get others in the class interested in these stories, so they are to look for stories that not only interest them but also would interest others.

After students have had one or two class periods to go through the collections, each student picks out a favorite, shares it with two other group members and then participates in some of the following activities:

- Discuss the story and one character in it enough so that the group can find commonalities or connections between the characters from the three different stories. The three students then create a script of a conversation that could take place among the three characters from different stories.

- Students create a rap or a poem advertising the short story they liked.

- Discuss how story A would be different if a character from story B or C were put into it. How might this additional character change the story?

- Students complete five to ten statements about their story that begins with "If you want to read a story that" and ends with "then read (name of story) by (name of author)." An example is:

  If you want to read a story that:
  1. is moving and involving
  2. makes you angry at parents who abuse their kids
  3. helps you better understand teens who look different and act slow
  4. helps you understand how childhood events can still affect adolescents
  5. teaches you about what it takes to participate in a triathlon
  Then read "Superboy" by Chris Crutcher.

- If you're interested in analyzing how story elements work together, make a chart illustrating how significant each of the following elements were in your short story: plot, theme, setting, point of view, characterization. Explain to your group members why you consider some elements very important, some not very important, and some not at all important.

- If your group wants to see how the writer created the impact made in the story, brainstorm a list of elements that speak to the style and the way the story was written. Such a list might include: great use of imagery, several points of view shown, extensive use of foreshadowing, excellent use of dialog, variety of sentence structure. After you have created a list, discuss what these devices or elements did for the story.

If all students are reading from two or three collections, students can form groups based on which story they would like to work on for a Short Story Fair and complete many of the following activities which will culminate in the class putting on a Short Story Fair.

- The group develops introductory questions that they think will help interest other students in reading the story.
- Students create a short written testimonial or video clip explaining the impact the story had on them, the themes that struck them as important, the questions it raised in their minds, and the things it encouraged them to think about.
- Students put together an advertising campaign on their story. Posters are made and displayed in the classroom, buttons or badges are made and passed out, and a radio commercial on their story is taped.
- Students create a visual representation of their story and display it in the room. It can include such things as pictures or photos evocative of the story or a collage of images from the story.
- Students create a short, persuasive speech on why their story should receive the Pulitzer Prize. This is a good place for them to point out elements of craft and style in their story.

Teachers can invite other classes to the Short Story Fair to see the video clips, hear the commercials, and see the visual displays and any other work students have prepared. This class might vote on which short story they are now most interested in reading.

If a class reads several stories in common, students could do any of the following activities:

- Groups brainstorm kinds of awards that could be given to characters in the stories. Then they choose the most dramatic or impressive awards and tell the class which characters got the awards and why.
- Students write pamphlets about any of the issues raised in the short stories: "How Not to Fall in Love," "Being Alone and Liking it," "Ten Things Parents Absolutely Should Not Do in Public," "Signs of Deteriorating Mental Health."
- Students propose a new ending for one of the stories.
- Students work to figure out groupings. What themes are presented in these stories? Are the stories connected thematically or in other ways? Students explain their rationale for grouping the stories as they did.
- Students are asked: "Should some of these stories replace some of the ones in your anthology?" "If you were to put them in the anthology, what study or discussion questions would you raise?"

- Students write a script based on one of the stories. Students should remember to pick a story that they consider dramatic or important. Dialogue in these playlets should be faithful to the characterization of each person used.

For additional ideas on teaching short stories see Short Story Folders in Chapter 7.

Summing Up

The relationships among books and young readers are extraordinarily complex. As the reader will recognize, the techniques we have suggested are models which can be applied to many other genres, including nonfiction and drama. The critical point is that there are a great many sound alternatives to the teacher's standing in front of a class flogging students though a "discussion" of literary elements. Without diminishing the need to "teach" literature, we can engage students in reading in vigorous yet enlightening ways.

◆ EXPLORATIONS

◆ Try the book pass in the secondary or college classroom or the library. Talk with other teachers and students about what went well and what didn't, and come up with strategies to improve the book pass.

◆ Interview several English teachers or prospective teachers about their favorite young adult novels. Then interview students on the same topic. After lists are made up, exchange the lists among your interviewees so that students can see what the teachers like and teachers can see what the students like.

◆ Survey a college class you are in. Ask students what books they were assigned to read in high school English classes and which ones they actually read. Perhaps they would be willing to share their strategies if they pretended to read the book but didn't.

◆ Write about and then share your most memorable literature/reading experience in elementary, middle school, or high school. What kind of books were involved? Draw conclusions.

◆ Write down your memories of the kind of writing assignments you were asked to do in conjunction with the literature you read, how you did on them, and how you felt about doing them. Share your memories with others in a group and then draw conclusions from what you learn that can inform your own teaching.

◆ Talk to the school librarian about how young adult novels are selected for the school library and how he or she determines how much money can be allocated for them. Or if you have access to middle or high school students talk to them about how they select books for themselves.

◆ Try one of the activities from this chapter that you've never done before with a novel. How would you evaluate its success and worth? How did you change or adapt this activity for your class?

◆ After you have read a novel, skim through the activities in this chapter and pick the five you'd most like to do and the five you'd least like to do with your book. Write up a set of notes for a lesson. This can be a valuable resource to you when you ask students to become involved in books.

◆ Take a young adult novel you know well and create ten activities you could ask students to do with the novel. Try to make up five kinds of activities that are not suggested in this chapter.

◆ Look through an anthology used in secondary English classes. Create the plans for a thematic unit that uses material from the text as well as from young adult literature. Then create a series of assignments, activities, or discussion questions you could use with the unit.

◆ From the school or public library or Internet, make up a list of biographies you think students would find interesting. Design a short unit that incorporates biography, tapping into the kinds of activities suggested in this chapter.

◆ Design short activities or units that include tales to get students acquainted with the idea of using folktales and fairy tales in the classroom.

◆ Go to the public library and browse through the picture book section. Pick out three to five books you like and design activities you could use with these books in the secondary classroom.

◆ Select a novel, a poem, or a piece of non-fiction you have read recently. At the library find picture books that could extend or expand on the themes or issues in the other genre.

RELATED READINGS

Literature for Today's Young Adults 5th edition by Kenneth L. Donelson and Alleen Pace Nilsen (Longman 1997) offers a comprehensive look at the whole field of young adult literature. It includes the history of the genre, sections on the different types of fictions and nonfiction in the genre, and extensive book lists. Michael Cart's *From Romance to Realism: 50 Years of Growth and Change in Young Adult Literature* (HarperCollins 1996), a very readable book, discusses the growth of Y.A. literature. One focus of the book is the evolution of the themes and topics written about. Sprinkled throughout are Card's very pithy comments. *Teaching Young Adult Literature* by Jean E. Brown and Elaine C. Stephens (Wadsworth Publishing 1995) and *Reaching Adolescents: The Young Adult Book and the School* by Arthea J. S. Reed (Macmillan 1994) give teachers the kind of background information and classroom strategies they need to successfully use young adult literature in their classes. *Responding to Young Adult Literature* by Virginia R. Monseau (Boynton/Cook 1996) shows the power of what can happen when students are given the opportunity to read young adult literature in school, while *Reading Their World; The Young Adult Novel in the Classroom* edited by Virginia R. Monseau and Gary M. Salvner (Boynton/Cook 1992) addresses the issues of selection, pedagogy, and worth of the young adult novel. *Adolescent Literature as a Complement to the Classics* edited by Joan Kaywell (Christopher Gordon 1993) pairs classics with Y.A. novels and is chock full of literature-teaching strategies. For a more critical look at and analysis of young adult literature, try the Twayne Series. Each book in this series focuses on one author and his or her works

For teachers who would appreciate annotated book lists on Y.A. fiction and nonfiction, the National Council of Teachers of English has two very thorough books for secondary students: *Books for You: a Booklist for Senior High Students,* edited by Leila Christenbury (NCTE 1995) and *Your Reading: An Annotated Booklist for Middle and Junior High,* edited by Barbara G. Samuels and G. Kylene Beers (NCTE 1996). These books are regularly revised by NCTE committees. Also Arthea J. S. Reed's *Comics to Classics: A Guide to Books for Teens and Preteens* (Penguin 1994) not only includes extensive book annotations, but also has sections on sharing books, locating books, and on the reading preferences of teens. Frances Ann Day has two excellent books full of annotations that can help teachers find good multicultural literature. *Latina and Latino Voices in Literature* (Heinemann 1997) and *Multicultural Voices in Contemporary Literature* (Heinemann 1994) are packed with information on multicultural authors and their works.

Writers for Young Adults edited by Ted Hipple (Scribner's 1997), a series of three books, is a wonderful resource for students who want to know more about a particular author, what other books the author has written, and what other authors write in a similar style or on similar topics. These books contain essays on over one hundred thirty authors popular with young adults.

If the idea of using tales in the classroom appeals to you, look for Betty Bosma's *Fairy Tales, Fables, Legends, and Myths: Using Folk Literature in Your Classroom* (New York: Teachers College Press 1987) which focuses on using folktales in upper elementary and junior high classrooms.

To keep up on the latest in Y.A. books subscribe to *ALAN Review,* published three times a year by the Assembly on Literature for Adolescents of NCTE. In addition to over thirty book reviews each issue, a full range of articles on Y.A. literature appears regularly. The *English Journal* includes a good review column on Y.A. books, and *Language Arts* reviews children's literature as well. If you are interested in the critical issues surrounding children's and young adult's literature the *New Advocate* is a must-read magazine. Also IRA has a journal called *Signal* which focuses on young adult literature.

CHAPTER 7

ORGANIZING TO TEACH LITERATURE

Robert Scholes works to put the "teaching of literature" in perspective by challenging us to define what we think we are doing when we "teach literature." Until recently, English teachers saw their job in teaching literature as imbuing students with the country's literary heritage, teaching students how to take apart a text, and making sure students came to share their interpretation of a story. But other teachers are ready to push the curriculum in new directions; we hope you are among them. Since literature is written to make an impact, our jobs as teachers include giving room to students to examine the impact it makes on them, to see how one piece of text speaks to another, and to work to make this whole process help students "make sense of their worlds."

When we say we "teach literature," instead of saying we teach reading, or interpretation, or criticism, we are saying that we expound the wisdom and truth of our texts, that we are in fact priests and priestesses in the service of a secular scripture. . . . (But) (w)hat students need from us. . . is the kind of knowledge and skill that will enable them to make sense of their worlds, to determine their own interests, both individual and collective, to see through the manipulations of all sorts of texts in all sorts of media, and to express their own views in some appropriate manner. . . . (We) must . . . change the way that we define our task. To put it as directly, and perhaps as brutally, as possible, we must stop "teaching literature" and start "studying texts."

From Robert Scholes, *Textual Power* (New Haven: Yale University Press, 1985), pp. 12, 15, 16. Reprinted with permission.

We suggest that the teaching of literature is at least three-tiered. It involves:

- developing reading strategies and an awareness of the processes of reading. (See Chapter 5)
- interacting with and responding to the content of the literature (Chapters 5, 6, and 7 are saturated with examples)
- learning about the literature—the structure of stories, stylistic techniques, features of different genres , the social/historical context within the context of interpretation and response.

It is fair to say that in the past, learning about the literature has dominated the English class at the expense of making students aware of how to read more effectively and of encouraging students to interact and respond to the literature.

Following Scholes' advice to start "studying texts," we suggest, first, that the teacher move away from a lecture approach into an approach that values student interaction. Second, we suggest that teachers develop activities that encourage and validate student response, so students are dealing with the ideas in the literature, not just the elements or the structure or the historical background of the literature. As we discuss organizing to teach literature, we want to suggest the need for a balance among whole-class, group, and individual approaches.

THE WHOLE-CLASS APPROACH

Generally this involves assigning a single literary work—poem, short story, novel—to the class so that every student reads the same material. If the teacher assumes the role of lecturer or critic, the whole-class approach can be deadly dull. There is a danger of what we call the "plod approach," the chapter-by-chapter, day-by-day, week-after-week stretching out of a book. However, the common class experience with a work of literature can also provide students with models of response that can be carried over to their small group work. Further, reading books in common builds the language community of the classroom and can provide a touchstone for experiences for the rest of the year. Students can also add to each other's knowledge and perceptions by sharing in discussions, projects, and writings over a period of time. Whole-class books also can help balance what students would read on their own. Ethnic literature can be introduced through whole-class novels; students might not choose a book on the Holocaust on their own but could get involved in a book like *Number the Stars* by Lois Lowry or the *Diary of Anne Frank*. Students might be hesitant to pick up a book that deals with racism but could respond to *Roll of Thunder, Hear My Cry* by Mildred Taylor when they read it with a class. Teachers can also get students to try different genres such as fantasy (*The Ancient One* by T.A. Barron), introduce them to tales of enchantment (*A Knot in the Grain* by Robin McKinley) or look at what it's like to be considered dumb at school (*Freak the Mighty* by Rodman Philbrick).

More challenging books that deal with philosophical (*Heart of a Jaguar* by Marc Talbert) or moral issues (*The Giver* by Lois Lowry) are also books that students may

> The traditionalist asks constantly, "How can I make *Julius Caesar* meaningful to my students?" whereas the modernist asks, "Is *Julius Caesar* the best choice of reading for this group of students?"
>
> From G. Robert Carlsen in *Literature IS,* edited by Anne Sherrill and Terry C. Ley (Johnson City, Tenn.: Sabre, 1994).

need a nudge to read. Whole-class teaching provides an opportunity for the teacher to give that nudge and also creates ways for students to get involved with the novel at many levels.

Choosing a Book for the Whole Class

The use of literature as a common class experience calls for careful selection of books. G. Robert Carlsen would encourage us to ask is, "Is this a book that will engage virtually all my students?" It's important to recall that even though a title may appear on a great books list, unless it snares the vast majority of students in your class, you will likely fall into the plod approach and wind up having to "beat a dead horse" as well. Next you might ask: "What sort of response can I anticipate?" Are there issues and characters and actions that will lead to discussion? Can writing options be generated from the book? Are there research possibilities? Will the book give students a desire to read more and know more? Are there poems and short stories that could be used along with it? Are there films and TV programs touching on similar themes?

Teachers do not always consider such questions when they select books for their students. Choices often seem almost idiosyncratic but may often reflect the books that teachers studied in college. Additionally teachers often feel hamstrung when funds are low or nonexistent and they feel they must use the books from the book room.

Aside from these concerns however, many teachers are fearful about suggesting new books for student use. They may feel unqualified to pick out a quality book; they may believe that their job is to teach the old standbys; they may feel students' reading tastes are "deplorable," and believe their job is to elevate their tastes and expose them to "good" literature. We urge teachers to examine the beliefs they hold about texts and materials' selection and measure their beliefs against their knowledge of learning theory and the principles of literacy teaching.

How does one avoid the many problems inherent in selecting and teaching common literary works to an entire class? The key is often in the approach used and whether the teacher believes in transmission teaching or in teaching so students create meaning. Generally we have found the following principles keep student interest high.

- Use short pieces of text whenever possible.
- Don't ask students to answer teacher-generated questions after every piece or every chapter is read.
- Read aloud to your students often.
- Stop and ask students to dramatize or role play a scene just read.

- Keep the focus on student response, not on factual minutia.
- Give students time in small groups to address issues that come up during the reading.
- Vary whole group, small group, and individual activities daily.
- Have students use information in new ways—such as selecting a poem or picture that a character would like.
- Select books that speak to the interest of your students, written in language that is accessible to them.
- Pick and choose selections from the anthology that will make an impact on your students.

Introducing the Core Text

If a whole class is to be involved in a book, getting them interested in reading it is crucial. Teachers need to show students what to expect, build a sense of anticipation, or give a preview or a tasty tidbit of what is to come. The following suggestions are aimed at getting students to want to read the book:

- Read the title and ask the students to speculate about its significance. What does it promise? How does it pique interest or fail to?
- Begin with questions on issues that are part of the book. Before reading Hamlet, ask students a question such as , "If someone in your family was brutally murdered, how would you want the killer punished?"
- Create a situation that parallels one in the book and ask students to react to it—for instance, how might they interact with a kid with handicaps as Max did in *Freak the Mighty* . Then have them look for the way that a character reacted to a similar situation in the book.
- Bring in poems that set the theme or center on the emotions of some of the central characters. Mel Glenn's collections consist of poems mostly written from the point of view of students and it's easy to find poems in his collections that speak to many themes.
- Read the first few pages of the novel or even the first chapter. Have students predict the kinds of situations that will develop or speculate about what will happen to the characters, based on those first few pages.
- Read the first few pages aloud, asking kids to write about or sketch out the first images they see. What does Lennie from *Of Mice and Men* look like in their mind's eye? Could they envision the house in which Nick in *The Great Gatsby* lived? This technique promotes engagement and reinforces for students that experienced readers do see images and pictures in their minds as they read.
- Draw students into the novel by asking them to share experiences that parallel characters' experiences. For instance, ask them about negative or positive experiences with pets before they read such a book as *Shiloh* by Phyllis Reynolds Naylor.

- Make up startling or interesting statements about a key character. Before reading *Mr. Was* by Pete Hautman you could tell students that the second time the main character sees his grandfather, which is on the grandfather's death bed, the grandfather raises up, tries to strangle the main character, and then falls back dead.

- Give students a partial list of values that seem important to the character (acceptance, achievement, loyalty, honestly, etc.). Have the students rank these values from most important to least important and then look for the character who seems closest to or farthest from their own values.

- Read a provocative paragraph or scene to raise student interest.

- Pass out a survey or questionnaire or sentence starters that you composed based on the issues that surface in the book.

Once Under Way

Help students enter the story world. Students need to understand that experienced readers form pictures in their mind as they read; students need to be encouraged to do the same. Reinforce that we can all "see" the characters and ask students to work to "see" them by having them consciously talk about entering the story world. Have them imagine where the character is, how she might be feeling, expressions that might be on her face, what she is doing physically in the story at different points. To do this, students must use all the clues the author provides and then fill in or imagine the rest. Get in the habit of having students act out or role-play situations from chapters just read. Also encourage them to draw and/or write about what they see as they read.

Use response logs. We find this sort of journal writing effective in helping students prepare for class discussion. Logs are also a good way to help students understand what is going on in the novel by giving them a place to ask questions. Often these questions will be answerable by others in the class. Too, the questions students raise may not always be the ones you, the adult, would see as critical: "Why did Pip let his sister push him around?" Why did Cassie's grandmother make her apologize to Miz Lillian?" Nevertheless, such questions can often lead to the sorts of critical discussions you want to initiate. Response logs are a place for students to wonder, to comment, to predict, to question, to connect events to their own life.

Teaching single works to a whole class often invites productive small-group work as well. For instance, if one or more groups in the class opt to write a newspaper based on people and events in the novel, they can subdivide tasks and choose to write editorials, feature articles, or news, draw cartoons, create the top ten hits of the time period, construct ads, and so on. The rest of the class will be interested in the end product because it knows the literary work under discussion.

Here are some activities for small groups working on a common text:

- Create an eyewitness news team consisting of an anchor person, sportscaster, weather broadcaster, writers, and if possible, a camera crew using home or school video. Use events in the book as a focus for one of the broadcasts. If several groups do this activity, they can focus on different events in the text.

- Make a map of the locations mentioned in the story, including characters' houses and other prominent landmarks.

- Create dialogue for a scene that is alluded to but not actually presented.
- Do research on a topic related to the book and present the findings to the class. For instance, after reading *Toning the Sweep* by Angela Johnson, students can find information on how people come to accept an impending death, options to dying in the hospital, animals and plants that thrive in the desert, lynchings in the South, and how teens view their own grandparents. Students can interview people they know, use the library, and even create surveys in their quest to find answers. When presentations are given, the class has a stake in knowing about the topics.
- Take a main character and track his or her interests, likes, and dislikes through the novel or other work. Each group can take a different main character. They can come up with a list of books that their character might like, sharing book titles and justifying choices to the rest of the class.

While students are working in groups, the teacher can circulate from group to group, acting as a guide, which we also find a good way to monitor how well students are responding to the common novel as individuals.

SMALL-GROUP READING AND DISCUSSION

Although working together on full-length books can be a rewarding way to build classroom community, providing options for students in their reading is another way to encourage students to read widely. Often the teacher can find several students in any class who would like to examine a single book and work together or even create groups along genre lines when all students are reading different books. One group might all be reading horror, another science fiction or fantasy, another problem novels, and still another group reading books that are part of a series such as *Fear Street*. Small-group work also has the advantage of being self-supporting, with the group members, rather than the teacher, supplying the principal motivation and direction.

In moving toward small-group reading the teacher uses a multitext approach, having students read a number of works simultaneously rather than respond to a single text. Multitext teaching can be as complex as a totally individualized reading program, with every student reading a different book, or it can be relatively simple, with students in small groups reading two or three different books.

A convenient way to begin multitext teaching is to introduce several common readings to the whole class—four poems on a theme, three stories by a particular author— and then extend the range by having the students break into small groups to read different novels on the same theme or to examine longer works by the same author. Students remain in their groups for a period of time for reading and discussion, then meet with the class as a whole to share their responses.

Until the teacher knows many novels well and can initially give guidance and structure to these small groups, the task may seem difficult. However, if teachers give the same kind of task to each group until they know several novels well, the problem of preparing separate discussion questions for each group each day is solved. Students can:

[handwritten margin note: though observed teacher get lost in worksheets]

- Begin each small group with a sharing of questions and comments from their response log.
- Be responsible on different days for developing discussion questions.
- Make lists of the issues and themes presented in the book.
- Brainstorm a list of values and then rank the main characters in terms of which values are most important to them (see Figure 7.1).
- Discuss where they would most like to intervene in the story.
- Discuss what seems realistic or unrealistic in the novel.
- Talk about what's most difficult to understand in the novel and how the author could have made this easier to grasp.
- Discuss conflicts in the book and what characters learn through resolving the conflicts.

Each day of class need not be spent in small groups. The teacher can vary the format by having students write about some aspects of the book during class. Also, whole-class discussions on such topics as "the character who is hardest to understand" can help provide the variety needed in a class.

Character: Rank the values in order from most important to the character to least important to the character. If the character's values change, then rank the values both before and after the change.

_____ 1. Acceptance (approval by others)		_____ 12. Love	
_____ 2. Achievement		_____ 13. Loyalty	
_____ 3. Aesthetics		_____ 14. Morality	
_____ 4. Altruism		_____ 15. Physical appearance	
_____ 5. Autonomy		_____ 16. Pleasure	
_____ 6. Companionship (friend-ship)		_____ 17. Power	
_____ 7. Creativity		_____ 18. Recognition	
_____ 8. Health		_____ 19. Religious faith	
_____ 9. Honesty		_____ 20. Self-respect	
_____ 10. Justice		_____ 21. Skill	
_____ 11. Knowledge		_____ 22. Wealth	

From *Writing about Literature* by Elizabeth A. Kahn, Carolyn Calhus Walter, and Larry R. Johannessen. (NCTE/ERIC), p. 30. Copyright © 1984 by the National Council of Teachers of English. Reprinted with permission.

Figure 7.1   Literary Characters' Value Profile

As the above suggestions imply, the teacher does not simply turn the students loose to proceed any which way. By preparing group activities and helping students generate questions they can discuss, the teacher will help students find a sense of direction in their reading. As students become more experienced in this sort of small-group work, the teacher can reduce the amount of direction.

Literature circles provide a curricular structure to support children in exploring their rough draft understandings of literature with other readers. Literature circles encourage children to expand and critique their understandings about their reading through dialogue with other readers.

From Kathy Short, foreword to *Literature Circles and Response,* edited by Bonnie Hill, Nancy J. Johnson, and Katherine Noe (Norwood, Mass.: Christopher-Gordon Publishers, © 1995), p.x.

Using Literature Circles

Literature circles has become an increasingly popular term for the process of students getting together with other students to discuss a common text. In literature circles the focus is on inquiry and exploration, not on literary elements or agreeing on one interpretation. Instead of instructing students just to get together and talk about the book, which could cause chaos and uncertainty in many classrooms, teachers often familiarize students with the procedure in increments. One way to begin is to pass out note cards and as students read have them write down questions that they have about the book as well as the issues, characters, events they want to talk about. As students are moving to get into groups, the teacher can collect the cards and list five to ten of the student questions on the board and ask each group to begin with any of these issues. For instance, as students read *Izzy Willy-Nilly* by Cynthia Voigt concerns might include: Why didn't the kids treat Marco the same way they treated Izzy? How can her best friends leave her when she needs them? Izzy's dad didn't seem to handle the accident very well—let's talk about his reaction. Do we have a different attitude about drinking and driving? What things have you done because of peer pressure? What things do we take for granted? How important are looks, really? What would it be like to be crippled or handicapped?

Students must see that they are doing this work for a reason and that they will get credit for doing this work. To show students that we value the meaning they make through discussion, giving checks in the grade book to indicate participation is usually enough. As students get more familiar with this kind of discussion, they may find the work itself rewarding. It usually works best if students have a task they are working to complete through the discussion. So near the end of the class each group can be asked to share: common group perceptions of the novel, areas they had the most divergent views on, what the group's major concern was with the book as reflected through the discussion, what they enjoyed discussing the most or what they found out about the way other's viewed the book. Students learn more about their own and others' views as they share these kinds of responses with the whole class. Students may also benefit by writing in their response log how their understandings of the book changed and expanded through the discussion.

Some teachers who feel their students need more structure begin using literature circles by assigning roles to students so they can see more ways that the literature can be thought about or approached. Often the discussion leader is responsible for generating questions; another student works to make connections; another may look for passages to discuss or comment on. Several excellent books have been written which show literature circles in action in a wide variety of classrooms (see recommended readings). Some also spell out the many roles students may be assigned as they begin their journey toward completely student-generated literature discussions.

INDIVIDUALIZED READING

Individualized or "free" reading programs became popular at about the time the paperback revolution of the late 1950s and 1960s made inexpensive quality literature available. Up to that time, common class reading of literary materials was the dominant mode of instruction.

Like multitext teaching, individualized reading calls for new roles for English teachers. Instead of leading a class through activities aimed at eliciting a response and connection to the book, the teacher is often a book or reading resource, working closely with students to learn about and to suggest titles. Individualized reading programs also involve a fair amount of bookkeeping, and the teacher must develop some sort of management procedures to record student progress. Techniques range from cumulative reading folders that the students maintain themselves to large posters or charts on which the teacher or students can note the titles that have been read.

Launching an individualized reading program is not simply a matter of supplying books in profusion and letting the students "have at it." Most teachers find they need to supply additional structure to make the program work. Sometimes individualized reading can be linked to thematic or other kinds of instructional units. After the class has examined some common literary works, each student launches a personal reading program. In this way, the books read by individual students are related to the common interests of the class, creating a natural audience for sharing.

In some schools, individualized reading programs become formal courses, frequently with a title like "Reading For Pleasure." Such courses have been controversial and have come under attack from both parents and other teachers. "Why should kids get credit just for reading for fun?"is the question most often raised. As far as we are concerned the more fun connected with reading, the better. Given the wealth of reading materials available at all levels, K-12, there is no reason the reading act need be unpleasant. Too often, individualized reading is slotted into the reading course only, while other English classes continue with one anthology using the whole-class approach. In some schools the "Reading for Pleasure" class is associated with students of low motivation or low reading ability. When this happens, the free-reading course is seen as a last resort, a course to be recommended when the students cannot be compelled or cajoled into reading teacher-selected material. In short, individualized reading programs should be well integrated into the entire English or language arts curriculum.

Although individualized reading may sound like an unmanageable monster to the teacher, there are several ways it can be made to work in the classroom. One kind of plan is illustrated in Figure 7.2.

Another way to work individualized reading into the regular class is to give students occasional reading days in class. After they have read the bulk of the book at home, have them do group activities on their books once or twice a month in class. Whole-class gatherings for book sharing are an important aspect of individualized reading programs. During each marking period students can make presentations to the whole class to build interest in their books. If students know that reading is an integral part of the class and that it "counts" for something by being evaluated or graded, they are much more likely to be enthusiastic about it. Simply assigning book

[handwritten margin note: — how to incorporate young adult]

The following suggestions can be used for part of class time as students are working to complete a book of their own choosing. Students can be given time in class to read and to do other written responses as well as participate in the group discussions.

Day One: Before books are read you will be assigned to a group. On the first day in the group, so you can get a sense of each other, talk about books from the past that you really liked and got involved in as well as ones you didn't like or couldn't get involved in. Work to explain the reasons you could or couldn't get involved. After this introduction to the group, write in your response logs what you learned about others' preferences in reading material and how you think the group can help you get the most out of your book.

Day Two: Read the first lines of your book aloud and talk about what pulled you into the book or what made it hard to get involved. Discuss whether you are now really into the book, what that means to you, and how you measure or figure out when you're really into a book. Discuss who had the best first line or paragraph. Talk about your own reading process and how you get into the story world. An example would be: *the language of the fantasy sweeps me away from the first line. I relax, let the words wash over me and the pictures just jump out at me. I'm there almost immediately.*

Day Three: Gaps. Share any gaps you've already noticed. What does the author assume you will fill in for yourself? How did you do this? Share what the characters are like, how you imagine them, what they look like. To whom are you drawn? Who don't you trust?

Assignment: Work on the names of the characters in your response log. First, free-associate what the names of the characters mean to you. Then look up the meanings of the names in a dictionary or a book of baby names. Do your characters seem to fit their names? Why do you think the author named the characters the way he or she did?

Day Four: Issues/Themes. On what does your book seem to focus? With what problems or issues are your characters dealing? How are they reacting? What advice would you like to give one of your characters? What do you wish other characters knew about your character and his or her problems.

Day Five: Values. Fill out a value sheet (Figure 7.1) and compare your character's values to those of the characters in the other books in your group. From what your group members have said, which of these characters do you admire the most so far? Which one is hardest for you to understand?

(continued)

Figure 7.2 What Can I Have Students Do During Class Time if They're All Reading Different Books?

Assignment in response log: Fill out a value sheet for yourself, compare your values to your characters's values, then write in your response log the areas of similarity and difference between you and your character.

Day Six: Craft. What does your author do to keep the story moving? Does she use foreshadowing, flashbacks, starting at the end? What keeps you reading? Do you consider this author a good writer? Find a passage you consider well-written and read it to your group. Explain why you consider it to be good writing.

Day Seven: Connections. How does this book connect to you in terms of kinds of people in it, similar experiences you've had, similar feelings you've had? Have you had to deal with the same issues as the characters or met people just like this? Do you admire and/or understand why the character undertakes or does the kinds of things he does?

Day Eight: A School Visit. Think about your main character visiting your school today. How would he or she get along? What might be unusual about him or her in the context of your school? What kinds of people would your character choose for friends? What types of things would he or she do during lunch hour? What classes would your character take? What school rules would be hardest for your character to follow? In what sports, clubs, or activities would she or he be involved? After each group member has had a turn describing a character's visit to school, discuss which of your group's characters would have the easiest/hardest time fitting in.

Day Nine: Heroes and Goals. Think about people, living and dead whom your character would consider a hero or heroine. What characteristics or actions would your character admire? Explain to your group why you selected the heroes you did. Next think about your character's goals in life. What do you think your character most wants to achieve through his or her life?

Day 10: What have you learned about life and about the world through this book? Before you discuss this with your group, you might want to organize your thinking using the following fill-in. Before I read this book I didn't realize _____ but now I _____. Push yourself to fill out five to eight of this kind of statement before you share with your group, so you can really think about all you have gotten out of the book.

Day 11: Evaluating the Story Elements. Think about plot development, importance of setting, depth of characterization, scope of themes, and development of conflict in your novel. Before you discuss with your group, rank these elements in terms of which were most important or most developed in your novel. Share your thinking with your group. Did you notice whether or not different kinds of novels emphasize different elements? Did most of your novels emphasize the same elements? Which elements seemed least important?

Day 12: Analyze and Evaluate. Model your group talk after a Siskel and Ebert show where they give one or two thumbs up or down for movies. Before rating your book, think in terms of the impact it made on you, how good the writing and craft was, how well developed and realistic your story line was, or if anything got in your way of understanding or of being involved. After considering all the elements you can, share your rating with other group members.

Days 13 and 14: Work on projects. Everyone might create a word collage for their book so others can see at a glance what the book is about. You may then select a project from a list of options that you will either do alone or with another student. These projects will be presented to the whole class so everyone can get a feel for what your book was about.

Figure 7.2

reports without any other activities related to their reading or any other mention of reading in class does not produce the avid readers we would like students to be.

In addition, a free-reading program opens unique opportunities for the teacher to individualize in other areas. For example, while students spend time reading, the teacher is free to consult with individuals about their work. A conference with a student on his or her writing problems can take place during this time. Further, as student reading is individualized, it becomes easier for students to create their own projects and responses to the literature as they search for ways to share their excitement about their book to the whole class (see Chapter 5 for Alternatives to Book Reports).

INVOLVING STUDENTS IN LOCATING AND CREATING LITERATURE RESOURCES

Whatever we are doing in our English classes, we always strive to involve our students and we always hope that students will enjoy what we ask them to do. Having them participate in the creation of literature folders not only insures that they will find material they want to read, but is another way to individualize and allow students to select their own reading material. Of course, just having literature folders or books sitting on classroom shelves does not mean students will use them unless we build their use into our classroom plans. Part of the discussion that follows will not only explain how to have students create literature folders but also how you can fit this into the context of your classroom work.

Short Story Folders

Bring in old anthologies, single copies of short story collections, as well as all the library short story collections you can get your hands on. Assign your students the task of selecting three short stories that they like and that they feel go together in some way. Have them make photocopies of the stories unless they can rip them out of old anthologies. In the folder along with the short stories they place the following:

- A one-page explanation of why they selected the stories and how they think they are connected.
- Three challenges they issue to any readers of the packet. Examples include: I challenge you to find anything likable about this character. I challenge you to find anything slow about this story. I challenge you to find a more unforgettable character than___.
- A writing response to one of the following teacher-created options:
  - Write newspapers that might appear in the various characters' towns.
  - Have a character from one story interview a character in another for a newspaper report or a magazine feature article. This can be done through writing or role-playing.
  - Assume that several of the families that appeared in the short stories move into the same neighborhood. Who would live next door to whom? Who would live way down the street? Who would associate with whom? Why?

- Fit selected stories into a time line representing a central issue. How have human rights, women's rights, views of freedom, or images of violence changed over time?
- Design a proposal for a new public broadcasting series based on selected stories.
- Three to five writing options they have created.
- A discussion of the elements of plot, theme, setting, and characterization explaining which elements seemed most important in which story.
- A list of characters they liked best or were most sympathetic to and why, followed by a list of characters they disliked.

When packets have been completed, teachers can use the packets as assigned parts of class work. The teacher could ask each student to read one packet a week during those stray moments when they have completed their work. Or teachers could have small groups respond to packets together.

After reading a packet, the reader briefly writes about the connections he or she saw among the stories, responds to one of the challenges, selects either a teacher-generated or student-generated writing option to complete, and responds to the creator's view of which elements were most important and which characters he or she liked.

Research Packets

To whet students' appetites to know more as well as to help them learn that research can be fun, have each student create a research packet which is actually a collection of resources and annotations on a specific topic. Students can be given the following directions:

> Your job is to prepare an exhaustive list of the resources in the library and the community that could be used to gain information on your topic. Include such resources as community organizations, university departments, knowledgeable people, where students can go on field trips to gain an understanding of the issue. From the library you can find what resources are available on the Internet, what web pages may help with information on the topic, what fiction and non-fiction addresses the topic, what CD-ROMs or laser disks, films or videos, music, or art might provide information on the topic. Your resource packet should be organized by type of resource and should include brief annotations (or explanations) of each resource as well as complete bibliographic information. Your booklet should include a minimum of three resources from the community, 10 from the library (books, magazines, filmstrips etc), 5 from the Internet, and any combination of 5 resources that include films, music, art, or CD-ROMs.
>
> As you begin your quest to amass helpful resources, keep notes an all parts of your journey. This record of your research will be almost as helpful to students as the resources themselves. Include in your record the "map" of your topic, how you started, what you looked up first or went to, what key words you used, what led to dead ends and what resulted in getting good resources. This will be part of your packet.
>
> When your packet is complete, make an attractive cover and fasten the whole thing together in some way.

Besides turning in your resource packet, you will also write a short paper explaining what you learned about research and what you learned about your topic simply by searching for resources on it.

These research packets can be used in several ways:

1. As part of a unit that introduces students to research and works to broaden their view of what resources are. Give one resource packet to each student. Create questions you want them to read for such as: which packet was most interesting, which kind of source hadn't you thought about or heard about before, etc. Students read all the packets in their group. After discussing the packets with each other, they report to the class which packet they found most interesting, which packet had the most diverse resources, which packet had the best topic,which packet had the most helpful explanations on the research procedures used etc.

By working with packets with solid resources, students see more possibilities for the kinds of resources that exist on a specific topic.

2. To evaluate the effectiveness of the resources. Give each student a packet and have him or her evaluate the resources in terms of which ones give the best information. To do this they will have to go to the library and read or view the actual source. Have them investigate about five sources for this study, rank the sources from high to low, and write up reasons for their rankings. They can share their findings in small groups so students will get a broader view of what makes a resource a good one.

Selecting Non-Fiction Books for the Class

Libraries are usually crawling with terrific non-fiction books. There are books on extraterrestials, books on loathsome-looking insects, books on ghosts, books on how bridges are constructed, books on coping with divorce. Each week assign two different students to go to the library, select, and bring back to class two books they think are fascinating. Allow the students a few minutes to show the class the books and explain why they selected these books. They can do this on the day you set aside for this purpose each week while you are taking attendance. Place the books on a shelf where students can have access to them when they are working independently or when they have completed their work for the day. Have students read parts of at least two of these books per month and write a response to them in their logs. Be sure to give credit for completing this work.

Having students create packets that other students can use helps the busy teacher bring fresh new material into the class.

THE TEACHER AS READING RESOURCE

As one moves toward involving students in their own reading, the teacher needs to help each student find appropriate reading material. The reading process is supported powerfully if a teacher is present at the right times to suggest titles, without pressuring the students to accept recommendations.

In sheer quantity, the resources that should be made available to students are staggering. Paperback catalogs and book lists provide literally thousands of book titles that are appropriate at various levels of school. Moreover, at last count some thirty-five thousand magazines were published regularly in this country, many of which are useful to a teacher of English. Add to that the newspapers, brochures, pamphlets, fliers, and booklets that are readily available and should be brought into a class at the appropriate times. A teacher must also know nonprint media in order to serve as a resource person on films, television, recordings, and radio.

This variety means that the English teacher must be "bibliographically agile." If a student develops a sudden interest in cacti or Strindberg or stage direction or poetry, the teacher should be able to help locate material that will satisfy those interests. Teachers of literature must know far more than the books covered in four years of college English. They must know and have access to many reading resources that may interest any growing members of the community of language. (In the previous chapter we mentioned several book review and selection guides to books appropriate for young readers.)

However, for many teachers, the problem is not so much locating titles as getting the actual books into the classroom. Book budgets are slim and are often consumed by the purchase of adopted anthologies. Libraries are poorly "booked," and in some cases the stereotypical librarian who doesn't like to have books circulate is still running things behind the desk. How do you bring more literature into the classroom?

- Contact your local paperback distributor for free or sample copies and for unsold back issues of newspapers, magazines, and even books.
- Call your local newspaper. They are usually willing to give copies of back issues out free to teachers. It usually involves driving to the newspaper's building to pick up the papers.
- Visit garage sales. Often you can find quality paperbacks at rock-bottom prices.
- Visit the Salvation Army stores or used book stores. Although the selection isn't wide, there are usually several young adult novels available as well as fascinating non-fiction titles.
- Watch for local library sales. Community members donate books and libraries get rid of books they don't think they need. Relatively new young adult novels are often available.
- Look in the book room for old, no-longer-used anthologies. Rip them apart, keeping the poems, short stories, and plays to which your classes respond favorably.
- Seek contributions of reading material from the community and from the students. Many paperbacks rest unread on home bookshelves, and they can easily be obtained for school.
- Encourage students to buy from the paperback book clubs such as Tab or Troll. For every book a student purchases the teacher gets "points" which can be turned in for books for the classroom.
- Have a dime book sale/drive. Students get ten cents credit for each book they bring in. At the sale they can spend it on books others brought in which only

The teacher — how to increase your library — (handwritten margin note)

cost ten cents. Students who don't bring books in can still get a book for the bargain price of ten cents.

Overall, our advice to the teacher who is just moving into the area of individualized reading is to start small and then expand. Initially, a classroom library may contain only twenty-five to fifty titles. That number can be gradually increased as the teacher locates new book sources and becomes more skilled at keeping track of individual student readers.

THE TEACHER AS READING PROPAGANDIST

Implicit, too, in the multitext and individualized programs is the role of the English teacher as book promoter, one who unabashedly "sells" literature and reading to young people, telling them about books, placing books in their hands, reviewing books, sharing responses. One clue to the importance of this role is suggested by the success of TV novels. Such books as the Star Wars spinoffs sell well as a result of the publicity they receive. Apparently, most readers want to know something about a book before they plunge into it.

To propagandize about literature one can:

- Put up attractive book posters advertising interesting reading, which are often available at state and national conventions where booksellers have displays.
- Include many short books in your class library.
- Habitually include free or individualized reading as part of any English course.
- Have "hot" books available to the extent that the school and community standards will allow it. Also look in the school library for new books that you could bring to your students' attention in your class.
- Include series books: *Fear Street, Nancy Drew, Sweet Valley High, Star Wars.*
- Provide book talks periodically, telling students what's available in an area or field. If you don't like to do book talks yourself, call on your librarian.
- Make audiovisual versions of books readily available: audio tapes, filmstrips, videos.
- Start a book club that meets during lunch hours or after school where book lovers can talk about the books they are reading and recommend books to each other.
- Share Internet addresses of book resources so students with access to the web can find out about even more books. One such address is **Young Adult Reading** <http://www.spruceridge.com/reading>. Publishers are putting sites on the Internet which include information on their newest books. The HarperChildren's site is at <http://www.harperchildrens.com/index.htm>.
- Entice your students to read excellent young adult novels by showing them books in the reference section in the library that focus on authors and their works. Scribner's *Writers for Young Adults* edited by Ted Hipple is a series of

essays on more than one hundred young adult authors which give readers a taste of what kind of books the authors write, some tidbits about their lives, as well as evaluative comments about their work.

ORGANIZING THE LITERATURE PROGRAM

> We need to develop programs that emphasize students' ability to develop and defend their interpretations of literary selection, rather than ones that focus only on knowledge about texts, authors, and terminology.
>
> From Arthur Applebee, "The Background for Reform" in *Literature Instruction: A Focus on Student Response*, edited by Judith Langer, p. 12. Copyright © 1992 by the National Council of Teachers of English. Reprinted with permission.

Over the years, four principal ways of focusing literary study have predominated in the colleges and the schools:

1. The historical/chronological approach, featuring survey and period courses and a concern for literary history. (Often these surveys are done by individual nations, e.g. British literature.)

2. The author approach, with a concern for the collected works of a single writer and the relationships between the writer's biography and evolution as a writer.

3. The genre approach, which directs literary study through the examination of the principal forms of writing: poetry, essay, drama, fiction.

4. The masterpiece or great books approach, which unifies its study through the choice of widely accepted classics.

In any college or secondary school curriculum, one often finds a number of courses based on one of these four organizing features.

Although each of the above approaches may have value for the literary scholar, we suggest, as Applebee implies, that each takes the content of literary scholarship rather than human experience as its starting point. If one is teaching a genre unit such as poetry or drama, the common denominator of instruction is still the elements of a literary form, leading the teacher inevitably to such questions as, "What is the definition of poem?" "Why is Dr. Zhivago a 'better' film than Gone with the Wind?" "What is drama?" In a survey or period course, discussion emphasizes historical matters, concentrating on knowledge of times and writings. Each of the other approaches similarly initiates discussion in terms of critical content, and the students' personal involvement necessarily gets second billing.

To some extent, a fifth approach, humanities, has broken the tradition of criticism-centered courses by focusing on issues and ideas. Yet in practice, humanities courses are often simply grand survey courses in the historical/chronological mode, or they reduce truly interdisciplinary questions to a comparison of artistic genres.

We would like to suggest other ways to organize the teaching of literature.

1. *Thematic approach.* In this approach we start with a big theme (see Figure 7.3) or idea or question. For instance, to examine the concept of war, the teacher can begin by pairing *The Red Badge of Courage* by Stephen Crane with *Fallen Angels* by Walter Dean Myers so students can see war up close. Of course, in these novels there is a lot of conflict in the minds of the troops as to how they feel about their own participation, so that is talked about. In their literature logs students react and respond to what they are reading and discuss in small groups such things as how difficult or easy it is to follow what is happening in the books. You can bring in the writer's craft here as students work to figure out why Crane's novel seems so disorganized. Students usually come back to the content he is writing about and often can see that his novel is almost flashes of scenes. After doing further work on the novel, dealing with characters and figuring out what is happening, ask students to find lines of text that are so vivid they can be turned into found poems. This is a very effective way to teach imagery and the impact it can have on a reader.

The important thing to remember is that though this is a thematic unit, the purpose is not simply to identify the theme of war in the pieces examined, but to use the theme as an umbrella under which lots of texts and experiences can come together. Another part of the unit can be the dramatization of war poems. Bring in six to ten poems, have students divide into groups and work to visually and orally represent the meaning of the poems through the presentations. Other material that can be brought in includes videos dealing with war, such as *Born on the Fourth of July*, that will give students lots to think about. As end projects students can interview people associated with the Gulf War, the Vietnam War or the "peace action" in Korea. Students can write poems, stories, essays, or editorials on war. They can perform scripts they have written in response to the novels or participate in a talk show on the effect participation in a war has on people.

Thematic units are one way to think about and organize material in the language arts class that first focuses on issues and problems and second on literature. If a literature

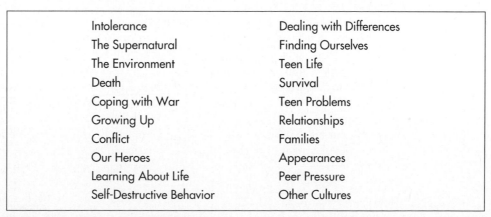

Intolerance	Dealing with Differences
The Supernatural	Finding Ourselves
The Environment	Teen Life
Death	Survival
Coping with War	Teen Problems
Growing Up	Relationships
Conflict	Families
Our Heroes	Appearances
Learning About Life	Peer Pressure
Self-Destructive Behavior	Other Cultures

Figure 7.3   Themes in Reading

program begins with people and ideas rather than literary patterns, types, or histories, the teacher can effectively involve students' experiences in the reading process. By centering on ideas or topics rather than a form of literature, the teacher is free to bring in multiple resources in many forms and media and to provide direction for reading by allowing students to read for their own purposes.

Despite the dramatic shifts in interest in literary theory in the past thirty years, secondary and post secondary literature teachers in general continue to employ methods reflecting New Critical orientations. . . . Teachers continue to focus primarily on "close reading" of literary texts, on the assumption that such texts are invariably integrated or organic wholes. Or in the "formalist" approach found in traditional textbooks, students focus on how the specific aspects of texts—setting, character, plot, language, and theme—fit together to form a coherent whole. Such approaches are often assumed by their practitioners to be merely "common sense" (as John Mayher calls it) of literary study, and to be untouched by "theory."

From Richard Beach, *A Teacher's Introduction to Reader-Response Theories*, p. 2. Copyright © 1993 by the National Council of Teachers of English. Reprinted with permission.

---

2. *Novels approach.* Many teachers organize their teaching around novels. Although this approach has elements of the thematic approach in it, the organization begins with a novel, not a theme, and the teacher uses the novel as a starting point and a touchstone for the work the students will do. Teachers select novels they think students will be able to get involved in, and focus on using the novel as a way to make contact with issues important to teens, to push them to explore the issues, and to get them to think about the issues in terms of themselves. Additionally, of course, is the focus on extending literacy skills, to encourage students to write in different genres, in different voices, to ask them to do things they haven't done before—like selecting a scene to be scripted.

When teachers use novels as their organizing device they are usually concerned with finding ways to connect literature with life as they extend their students' literacy skills. Literary elements are used to help students talk about the novel, not as terms that the novel illustrates. The important thing is to allow students to explore the impact the novel makes on them, not use the novel to teach terminology.

Although a unit based around a novel can be found in Chapter 3, very briefly here are the steps most teachers take to involve their students. First they find a novel that they think will involve their students and one that has many issues and themes in it. For instance if the book to be read is *The Crazy Horse Electric Game* by Chris Crutcher (which deals with a protagonist who is an athlete until he sustains neurological damage from a boating accident), some of the issues are: losing a skill, conflicts with parents, running away, death, alcoholism, drugs, sports, the role of school in a teen's education, child abuse, boy/girl relationships, dealing with divorce. Next, beginning activities are planned to awaken student interest. A newspaper or magazine story could be brought in that describes an accident which caused physical disabilities such as the actor, Christopher Reeves', riding accident. Students can be asked how they think they would respond to an accident such as this and how they think Reeves learned to cope with his extensive disabilities.

Possibilities for group work can be sketched out next. Some options include: script a scene and act it out, explore poetry, find newspaper and magazine articles which speak to the setting, character, or themes in the novel, interview characters, write poetry in response to a character or event, share dialogue/response journal with another classmate. Writing options and projects are sketched out next. Students could be Willie on the Oprah Winfrey Show talking about "emotionally abandoned children." As Big Will, students could write an obituary for "dead" Willie, they could write two or three more chapters, or make a soundtrack for the book, selecting one song per chapter. They could pick a theme from the book and create a collage which illustrates this theme. They could write a series of letters from one character to another or create a map of a character's emotional progress. Research possibilities include physical disabilities, alternative schools, post-accident trauma, gangs, alcoholism, LSD. This thumbnail sketch shows some of the richness of this approach and a few of the many possibilities that could be used in organizing this way.

3. *Experiential or inquiry-based approach.* In this kind of teaching, a piece of text is usually used as a starting point for writing and discussion. Students work to raise questions that they want answered (see examples in Chapter 3). For instance, an inquiry-based unit might start with the reading of Gary Paulsen's *Hatchet* or *Woodsong* and then move to other kinds of survival. Students write about things they have survived such as illness, the death of a loved one, a divorce, trying out for a team, or being rejected by friends. After papers and topics are shared students select a topic they want to know more about and that interests them.

At this point they move out to do interviews and other kinds of inquiry on the kind of survival they are researching. Some want to know how others have survived racism, abuse, alcoholic parents, traumas of high school, sickness, death of loved ones, injury etc. Students use both fiction and non-fiction to learn what others have experienced and to gain information. One of Diana's students focused on surviving the death of a close friend. She read a novel about a teen surviving the death of her best friend, interviewed young people who had experienced the death of a friend, found poems on the topic, read self-help books, and viewed videos. Her report to the class was moving and memorable. Literature in the inquiry-based unit is USED as teens further their knowledge and experience. They look at the literature analytically when they write and talk about whether an author's treatment of a topic, such as dealing with death, was realistic and reflected what is known about grieving. Literature and reading and writing and interviewing and researching are connected to life concerns. This approach helps students see literature and texts as something to read and talk about and as something connected to their lives.

4. *Modified author or chronological approach.* In the first years of teaching, having five different classes and three different preparations is overwhelming. Thoughts of best practice and creative curriculum design may take a back seat to simply surviving the experience. Since it is difficult to spend time looking for resources beyond the text at this point, start with the anthology. If at all possible with your several preparations, read ahead the first time you use the anthology so you can get a sense of what is coming. Think about the major ideas and issues that are dealt with through the literature and try to think of other resources you can bring in that in some way relate to the literature. But don't put the whole burden on yourself. Use poetry hunts by having students go

through the poetry collections from the library for usable poems. Also, the first time through an anthology, bring in collections of short stories. The library in your school probably has several. Or there might be old anthologies or old short story collections sitting dust-covered in the book room.

Use student input so you don't have to do all the work. Have them generate themes and ideas from the material you're reading. Bring in newspapers once every few weeks and ask students to go through a batch looking for editorials, feature stories, and news stories that might relate to what you are exploring. Actively involve the students in the process of creating units. Explain to them that you want to include more than material from the text, but that you will need their help. Set aside days in class to do this work and find ways to give students credit for all this reading and hunting. After a few years of using student help, you should have plenty of resources from which to draw so you can vary what you do.

We call this approach a modified author or chronological approach, because we encourage you, as you organize around the text, to change the typical ways of proceeding. First of all learn to use the text, but don't let the text use you. Just because something is in your text does not mean you have to use it. If after reading a poem, or essay, or short story in the text, you feel it will have little to say to students, feel free to skip it. Maybe at another time you will see worth in it. Also just because weighty introductions to sections in the text focus on such things as Romanticism, don't feel that this need be your approach to the selections that follow.

For instance, if teachers find themselves in the position of teaching the early parts of American literature, they can mute the impact of a strictly historical/chronological approach by finding ways to involve students and by showing them connections between the literature and their own lives.

Thus, before tackling Benjamin Franklin's *Autobiography* and Jonathan Edwards' *Resolutions*, which focus on how these authors wish to improve their lives, the teacher can raise questions about how important self-improvement is in today's society. Students can:

- Brainstorm all the ways in which our society is involved in self-improvement (aerobics, weight loss, finding inner peace, how to live without a man or woman).

- Read the selections with an eye to picking out the similarities and differences between what the authors think is important enough to change and what we think is important to change.

- Pick out five of Edwards' resolutions students strongly agree with and five they think are not important.

- Discuss what we can learn about the values and concerns of a people or a person by what they want to improve about themselves.

- Make up reading lists for Franklin and Edwards to help them achieve their goals (for example, Franklin might benefit from a book called *The New You—A Temperate Approach to Eating*).

- Think of the things they would like to change about themselves or their lives that could be accomplished by the end of the school year and then write a paper (possibly in the form of resolutions).

To cite another example from early American literature, students can look not only at issues but also at examples of a particular kind of writing and then begin activities based on that kind of writing. Thomas Paine's "The Crisis" and Patrick Henry's "Speech in the Virginia Convention" can be used as a springboard to persuasive writing or speechmaking and to a look at the ways we can be persuaded by the media today. Students can:

- Rewrite Patrick Henry's speech in modern English.

- Write a paper persuading the teacher of the need for more lenient or less work.

- Discuss why political speeches are in a literature book and why we no longer seem to treat speeches as literature.

- Discuss the media that our contemporary society used most to convince people on political matters.

- Explore the issues that concerned Henry and Paine. Are there issues today that can make Americans equally impassioned?

- Debate whether the kinds of persuasive devices that were used by the early Americans work today.

- Bring in ads they consider effective. Then, using their knowledge of the early Americans, explain how they might have responded to the same ad. For instance, would the appeal to be like everyone else work for them? Students might rewrite the ad in such a way that the product would appeal to those early Americans.

The new teacher should work to focus on making connections to students' lives and experiences and on discovering the relationships between the different pieces read.

5. *The Reading Workshop Approach.* Thanks to the work of Nancie Atwell and others, many literature programs are organized around the reading workshop. In the reading workshop, all students are usually reading novels of their choice. This is the major way this approach differs from Literature Circles in which groups of students read the same books. See Figure 7.2 for ways to get started with this approach. Students read, discuss, and advertise their books to other class members, creating excitement about books. Since most teachers don't feel they can conduct reading workshops at the expense of everything else, many set aside two days a week in which students read quietly, talk in groups about their books, and work on projects related to their books. Often classes such as this allow presentation time in which students share parts of their projects or do oral presentations which may include the scripting of an especially engrossing scene. As students get used to the small-group discussion aspects of this approach, they need less and less structure for their discussions, preferring instead to chose what they talk about each time.

UNDERSTANDING WHY YOU TEACH LITERATURE

As you can see from the way we describe interactions with literature, we don't believe the purpose of reading literature is to locate and identify literary terms. We don't believe the purpose of reading literature is to show how this or that piece of literature exhibits the characteristics of Romanticism or Classicism. We don't believe the purpose of reading literature is to learn history through the literature or to only use the literature as an example of what was going on in society at the time. We don't believe the purpose of reading literature is just to write papers with thesis statements. Nor do we believe the purpose of reading literature is to analyze the author's style and craft.

Literature was written to make an impact. Readers must talk about the literature, argue about it, look for points of agreement and disagreement with the author, look for ways it connects to their lives. We must keep this at the heart of what we do in the literature class and find ways to value and evaluate the meaning our students make through literature.

Literary Theory and Purpose

People don't teach literature poorly on purpose. Many literature teachers who "tell" what a book means, have gotten praise for their approach from colleagues and often from students. However, we assert that such teachers could benefit their students if they examined their beliefs about the purpose of literature and brought to light the assumptions on which they are basing their teaching. According to the research of Arthur Applebee, teaching literature has not changed much in the last thirty-five years. Secondary and college English teachers, whether or not they are aware of it, are still mainly using a New Critical approach which operates on the belief that specific methods have to be followed to elicit the right meaning from a piece of literature.

Too often, teachers who use this approach communicate to students that literature is about finding the same meaning that some superior intelligence decided on—not about seeing what the piece means to the reader and how the reader can connect it to his or her life. Teachers who use this approach sometimes seem to forget that literature is written to have an impact on the reader and that mucking about to create meaning by examining this impact is more important than agreeing with a critics' interpretation. When teachers elevate the opinion of "others" they often show they lack confidence in making literary judgments themselves. They also forget that to develop an interpretation, a critic did a lot of mucking about first, and then made his or her "best guess" about the piece.

Often because of their dependence on this approach, teachers lose their ability to respond to the content of the literature, responding instead only to the craft and to how a piece was put together. In our view, discussions of craft should be used as another way into the literature, not as a fence to put up between the literature and the reader. Only to analyze and discuss the hows of a piece robs the reader of a literary experience and deprives the reader of an opportunity to respond to and discuss the content of a piece. Imagine asking students to read Alice Walker's *The Color Purple* and then only talking about it in terms of the techniques the writer used, without ever talking about what the writer is writing about! Too often this kind of literature class only deals with how an effect was accomplished, not what the piece has to say. This seems to be a misuse of literature.

As teachers evaluate their own stances toward literature the three elements that come into play, according to Kathleen McCormick, are the place of the text, the place of the reader, and the place of the social/cultural context that shapes the transaction between the reader and the text. Teachers who teach from a New Critical stance place authority within the text and the text becomes the most important of the three factors. Although there are many, many literary theories, we are only briefly touching on the two that seem to provide the broadest contrast.

The other major theory is the reader-response approach which places the authority in the reader. Reading is viewed as an interaction between the text and the reader. When this interaction occurs, meaning is made. Texts spring to life when their words enter a reader's mind. This view comes from the work of Louise Rosenblatt, who first articulated this way of reading in the 1930s. Most of our explanations of approaches to literature in this text, are grounded in Rosenblatt's work. But teachers who deal with literature often fear embracing this approach because they think it means they must accept every student response as valid. These teachers should be aware that asking students to go back into the text to explain the source of their response is a common practice in classrooms where reader-response is in operation.

"I argue that both texts and readers can be seen to possess *repertoires,* a subset of the larger culture's discourses, beliefs, values, and ways of understanding the individual and the world. I contend that readers can become critically literate, active readers only when they are able to analyze the ways in which their own and texts' repertoires are embedded within the larger culture. I therefore argue that pedagogies need to be developed that can engage students in three interconnected areas of study. First, students must become able to analyse how they themselves are culturally constructed as subjects-in-history—this is, how they are both constructed by (or 'subject to') larger cultural forces and how they are also capable of taking autonomous action within those forces. Second they must learn to analyze how texts are likewise culturally constructed. . . . Third, they can then use such cultural and historical analysis to develop and defend critical positions of their own."

From Kathleen McCormick, *The Culture of Reading and the Teaching of English* (New York: Manchester University Press, 1994), p. 9. Reprinted with permission.

McCormick encourages teachers to help students become aware of all the stances and perspectives they read from, to take the socio-cultural background into account. The point of considering the socio-cultural is to help students understand that every piece of literature is written from a point of view and is based on assumptions, that nothing written is simply "the way it is." When they react and respond to literature, different pieces of their background and belief systems come to the forefront and influence their take on a piece. When students respond to books, it is important that they know which role as a reader they are predominantly using when they read. If an African-American reads *Of Mice and Men,* he may react strongly to the treatment of Crooks, the black stable hand. This may be central to his response and the entire way he views the book would be shaded by it. Or when a female reads the book, she may respond very strongly to the fact that Curley's wife isn't given a name and is judged harshly for trying to be friendly with the farm hands. So our socio-cultural background influences the way we respond to books. In one reading our spiritual stance may lead us to view a character a certain way, in another book our strong views on organized labor may be the lens through which we mainly see the plot. The importance for students in identifying and being able to articulate their stances is to help them see how they are situated in terms of the text so they can better understand their own responses. The importance for the teacher is in recognizing that each point of view from which we read will cause readers to see texts differently, but no less validly. Whether we grew up in a rural, suburban, or urban area, whether we are male or female, whether we are Latino, African-American, Asian, or Caucasian, whether we had a strong religious upbringing, whether we came from a poor or wealthy background, whether we were taught to value sports or not, whether we were an only child or one of many—all these things can affect the way we view stories and the characters in them. Our goal is to help students recognize all the factors that go into their response so they may better know what they are reacting to and can better explain and question their own responses.

INTEGRATION OF THE LANGUAGE ARTS THROUGH LITERATURE

It is no doubt clear by now that the literature programs described here are, in essence, language arts programs—they involve at least as much composing, speaking, and listening as they do reading and literary study. This integration seems to us highly desirable: teachers should encourage a natural flow from one form of language to another. By offering writing options as part of a literature unit, the teacher makes the *producing* of language a comfortable outcome of *consuming it*. Similarly, when reading is focused toward an actual task—learning something or persuading someone—it too becomes natural and purposeful and leads easily to related language arts activities.

In fact, it is perhaps inaccurate to call these English units at all, since they involve experiences outside the dimensions of the traditional English course; they are genuinely interdisciplinary. In the history of education, English has often been an umbrella subject, with the teacher trying to hold the umbrella straight while teaching basic reading, the history of Western civilization, spelling, the business letter, the necessary skills for success in college, and the differences between Elizabethan and Petrarchan sonnets. We suggest that integrated literature units, particularly with a thematic emphasis, provide a way to pull together diverse demands, while actually enlivening study and providing students with useful training for other fields. There seems to be no reason the English teacher should not incorporate the materials of science, history, math, business and industry, politics, psychology, sociology, vocational education, art, music, journalism, and theater, since they can be used to provide a genuinely humane, broadly practical literature and reading program.

◆ EXPLORATIONS

To run a good literature course, one must be bibliographically agile, knowing sources. Teachers need not always know the fine details of what is in the literature, but the knowledge must be sufficient to allow them to make recommendations with confidence. Here are three projects a teacher can undertake to develop bibliographic agility:

1. Spend time browsing in a paperback book store looking at books that might be useful with students. Don't limit your thinking to traditional literature. Check out the sociology section, the history paperbacks, the joke books, and the science section. Examine the handicrafts department and the sports books. Check cookbooks. Practice scanning for content so you can form quick, reliable judgments about a book's applicability.

2. Do the same with the magazine section of a bookstore. There is a phenomenal number of magazines on which you can draw regularly. Check such titles as *Gem Collector* or *Czechoslovakia Today* for possible use.

3. Learn about pamphlet and brochure sources. Enormous amounts of such material are printed each year in this country. For starters, familiarize yourself with the publications available from the Superintendent of Documents in Washington, D.C., and from your state's printing office. Then check travel agencies, public service institutions, universities, county agriculture agents, and the pamphlet files at your local library.

- Pick a topic that you think would interest students of the age you like to teach, and create a list of related books of increasing sophistication and difficulty. It might be interesting to start with picture books.

- Learn how to give a book talk. Focus on spending only a minute or two on each book, giving your listeners only a few sentences that will raise their interest and curiosity.

- Try letting a class (or a few students) embark on a totally free reading program, with you serving only as a guide or coach. Stay with it long enough to see patterns of growth and development emerging. Do students grow as readers when left on their own? Do they enjoy the program?

- Design a record-keeping system for an individualized reading program.

- Get together with two or three other teachers and build a resource unit, just to find out how it's done and how much or how little work it involves. Flip a coin to see who gets to test it first.

- Study a conventional literature anthology in terms of its adaptability to thematic teaching. For example, if you find a British literature anthology that is organized chronologically, consider ways in which its literary selections could be restructured along thematic lines.

- Create introductory activities for a novel you know well. The next time you use the novel, see which activities work best at piquing student interest.

- Sketch out plans for a two- or three-week unit on a specific novel. Include several activities for whole-class novels mentioned in the chapter and create several of your own.

- Look through an anthology and find two or three selections you could do a mini-unit on. Generate as many teaching ideas as you can on these selections.

- Read more about literary theories and share your ideas on what each theory believes about the place of readers, texts, and socio-cultural context. What implications does this theory have for the classroom? Share your ideas with other group members and look at what you can take from each of the theories to help students find ways into the literature.

- Observe a teacher over a short period of time as he or she deals with literature. Work to dig out the assumptions on which that teacher is basing his or her approaches and plans. Which literary theory does the teacher seem to embrace?

RELATED READINGS

Many books in this burgeoning area of literature instruction can push your thinking and help you sort out your assumptions about literature teaching. They include Robert Scholes' *Textual Power: Literary Theory and the Teaching of English,* Kathleen McCormick's *The Culture of Reading and the Teaching of English,* Gordon Pradl's *Literature and Democracy, Knowledge in the Making: Challenging the Text in the Classroom* edited by Bill Corcoran, Mike Hayhoe, and Gordon M. Pradl, and *Literature Instruction: A Focus on Student Repsonse* edited by Judith A. Langer. To read more extensively on the reader-response theory we suggest *The Experience of Reading: Louise Rosenblatt and Reader-Response Theory* edited by John Clifford and *A Teacher's Introduction to Reader-Response Theories* by Richard Beach.

The *Language of Interpretation: Patterns of Discourse in Discussions of Literature* by James D. Marshall, Peter Smagorinsky and Michael W. Smith. and *Literature Circles: Voice and Choice in the Student-Centered Classroom* by Harvey Daniels focus on discussion and talking about literature. *Literature IS . . .: Collected Essays of G. Robert Carlsen* edited by Anne Sherrill and Terry Ley looks at literature and programs in terms of teens and their interests. *Learning the Landscape: Inquiry-Based Activities for Comprehending and Composing* and *Recasting The Text: Inquiry-Based Activities for Comprehending and Composing* by Fran Claggett, Louann Reid and Ruth Vinz, which could be used as student texts, focus on ways students can relate and respond to literature. *Transactions with Literature: a Fifty-Year Perspective* edited by Edmund J. Farrell and James R. Squire not only summarizes research on the teaching of literature but also looks at books and classroom practices in terms of what is done in literature instruction. Other books that focus on literature instruction are *Passages to Literature: Essays on Teaching in Australia, Canada, England, The United States, and Wales* edited by Joseph Milner and Lucy Milner, *Exploring Texts: The Role of Discussion and Writing in the Teaching and Learning of Literature* by George E. Newell and Russell K. Durst, and *Literature and Life-Making Connections in the Classroom* edited by Patricia Phelan.

CHAPTER 8

TEACHING WRITING

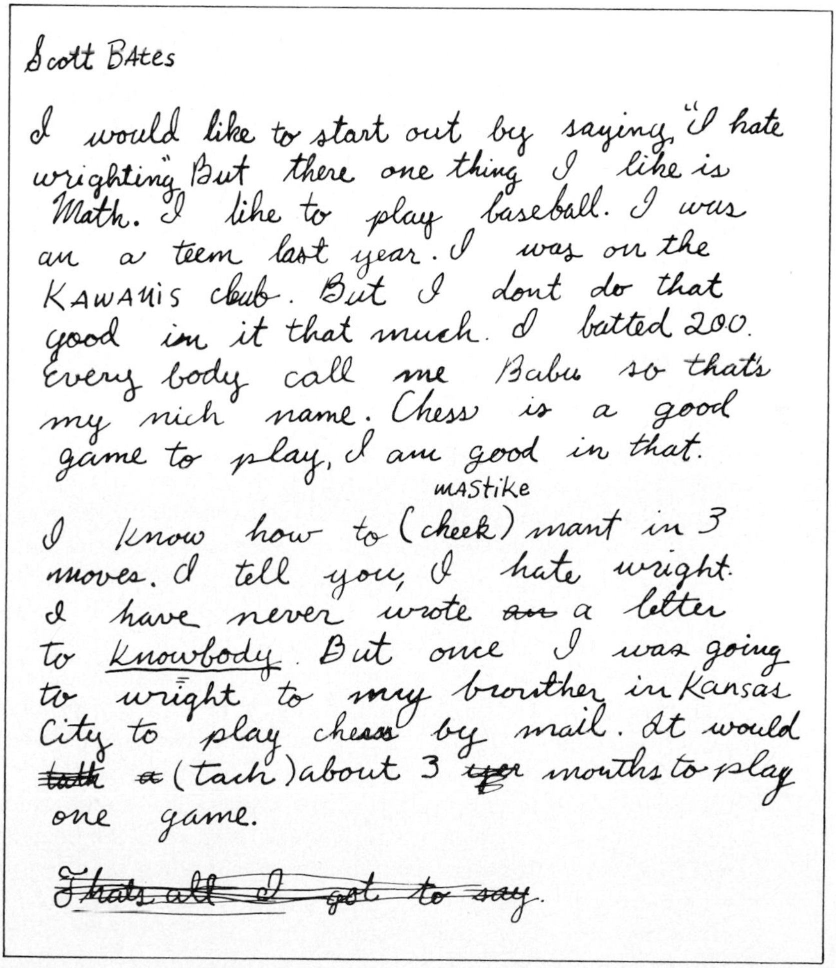

Scott Bates

I would like to start out by saying "I hate wrighting" But there one thing I like is Math. I like to play baseball. I was an a teem last year. I was on the KAWANIS club. But I dont do that good im it that much. I batted 200. Every body call me Babu so that's my nich name. Chess is a good game to play, I am good in that.

I know how to (cheek) mant in 3 moves. I tell you, I hate wright. I have never wrote an a letter to knowbody. But once I was going to wright to my brouther in Kansas City to play chess by mail. It would tuth a (tach) about 3 yer mouths to play one game.

Thats all I got to say.

Figure 8.1 "I hate wrighting."

Well, Scott Bates, you are not alone.

Even the most dedicated of writers have times when they, too, "hate wrighting." The assignment to "write a paper" can strike fear into the heart of even the most successful of students, and writing assignments often reduce many people to a state of procrastination, if not downright misery.

When we poll students in both schools and colleges, we find that although many may express some doubts and reservations about their ability to read and respond to literature, their insecurities about writing are deep and profound: "My grammar is no good." "A teacher told me I have good ideas but cannot spell." "I can't think of anything to say." "Who would want to read my writing anyway?"

The last question provides the lead into the approach to composition that we take in this book. The answer is, "*We* would like to read your writing, and so would a lot of other people." Let's take another look at Scott Bates, the writing hater. Granted, he has some technical or surface errors, what he calls "mastikes," but a *most* interesting kid emerges in this piece. *Anybody* would like to hear his stories, to read about them, to learn more about him. "So how are your prospects for baseball this year, Scott? Did you feel kinda bad about batting .200?" (Steve once batted .000 for an entire season in the *minor* little leagues, so he can relate!) "Chess, huh? How did you learn to play chess? How did you get so good at it? You wrote, 'That's all I got to say,' but then scratched it out—*good,* because we know you have lots more to say about baseball and chess and probably ten million other things."

We want to argue that for Scott and for every other user of language, writing ought to be no more challenging and painful than learning to play chess or maybe upping your batting average from .200. Scott shows some fundamental human traits: He is a learner; he is a thinker about experience; he uses language to express his needs and interests and knowledge. He may never write .400, which would be the literary equivalent of a Bronte or Seuss or Woolf, but there's no reason to suppose that he doesn't have the stuff of a writer in him—a kid who can be a good competitor at the compositional home plate and can bang out solid hits with regularity.

A writer at a different end of the spectrum is Marie Teal, presently a middle school science teacher in Elko, Nevada. In Figure 8.2 she describes some of her early experiences with writing that led her to become a self-confessed "perfectionist," more interested in the surface appearance of her own writing than its content. Marie was obviously a successful student, who got good grades, and a competent writer. Yet she grew to fear writing and to engage in a kind of procrastination that many readers, even those with high confidence in their writing, may recognize.

Why does writing cause people such grief? To some extent, the answers lie within the nature of the process itself. It's hard work to shape and fashion one's ideas in language, and, as Scott notes, it's slow work, even with the benefit of the highest tech word processors. It is also risky in its way, for when we offer our ideas in language, we are exposing ourselves for public scrutiny. People may not *like* what we write or say; it may make them angry with us, or it may make us look like fools in their eyes. The very features that make writing so valuable as a source of human expression give

I am not sure at what age I began to "fear" writing. I remember elementary school primarily providing reinforcement for good penmanship. The content of your writing was not critical; it was important that the paper be neat and tidy. I remember having one of my papers displayed in the fifth grade because of its neatness, and I was so proud.

Following elementary school I began writing papers that were considered for content as well as structure. I don't remember any negative feedback, but, for whatever reason, I began to develop a certain perfectionist attitude about my writing. This led to procrastination of my writing. I was shameless about putting off my writing assignments until the last minute. I always managed to hand in adequate papers—my grades were good. By delaying the work, however, I managed to accept the "inferior" quality of my writing because, after all, that's the best I could do in so short a time.

—Marie Teal
[Reprinted by permission of the author]

Figure 8.2   Confessions of a Writing Perfectionist

it the risk of public embarrassment to weigh against the potential for moving an audience, shaping others' ideas, and swatting a linguistic ball out of the park.

But equally important, we think, has been the effect of schooling on composition, for until quite recently writing has been taught through a traditional method that emphasized correctness over substance, that elevated "mastikes" to the level of high sin, that discouraged novice writers from expressing themselves openly and freely. The experiential model, by contrast, begins with experience—whether chess or checkers, baseball or swimming or reading, personal traumas or public successes, hopes or dreams, jokes or confessions—and moves into language development from there, arguing that, with the support of a good teacher, virtually all students can find ways to compose articulately and to receive high praise from the folks in the grandstand. Indeed, in recent years, thanks to new methodologies, the ranks of the writing haters have been seriously diminished as young writers compose in print and non-print media, in speech and writing, and present their polished work to an audience.

You may have noticed in the paragraph above that we have used the word *composing* along with *writing*. The new theory says that the two are not identical: *Composing*, or creating in language, is broader than writing and so is the school's focus broader than *writing*. We've come to see that speech is composing, along with dramatic play, media creation, and including paper and pencil print. At its best, composing theory even includes reading, for as we have come to see, reading is a matter of *making meaning* not just passively absorbing texts. In the experiential classroom, reading and writing flow into and from one another, and students compose in myriad forms: speech, prose, poetry, fiction, drama, and so on.

Evidence of the nature of the experiential theory can be derived from some additional reflections by Marie Teal, who, after college and before becoming a teacher, worked for ten years as a chemical engineer [Figure 8.3]. There are several features of her experience that warrant commentary. First, as an engineer, she was writing "for real," rather than a school or college practice exercise, and this meant composing for

I thought I was doomed to be a frustrated writer. I completed my engineering degree and with several laboratory reports and research papers behind me, I headed for my first job. I never realized in college how much writing an engineer must do! I went into engineering to perform interesting and detailed calculations, not to write so many reports, letters, and memorandums! But write I did.

After about two or three years on the job, I met with my supervisor for a routine performance evaluation, and much to my surprise, one of the items he noted was that I was an "excellent writer." I had never seen myself as a writer before, let alone a good writer. I was amazed.

I continued to improve my skills in technical writing during my years in engineering. I am now trying to improve my literary skills as a writer of short stories and essays. I have long toyed with the idea of writing children's stories. I realize that I will need to do what I did in the past with my technical writing, and that is to write, write, write!

—Marie Teal
[Reprinted by permission of the author.]

Figure 8.3   Learning Writing on the Job

a genuine audience of her peers and supervisors. In addition, she was writing in actual discourse forms—reports, letters, and memoranda—rather than schoolhouse themes or "compositions." There was *substance* to her writing those "interesting and detailed calculations" that had to be explained in writing to others, a base of knowledge and information that informed her prose. Finally, there was practice, much writing, not just for the sake of learning to write better, but for the sake of accomplishing the goals of all language: to inform, to communicate, to report, to move others toward action. Although Marie's writing was in a technical domain, much of her learning is applicable to any area of composing, including creative writing, as shown by her interests and insights into moving into the writing of children's literature.

WHY WRITE? WHY COMPOSE?

Despite its complications, complexities, and generally bad reputation with students, writing, to us, remains absolutely central to the English language arts program. We argue that it is important for a variety of reasons, not the least of which is that, under the proper teaching conditions, writing *doesn't* have to be painful and can be a rich and deeply satisfying experience. Close to the writer him or herself, composing is a crucial way for people to clarify their ideas and thinking. Although there is some inaccuracy to the old adage, "You don't understand a thing until you can write it," there is wisdom as well. Many people find that composing not only clarifies their thinking, but actually leads them to discover ideas they didn't fully realize they had. (You've probably had the experience of starting a paper, thinking you had it under control, either to discover that you knew less than you thought you did or, marvelously, that the paper took on a life of its own, leading you off in surprising directions.) Writing is, of course, an extremely practical skill, for chemical engineers and teachers, for preachers and salespeople, for people in the street and executives up on the eighty-sixth floor. Although electronic devices—word processors, faxes, e-mail, the net—have made communication easier and faster, there still is no substitute for the skill of being able to marshal ideas and to express them verbally. The usefulness of writing in school is pretty much undebated, even to the point that students who are skilled writers have distinct advantages academically over other students. But we hasten to add that writing is more than a "service skill," the English language arts more than a service course. Writing is far more than just getting ideas down on paper; composing is more than translating ideas into words. Virtually the whole of human experience reveals that we use writing as a way of developing and exploring ethics and values, of probing into questions that perplex and puzzle, as a way of forming deep and lasting social relationships. The word "literature" is often misused to mean the stuff that gets packaged in textbooks or sold at the bookstore, for student writing, too, is literature, expressing the same vast range of human emotions and experience. Finally, in this brief paean to writing, we want to make the bold claim that composing may, in fact, be the most fundamental of the liberal arts. It certainly encompasses most of the language arts (one reads as one writes, one speaks one's way to writing), but it is truly and naturally interdisciplinary—there isn't a subject in the curriculum, in the universe, that doesn't have deep roots in language and where students cannot successfully enhance their learning, knowledge, and understanding through composition.

WRITING AS PROCESS

Much of current development in theory and practice comes from the recent understanding of writing as *process* rather than *product*. The late Wallace Douglas of Northwestern University (to whom this book is dedicated) was one of the pioneers in this movement. While directing the Curriculum Center in English at Northwestern in the 1960s, Douglas studied the history of writing instruction, from Plato and Aristotle through the dominant school textbooks, and saw that it was placing inordinate emphasis on the form and shape of finished writing—the product—rather than on how writers go about making successful pieces—the process. He wrote about the astonishingly complex body of skills that a student/writer must master, from the physical act of penmanship through the stages of gathering ideas, getting them down on paper, revising, proofreading, and receiving the response of an audience. Douglas studied the works of professional writers as described, for example, in the *Paris Review* interviews with distinguished twentieth-century writers, illustrated through their collected notes and drafts. He conceived of a multistage view of the writing process, from idea to finished page. Douglas's observations were echoed by others in the field, particularly in the 1970s by Donald Graves and Donald Murray at the University of New Hampshire. During the past several decades, the idea of "writing as process" or the "process approach" has become both famous and infamous, practiced widely by K–16 teachers while being frequently challenged by adherents to the traditional or product model.

Like any creative effort, writing requires energy and time. Few writers are able to dash off something in final form, and most of us find writing rather a struggle. Further, in writing, people put something of their soul down for scrutiny by others; there can be a feeling of exposure in writing, especially if an audience is sharply critical.

At the same time, there are many processes in a young person's life that require complex skills, an investment of time, or public exposure: mounting a butterfly for a public collection, putting one's sheep or pie on display at the 4H fair, playing a sport, playing a musical instrument, going on stage. Although writing differs in many ways from these activities, there seems to be no reason students should find the single task of composing much more difficult. One key variable is that the skills described above are generally taught through a process model, a learn-by-doing approach. Of course there are some practices and drills—the musician practices scales, the volleyball player is drilled in serves and spikes—and there is plenty of coaching and correcting involved, but much of the instruction is centered in the process: learning how to volley by volleying, learning to raise sheep by raising them, playing in an orchestra, mounting hundreds of butterflies.

The writing process model is summarized in Figure 8.4. Although conceptions and terminology for the process differ, we see writing as proceeding by stages: prewriting (where people find purpose and gather ideas), drafting or the writing act itself, and postwriting (revising, copyediting, and publishing). (See the bibliography works by Graves, Elbow, Moffett, Atwell, and Murray.) We want to observe that writers experience these stages in many different ways and that, as Murray notes, the process is "recursive," meaning that even as we revise we are "prewriting" new material; even as we draft, we revise.

To be sure, not all pieces go through all stages. Kids need choices about which pieces they take through the publication stage. And, unfortunately, we've seen

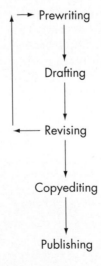

The Process of Composing

Prewriting

Drafting

Revising

Copyediting

Publishing

Figure 8.4   The Process of Composing

teachers become slavish adherents to the writing process, insisting that *all* students take *all* papers through *all* stages. In that setting, students come to see "writing process" as a series of tortuous steps they are flogged through with every piece they do.

One student may enjoy the security and order of writing detailed notes before beginning to draft, while others (for good or bad reasons) may prefer to write off the tops of their heads, essentially prewriting and drafting simultaneously. Some kids are perfectionists who feel the need to get the draft down perfectly (sometimes to the point of writing and rewriting the first sentence endlessly), in which case drafting and revising become more or less simultaneous or concurrent. In the Explorations at chapter end, we'll invite you to characterize your own writing process to see how you fit the model, while cautioning you to realize that what works for you is not necessarily the only approach. Teachers need to be very cautious about imposing their own conception of the process on diverse minds and individuals.

In our scheme, there is an important distinction between *revising* (by which we mean making changes in content, structure, and language) and *copyediting* (our term for the cleanup or surface structure phase—spelling, usage, mechanics, typography). This distinction will be discussed in greater detail in the next chapter; for the moment, it suffices to say that in this chapter we want to focus on that prewriting, drafting loop, the getting-it-down stage, to discuss revising and polishing a bit later.

The term *publishing,* which is also relegated to the following chapter, does not necessarily mean appearing in a book, newspaper, or magazine. Rather, we take publishing in the sense of "making public." Much (but not all) writing craves an audience, for reasons that we've made clear in discussing the experiential approach. Although diaries and journals are often private records and recollections, most of the time that we write, we want (or are required) to reach an audience. The boss wants a chemical engineer's lab report; the poet wants to present to a readership; the prof or teacher insists on reading the examination; the lover wants to wow the significant other with a letter or other public expression.

The writing process approach suggests, in simplest terms, that composing needs to be a *wholistic* process. Despite the artificialities of the school classroom, we need to let the writing process operate as it does in nature, from idea gathering to finding an audience, as a dramatic process where live "performers" compose with genuine purposes and motives, pushing their language to its fullest limits in order to have the desired effects on an audience.

JOURNALING AND FREEWRITING

Two interesting exceptions to the "I hate writing" syndrome are *journals* and *freewrites,* both of which, at first glance, might seem to violate the principle of wholism that we just articulated. Journals are a reflective form of the diary, not just a log of experience, but reaction to that experience. Freewrites may be done in solitude or in class, but often involve fast-and-furious impromptu writing; they may serve as brainstorming (prewriting) for a paper or be a response to classroom instruction, say a brief on-the-spot reaction to a poem or lecture or film.

taking pressure off

The consistent elements of journals and freewrites are that they give students a *choice of writing topics* (by inviting personal reaction), that the writing is *private* or *semiprivate* (the teacher may be the only reader other than the student), and *is not revised and graded* (the writing process is completed at first draft).

In the experience of most teachers, student response to journals and freewrites have been almost universally positive. So-called nonwriters seem to enjoy writing journals, while many writers tee off on freewrites, pumping out page after page of work. Teachers generally enjoy reading this material, especially since they don't have to grade it, and they report seeing great growth in student fluency. Thus although journals and freewrites may seem to truncate the writing process, they are quite true to it. Figures 8.5 and 8.6 suggest some of the ways in which these tools can be used in the classroom.

Diana did some classroom research on journal writing with a group of tenth graders who had previously failed English. She came to the following conclusions:

• Journals and freewrites are an important tool for use in the English language arts classroom, especially for disaffected students and those who do not feel particularly confident of their writing (and English) skills.

Using *journals,* students can:

- record and respond to daily experiences
- react and respond to books and literature
- log and discuss work done on classroom projects
- react to local and world events (say, in response to the daily newspaper)
- carry on internal dialogues (the "split column" journal where students write observations in the left column and their reactions in the right)
- better understand classroom content material (summarizing and paraphrasing, raising questions)
- provide a "track" of their intellectual journeys and life journeys

With *freewrites* students can:

- provide teachers with on-the-spot feedback
- demonstrate learning or misunderstanding of class concepts
- respond immediately to films, poems, stories, events
- brainstorm writing ideas
- create hasty but unpressured drafts of papers
- explode on topics, angers, irritations, sensed wrongs
- effuse in moments of happiness and satisfaction
- engage in self-assessment of their work

Figure 8.5   Journals and Freewrites in the Classroom

• Supplying topics is important, especially with students who feel they have "nothing to say." (Some of our favorite starting points for journals are provided in Figure 8.6.)

• Teacher response to journals and freewrites is important, but it should be non-judgmental and focus on content, not grammar. The need for teacher response seems to diminish with time; that is, increasingly students write for themselves, provided they know that the teacher cares and will respond.

• When students feel the topic is important, their writing is at its clearest and most focused.

• There are different purposes for writing. Journals and freewrites allow students to explore those purposes (and different aspects of their lives) without the immediate fear of being criticized for comma placement.

• Students should write about problems of direct personal experience before moving on to larger topics. They cannot be forced to be exocentric. When they are grappling with problems in their own lives, they simply cannot pay attention to anything else. There must be a bridge between problems with a girlfriend or boyfriend and the language of Geoffrey Chaucer. (Readers will promptly anticipate what that bridge can be: It involves treating Chaucer as the sometimes bawdy writer about real life rather than as fodder for linguistic or literary analysis.)

- What's *wrong* here today? (When you sense that everybody is in a crabby mood.)
- What's the best thing/worst thing that's happened to you this week?
- What questions *aren't* we discussing here?
- Read any good books, seen any good TV lately?
- My [girlfriend, boyfriend, father, mother, brother] is driving me nuts.
- If I ran the school, I'd _____.
- It's unfair that _____.
- Twenty-five or fifty years from today I see myself _____.
- My gut response to the poem we just read is _____.
- The world issue I think that's most important is _____.
- It probably wouldn't make any difference if I _____.
- How I feel about confronting other people.
- How I feel about confronting myself.
- How I feel about _____.
- The last good laugh I had was _____.

Figure 8.6   Our Favorite Journal and Freewrite Starters*

*We hasten to add that we do not think that students must always or mostly have journal and freewrite "prompts." These are "starters" that we use early in a class to give students a sense of what is legitimate and interesting to write about. As time goes by, students themselves provide most of the topics.

• Students need to be encouraged not to worry about the correctness of their writing in journals and freewrites. Of course, a certain amount of correctness is required for this material to be readable, and Diana found that some students had difficulty not worrying about correctness, thus inhibiting their writing.

Journals and freewrites should be done frequently; some teachers even believe they should be daily. They can be used for a few minutes at the beginning or ending of a class or required as part of outside work. Entries can be turned in one-at-a-time for quick response by the teacher or accumulated in a notebook or file or portfolio for periodic review, depending largely on the teacher's inclination and time schedule. We've generally found that although responding to this writing obviously takes time, it is one of our most enjoyable tasks, for in journals and freewrites you catch students at their natural and youthful best.

WRITING: PERSONAL AND CREATIVE

How can we extend the freedom, flexibility, and good writing of the journal and freewrite to other composing activities? It is a cliché that "the best writing comes from personal experience," but a cliché that rings true to us. The idea can be oversimplified, as in the "My Summer Vacation" theme that draws groans from kids in school and adults in memory. Writing about vacations is not necessarily a bad idea, but the in-school version tends to create a routine travelogue rather than deep engagement with experience.

Writing instruction works best when students draw on not only personal experience, but also what counts as *substantial* experience for them. Writing involves self-discovery and satisfies a person's need to communicate. It provides a way for students to sort through their experiences, to make sense of their world, and to share their observations with others. When students are deeply engaged in this process, it is often revealed in the intensity and vibrancy of their language. It is important to add, too, that "personal experience" is *not* limited to boy-girl relationships or what-I-saw-on-the-way-to-school. At its best, school experience—in geography, in math, in languages, in music—is also personal experience, a part of the student, and subject for writing.

Another way to phrase this is to borrow another cliché, one too often ignored in practice: "All writing is creative." The distinction between "creative" composition and its opposite (uncreative? noncreative? counter creative?) is an unfortunate one, "creative" being seen as poetry, stories, and plays, the other stuff being what's left— exposition, persuasion, the essay, the "theme," and the "composition." There are obvious differences in form and process between composing a poem and composing an essay, but the similarities are great. Creative, or what we prefer to call *imaginative*, writing involves a writer's successfully assimilating personal experience and sharing it with someone else. A good memo, for instance, can be an imaginative work; the results of a teacher-imposed sonnet-writing lesson often are not.

Moreover, the false dichotomy of creative/other leads to other fragmentation: poetry writing is seen as a frill with exposition as a "basic"; writing about academic topics becomes dull and perfunctory; students fail to employ their fullest range of imaginative skills in the fullest range of discourse forms. We're increasingly convinced that the differences between journal writing and academic writing, between inventing a short story and explaining a scientific process, are not as great as are supposed. While the forms and techniques may differ, the fundamental nature of the writing process, to us, appears to be a constant.

TO ASSIGN OR NOT

Evoking personal, imaginative writing in the classroom is not easy. Students are accustomed to look for "what the teacher wants," for in the past, this has been the route to successful grades.

One important debate in our profession these days centers on the idea of writing *assignments*. Some writing specialists are advocates of having students *always* come up with their own writing topics. While the teacher may provide some ideas and suggestions, the students are generally asked to come up with their own idea. Proponents of this approach generally admit that the first few times this is done, students may struggle a bit, looking to the teacher for ideas. But over time, it is claimed, they come to rely on their own inner sources for writing. And, they also claim, students eventually come to have greater ownership of these topics.

We have experimented with this approach and find that, to a degree, the claims are valid. But we have also found that when students come to us with their imaginations closed down, the "open" invitation to write may just bring about blankness. Further, although we invite and celebrate students' choices of topics, we also see room for teachers to extend the range of demands and experiences that go on in the classroom.

Thus, in contrast to some people in the profession, we make those things called "assignments." Prior to the advent of writing process theory, assignments were often constrained and artificial: "Write a one thousand word essay discussing Shakespeare's view of the human condition." The traditional assignment was often arbitrary in its scope (why 1000 words on this topic?), lacking in audience (who is to read this paper?), and academic in purpose (does the assignment really ask for a student opinion or merely regurgitation of text ideas?). The assignment might have been designed to teach a genre (write a short story for Tuesday) or logic and organization (a "comparison and contrast" theme or a "hamburger essay" (with introductory and concluding "buns" and an internal burgeresque stuffing).

Young people bubble over with ideas and experiences they want to share with one another and with adults. Yet, when given a blank sheet of paper and a writing assignment, they often claim they have nothing to say. Part of the problem is that the assignments teachers offer are themselves frequently dull and uninviting. While we do not feel that every assignment given to students must be wildly innovative, novel, or clever, it is evident that the assignments the teacher offers define the dimensions of composition for the students. If assignments are of the 500-words-and-three paragraphs variety, students are obviously limited in what they will accomplish as writers.

Some of our criteria for good assignments include the provisions that:

• A good assignment should grow from a *context*, whether students' lives, world issues, or academic subjects, and it should grow from students' engagement with that context. In other words, we don't think it's valuable for students to, say, write an analysis of nuclear fission unless that writing is somehow grounded in experience, say current problems of nuclear disarmament or nuclear waste disposal.

• A writing assignment must be done with *purpose,* and this is seldom something that the teacher can impose on students, so a good deal of prewriting work must be done to ensure that students have deeply and satisfyingly engaged with their subject.

• Having purpose also implies that an *audience* is part of the scene, preferably an audience other than the teacher, so that student's writing goes someplace (a topic, again, that we'll take up in the next chapter).

• Writing should be done in real writing modes or forms, not always the school "paper" or "composition." Figure 8.7 suggests what we call "some neglected forms of composition." Real writers don't write "themes" or "assignments"; they write essays and lab reports and editorials and poems. A key element to our assignments, then, is to offer real-world discourse forms to the students, not only that, but to offer a number of options and choices as well.

There is no single composition assignment appropriate for all students. Steve discovered the idea of presenting multiple assignments—writing options—as a result of a bad time in a high school sophomore English class. At the time, he was trying to extend the notion of the journal approach to other assignments as a way of getting students to write more engaged work. He took the obvious route of establishing a freewriting day for the class—one day each week when the students could write about anything they chose. The results were discouraging. The students sat around fussing and twitching, and most of the writing they produced was mediocre. They kept claiming they had nothing to say, and Steve couldn't persuade them otherwise.

So he began developing lists of writing options for freewriting day. Each week he sketched out a half-dozen writing possibilities—some dealing with current events and ideas, others suggesting starting points for personal narratives. He tried to build in choices for writing poems or plays or stories as well as ideas that would lead to expository writing. He tried to find something that would appeal to everyone. And he developed what he called the "wild card" suggestion: "If you don't like any of the above suggestions, come up with a topic of your own."

The tone of the class improved enormously. Interestingly enough, the change seemed to result less from the actual topics designed than from the fact that Steve was helping the students see *possibilities* for writing: *contexts, audiences, purposes, modes.* Whether the students used a suggested topic, modified them for their own purposes, or rejected them to strike off in new directions, they were discovering new avenues and possibilities. By offering options, he was saying, "These are some of the things you can do with language." We have used this approach ever since with young writers in arts workshops, with high schoolers, with developmental college freshmen, in an advanced expository writing situation, and even for advanced graduate students studying the history of rhetoric.

To illustrate the wealth of options available on almost any subject, we want to play around with a thematic topic, "Human Relations." It is admittedly an abstract-sounding

Journals and diaries

Observation papers

Profiles and portraits (friends, enemies, adults, public figures)

Interviews

Sketches (notebook jottings, gleanings)

Reminiscences and memoirs (high or low times, serious or fun)

Autobiography

Confessions (real or fictional)

Dramatic monologues (written, improvised, recorded)

Slide presentations

Videos and films

Radio plays

Photo essays

Editorials

Columns (political, advice, how-to)

Stream of consciousness

Satire

Children's literature

Poetry, poetry, poetry (free forms and structured, rhymed and unrhymed, haiku, concrete poetry, light verse, limericks, song lyrics)

Policy or position papers

Fiction, fiction, fiction (short story to novel, sci-fi, period stories, fantasy, true-to-life, adolescent stories, grotesque and gothic)

Light essays (Thurber, E. B. White)

Plays, plays, plays (short scenes, one-acts, improvised, full-dress productions)

Advertisements

Commercials

Imitations

Jokes

Posters

Fliers

Independent newspaper

Literary magazine

Telegrams

Aphorisms

Figure 8.7   Some Neglected Forms of Composition (or, Must they *Always* Write Essays?)

theme, but one that can be made concrete and relevant through a carefully designed range of writing assignments and student choices. We might begin the unit by saying:

> Because you guys seem so concerned with problems and issues of getting with other people, we will embark on a unit on Human Relations. We will each look at different aspects of the topic, then we will read and write about other areas of concern or interest to you, and we will present our findings and products to other English language arts classes that meet at the same time as our class meets. To begin the unit, we want each of you to do a quick write on: "Why do people have so much difficulty getting along in the world today?" In small groups, you can share your quick writing, begin the discussion and then brainstorm all the topics and ideas and situations that occur to you about aspects of human relations. What kinds of problems interest you the most?

As students generate these lists, topics will emerge. On the chalkboard or an overhead, the teacher writes down the class's ideas and concerns. The next day students discuss the topics and decide which areas appeal to them most. They can come up with suggestions on writings, research, projects and presentations. For example, they might choose to do informal research first: Without even suggesting the kinds of writing that could grow from imaginative literature, we'll suggest some ways in which students can explore the topic:

[handwritten margin note: begin with a question, to spark students]

> For hundreds of years people have chosen to live in communes, intimate gatherings of people who share common ideas or beliefs. Read about some of these communities and write a report on the human relationships that are involved.

> Read about some of the nineteenth-century experiments in communal living that were conducted in this country (the Oneida community, for example) and look into some of the reasons these experiments did not succeed.

More imaginative possibilities exist:

> Suppose you were the ruler of a country in which the inhabitants were constantly squabbling with one another. What kind of decree might you issue to force people to get along better?

> Write a science fiction story in which monkeys learn to get along with one another and as a result take over the earth from quarreling human beings (an obvious spin off from the *Planet of the Apes* classics).

The topic lends itself to imaginative writing assignments (not that the above don't require imagination):

> How do you feel when you are in deep conflict with another person? Try to express that feeling through a poem.

> Write a short play in which you show a family that cannot solve its human relations problems. What happens in the end?

It can lead to speaking assignments (after all, "composition" can be done in spoken words as well as writing), including the old debate chestnut:

> Resolved: Parents nowadays are too permissive toward their children.

One could develop possibilities for drama and media as well:

> Videotape an episode from a soap opera called "The Cozy Corner," the continuing story of a family in which all the members dislike one another.

We can move the topic into interdisciplinary fields:

> At the library or through the internet, collect statistics on family membership in America. What percentages of young people live with one parent? with two? How many children, on average, are in the American family? Is it growing or shrinking? Show your results on a graph.

> Get some help from the media center and locate some articles on the chemical bases of psychological problems or disorders. Can our behavior be explained by chemical imbalances? Write a science report on the topic (or, perhaps, write a sci-fi story about a society where human relations are controlled by drugs and chemicals).

And lastly (but not exhaustively), we might encourage the students to do some community-based writing about Our Town:

> What agencies in our town are designed to help with "human relations" problems? After finding out about some of these places, work up a set of interview questions and meet with the director. What problems do they solve? Perhaps you could tape and edit the interview or write it up and present it to class. Alternatively, perhaps you can invite the director to class to be interviewed by you and the rest of us.

One could go on and on: This topic could lend itself to satire, reminiscences, editorials, policy papers, commercials, posters, fliers, and so on. We've given a detailed secondary school example here, but elementary children are equally capable of exploring an equally broad range of topics. Moreover, we've found that when students are working on different topics, they naturally generate an audience for one another. The dullest writing in the world is produced by thirty-five students writing on a single topic; with options, there is always a sense of curiosity: "What is so-and-so writing about?" "When can we hear your sci-fi story?" "Will you perform your play for the class?" The logistics of managing this diversity is something we'll take up shortly, along with ideas on sequencing writing ideas and suggestions to promote growth and development among your novice writers.

WHEN THEY (AND YOU) RUN OUT OF IDEAS

No matter how creative the English language arts teacher may be, and whether students are mainly developing their own topics or drawing on the teacher's options, there comes a point in any year when they feel creativity ebbing and they can't think of any writing option that sounds even remotely appealing. This is the time to turn from whatever is going on in the classroom and look to some less-often-considered sources for writing ideas.

Children's and Young Adult Books

One such source are books written for young people. Many books can be used to model a form or kind of writing. If a book explains everything there is to know about caterpillars or butterflies, students can follow the format of the book and tell others all the wonderful things about their own favorite topics. They can write of video games, synchronized swimming, pets, members of the opposite sex, or even the more serious topics of world peace, clean air, and honest government officials. Make it a habit to cultivate the acquaintance of the person who acquires children's and young adult books at your school or local library. Keep an eye out for new titles, and maybe even strike a deal where you are the first on your corridor to have access to the new books. Use them for whole-class, small-group, or individualized reading and watch interest in writing grow.

Surfing the Web

If you have access to the internet or to a commercial on-line computer service, let your students log on and browse for topics. We've been consistently surprised as we watch young net surfers, at the range of topics that provoke interest, at what will catch young people's attention. About the time this chapter was written, Steve was working with a high school student who had expressed an interest in "spirituality," though she didn't quite know what she wanted to learn. Net surfing, she found a New York Public Library web site featuring "world religions" and said she wanted to know more about that. From there, she made connections with a university philosophy and religion program, and before the Internet session was over, she was downloading articles on Zoroastrianism and Sufism, two religious systems about which few adults know very much, and had fired off an e-mail letter to a university Young Zoroastrians' club seeking more information. Did she have any trouble writing? You bet not.

Figure 8.8 lists some of the search categories available through a popular on-line service. Clicking on any one of those categories opens up literally thousands of items—books, magazines, discussion groups, bulletin boards, cross references. Not only does the internet provide a wealth of information, there are innumerable opportunities for students to use writing skills by corresponding through e-mail, asking questions at web sites, and contributing to chat rooms and bulletin board conversations.

The Newspaper

Steve once attended a newspapers in education workshop where the presenter argued that all you need to teach any subject is the daily newspaper. Teachers should make a list of topics to be covered in any class—English, math, science, history—and keep that close by as they read the morning paper and have a cup of

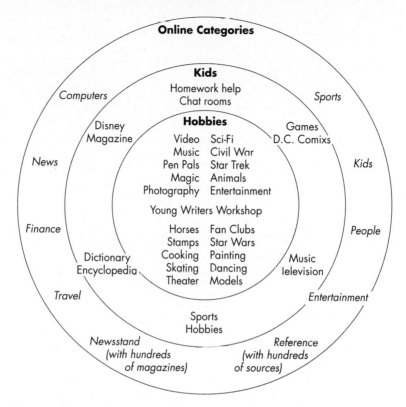

Figure 8.8   Surfing the Net for Writing Ideas and Interests

coffee. Clip and save any newspaper article related to the topic. Steve has tested this claim, and it pretty much proves valid. In fact, he has conducted teacher workshops in a number of states using *this morning*'s local newspaper to show that one can easily come up with twenty-five, fifty, or even a hundred writing ideas each day, day after day, no matter how small the paper. Every section will reveal ideas: news stories, letters to the editor, columns, advertisements, classifieds, sports, arts and leisure, and so on. Figure 8.9 shows a sample list, and, to prove the point, that list comes from the morning newspaper the day these words were drafted.

Create Lists as Starting Points

Lists are a quick way to get students involved in writing and in finding fresh things to write about. Ask students to make a list of "Everything Anyone Would Ever Want to Know About X," where X can represent computers, games, talk shows, brothers and sisters, chores at home, getting along with parents, dealing with divorce, succeeding in school. Students can share lists in groups and then jot down additional ideas.

television rating systems	the weather
owning your own business	high school sports scandal
country music	the Pope
divorce	aging and health
aurora borealis	Herbert Hoover
Pentagon coverup	Hong Kong
drug smuggling	space flight
plane crashes	rights to privacy
Iraq	oil
chemical warfare	Israel
the United Nations	Africa
Haiti	Coca-Cola
terrorism	the justice system
charge cards	back pain
breast cancer	Ritalin
golf	nose hair trimmer
minority representation	Voice of America
Spain	North Atlantic Treaty Organization
citizenship	law suits
pets	sonic booms
veterans	conflicts of interest
cable TV	speeding in school zones
cross-country skiing	profanity
women's athletics	role models
Hawaii	school overcrowding
storytelling	murder
volunteerism	velvet
environmental cleanup	highways
dog biscuit cookbook	coffee machines
eating raw eggs (bad idea)	pacemakers
fur coats	furniture refinishing
know-it-alls	female baldness
love	spelling lists
trade deficit	downsizing
corporate waste	the price of gold
computer companies	adding excitement to writing
retirement	investment schemes
starting your own business	celebrity privacy
floods	famine
voter apathy	Save-the-Children
teaching about socialism	teaching about capitalism
first aid at home	dangerous pets
wrestling with eels	urban infrastructure

Figure 8.9   Surfing the Newspaper: Topics Gleaned from Today's Paper

Short Answers

Ask students to write quickly and then share their writing: earliest memory, a time when you learned something new, the hardest thing about school, what adults should realize, the key problems in the world today. Answers are shared orally, followed by a freewriting on topics or concerns that came to mind as students heard their classmates' ideas. From these short answers, longer topics can emerge.

Fill-Ins

Diana's experience is that all kids will respond to these kinds of blanks because they seem easy, non-threatening, and interesting.

> When I think of X I . . .

where X can be teachers, parents, friends, music, school, adults, and so on. Papers can be passed around in small groups, and, again, lead to amplification in the days that follow.

COACHING THE WRITING PROCESS

Writing is, in many respects, a learn-by-doing skill. If you doubt that, recall that young children learn to speak by living in a language environment. Although writing involves the additional problem of sound/symbol relations (that is, transcription, spelling, and mechanics), what Marie Teal said about learning this skill is correct: "write, write, write." Of course, for learning to be most successful, it should be done in a supportive environment. For that reason we introduce the metaphor of teacher-as-coach of the writing process.

That children learn to write by writing has been recognized as pedagogically sound for well over one hundred years. Yet curiously, when it comes to actual practice, some teachers seem to retreat from the wisdom of this learn-by-doing philosophy. In fact, they seem to be willing to go to great lengths to *avoid* actually having students write. Thus students engage in vocabulary study, spelling work, outlining practice, sentence composition, sentence construction, and error correction, but little actual writing. Part of this reaction on the part of teachers is self defense. If you assign writing, you have to take time to comment on it—a problem that will be discussed in the next chapter. But a more basic cause of teachers' not relying on actual practice is that they assume students will write badly unless given all kinds of preliminary instruction on writing form: how to write an essay, how to compose a paragraph, how to vary sentences.

The same sophomore class described earlier helped Steve discover that teaching about writing is less important than helping students—coaching them—as they shape their ideas in language. While exploring various writing options, students had been encouraged to try different forms—reviews, poems, stories, position papers. It dawned on Steve one day that although the students were successfully composing in these forms, he had never given any lessons on how to write them. How had the students learned to do it?

There seemed to be two sources for these skills. First, many of the students had an intuitive sense of forms based on talk, reading, and TV viewing. Stories have beginnings, middles, endings, surprises, and climaxes; the students had all read or seen editorials, columns, plays, commercials. Thus they had a surprising knowledge of writing forms just from being part of a literate environment. The second source was questioning. When students did not know what something was, they asked: "What's a haiku?" "What's satire?" "Do poems have to rhyme?" "How do you begin an editorial?" These questions obviously opened the door to coaching.

But for the students who don't have prior knowledge about composing in a specific form the teacher can help by bringing in many examples of the form in question such as a collection of fables. After these are read, students in groups can brainstorm and generate a list of the characteristics or conventions of the genre. For instance after reading several of Arnold Lobel's *Fables* students will notice that they all involve animals, they all use dialogue, they all end with a moral and so on. Once students go through this process and articulate the characteristics, they will feel more able to write in the form.

We also have learned that questions about writing are best answered in *operational* not *definitional* terms. When students ask, "What's satire?", they do not need to be told, "Satire is a poem or prose work that holds up human vices, follies, etc. to ridicule or scorn." What proves more useful is advice on how to *make* a satire; "Well, suppose you wanted to make someone you disliked look foolish? One way might be . . ." Or perhaps better, "You know those stories in *Mad* magazine poking fun at a movie or a politician? Well, . . ."

How do we know when to intervene, to coach, to offer suggestions? How much do we say? Much of this must simply evolve with experience—as you teach writing from an exploratory or experimental approach, you'll start to find rules of thumb.

A particularly useful strategy is to play the role teacher-as-writer: for you to write some or many papers and projects with your students as a way of discovering what sorts of problems are likely to be encountered along the way. While teacher workloads probably prohibit you from writing *all* assignments with your students, we urge you to write your own assignments and activities regularly. Share your frustrations and triumphs as you gather ideas and wrestle with materials, getting them down on the page. Read some of your writing to your students and get their response (a scary enterprise the first few times you try it) as a way of modeling how such things are done.

Other ways of coaching through the writing process will also emerge as you engage students in hands-on writing. The following are among the techniques and strategies we've picked up over the years:

In *prewriting*:

• Build an atmosphere of support by regularly and sincerely showing interest in kids' ideas. You may have heard the same idea from dozens of young people, but each kid puts his/her own twist on it, and each predictably needs good adult response. Legitimize ideas: "That's *interesting*, tell me more!"

• Assist students in finding prewriting strategies. Some novice writers can use freewriting to generate ideas; some like lists or cluster diagrams; some work best

try to write — assignments w/ students

with brainstorming while others need a pretty accurate outline before proceeding. Share prewriting strategies in the class and encourage students to develop and talk about their own.

• Flood the classroom with writing ideas and suggestions. Occasionally chalk ideas on the board. Bring in the newspaper and browse through it aloud suggesting topics for writing.

• Think of class reading and literature as a constant source of writing ideas. We don't want to kill off literature by *always* making students write about it, but the books, stories, poems, and plays you bring to class suggest jumping off points: "Has anything like this ever happened to you?" "What do you think of the moral issues involved here?" "Is the ending satisfying—could you write a better one?"

• Talk about your own writing blocks and the fact that professional writers, too, have times when they find it difficult to come up with ideas. Demystify writing.

• Encourage a great deal of prewriting talk in your classrooms. Talk is easier than writing—work things out orally in advance.

• Allow time for rumination and germination; don't be impatient if students cannot write on demand. Not all procrastination is necessarily due to spurious causes, and most of us require some "incubation time" for our ideas.

In *drafting:*

• Share "getting started" strategies. Freewriting works for many—just getting it down , *anything, something,* for revision later.

• Encourage talk and conversation while drafting takes place, for it helps many writers clarify writing ideas to talk with others periodically as they write.

• Share your own writing in process.

• Encourage computer use in drafting—at home, in the school computer lab, in the computer(s) in your classroom.

• Be available for mini-conferences as students draft. Encourage them to ask questions as they write. For those who are shy, circulate around the classroom and ask questions, "How's it going?" "Need any help?"

• Treat drafts as tentative, as experiments. "You can always fix it up later."

• Remind students that they need not worry about correctness at this phase. "You can fix that up later, too."

• Let students write at their own pace, within reason. Some will be speedy drafters; others must take their time.

THE WRITING WORKSHOP

To the beginning teacher, in particular, what we have described thus far in the chapter may seem kaleidoscopic, a whirlwind. We've suggested providing lots of writing options and topic choice, which implies many students working on a variety of writing projects. We've suggested letting students find their own approach to the writing process, whether prewriting or drafting. We've said that students should be keeping writing journals and doing freewrites, that they should be talking with one another, that they should be holding frequent conferences with you. This seems, at first glance, to be chaotic.

Composing is not a neat, orderly process; it *is* highly idiosyncratic. Writings cannot be stamped out like lipstick cases or hubcaps; the process cannot be mechanized; students must find their own style of working. Some writers produce a polished first draft; others pump out a hack draft, a cross between notes, freewrite, and essay—all to be polished later.

The teacher can accommodate individual styles by organizing the class as a writing workshop. Within the workshop—a block of time set aside for writing—many diverse activities may be happening at once. On any given day, some students may be starting new projects while others are finishing up. A few people will be nearing the publication stage, while others may be displaying and distributing completed writing. A workshop mode encourages students to select new writing options, since it does not pressure them to complete a standard essay in a set time period. It also provides great freedom for the teacher, who can serve as a roving consultant—supplying help when and where needed—rather than as a hall monitor watching thirty people writing in silence.

In the course of a writing workshop, students may:

- Talk with one another about writing ideas and possibilities.
- Confer with one another and the teacher as part of prewriting.
- Prewrite papers in pairs or small groups, talking through writing ideas before committing pen to paper.
- Work in small editorial groups.
- Work alone on drafting and redrafting.
- Conference with the teacher about specific writing problems; help one another with problems.
- Read writing on similar topics.
- Copyedit writing for publication.
- Illustrate, print, and distribute their work.
- Read finished writing to small groups or the whole class.

The workshop is developed gradually. Only after a period of time will it reach its peak of independent operation. For teachers who have never used the writing workshop approach, one easy way to begin is simply to give students one day a week to write in class. Time can be spent at the beginning of the class interesting students in several kinds of topics. Once students are excited or have concrete ideas, they are often ready to write. The teacher then gives the students the time they need. For students who finish early, have another step or activity planned so they will know exactly what to do, probably sharing completed work with others.

The teacher usually begins writing workshops by having all students do the same sort of task, perhaps "getting started" activities, journal writing, or short common assignments. As the students and the teacher become accustomed to working together, the class can be differentiated. Perhaps some students will use the time for first-draft writing, while others will want response from a group. Still others may want to meet with the teacher while others will be working on publishing their work. We have also found that providing writing options is a good way to launch the workshop, since it invites individualized work from the beginning. Other teachers have had success with such workshop activities as freewriting, contract learning (see our chapter on grading), independent study, idea posters, a composition idea box at the back of the room.

Many teachers find it helpful to give each student a writing folder that is kept in the classroom. It will contain notes, drafts, and completed work. On writing workshop day—soon, perhaps, to become several workshop days—students first pluck their folder from the file. This helps keep the whole process organized and allows the teacher to assess rapidly where students are with particular projects. The folder can also include a log of student writing projects for the term. For assessment purposes, the folder can eventually be turned into a *portfolio,* a collection of pieces that the student and teacher agree best represent work done in the class.

The spirit of the writing workshop is one of exploration and discovery, not drudgery. We encourage our students to see this as good productive time and as a time to write freely and openly, to get advice from others, to revise freely, to move toward completion of successful writing acts, and, above all, to become masters of this complex thing called "the writing process."

SEQUENCING WRITING ACTIVITIES

Many teachers are skilled at developing good writing assignments, yet their activities frequently stand alone, bearing no discernible relationship to one another. Frequently this problem is a side effect of isolating composition from other parts of the curriculum. If writing is a Fridays-only activity, the assignments may be gimmicky, one-shot affairs. The pervasiveness of this approach is testified to by the popularity of professional articles of what-shall-I-do-on-Friday lists of writing ideas. Although one learns to write by writing (and even isolated topics are better than no writing at all), writing ought to be assigned in ways that promote sustained growth as well. To this end, it is important to sequence the kinds of writing one expects from students. In concert with other aspects of the English language arts program, the following are some common ways to put some coherence into your writing program. Our criterion for selection is that each of these is consistent with the experiential principle of starting with students' present linguistic growth and maturity and guiding them along natural patterns of growth.

Self-Directed Sequences

We have voiced our reservations about totally self-selected writing "programs," which seem to us to have the disadvantage of leaving students in a vacuum, in terms of recognizing the validity of their own experience. They simply fail to educate writers in the range of possibilities open to them. Nevertheless, there is much to be said for a structured variation, where teachers encourage students to explore their ideas and experiences systematically and nudge them toward wider and wider ranges of achievement and interest. Theoretically, if students simply write about their immediate concerns and interests, and if they are normally and naturally inquisitive, growing people, sooner or later the entire range of human experience will fall within their writing ken. Practically, they might need some help.

In a self-directed sequence, for example, the teacher might from time to time provide students with interest inventories or surveys (see Figure 8.10) to prime the pump. Freewrites about writing itself can periodically provide structure and rhythm

ideas

ABOUT ADOLESCENCE:

What are the advantages and disadvantages of growing up in our town?
What do you expect from your parents as they raise you? What do they expect from you?
How do you expect your relationship with parents to change in the future?
Whom do you trust and why? How do people earn your trust?
What are the biggest worries you and your peers have? How much peer pressure do you experience? What does it pressure you to do?
Is your generation better or worse than previous ones?

ABOUT SCHOOL

In what ways is school relevant/irrelevant to your life?
What do you think of the idea of home schooling?
Do we need school uniforms? Should the pledge of allegiance and/or school prayer be part of school routine? Do we need armed security guards in the schools?
Are grades accurate judges of performance? Is school too demanding? not challenging enough?
How could we improve schools for you?

ABOUT YOUR VIEWS OF THE WORLD

What do you see as the most pressing problems the world has to solve in your lifetime? What role do you see for yourself in trying to solve those problems?
Where do you personally see yourself in the future? What will you do? What will you be like thirty to fifty years from now?
Do you think democracy works? Have you thought about other kinds of political systems? What works in our current system? What needs to be improved?
Do you think world peace is a possibility in your lifetime?
What is your attitude toward people different from yourself? How do you get along with people from different cultures or backgrounds?
What do you think you need to learn or know in order to be prepared to face the world?

Thanks to the practicing teachers in University of Nevada English 631, "Childhood and Adolescence in Literature and Life," who developed these questions in preparation for a panel discussion with young people.

Figure 8.10   Questions for Self-Directed Writing

to the process: What have you written recently? What do you find satisfying about it? What new topics do you want to explore? In what ways do you think you'd like to develop your writing skills? Contract grading, widely used in school and college classes, also provides structure: Students determine in advance, and in negotiation with the teacher, what kinds of assignments they will complete in order to earn grades or points. Portfolio assessment, where students collect and self-assess their writing can work in this way, too, and in some school systems, student portfolios must include a range of writing produced over time—essays, narratives, biographies, imaginative writing—as a way of ensuring that students don't get stuck in a rut.

Inner Worlds to Outer Worlds

A structure that we have used frequently in both school and college writing courses draws on the research of James Moffett, James Britton, and others, suggesting that writing should probably begin with the personal and expressive before moving toward the academic and abstract. Interestingly enough, although this cycle is maturational—with the youngest students naturally inclined to egocentric writing, with older students moving outwards—it can be repeated over and over. For example, we find that at almost any grade level, students can benefit from a good dose of personal and journal writing initially as a way of securing and gaining confidence in their writing voice, before moving out to explore the world around them. (Note, too, that the sequence of questions in Figure 8.10 follows the same pattern, from "Who are you as a young person?" to "What do you think about the world out there?") At the same time, the sequence cannot be treated rigidly. For instance, many senior citizens have a great need to return to personal, expressive writing toward the end of their lives and come to care very little about that large impersonal world beyond their immediate experience.

In practice, an inner-to-outer-worlds sequence might begin by having the students write stories and autobiographies—the stuff and experience of their lives—before having them look at people and places close by that influence and shape their lives. Depending on their age and maturity, students may then be able to explore issues and topics of family and community, eventually tackling relatively abstract issues and problems of values, their own, those of their community, those of the world at large.

Local to Global

Related to the inner-to-outer sequence is one that starts close to home. In "reading and writing the culture workshops" conducted in small towns and large, and in countries as different as England, Australia, and Taiwan, Steve has discovered that studying the culture, geography, history, and problems of your town invariably leads one to explore broad issues in culture generally, issues with global implications and concerns. Depending on their age, experience, and maturity, students will increasingly move beyond immediate concerns to look at the larger world. In this approach, students start with local resources: neighbors, elders, museums, businesses, or government. They come to know "who are the people in your neighborhood" (to use a line from Sesame Street) and to discover their links to humankind by understanding the people close by. The approach is also informed by the "Foxfire" project of Eliot Wigginton, where young people discover and record arts, crafts, and traditions that are known by the elders in the community, and by the schools-without-walls and de-schooled society movements (see the Bibliography for Wurman and Illych), which suggest that much of what one needs to know and learn about the world can be found through communty-based resources.

In a "Reading and Writing the West" institute at the University of Nevada, Reno, teachers quickly learn that issues central to life in northwestern Nevada (e.g., water and land use) are linked to national issues (environmental resources). They can even be traced to key issues in U.S. history (Thomas Jefferson's view of the frontier to be tamed and ordered) and ultimately to global concerns (such as Buckminster Fuller's discussions of our stewardship of Spaceship Earth, or whether the United States has an obligation to subjugate its interests to those of the United Nations). Teachers in this program have, in turn, adapted the local-to-global approach in their own schools, including a K-6 schoolwide program where kindergartners explore their neighborhoods, the third graders look to community, and the fifth and sixth graders start to look and write about concerns beyond the boundaries of their own state.

Literature Driven

We hope that at this point you are committed to an approach to literature and reading that seeks student response to books that are appropriate to your students' reading skills and interests. In such a literature program, writing sequences naturally follow response to literature as students engage with texts. They write about their reactions to the ideas and stories in literature, move into writing about their own experiences, engage with issues and ideas, and even write about the literature as art, moving in the direction of informal literary criticism. In some respects, a literature-based program will also follow the inner-to-outer-worlds approach, since we want students first to develop strength and confidence in responding to literature in personal terms before moving on to more abstract discussions about books. Particularly valuable are writing activities that grow directly from *thematic* units, whether focused on *dinosaurs* (just think of the great writing topics here, from science writing to fantasy) or *human values* (essays, poems, plays, stories, credos). More conventional approaches to literature, including the conservative chronological/historical, can actually be enlivened through carefully developed writing activities. (Imagine you are in the audience while Jonathan Edwards delivers "Sinners in the Hands of an Angry God." Write a letter back to Edwards. You can do this by putting yourself in the buckled shoes of a colonial New Englander or the winged Nikes of a 21st century time traveler.)

Writing Across the Curriculum

English language arts teachers have campaigned for several decades now to have writing taught "across the curriculum." It makes no sense, we say, for us to teach writing skills if they are not practiced in other disciplines. To their credit, a great many teachers in other fields (as well as elementary teachers who cover all disciplines in self-contained classrooms), have come to recognize the value of using writing. It turns out that writing across the curriculum not only reinforces "English" skills, but actually helps students learn content material *better*. Students who write about history or science or art come to synthesize those fields more fully than students who simply answer study questions or fill in the blanks. English language arts teachers can approach writing across the curriculum in several ways. One can, within the friendly confines of the English class, encourage writing in various disciplines. In a self-directed student program, for example, teachers can encourage the kids who like science to write about it, the ones who like music or sports or art or dance or technology to explore those interests in writing. English language arts teachers can also coordinate their teaching with other fields. If you learn, for instance, that the social studies teacher is doing a unit on "capitalism," you can develop writing activities that are related (e.g., writing to or interviewing a local investment counselor, or surfing the net and researching what's available to the individual investor through electronic media). You can also offer your assistance to colleagues in designing writing activities, for often teachers in other disciplines are limited to fairly dull and ordinary textbook writings, e.g., "Describe the nature of the atom." The English language arts teacher can help them think of imaginative alternatives, e.g., "Write about the atom from the perspective of an electron—what do you see and experience?"

A NOTE ON PREPARATION FOR COLLEGE

Until the 1960s, writing instruction in the United States was largely dominated by a college-preparatory model. Driven by grammar/rhetoric handbooks, it "sequenced" writing from small particles to larger stretches of discourse, from grammar and parts of speech, through the topic sentence and paragraph, eventually leading to a staple of the curriculum: the research paper. Obviously the sequences of writing assignments we suggest differ from that pattern. We would like to see students write more and more in diverse forms and genres, to write imaginatively, to move freely and flexibly between personal and abstract writing, between essays and so-called creative forms. To some, this may seem to neglect the needs of the college-bound student. However, we would like to suggest that, to the contrary, the sort of approach advocated here is highly attentive to the needs of the college-bound student as well as to those who plan to enter the world of work immediately and certainly to all students who will obviously need to compose for the rest of their lives to participate fully in family and community.

We have earlier argued against the distinction between "imaginative" and "other" writing. We would also like to abolish the false dichotomy between "research" or "academic" writing and "personal" and "imaginative" writing. For whether or not one is writing about memories of past experiences or priorities for community or world development, one is doing *research*, looking at the data of experience, sifting through it, making sense of it, getting it down on paper. Sometimes that research will primarily take place in one's memory banks (a characteristic of "inner-worlds" writing); often it forces the writer to look outside for more information ("outer worlds"). The kinds of activities we have described in this chapter obviously include some need for traditional library research as well as interviews, observations, internet surfing, and myriad other kinds of data gathering. We argue that the student who is confident of the writing process and has composed in a wide range of forms and genres will do just fine in college and business and will have the adaptability to pick up the traits of particular writing forms, whether the form of the chemical engineering report in business or the idiosyncrasies of footnoting in a college anthropology or physics class. What matters is the ability to learn and to compose, not the explicit knowledge of particular writing forms.

A writing activity that seems to us to illustrate the preparatory value of the writing process approach is the "senior project," popular in high schools all over the country. Originally developed by teachers in Medford, Oregon, the project requires students to select an area of personal or community interest early in their senior year. With coaching from the English language arts teacher, teachers in other subjects, parents, and community members, students complete "the 3Ps": a Project, a Paper, and a Presentation.

The project involves them in real-world, hands-on learning: working at a day care center, helping in a park development project, serving as an apprentice at the symphony orchestra. Through outside reading (including imaginative literature), interviews, networking, students develop a paper about their chosen area, possibly a traditional research paper, more likely an imaginative alternative: a feature article for the newspaper, a collection of poems, a novel, or a symphony. Finally, students present their work to a panel consisting of teachers, parents, and fellow students. The projects are often dramatic—a reading, performing a play—and draw on media or visual aids—posters, videos, photo displays, and so on. We think this is a marvelous end to a school program, clearly drawing on and synthesizing a host of literacy skills.

And this is not a project that can be "crashed" toward the end of senior year. To succeed, students need to have been engaged in a process-centered writing program for years, back to the foundation years in elementary school, expanding through the turbulent years of the middle school, deepening and being enriched throughout senior high. We leave it to the reader to consider whether students who complete the project are adequately prepared for college, for business, for *life*.

◆ EXPLORATIONS

◆ Think over your career as a school and college writer, and possibly as a writer-on-your own. What are the successful experiences you have had as a writer? What were the conditions or the "assignment" that led to the writing? Share your criteria with other teachers and develop a rationale for these criteria. What do you know from theory that supports your position? What elements of best practice are embedded in the criteria?

◆ We've suggested the basic stages of the writing process—prewriting, drafting, revising, copy editing, publishing. Do some freewriting on your own composing process. What kind of a writer are you? What techniques and strategies have you developed to gather ideas? Do you draft rapidly or slowly? Is revision easy or difficult for you? Ask students to do the same mapping of their writing processes. Lead a discussion in which you explore the range of different processes and strategies that people explore.

◆ Start a collection of writing ideas or activities, preferably in collaboration with others to create a shared resource bank. Although we've warned against isolated or gimmicky assignments, it pays to have a collection of good activities. One idea we've found helpful is to put writing ideas on index cards or keep them in file folders, a starting point for individualized writing activities.

◆ Develop additional sources of ideas for writing topics. How would you develop composing activities from:

- oral storytelling (e.g., ghost stories, strange happenings, close encounters, close escapes)?

- artifacts (odds and ends brought in from home: photographs, kitchen objects, stuff from the junk drawer, objects for garage sales)?

- interviews (with relatives, friends, doctors, lawyers, teachers, sports figures)?

- group poems (students brainstorm for words on scenes from nature, powerful emotions—see Wordsworth—ideas recollected)?

- surveys (student-developed questionnaires about smoking, interracial dating, sexual harassment, peer pressure, etc.)?

◆ Choose a topic or theme or issue—love, war, identity, politics, pets—and develop an exhaustive list of composing ideas for it. How can your topic be developed as:

short story	video script	essay
play	letter	sculpture
graffiti	satire	feature article

Use the list of writing forms in Figure 8.7 as a guide.

◆ Choose one of your favorite literary works and develop a list of writing ideas about it. Aim to produce a list that would provide an interesting option for every student in a class (an optimistic if not totally realizable task). Which activity appeals most to you? Do it. Does it meet your expectations?

◆ Choose a concept in a discipline outside English, say, "the triangle" in geometry or "the nature of electricity" from physics. If you were teaching that subject, what sorts of imaginative writing assignments might you create to help students learn the material more satisfactorily? How many different ways of writing about each concept can you come up with?

◆ Scan your daily newspaper and generate a list of at least fifty writing ideas. Or, introduce the idea to a group of students and have *them* develop ideas for exploration through writing. Suggestion: Have the students also clip stories, photos, cartoons, ads, classifieds and paste them on a sheet of paper, along with writing ideas. You've got the beginning of a writing idea file.

◆ Fire up a computer, log on, and surf the net looking for interesting writing ideas for your students. Download interesting stuff and file it away, or compile a directory of web sites for your students' recommended browsing.

◆ Develop a sequence of writing topics or activities for a group of students you're interested in working with. Given what you know of how young people approach, love, and hate "wrighting," what will you have them write first? what next? What sorts of sequences would move them from where you perceive them to be to where you think they can arrive?

RELATED READINGS

The production of books for teachers interested in writing instruction has mushroomed in the past several decades as teaching writing has come to be seen as less a chore than an opportunity. Boynton/Cook and Heinemann are publishers who, along with the National Council of Teachers of English, have produced a number of excellent texts. We recommend that you obtain their catalogs and get on their mailing lists. For basic reading on writing, we recommend any of the books by the leaders of the revolution in writing cited in the bibliography: James Britton, Peter Elbow, Nancie Atwell, Donald Graves, Donald Murray. Ralph Fletcher's *What a Writer Needs* is a book for the teacher as writer and the teacher as writing teacher. He shares his passion for writing as he shows us ways of sharpening our own craft and the craft of our students. *Critical Teaching and the Idea of Literacy* by Cy Knoblauch and Lil Brannon has the potential to take one's composition teaching to a new dimension by placing it in the broader scene of political and social empowerment as fostered by education. Particularly valuable is their critical discussion of the "expressive" literacy movement of the past several decades, which is closely linked to what we call "experiential" learning. Knoblauch and Brannon are refreshingly candid in discussing its successes and failures as well as its political stance in opposition to conventional writing pedagogies.

CHAPTER 9

WRITING FOR THE HERE AND NOW

In this chapter we turn to the second half of the composing process: what we're calling *revising, copyediting,* and *publishing.* We remind you that the process of composing is not neat and linear. The "stages"—from prewriting and drafting through publishing—are really not very separate from one another, and most writers cycle through the stages in a variety of ways. Although we have chosen terms from the printing industry like "copyediting" and "publishing" to describe the latter stages, we want to emphasize again that *any* act of composing, whether making a speech, painting a picture, or making a video, has similar steps.

Revising is a central part of writing. Few people are able to get their thoughts down just right the first time, and writers toil and trouble themselves to find just the right word, the right phrases, the right ways of organizing their work. We make an important distinction between this act of *revising*—working with content and language—and *copyediting,* the term we use for the preparation and cleanup of final copy, including such matters as spelling usage, and mechanics. For a great many student and adult writers, worry over correctness has diminished the importance of revising, which is where one actually does the substantial work of making a piece say what one wants it to say. Copyediting (or *cleanup* or *proofreading* if you prefer) precedes the *publication* or *making public* of a work, sending it out to an audience for response, reaction, and action.

Revision is an act (often done in collaboration with other people) that leads to substantial changes in both the surface and deep structures of a work. Above all, it is directed toward an *audience* or readership.

WRITER AND AUDIENCE

The concept and pedagogy of *audience* in the English language arts classroom is a complex and interesting one. We'd like to say in simplest terms that for students to be motivated to write, revise, and even copyedit successfully, they must write for an audience, or, as Samuel Thurber said one hundred years ago, "No language is learned except as it performs the function of all speech—to convey thought—and this thought must be welcome, interesting and clear. There is no time . . . when language will be learned in any other way." (See Prologue.) In his book *Growth Through English*, John Dixon observed that one doesn't learn to write through the "dummy run" or practice exercises; rather students must write on genuine topics for real audiences, receptive readers or listeners who will respond to what has been written. In his important book on the process of writing in the British schools, James Britton observed that for too many pupils the only "audience" for writing was the teacher—all too frequently the "teacher-as-examiner" rather than a genuine reader and respondent.

Although these notions about audience are an important part of our pedagogy, we also must caution about over generalizations. We've taught fluent, competent writers who were deathly afraid of sharing their writing with the most sympathetic and receptive of audiences. We've seen students proudly put their writing on display only to be devastated by a candid but negative comment from a passer-by. We've had students who delight in the privacy of the writing journals and those who hate journals "because nobody ever reads this stuff." We've seen our best efforts at making the writing class audience-centered go awry because students don't always regard one another as real or genuine readers. Some of our best writing activities have included "real" audiences—write to the mayor! write to the newspaper!—and have fallen flat because, after all, school is still school, and "we have to write this to get a grade."

Nevertheless, with those qualifications, we'll assert that a readership—an audience, somebody to read your poem, to react to your diatribe, to respond to your video or painting, to rebut or shout "huzzah" over your speech—is essential to the veracity of the writing process. As a rule, students write *better* for genuine audiences than they do for the teacher-centered, turn-in–500-words-on-Friday assignment (and that generalization even includes student performance on spelling and mechanics). In their book on *The New Literacy,* Paul Morris and Steve discovered that when motivated to write and communicate, adults and youngsters have powerful ways of learning how to reach an audience. Writers aggressively master new information (e.g., the nature of the 500 megahertz broadcasting system for a report to the governor) and new writing forms (the nature of the foundation proposal driven by the need to raise funds for a community group). The trick is to find ways to turn the writing *class,* with all of its incumbent school-created artificiality, into a place where the vitality of audience reigns. (Let us also add parenthetically that the artificiality of school also creates the opportunity for the English language arts class to become a true community of learners, where students are their own best audience!)

Figure 9.1 presents our view of this complex relationship of writer and audience within the classroom. In an active writing community, fellow students often serve as the audience for what others write, but they also serve as friends, confidants, critics, and audiences standing in for the public outside the classroom. The variety of these roles makes it extremely valuable to engage students as editors of one anothers' work. A good

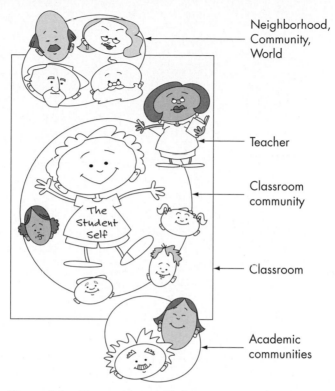

Figure 9.1 Classroom and Audience

reading group can serve as a surrogate audience ("Well what do you think the principal would think of that?"), as editors ("Really, I think you need more information in paragraph two."), and as friends ("There's no way they're going to let you say that!"). The teacher stands somewhat outside that peer relationship by virtue of age and authority, but under the right circumstances, the teacher can become an almost-full partner in the writing community, writing along with the students, participating in the give and take of classroom discussions, wearing teacherly authority lightly and helpfully.

Beyond the classroom itself are innumerable audiences in the neighborhood, community, and world. Although we'd like to be able to say that academic communities are part of the "real world," the fact is that many of our students must prepare to write for the constrained audiences of academic-as-authority. Thus we show academic writing as a distinct circle in our diagram. Sometimes, and optimistically, the academic authorities know enough about writing and learning to engage students in a discourse community where one learns to write and talk the language of a field or discipline by entering into it. But we know (and the reader will recognize) that in many cases the authority will be serving primarily in Britton's teacher-as-examiner category, treating writing less as "communication" than as "evidence of mastery" of particular knowledge.

The "student self" at the center of 9.2 is actually a very complex person, a person of many selves, a person who serves as both writer *and* audience for his or her own work. We've zoomed in on these multiple selves in Figure 9.2 to show, for instance,

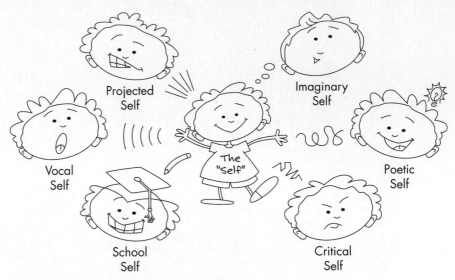

Figure 9.2 The Self as Writer and Audience

that most kids have a *school self* that may differ greatly from the self that hangs out at the mall. Our students have selves that are projected in a great many different ways for various roles and in multiple voices (or *vocal selves*, what the rhetoricians call our *personae* or *masks*). There is often an *imaginary* self to whom we can address *imaginary* and *imaginative writings* or *fantasies*; there is the *poetic self* that makes quantum leaps in words and ideas and the *critical self* that not only nags us about our moral and ethical *shoulds* and *oughts* but sometimes gets around to making us correct spelling and punctuation errors in our papers.

The reader can project many other selves onto this diagram, but lest we overstep our bounds and turn this into a psychology text, we simply want to offer our observation that student writing to and from these various selves is a rich form of activity that exists in balance with writing for larger and outside audiences. Ideally and over time, as students write for audiences "out there," they assimilate writing styles and processes so they become increasingly skillful as judges of their own writing, just as by enlarging the range of that multivariate critter we call the self, they become increasingly responsive to the writing and ideas of others.

The concept of self-as-audience also helps us understand such phenomena as different as the devoted writer-of-journals and the kid who hates to write "private" journals, as different as the student who writes great poetry and short stories but does poorly on essay exams, and as different as the students who both thrive and wilt in classroom editing groups.

THE CLASSROOM AS PUBLICATION CENTER

In the previous chapter, we emphasized the need to expand the range of discourse forms that students explore. Traditionally, schoolroom discourse actually narrows as students grow older because of increasing concern for academic and job-oriented writing. As we said, we want *all* students to write more than academic essays, term papers, and job applications. The literate student/citizen will write fiction and non-fiction, research and observation, poems and poetic prose, scripts and dialogues, private and public reflections. The obvious corollary for this chapter is that extending the range of discourses also and naturally extends the range of audiences students encounter. To accomplish this symbiotic expansion, we need to think about the classroom as a "publication" center, or what we'd prefer to spell as a "public-action" center, a place where words and ideas fly about, eventually finding a public forum through speech and writing.

Way back in the middle of the nineteenth century, a farsighted high school principal, John S. Hart, of Philadelphia Central, had a policy that the school would support *any* student publication that showed it could attract a modest readership of about a hundred readers. Over the period of a decade, Central had at least a dozen school newspapers, plus a wide range of magazines and other student publications. Hart's wisdom was in seeing that writers need audiences. When these audiences are provided through publication, student writing improves dramatically, in both content and correctness. Diana has taught and enjoyed journalism and has put in her long days of prodding the staff into getting out *the* school newspaper, but we'd like to see the range of public-action opportunities dramatically expanded in the schools, for all kids, not the motivated minority who staff the school paper. Interestingly, the computer revolution has placed the tools of publication closer than ever to the hands of students and teachers.

"Freedom of the press," it is said, "belongs to the person who owns one." That is, despite efforts at democracy in the media, the material that gets out to the public invariably reflects the biases and interests of the owner, the boss. Today, thanks to personal computers, desk-top publishing programs, laser and ink-jet printers, and the World Wide Web, virtually every one of us is a potential publisher. Students *don't* have to go to the high school principal to get funds to publish their work (although such support is still highly desirable), for they can run off a few gorgeous copies on a color printer or upload their ideas to a web site that may be visited by thousands of readers. Further, we are strong believers in the efficacy of one-of-a-kind publications: the letter to a public official, the original holiday greeting card, ninety-five theses tacked on the door in Wittenberg.

There are myriad ways in which the teacher can provide students with a readership. Some work is best "published" by being read aloud to the class, either by the author or the teacher. Some writing can be read and tape recorded to become part of a class library of recorded literature. Students' work can be posted on the bulletin board, submitted to a class or school newspaper or magazine, circulated in manuscript form, issued as a one-page information sheet, or printed and bound into a one-of-a-kind or twenty-of-a-kind booklet. Figure 9.3 presents a list of some avenues of publication that are open to your students. Plan to add to that list as other ways of presenting your students' work occurs to you.

It is important to note that every form of writing and each kind of publication makes particular, specialized demands on the writer. Students should have an audience in mind when they are writing, but often the best form of publication may not be apparent until after the writing has been completed. A short, witty poem that might bring a good laugh to the class when read aloud may die if set in print. A play that has absorbed a student's attention for several weeks surely deserves presentation,

Notes, journals, logs, and diaries*

Small group readings and writer's workshop

Reading works to younger students

Newsletter to parents

Class book or publication at the end of a unit

Bulletin boards (also clothesline displays, writing "kiosks," display centers)

Fortune cookies**

Group compositions done on the chalkboard or butcher paper

Theme-of-the-day posted at the front of the class.

Letters, letters, letters: to friends, to community members, to distant readers

Skits and improvisations

Reader's theater presentations of student writing

Parents' night readings

All sorts of books, booklets

e-mail

The Internet

Posters and displays

School literary magazine

Writer's club or center

Readings to senior citizens

Community events and displays

Videos

Photo albums and displays

Recordings of all sorts

T-shirts

Debate: classroom, school, community

School/city council

School "public address" radio

Cable TV and public access

*Recall that writing-for-the-self is also writing for an audience.

**We've *done* this. For a description of myriad arts and crafts projects using writing see, Stephen and Susan Tchudi, *The Young Writer's Handbook*. New York: Scribner's, 1984.

Figure 9.3   Ways of Publishing Student Writing

but it may work better as a reader's theater or radio play than as a stage production. As an expert on writing, the teacher can help the student find the most productive forms of publication. (We'll discuss more of these nonprint forms in Chapter 12.)

How would you "publish" this paper by Roman Cirillo, an eighth grader?

HOW AIRPLANES FLIES

Few people know why or how an airplane flies. The explanation is very simple. There no mysterious mechenism or machinery to study. You don't have to take a plane apart or crawl around inside to understand why it stays in the air. You just stand off and look at it. Airplanes flies because of the shapes of its wings. The engine and propellor have very little to do with it. The pilot has nothing to do with making the plane fly. He simply controls the flight. A glider without an engine will fly in the air for hours. The biggest airplanes will fly for a certain length of time with all the engine shut off. A plane flies and stay in the air because its wings are supported by the air just as water supports a person. Toss a flat piece of metal on a boat. Toss a flat piece of metal on a pond at it will sink at once. If you bend it through the middle and fasten the end together so its is watertight, it will float.

OK. there are some problems with the draft. It lacks some clarity and focus and leaves the reader behind from time to time. But if one looks past the surface errors and the occasional meander, "How Airplanes Flies" is a clever explanation of flight. The paper has a strong, clear, intelligent voice. One can hear Roman's patient instruction to someone who is ignorant of the principles of flight: "You don't have to take a plane apart or crawl around inside to understand why it stays in the air. You just stand off and look at it." Roman is a good teacher, and his explanation of how shaping metal enables the plane to fly is skillful, although incomplete. Roman might well flunk a test on analogies, similes, and metaphors, but he makes excellent use of analogy in relating how something floats in an invisible substance—air—to an observable phenomenon: a boat floating on water.

In its present form, however, the paper will probably not find much success with an audience. It has too many problems of clarity, too much drifting and backtracking, for a reader to stay with it for long. So how would we revise it for publication?

One possibility would be to show Roman one of the wonderful books by David McCauley on *How Things Work,* so he can see how an artist/writer combines sketches and words to describe complex technical phenomena. This might lead to an essay with illustrations to be posted on the bulletin board or included in a class booklet. Our hunch, however, is that a more profitable route might be to draw on Roman's obvious oral and teaching skills to have him present a demonstration to the class. He might bring in a dishpan and some aluminum foil to demonstrate flotation. Perhaps he can bring in some model planes, a glider, or some photographs of planes (we guess that he probably has such materials at home already) to amplify his talk. Or perhaps he could prepare a two-panel poster display comparing water and air flotation. The point, again, is to provide Roman with an audience, a "readership," a forum for "public-action" where he can present his ideas. And clearly, the mode of publication will have implications for how Roman revises his work.

Must everything a student creates be "published"? Should every scrap of writing ever written be revised and polished for public presentation? Of course not. As we've noted, writing serves a wide variety of functions for the writer, and an audience is not necessarily required to round out the process. At the same time, it is our experience that people do crave audiences for the language they create. In Chapter 1, we described "experience" as a kind of "engine" that drives the communication process. We might add the metaphor that *audience* and *publication* are a kind of vacuum cleaner at the other end, irresistibly drawing communication out of people.

WRITING FOR THE HERE AND NOW

Before we link the concept of publication to ways and means of evaluating student writing, we want to develop briefly the philosophy of writing assessment that underlies our approach. Writing assessment has traditionally struggled with a dichotomy of content versus form: students' ideas *versus* writing structure, the free expression of ideas *versus* surface language. This dichotomy, in turn, creates the problem of what to "do" with student drafts. Does one praise ideas and ignore errors? Correct the errors? Make students correct the errors? How do we support the ideas students generate while still maintaining standards? These perplexities have historical roots that can be traced back to the time when writing became a regular part of the school curriculum in the mid-nineteenth century. In his 1850s textbook, *Aids to English Composition,* Richard Green Parker was one of the first to comment on ways of evaluating writing:

> Merits for composition should be predicated on their neatness, correctness, length, style &c.; but the highest merits should be given for the production of ideas, and original sentiments, and forms of expression.

In some ways, Parker's approach to the problem seems quite contemporary, emphasizing "the production of ideas" rather than dealing exclusively with mechanical correctness and neatness.

However, like many teachers who followed, Parker seemed to find it easier to correct mechanical errors than to wrestle with abstract and nebulous concepts like "original sentiments." His text showed far more concern for pointing out "deficiencies" than for rewarding "merits." A theme-grading guide at the end of the text dealt almost exclusively with the kinds of errors that could be indicated in the margins of a paper with "shorthand" symbols, "arbitrary marks" of the kind "used by printers in the correction of proof sheets." Parker may have been one of the first teachers to recognize the practical impossibility of writing detailed corrections on a student paper and to resort to proofreading symbols as "shorthand" or a shortcut in processing large numbers of papers. (In our own time, we've even seen a variation of Parker's proofreading symbols: little cartoon stamps with error messages on them, e.g., a picture of a duck saying "AWK!" to alert the child to his or her compositional awkwardness.)

How would Roman Cirillo fare under Parker's system? Obviously he would receive a few AWK!s and several AGR!s for "agreement," for he surely has some trouble getting singular and plural verbs to agree. But do surface errors begin to get to the heart of the weaknesses and strengths of Roman's piece? We think not. His "original sentiments" seem to us important, and we'd be most reluctant to clutter his draft with error messages when, in fact, we think he is doing some interesting and valuable composition.

As we struggled with these theme evaluation questions ourselves and studied the history of our profession, we came to the concept "writing for the here and now." We have observed that few people write just for the sake of learning to write better some time in the future. Yet much theme evaluation stresses getting students ready for the next time they write, rather than helping them find success in the present.

For instance, with his talk of "merits" and "deficiencies," Parker sounds rather like a preacher trying to prepare his flock for the hereafter. Much composition evaluation has been based on this model, the assumption that if students write enough themes and receive enough evaluation, they will, some time in the near or distant future, write The Perfect Theme that will be their pass through the Golden Gates of Composition.

A friend who is in publishing helped us see that professional editors are *not* necessarily interested in teaching authors to write better "next time." When a manuscript arrives, an editor looks through it, makes comments, calls for some revisions, and submits changes. All this "instruction" or commentary is devoted to the aim of getting out a successful publication—now! The editor remains theoretically indifferent to whether or not the author's writing improves in the process. However, many authors (and we're among them) freely acknowledge that the editing process does help them write better, and many writers depend quite heavily on their editors for advice. The moral here is that by concentrating on the present, the "here and now," editors help writers find success, and that success often does carry forward to future writings.

Thus we advocate the same general attitude toward student composition. We think the teacher needs to be *not* a proofreader or a dispenser of merits and deficiencies, but a person who is concerned with helping young writers obtain success with their work—now! The commercial editor, of course, works with adults who are reasonably accomplished writers to begin with. Because teachers work with young people who are in the process of growing, the concerns and editorial strategies will be more complicated. At times the teacher should be an editor, dealing with strengths and weaknesses in papers, particularly, as publication time approaches. At other times in the writing process teachers must serve in more sensitive roles: respondent, interested human being, friend, adviser. The roles will differ with the student, the circumstances, and the state of the writing that the teacher receives.

This does not mean that a teacher must abandon all standards and accept everything with praise (a common myth concerning "progressive" teachers who are all praise and no constructive criticism). The teacher does need to have criteria for "good" and "bad," and certainly a teacher needs to be well-read in both student and adult writing to develop an extended sense of the possible, but these criteria should be applied as a way of helping students find success *now*.

Figure 9.4 offers a "Flow Chart" for assessing student writing that shows how the "here and now" philosophy operates. For each of the stages of the writing process (and again, dear reader, we remind you that the stages are far less discrete than implied by a boxy diagram), we suggest some of the roles that you can play as an editor/manuscript manager/adult friend/respondent/concerned critic/writing specialist/proofreading master or mistress.

You'll note that our chart includes assessment that takes place in the prewriting and drafting stages. As we've implied in the previous chapter, the teacher's responsibility needs to go far beyond merely making assignments and then waiting until papers arrive to be "corrected." Teachers must be deeply concerned, for example, at the prewriting stage that students are, in fact, engaged in the topic, have ideas to write about, and have a sense of purpose and audience in writing. Too, there are many opportunities, especially in the writing workshop, for the teacher to intervene during the act of writing to help the students make certain the work is on track, to help them anticipate problems, to make that first draft just as good as it can be. Our focus in this chapter, however, will be principally centered on writing for the here and now as it can be implemented by the teacher once students have prepared a draft.

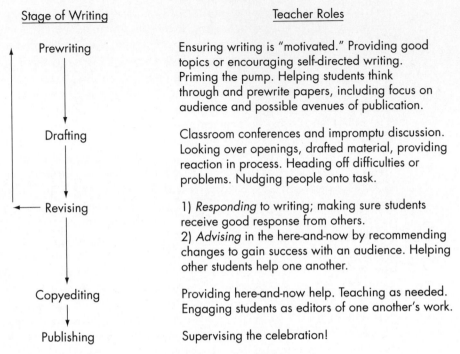

A Flow Chart
for Assessing Student Writing

Stage of Writing	Teacher Roles
Prewriting	Ensuring writing is "motivated." Providing good topics or encouraging self-directed writing. Priming the pump. Helping students think through and prewrite papers, including focus on audience and possible avenues of publication.
Drafting	Classroom conferences and impromptu discussion. Looking over openings, drafted material, providing reaction in process. Heading off difficulties or problems. Nudging people onto task.
Revising	1) *Responding* to writing; making sure students receive good response from others. 2) *Advising* in the here-and-now by recommending changes to gain success with an audience. Helping other students help one another.
Copyediting	Providing here-and-now help. Teaching as needed. Engaging students as editors of one another's work.
Publishing	Supervising the celebration!

Figure 9.4   A Flow Chart for Assessing Student Writing

RESPONDING TO STUDENT WRITING

We see the obligation of the teacher in assessing student writing as falling into two general categories: *response* and *advice*. Of the two, response seems to us primary. Response presents a reader's reaction to a text—it is why we write, what we seek as writers. In his wonderful book, *Children's Writing*, David Holbrook suggested:

> When anyone is really working on his inner world, he becomes excited—for he is making important discoveries and gains. . . . Expression will convey the bodily feelings of experience, and the "inscape" of an inward effort. So if we are responsive, we can usually feel this excitement in the words (as we can usually feel this excitement in a piece of music. . . . (p. 46))

What Holbrook is telling us—*challenging* us to see—is that the editorial process begins for the teacher by seeking out the points in a piece of writing where the student/author is really working hard on expressing experience. In this respect, the role of the teacher differs from that of a commercial editor, who moves more rapidly toward the *advisement* stage; but even there, the first impulse of most writers is to ask of their editors, "What did you think of it?", "How did you like it?" rather than

"What editorial advice do you have to offer?" Holbrook further challenges us by saying that even in the least successful student work, there will be moments of power and feeling, and it's our role as professionals to find those moments. Diana's and Steve's own teaching experience bears this out. If one is freed from being a proof-reader, grammar checker, or editorial advisor (at least for the moment), it's easy to find delightful spots in virtually everything a student writes.

But what if you read a piece of writing, once, twice, thrice, and just find it life-less? Traditionally, when teachers have received flat, dull, colorless writing, they have blamed it on the student: "You're not trying hard enough. Do it over!" We think that blame is often misplaced. Students seldom deliberately set out to create lifeless writing. Generating dull writing is boring indeed, and few people outside the faceless bureaucracies of government would choose to do it.

In many cases, the cause of dull writing can be traced more or less directly to the assignment or to an unfavorable classroom climate. Perhaps the assignment was poor—too complicated, lacking an audience, too "schoolish," irrelevant, or just plain silly. (Another good reason to write along with your students from time to time is to test the vibrancy of your work in reaction to your own assignments. If you find the topic or assignment dull, the odds are pretty good that it will miss the mark with the students as well.) Whatever the cause, if the writing lacks voice and energy, our "here and now" philosophy calls for some kind of conferencing with the student. "Look, I had the feeling you didn't enjoy doing this. Am I right? Let's see if we can rework the project so it is more engaging for you." On a number of occasions we've simply abandoned projects for individuals or whole classes when the drafts are dead on arrival. We find it better to bail out and start anew than to flog and slog our way through a topic that isn't working.

To some that attitude may seem cavalier and "permissive." "In life," critics have said to us, "not all assignments are fun and engaging. There are times when you simply have to sit down and pound out the work. Dull? Too bad."

We recognize the validity of that argument and have, over the years, pounded out our fair share of uninspired prose. But we counter-argue, first, that "life" is quite ready to teach those lessons to students (if, in fact, the lesson hasn't been learned), and, second, that the "here-and-now" approach emphasizes teaching writing through success, not failure. Third, we also include in all our classes warnings about the pressures of required writing, and we help our students think of strategies for approaching such topics, not with a spirit of doom and dread, but as an opportunity to turn one's skills loose on a difficult assignment. Chiefly, however, we want to work on polishing writing that is destined for success and, we see the success-making as our job and commitment.

To respond to student writing simply means to react to a paper openly and directly, reacting as a person rather than as a "teacher." This is a reaction to content, ideas, and "original sentiments" shared with the student, rather than a set of future-directed instructions for improvement. In responding, teachers can tell how they reacted to a paper ("I strongly felt the fear you described when the storm hit."); they can share similar experiences ("I remember a time like that in my own life."); they can agree or disagree ("I can see your point and think you make the argument well, even though I still don't buy it!"). The option to disagree and to express the teacher's opinion is important here. We're not recommending that you respond with bland niceties. Of course, there are times when you might pull your punches, and not devastate a student because you don't agree with something he or she said. But you'd probably pull those same punches with an adult, colleague, family member, or drinking buddy under the same circumstances. The point is to be human, not to be a mechanical pedagogue.

In that respect, teachers differ from the ordinary reader in another significant way. Teachers should be willing to ignore all kinds of graphic, rhetorical, and syntactic problems that a regular reader might find frustrating or disagreeable. Teachers will fight to dig out the meaning of a page. They will puzzle over idiosyncratic spellings, ignore the run-on sentences, forget about the fact that statistics and supporting evidence are missing, and struggle to uncoil long strings of loops that pass for handwriting. This is not to suggest that such problems are blithely ignored in the long run. The key point is that response in the here and now should not be confused with copyediting.

Perhaps the best model for the kind of response we advocate is the letter one would write in reply to a note received from a young relative—daughter, son, niece, nephew. Few of us would turn such a letter into a commentary on rhetoric or syntax. Rather, we'd cut to the heart of the issues being raised and do our best to react to them sensitively and intelligently. Student writing deserves the same sort of response from the teacher.

THE TEACHER AS EDITOR

Some teachers we've encountered have adopted a praise-*then*-criticize philosophy that we find a distortion of the here-and-now approach. "Nice paper, Charles," reads the vague opening comment, "but you have three typographical errors and no conclusion." It's a lot easier to be detailed about what's wrong with a paper than to describe, in detail, what a project is doing well or successfully. Figure 9.5 is a collection of phrases that Diana found in her own editorial comments on students' papers. Notice that she is not only free in praising students, but gives them reasons for her appreciation of their work, so they understand why things are working in the here-and-now. When she hits problems in a paper, she doesn't describe these in pejorative terms ("What a terrible paragraph!") but works to show the students why her reading went astray and what the student might do to solve the problem. Even her comments on mechanical matters such as spelling and punctuation are linked to her response as a reader: an unwieldy sentence is not "ungrammatical," but causes problems in understanding. Because the editorial advice is linked to description and explanation in the here and now, students can link the general characteristics of writing to their own specific ideas.

How *much* does the teacher say? Research in the English language arts (see Flood et. al) indicates pretty clearly that exhaustive commentary on student papers is not likely to be digested or assimilated. Students quickly become overwhelmed with advice. Moreover, from a practical perspective, teachers simply don't have time to write out the sorts of exhaustive comments and error corrections that were once fashionable. Our approach, also supported by the research, is to focus commentary on one or two issues or problems in a particular paper. The here-and-now approach gives us our criteria for selecting the problems: "What one or two pieces of advice can I give the student that will do the maximum to help her/him find success with this paper *right now*?" Sometimes that will lead us in the direction of story line or beginnings; at other times it may lead us to focus on grammatical problems that

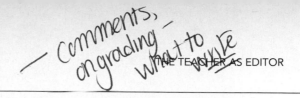

GENERAL

1. Strong writing voice—I can *hear* someone behind those words.
2. I can picture this!
3. I know just what you mean—I've felt this way, too.
4. My attention started to wander here—maybe you could be more specific.

BEGINNINGS AND ENDINGS

5. Strong introduction—it makes me want to read the paper.
6. Your ending came so quickly that I felt I had missed something.
7. Your wrap-up really captured the whole mood of the paper.
8. The conclusions seemed a little weak—I felt let down.

ORGANIZATION

9. This was very well organized. I could follow it easily.
10. I'm confused about how this fits in.
11. I'm not certain what the focus of the paper is.
12. How is this connected to the sentence or idea before it?
13. This paragraph seems overloaded—so much happens so fast I just can't follow it.

CLARITY

14. I don't see the whole picture. Can you add detail?
15. Good description—I could make a movie of this.
16. Great physical description, though I would enjoy seeing even more.
17. Tell me more about this.
18. An example here would help me see this person more vividly.
19. I'm not sure what you mean. Let's talk.

LANGUAGE

20. What a truly wonderful descriptive sentence!
21. This sentence is a whopper! You probably need to break it up.
22. Good word choice—it really captures what you are saying.
23. Your language seems strained here; I don't hear *you* talking and that distracts me.

USAGE AND MECHANICS

24. Ooops. You changed tense and confused me.
25. You switched from the third person to first. I can understand it, but it does distract.
26. Did you run this through your spell checker?
27. You seem to be capitalizing words randomly. We need to work on this in the writing workshop.

Figure 9.5 Commenting on Student Writing

induce confusion in a paper. Obviously, differences in age and experience of the student call for different responses as well; what might be appropriate for one student may be inappropriate for another. Such decisions are the sorts of things one learns to make through the experience of teaching, of working with a wider and wider range of students, of learning what kids care about and don't, and of seeing how they assimilate ideas, comments, and suggestions in their work. While that may seem a bit evasive on our part, as if we are passing the buck to you, the reader, we want to remind you again of the subtitle of this book: *exploring* and teaching the English language arts. If there were a formula for responding to and editing student work, we'd give it to you. Most important, we think, is to keep in mind the pedagogical ground rules we have outlined here, slightly rephrased:

First, *guarantee* that every piece of writing a student has taken the trouble to create receives the benefit of a good, humane, articulate response.

Second, filter your editorial suggestions through the here-and-now screen. Will this comment help the student make this paper more successful right now? If the answer is no, leave it out.

ON NOT WRITING ON STUDENT THEMES

In the previous section, we've described what is a more-or-less time-honored approach to writing instruction: The students write; the teacher collects the papers; the teacher takes them home and writes comments, and returns them, presumably promptly. Unfortunately, the model is also linked to the negative stereotype of the English language arts teacher waddling out of the building on Friday with shopping bags full of themes to "correct" for Monday. Indeed, one of the greatest barriers to teaching writing is the reality of that stereotype, the realization that we can't possibly respond to all the work generated by students if we're doing our job. Further, the writing research is sometimes discouraging about the effects of carefully detailed written comments on student papers, and it's widely known that students ignore the comments.

An alternative worth exploring, then, is *not* writing on student themes, and there are some strong arguments in its favor.

Aside from the fact that teacher-written comments are not always heeded is the fact that for some teachers, scrawlings on student writing is seen as violating or graphically spoiling the students' efforts. Although we don't share this philosophy fully, we know of teachers who *refuse* to write on a paper turned in by a student ("After all, do *you* like it when people mess up something *you've* worked on diligently?"). Some teachers have also taken to writing all their comments on post-its, which, like commercial editor's "flags" can be removed from the paper, leaving the student's work intact.

More effective, we've found, is to shift the direction of commentary away from written comments toward oral language. We do this by taking advantage of the time available in the writing workshop. As described in the previous chapter, the writing workshop is a time—a day or several days a week—set aside for writing. Students are encouraged to proceed at their own pace, so they may be working simultaneously on plans, drafts, and revisions, often working on several written pieces. The writing workshop provides an opportunity for the teacher to provide response and feedback orally through miniconferences, a very effective and efficient use of time. While the principles of response and editing we've suggested hold true in the writing workshop, the give-and-take of conversation put a practical here-and-now edge on the comments. "I love this opening. I can't wait to see where you'll go next." "You were going great on this yesterday, but now you've hit a snag. What's going on?" "Here, you've got a punctuation problem; let me show you how this works."

At least one advocate of this sort of conferencing, Roger Garrison, boldly states that English language arts teachers should *never* take papers home, that teachers have assumed an unnatural burden and that organizing a class around the workshop eliminates that need. We've explored this approach; we've even announced to classes at the beginning that we would not be taking their papers home, that all our response would be given in class. Although we enjoyed this style of teaching and found it productive, we also felt the need for written response as well and sensed that students wanted it too. There is something binding about written comments that no amount of oral conferencing can replace. Moreover, we discovered that in oral conferences we were sometimes handicapped by not seeing the big picture of a whole piece of writing, something that is most obvious when one sits down and reads a paper alone, rather than in a class where thirty other people may be clamoring for one's attention. An Aristotelian golden mean seems possible: combine conferencing and pedagogically sound written comments.

Some teachers like to schedule conferences as meetings between teacher and student, perhaps at the teacher's desk. This is a highly productive approach, but it's difficult—especially in the secondary classroom—to have regular semiformal meetings with every student. We especially like the idea of the miniconference, conducted as the teacher circulates around the writing workshop, making a comment to one student, asking another a question, answering a question or two from a third. In this way, the teacher can comfortably meet with each student in every workshop session. Another workable approach is to hold longer or more formal conference at intervals for the purpose of reviewing works nearing completion or several student writings in a portfolio.

So, understandably, we do all of these variations: Lots and lots of oral conferencing formal and informal, augmented by written responses to student work, especially as a piece nears completion and is ready for the publication phase. But oftentimes, we find that students want more: more suggestions on how to go about something, more models of a specific genre, more specific strategies that can help them confront a particular problem. Or, we have students who, despite conferencing, are not interested in revising, perhaps because of discouragement about writing generally or because they have no real idea where to start. This is where mini-lessons and modeling come in.

If we find our students disappointed, say, in introductions to their stories, we might structure a brief activity focusing on beginnings. For instance, Diana will bring in an armload of children's picture books, have students work in groups looking at introductions, and have the groups articulate what makes the introduction interesting to them. When students work to create their own categories, they seem to remember them better and often use the types of introductions they liked in their own papers. Barry Lane's excellent book, *After the End: Teaching and Learning Creative Revision,* is packed with wonderful mini-lesson ideas and strategies. His procedures have the ability to captivate even the most reluctant reviser.

PEER-GROUP CONFERENCING

Our writing in this chapter has, thus far, focused mostly on the teacher's role in evaluation and assessment of student writing. We think the response of the teacher is essential to model what's possible for students. Too many kids come into our classes never having had much response to their work, thinking they are bad writers and thinkers because somebody has red-penciled their grammatical or spelling errors and never told them their writing was good. So part of our function as teachers, we feel, is to show students what heartfelt response is like, how a good editor advises without insulting and coaches without dictating. Our response also helps students see what's important in writing, that we value their ideas as young thinkers, that we are delighted by their language, that we respect them as emerging writers.

But a key tenet in writing process theory also emphasizes the role of the classroom community in assessment: that students are quite capable of responding productively to one another's work. Launching peer group response sessions is tricky. If students do not have experience in the writing workshop, they may find themselves speechless in small group conferences, limited to vague gushes or condemnations ("great," "not-so-great"), or worst, imitating red-pencil teachers and destroying one another's confidence in writing. There are a number of strategies for making peer group response to writing highly productive and successful, and we have summarized some of our suggestions and recommendations in Figure 9.6. Our bibliography also includes several books that are devoted to the art of developing a peer-approach to writing.

- Experiment with different-sized groups: pairs, trios, groups of four or five.
- Experiment with self-selected groups or teacher appointed groups—there are advantages to each.
- Carefully introduce peer groups to your students so they understand precisely what is expected of them.
- Decide whether you want students to read their papers aloud to a group or to circulate copies for response. (Both have advantages, as you'll see.)
- Don't let authors "explain away" their papers in advance, making excuses, explaining problems. Let the paper carry its own weight.
- Teach the distinction between *responding* and *advising* developed in this chapter. Always have kids respond first.
- Don't expect professional quality "advice" from student writers; let them give here-and-now suggestions on what works best in a paper and how it could be made to work better for them as readers.
- Focus writing peer groups: This time work on beginnings, next time on endings, then on description, then on support for arguments, etc. Focused groups work more successfully than those that simply gather to dissect a paper.
- Monitor groups *very* carefully. Intervene if writing groups are dysfunctional or hurtful or unproductive.
- Encourage students to appreciate and understand the contributions of their fellow group members as part of a living, languaging community of learners.

Figure 9.6   *Making Peer Writing Groups Work*

Again, we would encourage you to employ a variety of approaches to these stages of revising student writing. When our own writing workshops are working most successfully, a freeze-frame of the classes might show a great range of activities going on: Some students working in pairs to respond to each others' rough drafts; a group of four or five students in a writing circle responding to or making editorial suggestions; a few kids working alone on revision, using the teacher's written suggestions as a starting point. The teacher in this freeze-frame actually appears as a kind of super hero or heroine in a number of places at once: holding miniconferences with individual students by responding to an opening sentence for one paper, a concluding sentence for another, helping a student copyedit a piece, working with another on a desktop publishing program, chatting with one of the peer reading circles, conducting a mini-lesson on punctuation or spelling with a student who needs particular help.

COPYEDITING AND CORRECTNESS

For too long, we think, textbook writers and composition teachers have blurred the distinction between revising—changing content and form—and copyediting or proofreading—polishing matters of spelling, mechanics, and usage. In their zeal to make students into writers of standard English, teachers have pounced on copyediting problems as early as the first draft, blithely pointing out errors in words and sentences that may well disappear entirely during the revision stage.

Let us make it clear that we don't take the question of correctness lightly. It is too obvious that the general public expects its teachers to produce students who are masters of this somewhat slippery creature called Standard English (whose nature we will discuss in the next chapter). We think that the emphasis on surface correctness is dramatically overstated (after all, does it *really* matter in the cosmic scheme of things if an expression is spelled "a lot" or "alot"?). Nevertheless, nothing will make the public see red or purple more rapidly than a mispelt word in a letter to an editor; nothing will bring down parental wrath upon an English language arts teacher more quickly than a paper sent home without errors marked and corrected. We need to acknowledge that much of the public and media overconcern for correctness is a direct result of what has happened in English language arts classes, where such matters of linguistic etiquette came to loom large in the minds of students.

The here-and-now approach, offers teachers a reasonable approach to these issues. We know from research that blanket correction of errors doesn't work. We know from media reactions that teachers appear to let errors go, to apparently not care whether students write with surface correctness. Our middle ground calls for us to put correctness in context: first, within the context of the writing process itself, and second, within the context of an experiential framework.

Within the writing process, the here-and-now approach clearly implies that discussion of mechanical and stylistic correctness should be delayed until the end, leaving students free to do the basic writing and revision of papers without hesitation because of uncertainty over rules of correctness. Only after students have revised their writing into a form that satisfies them should the teacher open the discussion of mechanics and usage. Even then, one should not charge in to red-pencil every error. Rather, the teacher (and peer editing groups) should concentrate on helping students put their papers into a form that will not confuse, irritate, or distract the readership. The teacher can point out that some audiences are offended by unclear handwriting or by language that doesn't conform to certain standards. The teacher can also note that failing to conform to some standards creates communications problems. At the same time, one might observe that doctors are notorious for their poor penmanship and that hasn't penalized them on the socioeconomic scale, or that minor errors in alot of communications will passed largely unnoticed by a readership. We've found that most students can appreciate these realities of the writing act and that many are willing to participate in a copyediting session to get their papers into a form that will not cost them their readership.

But what problems does one work on? Should we tackle "alot" or the run-on sentence? Flagrant disregard for Capitalization Rules or Dangling Modifiers? To some extent those questions are answered by the maturity of students, and the teacher will develop a strong sense of students' readiness for particular concepts.

More important, we think, is that the teacher (and peer editing groups) apply the here-and-now criterion: What is required to put *this* paper into an audience-acceptable form at *this* time? For instance, if a piece of writing is to be read aloud or tape-recorded by the author, work on spelling, punctuation, or capitalization is largely a waste of time. Even if the piece is misspelled, semilegibly written, and totally unpunctuated the author can probably read it, and pointing out those writing problems will contribute nothing to its success. If, on the other hand, the student is writing a letter to the editor of the local paper, common sense dictates that the teacher should pitch in to help the student catch any and all surface errors.

To link our discussion to that of audience, we want to reiterate that in our experience, students understand the realities of audience response to correctness problems, and students are, in fact, willing to work on correctness. We also find that in most peer editing groups, pooled knowledge of conventions is enough for the students themselves to do the work of copyediting. A tip sheet on copyediting that we have used, in variations, with groups of younger as well as older students is given in Figure 9.7.

We also mentioned that it is important to put copyediting in the broader context of the experience model of language learning. And now we have to confess that we have been slightly misleading in our discussion of the here-and-now approach. We implied that one should *never* think about solving future writing problems but should *always* concentrate on the present. But two-facedly, we have to acknowledge that *any* teacher *must* be concerned with more than teaching for the moment. We *all* want our students to master the skills they will need for college and jobs and life; in the long run, we *do* hope they will write perfect Golden Gate themes!

But the key to such growth, is, ironically, that by focusing on the here and now, teachers are most effectively preparing students for the there and then. As we discussed in Chapter 2, the experiential approach encourages young people to grow by extending the range of their experiences and by extending the kinds of languaging they do about those experiences. Younger children generally write about very close personal experience to audiences close at hand; older youngsters learn to write in more and more abstract ways for larger and larger audiences. We suggest that if one keeps the here-and-now approach in mind, over time, the growth and development we seek will take place. The young 'uns will develop the skills they

- Copyedit your work only *after* you have completed work on the writing and revision itself. In other words, first say what you have to say, then check for correctness.

- Read your paper aloud to yourself. (Or if you're in a room with others, read the paper word-by-word with your lips moving.) Some people even like to run a ruler beneath each line to make certain they don't skip over any words. Reading a paper aloud will often show you a number of errors and problems.

- Check your paper over for problems with *spelling, capitalization,* and *punctuation.* The trouble with these critters is that often your own mistakes will look alright to your eye. Check the margin near any item that you think might be wrong. Better still, get somebody else to proofread your paper for you; four eyes are better than two. When in doubt, get help, either by asking your teacher or by looking up things in a reference book.

- Check your paper one more time for problems with *usage.* These are things like "It's I" (or me?), "he don't" (doesn't?), lay or lie, sit or set. Here again, you know which of those items cause you trouble. Ask for help. Get a friend to proofread for you.

- A good idea is to jot down items that keep coming up in your work. For example, if you *always* have trouble spelling "necessary" or "recommend," write those down in a special place in your notebook. Similarly, if you can't remember when to use Capital letters for names of things, write down the rule in your notebook.

- Remember that a good job of copyediting is important to make certain your writing receives the response it deserves.

Figure 9.7   A Guide to Copyediting

need to transcribe their own stories using standard spellings; the older ones will master the more complex skills of writing for mature audiences. All the teacher has to do is focus on the here and now and provide the support students need, while increasing the range of opportunities youngsters have to try out their experiences and their skills.

STUDENT SELF-ASSESSMENT

As we have described them, these considerations concerning revising and copyediting may seem too elaborate and time consuming for an elementary teacher with five or six subjects to cover or a secondary teacher with five or six classes and 150 or more students. However, we have found that focusing assessment on the here and now actually speeds up the process and provides more time for the teacher to take up other classroom roles. For example, it takes less time to write a note of personal response on a paper than to mull through and write out detailed, pedagogically oriented evaluative comments. It is much faster to offer direct editorial advice keyed to specific publishing situations than it is to puzzle over the adult errors one will selectively attack *this* time.

In addition, as a class grows in the course of a term, the students can take over more and more of the process. All this creates more time for the teacher to miniconference, working on a one-to-one basis with students who seek help. There are also specific strategies that you can take in the process of having students assess their own work. You can:

- encourage students to talk to you and to one another about problems *while* they are writing.
- let students propose alternative topics to yours in the event a fire has not been struck.
- engage students in thinking about audiences for their work.
- work hard at helping peer writing groups function successfully.
- work at encouraging students to assimilate the editorial skills they develop in their writing groups.
- leave copyediting to the students.
- identify students who have good copyediting skills and encourage others to consult with them.
- encourage students to develop criteria of excellence for the work they are doing by putting themselves in the position of the audience and asking the questions *it* might raise.
- have students start notebook pages with the errors they commonly make.

THE DILEMMA OF GRADING STUDENT WRITING

What we have written in this chapter is also mightily complicated by the grading system as it operates in most schools. It's well and good to respond to writing in the here and now and to urge students to take responsibility for the quality of their own work, but if papers are graded, if the teacher is seen as the final authority dishing out grades, it is difficult to push students toward confidence and autonomy. Veteran teachers commonly report observing students who receive a paper back, ignore the comments on the page, check the grade, smile or frown, and toss the paper away. We need to dissociate writing from grading, but that is difficult to do in grade-oriented school systems.

At the time of this writing, Steve was finishing a three-year term as Chair of NCTE's Committee on Alternatives to Grading Student Writing. The committee consisted of interested educators from all over the country and its work culminated in a book on this topic mentioned in the bibliography. In a nutshell, the Grading Alternatives Committee concluded that:

1. There is no substitute for *response* to student writing, that the effects of grading can be blunted to some extent if students receive full and humane response to their work from teachers and peer readers.

2. Grading student writing is most harmful when criteria for grades are not clearly stated in advance, when students write blindly without knowing what the grader will reward or value.

3. Students need to be involved in forming criteria for grading; that is, even as assignments are made, students should be involved in discussing the expectations for the assignment, what will constitute success, and how success will be measured.

The Committee also agreed that the worst sort of grading is that which places a letter grade on a paper without much explanation or justification: "A. Great work!" "C. Not that great!" Surveying teachers nationwide, it came up with a number of ways in which teachers can avoid this sort of traditional grading in the writing class, including:

1. *Credit/No Credit* or *Pass/Fail grading.* In this arrangement, criteria for a good or "creditable" project are stated in advance; if students submit quality work, they receive credit for it. A popular variation on these approaches is the *Accept/Revise* grade, which, instead of "punishing" unsuccessful or incomplete work with a "Fail"or "No Credit," allows students to revise papers until they reach an acceptable level. In any of these systems, teachers generally award "points" or grade increments for successfully completed work, e.g., 10 points for a successful paper (with 100 points leading to an A for a semester), a plus (+) for a successful paper (raising grades from, say C to C+, C+ to B−, and so on).

2. *Contract grading.* Here students propose an amount of work and a grade to be received when it is completed. The teacher sets up general parameters, e.g., writing an essay weighs in at a C while a full-scale research paper might carry an A. Students then argue for the merits of the work they have completed.

3. *Negotiated grades.* Both student and teacher grade work independently. Often they will concur about a grade, in which case its validity is established. If there is a wide range between grades, they meet in conference to discuss and iron out the differences in their perceptions. (See particularly Boomer.)

4. *Rubrics and trait scoring.* The teacher and students create a list of traits or characteristics of a good piece of writing, e.g., content, style, originality, correctness. These traits may be weighted (e.g., 30% for content; 10% for correctness). The teacher (and sometimes the student) rates papers on a continuum of, say, 1 = poor to 10 = outstanding. Rubrics provide more detail than conventional grading and are overwhelmingly preferred by students to the traditional letter-only grade.

5. *Portfolios.* Perhaps the most popular alternative to grading individual papers is to grade portfolios, or collections of student writing. At the end of the term or semester, students collect their work, identify pieces they think are best, and write self-evaluations of their work for the semester. Grades are then given on the basis of the whole collection, its balance and breadth, its evidence of growth and improvement, or other criteria established by teacher and students.

◆ EXPLORATIONS

◆ Assess yourself as an audience for writing and other forms of communication. That is, keep track of the ways in which people reach you as an audience. In the morning shower you are the audience for a label on dandruff shampoo. In the car, you are a (button-pushing) audience for dozens of radio stations—how do they hold your interest? Make note of written communications you receive: e-mail, letters, brochures, pamphlets; list the ways in which people reach you orally—conversation, lecture, radio, telephone. Then consider how each of these audience functions might be made part of your writing program. Sometimes students can create in "real" media for "real" audiences (e.g., writing a letter to a politician), but you may find it equally productive to have them create for simulated media and audiences (e.g., starting a schoolwide "radio" network using the public address system).

◆ Learn more about the ways in which electronic media put "publishing" within the range. You probably already know word processing and how to gussy up your papers to make them look interesting. Explore desktop publishing systems and master one. Learn to create an internet web site. Visit your local copy shop and learn about all the intriguing ways printers have developed to put messages on mugs, calendars, bumper stickers, sweat shirts, and pencils. Which of these media could be incorporated in your audience-centered writing class?

◆ Discuss and debate the central assertion of this chapter, that writing for the here and now eventually leads to writing for the then and there.

◆ Some unresolved issues and debatable questions:

What is an "error"?

Do people learn by having errors pointed out to them?

How should response and revision and copyediting change as students mature?

Need a teacher respond to or evaluate *every* paper assigned?

Share your views with others and create a list of your beliefs on these important issues.

◆ The most difficult part of responding to student writing is getting over one's negative feelings about "blights" in order to look at real content. Collect some student writing and talk it over with others. Share your ideas on the ways in which one could respond to the paper productively. Learn to look beyond surface errors.

◆ Meet with a small group of students and engage them in a discussion of what makes good writing. To what extent do the students already have criteria of excellence of their own? How do these compare to yours?

◆ Develop the resources for a classroom publishing center. Collect the papers, staplers, poster board, glue, etc. that students need to turn their writing into booklets, posters, bulletin board displays, greeting cards, magazines.

◆ Look into publishing opportunities for young people in your town, region, and state. Many areas already have numerous writing contests and awards. Check into the National Council of Teachers of English and its programs to recognize promising young writers. Check the library for magazines that accept writing by young people. Put your students into a position to write for publication as professional authors do.

RELATED READINGS

At the risk of seeming self-serving, we have to say that the state-of-the-art book on assessing student writing is *Alternatives to Grading Student Writing,* edited by Stephen Tchudi on behalf of the NCTE Grading Alternatives Committee. In addition to reviews of the research on grading and assessment of writing, the book offers over a dozen essays by practicing teachers K-college providing detailed discussion of how they organize their classrooms, respond to writing, and deal with the complexities induced by the grading system. *Encountering Student Texts,* edited by Bruce Lawson, Susan Ryan, and Ross Winterowd is a powerful collection of essays, including a number of discussions of ways of approaching, understanding, and interpreting student writing. David Holbrook's *Children's Writing* is a classic in that area as well, including a number of essays by less skilled writers, reproduced in the original handwriting as a challenge to interpreters. Some think Holbrook goes too far in his "Freudian" interpretations of children's writing, but his attitude of commitment and understanding is a benchmark in this field. Another classic is Peter Elbow's *Writing Without Teachers,* a pioneering book on peer group response to writing, with many practical approaches to engaging students productively in assessing one another's work. For those interested in portfolio assessment, we recommend *New Directions in Portfolio Assessment,* edited by Laurel Black, Donald Daiker, Jeffrey Sommers, and Gail Stygall. Ed White's *Teaching and Assessing Writing* is also an excellent summary of current practice, with emphasis on program assessment (as opposed to our focus here on assessing and responding to individual student works).

CHAPTER 10

EXPLORING LANGUAGE

While we were working on this edition of *Exploring and Teaching the English Language Arts,* a language issue that had been simmering for at least three decades came to a boil. Concerned with the low academic performance of African-American students in its schools, the Oakland, California, Unified School District approved a teaching program in "Ebonics," a coined term that combines "ebony" and "phonics" to describe what has been variously called "Black English," "African-American English," or AAVE (Afro-American Vernacular English). This is a dialect that is used some or all of the time in an estimated 80% of African-American

---

One of the things that is a very interesting thing to know is how you are feeling inside you to the words that are coming out to be outside of you.

Do you always have the same kind of feeling in relation to the sounds as the words come out of you or do you not? All this has so much to do with grammar and with poetry and with prose.

—Gertrude Stein
"Poetry and Grammar"

Polonius: What do you read, my lord?
Hamlet: Words, words, words.

—William Shakespeare
Hamlet

Figure 10.1 Language Epigraphs

households, and it is an unusual dialect that, unlike "southern" or "northern" or "Appalachian," its characteristics are fairly uniform from coast to coast, border to border, making it essentially a *national* dialect of English. Linguists studying this dialect trace its roots to African languages and have shown persuasively that it can trace its American origins to the slave trade, where slaves speaking a variety of African languages mapped grammatical features of those languages onto English, thus creating a unique dialect, or what some linguists claim is even a unique *language,* with grammatical rules and conventions that are, in fact, different from English. The Oakland Schools called for teachers to understand Ebonics, not condemn it as an inferior dialect, and to use it as an approach to improving language skills, much as a second-language teacher might use a student's native language background as a way to master the new or target language. Indeed, the title of the document adopted by the district was "The Adopted Policy on *Standard American English* Development" (Emphasis added. See bibliography: Chomsky, Dillard, Oakland, Smith, Smitherman).

To those who follow debates over language and dialects, the uproar that followed the Oakland announcements was more or less predictable, though highly unfortunate. Newspaper readers all over the country wrote in their opinions, usually negative, often ill-informed. In the Reno press, for example, one person wrote to complain that if African-Americans could have their own language, then he, raised in Tennessee, ought to be allowed to use his own "Hillbillyonics," where "bear" is pronounced "bar" and rhymes with the word spelled "fire" and pronounced "far." Another Tennessean wrote in later to complain that the first person was ridiculing her way of talking, and she didn't like that one bit. An African-American woman wrote to say that she had raised her children properly, not allowing the use of "broken" English in the home, and she didn't see why kids in Oakland should be treated any differently; but another African-American objected to the labeling of Ebonics as "broken" English, arguing that Black dialects work quite successfully for their purposes, serve as a unifying force in the Black community, and that it stands as a living monument to white oppression of Black people in this country. At the national level the Reverend Jessie Jackson initially condemned the movement as an effort to continue the suppression of Blacks by denying them access to Standard English. Then he reversed himself and said that Ebonics was OK if it was to be used to teach Standard English, not to celebrate Afro-American Vernacular English, which Jackson (not a linguist, mind you) sees as a broken and lower-class dialect.

Man in the rudest state in which he now exists is the most dominant animal that has every appeared on this earth. He has spread more widely than any other organised form, and all others have yielded before him. He manifestly owes this immense superiority to his intellectual faculties, to his social habits, which lead him to aid and defend his fellows, and to his corporeal structure. The supreme importance of these characteristics has been proved by the final arbitrament of the battle for life. Through his powers of intellect, articulate language has been evolved; and on this wonderful advancement is finally dependent.

—Charles Darwin
The Descent of Man

Figure 10.2 Charles Darwin

Before the end of this chapter, we'll return to the question of Ebonics and expand the discussion to all dialects, English as a first and second language, Standard English, prestige and non-prestige dialects, English as a national language, and the tricky problems of handling these issues in the English language arts classroom. For the moment, we want to comment that the Ebonics movement epitomizes the depth of linguistic *misunderstanding* that is afloat in society, and the vehemence of the debate was exacerbated by ignorance. We don't want to cast blame here, but we do need to point out that English language arts teachers have an important obligation to increase people's understanding of language. Our "program" for language study in this chapter will be, first, to define some terms to clear away possible misunderstandings, second, to discuss ways in which teachers can increase students' awareness of and competence in language generally, and finally, to discuss the specific issue of language "correctness."

GETTING BACK TO BASICS

Every few years politicians seem to reinvent "basics" and make their campaign theme "First Things First." They advocate "the elimination of frills" and promise a return to "old standards." In some ways, theirs is an appealing strategy that cuts to the heart of America's desire for efficiency, directness, and simplicity; and it often wins a good many votes, especially in an era when the public is widely dissatisfied with its public schools.

English teachers also hear this cry from time to time. "Let's get back to the three Rs in school." "Why didn't someone teach my secretary to spell or punctuate?" "We here at the State U find our new students are abominably weak on fundamentals." "Of course I want my child to read literature, but after all, certain other things must come first." Often the demand for basics is phrased as a broad, unanswerable question: "Given all the money we spend on the schools, is it really too much to ask that the graduates be able to speak and write the Queen's English properly?"

As the Oakland Ebonics debate suggests, language arts teachers are at the center of a basics debate. More and more parents have become upset about what they take to be a neglect of "basic skills" and have translated their concern into threats to limit funding. This, in turn, has pressured administrators and led to the movement to hold teachers accountable for listing fundamental skills and showing student improvement on test scores. Although to our way of thinking, standardized test scores have very little to do with student global performance in language, state after state, and, indeed, our federal government, seem to be as much interested in introducing tests as a threat to teachers and students as they are in actually remedying problems in the schools or funding comprehensive language development projects.

Like the appeal of the politician, a proclaimed interest in basics is very satisfying for many parents and administrators. Blue-collar parents are given a kind of assurance that their children will be able to rise in life; white-collar and suburban parents are reassured that their supremacy will not be undercut by "progressivist" English teachers who encourage "sloppy" speech and act as if "anything goes."

In a persuasive little book, *Basic Skills* Herbert Kohl has observed that traditionally, definitions of and demands for "basic skills" vary from one interest group to another. Kohl himself argues for a broad definition of basics, including learning how to use language successfully, how to compute, how to use tools and information. We like his emphasis on broad basics, but it is clear that in English language arts teaching, "basics" almost invariably means a narrow range of surface features in language, those associated with so-called Standard English.

English language arts teachers themselves have helped to create this overemphasis on surface correctness. Although they may not have been entirely certain of what they were trying to do in writing classes, they have stressed "grammar" and correctness—faithfully, consistently, without hesitation or doubt, year after year. It is unlikely that the emphasis on grammar has actually taught very much to students, but it obviously has made the graduates of our schools intensely aware of correctness. Thus parents are delighted to join in the demand for a return to basics, whether or not they ever learned anything from their own bout with grammar.

The hold of grammar over the English curriculum has been strong for over one hundred years. Beginning in the fifth or sixth grade, children have received intensive instruction in grammar at annual intervals for six or seven years. Few children seem to remember much grammar from year to year, and many students quite honestly tell the teacher in June that they don't recall having studied the noun in September, despite the fact that the entire month was devoted to it. A growing body of research argues against teaching of formal grammar as a route to improved language usage. As a result, many teachers have cut down on the teaching of grammar, sometimes to the dismay of the taxpaying public. However, the decrease in grammar teaching should not be equated with a decline in standards, and there is considerable confusion on this matter. Much of the conflict can be traced to what people expect the teacher of "grammar" to accomplish. Indeed, part of the problem simply concerns terminology, and some preliminary definitions are thus in order. Specifically, we will ask our readers to be very clear and precise in their use of four terms: *grammar, usage, spelling/mechanics,* and *dialect*.

GRAMMAR

Grammar is most simply defined as "a description of how English works." Through a process of analysis, the grammarian discovers the various components or parts of the language system and how they fit together. Grammar is a description of the language conventions that a speaker of the language has mastered in order to communicate with other people. Grammar is not a set of rules telling how one is "supposed" to speak, and it does not prescribe behavior. It simply makes note of the language behavior that native speakers have learned. Very few people actually speak "ungrammatically," because something that is ungrammatical does not follow the basic patterns of English and therefore cannot be understood by another person. This statement is ungrammatical:

"Nobody ain't and got me ain't got nobody yet I."

It was produced by scrambling a sentence to break up English word order. Here is the grammatical version of the sentence:

"I ain't got nobody, and nobody ain't got me yet."

Now, your ears may bristle at the use of "ain't" and the double negative, but this sentence follows normal English word patterns and it can therefore be understood by listeners, even though they might be somewhat offended or bothered by some of the word choices. Another word for grammar in this sense is "syntax": how sentences are constructed. Never mind the kids' joke that grammar is a "sin tax."

Unfortunately, grammar has long been seen as *prescriptive* rather than *descriptive*. As you may know from taking a linguistics class, the grammars of English that were first developed in the seventeenth century—where we get our grammar of *nouns* and *verbs*, *simple* and *compound/complex* sentences—were highly prescriptive, attempting to legislate how people talk. But at its best, grammar is a science of language, not a set of rules of behavior. It is not to be confused with *usage* or *dialects*, or, for that matter, with spelling.

USAGE

This term should be used to describe a range of socially significant choices available to a speaker within the grammar of a language. Either of the following can be understood:

> "I ain't got nobody and nobody ain't got me yet."
> "I haven't anyone, and no one has gotten me yet."

The difference between the statements is that each speaker reveals himself or herself to be a member of a particular social class. Usage is a sociological phenomenon, not primarily linguistic, which means that it is concerned with the perceived social level of the speaker rather than with understanding or communication of messages. Usage is relative, and it is neither correct nor incorrect in itself. We have to be candid: "Standard" usage is generally little more than the usage habits of the people in a country who are either (1) envied because of their superior breeding, intelligence, charm, and wit or (2) envied because of their superior wealth. The latter is more often the case. To some, this seems a cynical view of the nature of the "pure" form of our mother tongue. But the history of English shows that standard usage is a matter of convention, custom, and prestige; it is not an inherently superior dialect.

In the schools, our work has been enormously complicated by the blurring of the terms grammar and usage. You'll often hear that someone has "bad grammar" when what is meant is that he/she doesn't use the standard dialect. This misuse is damaging, for it implies that somehow studying grammar (how the language works) will change how people talk and write. As we'll see a little further on, that connection is at best problematic.

SPELLING/MECHANICS

iaintgotnobudyandnobudyaingotmeyethesaidafaintsmileplayinacrosthislips

Straighten that out, and you've got (or should it be "gotten"?) yourself an "A" for spelling and mechanics on your report card. Mechanics are simply writing or transcription conventions—capitalization and punctuation—that make it possible for one person to read the writing of another. Spelling is, well, spelling, a set of conventions for noting down words, which helps make connections between written and spoken English. These conventions are standardized and do not vary the way usage does. However, they are also arbitrary in the sense that they are merely symbols for aspects of spoken language.

For instance, the "period" used to be called a "full stop" because it marked where a speaker paused at the end of a grammatical unit. It could just as easily be called a "breather" and symbolized by an icon in the shape of a lung! Likewise, spelling is simply a way of attempting to represent speech sounds. English happens to use twenty-six letters of the alphabet to represent something like 250 English speech sounds. We could use different symbols altogether or strive (as some have) to create an alphabet that would represent these sounds unambiguously (an alphabet, say, where "s" always stood for a hissing sound and "c" for a hard glottal noise). Spelling is conventional as well; that is, over the years, "standard" forms have evolved. But it is useful to recall that this standardization has evolved with printing; in an earlier era, people spelt pretty much the way they felt like speling, and it didn't kreate partikularlie serious problems in komprehensun.

To recap, although spelling and mechanics are matters of convention and custom, they are nonetheless standard. A writer must follow them if he or she is to gain support of a readership. Teachers must be cautious about over-teaching these codes. An exciting area of research in elementary children's language learning shows that letting kids play with "invented spellings," spelling the way they think words should be spelled, does no harm and eventually helps children come to standardized spellings (Goodman, Weaver). The research (Flood) suggests that in the end mechanics and spelling are learned as much from reading as from direct instruction anyway, but more on that topic later.

DIALECTS

A "dialect," or perhaps better, a "variety" of English is a collection of features, pronunciation, usage, style, vocabulary that simply go together because people have grown up speaking in communities. Ebonics is a dialect of English; so is Yankee, Southern, Appalachian, Valley Girl, Brooklynese, and so on. (Actually even here we oversimplify, since the "Yankee" of Providence, Rhode Island, differs considerably from that of Boston, Massachusetts, or Weld, Maine, even though the three communities have common as well as idiosyncratic features.) *Everybody speaks a dialect,* although most people are blind to their own: "I speak just right; you talk funny." There are two important linguistic facts to recall about dialects (in addition to remembering that everyone—you included—has one):

1. *All dialects "work" just fine.* Every dialect serves its users quite nicely. Ebonics or Appalachian are not "broken" English. Southern is not a slower or inadequate form nor are the allegedly crisp Yankee dialects. New Yawk works just fine. Any dialect develops in response to the needs of its users and, within its linguistic group, function the way all language should: to powerfully express ideas, emotions, and experiences. (See Gertrude Stein's epigraph at the beginning of this chapter.)

2. *Dialects have varying levels of prestige.* Here's where the sticky wicket of "standard" rears its ugly head (to mix metaphors, but to do so in proper "grammar"). So-called "Standard English" doesn't work any better than any other dialect; but it does carry an official stamp of approval: it's the dialect of usage handbooks, it's the dialect of the news networks, it's generally the dialect that employers prefer. There

are consequences for not having mastery of it, and that's why the Oakland Unified School District was teaching Ebonics, not to trap kids in their linguistic community, but to give them some social mobility.

TEACHING GRAMMAR

For generations, teachers of English have presented lessons in grammar (the description of how English works), thinking they were teaching standard usage (the conventions of language followed by the middle and upper classes) and mechanics (the standard code of transcription conventions). The motivation behind this instruction has been to provide students with access to higher social levels. Thus students have been told such things as, "It's important for you to know grammar because you'll need it in life." It would be pleasant if life responded to laws like that, but not surprisingly, students have sensed that it doesn't and have gone on not learning the noun and the comma. It seems apparent that teaching rules and laws does not significantly change performance, and most research attempts to prove otherwise have failed.

Grammar may be the most researched topic in the English curriculum. Throughout the twentieth century, one study after another has unsuccessfully attempted to show some sort of relationship between grammar knowledge and what people do with language. We can't go into detail reciting the "gospel" on this research but strongly recommend that you explore some of the books in our recommended reading section that summarize the case against schoolhouse grammar.

Does this mean we should shelve grammar altogether? never teach it? never mention it? What about usage, then? Do we not teach it either? Do the schools refuse to let kids in on the secrets of the standard language, which, we've acknowledged *is* unquestionably the prestige dialect of English?

Gertrude Stein's playfulness with grammar helps us put those questions into broader perspective. Her "Poetry and Grammar" essay suggests that there is so much more to language than mere grammar, that we have to avoid being trapped in the quicksands of grammar, usage, and correctness.

That teaching grammatical rules does not change performance is a function of the relationship between rules and performance—not of the quality of grammar or the imaginativeness of instruction. That is, from time to time you'll hear or read of a wonderful new grammar or technique for teaching. Or you'll hear that "If only English teachers would try hard, grammar could be taught." Such methods don't bring about the correctness millennium because grammars are not designed to change usage habits. Teachers need to put the teaching of grammar in perspective for themselves and make their own set of judgments about what value it has in the schools. We will briefly present our own formula for putting grammar in its place by sketching out three areas where we think grammar is useful:

1. As a source of information about language and language learning for teachers. Grammar study, treated as description, not prescription, provides numerous insights into the language learning process, and it is a vital part of a teacher's background. In fact, it is through the study of modern grammars that one can most clearly see why the teaching of grammar does not promote language change. (See the recommended books at the end of this chapter for some introductory texts.)

2. As a source of terms and tools for talking about language. There are times when a knowledge of grammatical terminology provides a convenient way of talking about language. The discussion of language that will go on in the English class can sometimes be simplified through use of common terms. Thus we are not opposed to the occasional and periodic introduction of basic terms and definitions of grammar. In her excellent book, *Teaching Grammar in Context,* Connie Weaver argues that any teaching of grammar should be both *contextual* and *constructivist;* that is, the grammar should be treated as the occasion provides, with emphasis on helping students apply the ideas directly to their own work. However, we believe very strongly that the introduction of grammar-as-terminology should be done briefly, and the teacher should watch closely to see whether it is producing any positive results. After all, there are many ways of talking about language and composition, and grammar is only one of them. Often the time spent teaching grammar would be much more effectively given over to additional writing or speaking activities. We've found in our own teaching that we can talk about writing and literature in more specific detail by referring to content, rather than grammar. As Gertrude Stein might say, the thing that is interesting about nouns is that they are penguins and platypuses and loves and hates. Obviously, *some* students *can* employ the abstract language of grammar to discuss writing, to discuss literature. But the evidence is clear that not all students can operate from this intellectual frame. The brief introduction allows those who *can* to learn how, while not handicapping the others.

3. As part of intellectual inquiry. When divorced from concerns about usage and correctness, the study of syntax can be interesting for some students. Why is English a "word order" language? Does anyone know how German works? How does it differ? Who's studying Latin? What differences do you see between Latin and English grammars? We think that sort of study can help students gain a feeling for and an understanding of the nature of their mother tongue, but it should not be expected to eradicate "ain'ts" and "he don'ts" from the next set of papers.

EXPLORING THE DIMENSIONS OF LANGUAGE

In the debates over grammar and correctness, people sometimes lose sight of the fact that one of our goals as teachers of English is to help students gain more personal power through language. We want students to be articulate so they can explain their stances and feelings, to write so they can share their views of the world, and to read so they can get the information or the enjoyment they seek. We want them to be curious about language and to wonder how it works, to think about nonverbal communication and to be aware of its effects, to be willing to take risks with language by using new words and phrases, and to be aware of how language affects a reader or listener.

We are convinced that if students knew more of language beyond correctness—that is, if they better understood how language itself functions, they would be more effective writers and readers. Thus our approach to language in the classroom begins with the third of the values argued previously: "grammar" (or more broadly, "language") as a part of intellectual exploration and understanding. Lest that sound collegiate or abstract, let us say that we think this study should begin with kindergartners and extend all the way through college. We be talking with kids of all ages about language. "Now that's an interesting word! Where did you learn that?" "What are your favorite words and why?" "How many different ways of talking do we have in this classroom?" "Whoever told you that you have 'bad grammar,' because your grammar sounds just fine to me?" The language curriculum is never farther away than the next utterance you or a child make. We have our students collect what we call "language artifacts"—examples of language in use—and maintain journals or notebooks commenting on them. An artifact notebook may contain snatches of overheard conversation, the health warning from a cigarette pack, a political cartoon, or a comic strip. We regularly pause in our classroom deliberations to explore this marvelous human creation called language.

Many classroom explorations of alternative forms of language study fall in the general area of "sociolinguistics"—the study of language, human beings, and their interactions—an area that students find fascinating. Although knowledge of language and society will not automatically improve students' language skills, it often helps them deepen their feeling for language and how it shapes their lives. We propose that teachers explore language through "interludes," language lessons of ten minutes, a day, or a week. After students have finished a major project in reading and writing, pause to let them try some of the following language explorations.

1. Body Talk. Study "kinesics": how people interact through physical mannerisms. The concept of body language is intriguing (and even a bit frightening), and young people of many ages enjoy talking about it and exploring its consequences. How can you tell when somebody is shy or nervous? How do you know when somebody is not telling the truth to you just by looking at him or her? How do you size up a new teacher or a new kid on the first day of school? Play "Emotional Charades," where students mime basic emotions—love, hate, excitement, fear—using only facial expressions or physical movement. How can you tell when the teacher is in a bad mood? How do you know you're not welcome to sit with a specific group at lunch? How can you tell a parent is mad before he or she says anything? Some students may enjoy observing people at a distance and trying to record their nonverbal "conversations." By being aware of what this nonverbal form of communication can mean, students can more easily communicate, because they can more accurately read the responses of other people. Body talk also offers some interesting possibilities for film or video making and photography, both of which can supply visual data for class analysis and discussion.

2. The Language of Objects. The objects that people use and venerate tell a great deal about their value systems. Ask students to assume that your city has been covered by a giant lava flow and then unearthed by archeologists from an alien culture hundreds of years later. Have each student choose one surviving object that the aliens might find and do an analysis of the unspoken "language" of that object. What would the strangers conclude if they dug up the Golden Arches of a McDonald's hamburger palace? What might they learn from a snowmobile? from the architecture of a city? from one of its automobiles or from parks or factories? This activity encourages students to think, make generalizations, draw conclusions, and just figure out what an object alone can say about itself merely from the way it looks. (As a variation, have each student bring in an object he or she prizes personally and turn it over to a partner for analysis.)

3. Baby Talk. Psycholinguists who have examined the earliest stages of language acquisition have learned to write "baby grammars" that describe the young child's grow-

SOURCES OF LANGUAGE ARTIFACTS

- On the ground at your feet. Watch your step. Look for throwaway wrappers and writing on the street itself! Where are the grates that surround mall trees manufactured?

- Within eyeshot. Look around you. How many words do you see at any given moment? What do they say? What words are carved on buildings? Posted on billboards?

- In the newspaper. Explore *all* the sections of the paper for language artifacts: the sports page, the advice page, letters to the editor, classifieds for all sorts of products. (How many exercise machines are for sale this week? What does this tell you about the language of exercise in our time?)

- In the phone book. Check the yellow pages. How many businesses and industries in our town make their living as wordsmiths—producing language, getting it in print, mailing it out, getting it in front of the public? Also browse the "residential" entries and look for curious, interesting, and repetitive names. What does a name like "Smith, C." tell you?

- Study the language of C-span, the network that broadcasts governmental hearings, speeches, and the like. What can you learn about language from watching these leaders at work?

- Explore the worldwide web. What's the relationship of language to pictures on the web? How does language on the web differ from, say textbooks or library books or other materials you encounter every day?

- Your wallet or purse. What do your language artifacts say about you?

- The first utterance you hear after X o'clock. Pick a time and examine the first thing you hear or read thereafter.

- Talk radio. Disk jockey radio. Public radio. Radio commercials. Radio public service announcements.

- Lectures, events, concerts, art exhibitions, museum shows, and plays going on in our town. Any event, even a symphonic concert, is also a language act that you can study.

- Pets. Do they know their own names? Can you teach language to a pet?

- Stupid remarks. Why *do* people say some of the strange, curious, and, yes, *dumb* things that they do?

- Smart remarks. Write down the intelligent, informative, interesting, challenging and provocative things you hear. Write down quotable quotes. Why are these statements worth saving? How do they change your way of thinking? *your* language?

- Funny remarks. Humor is essentially linguistic in character. Collect witticisms, satires, "funny" moments, etc., and analyze the role language plays in the equation.

Figure 10.3   Language Artifacts

ing mastery of English. Ask students who have young brothers and sisters (age one to three years) to bring in some tape recordings of their speech. Split your students into groups and have them discover the regularities—the "grammar" of the child's speech. How does babbling seem to work? What kinds of words do children learn first? What patterns do they use for two-word strings? How do they seem to move from two- and three-word strings to whole sentences? While students should not try to duplicate the complex work of linguists in the field, studying baby talk brings about many insights into how human beings learn and use language. They will be able to see clearly that formal instruction is not the only way a speaker learns the rules of a language.

4. Tutoring. Locate some younger students who have reading difficulties and arrange for interested students from your class to read with and to them. Hold frequent discussions with your team of tutors to discuss their observations and problems. Some of your students may be interested in joining a group like Literacy Volunteers of America, which works with adult nonreaders. Again, encourage your students to share their observations about how language works and is learned.

5. Greetings. What do we mean when we say, "How are you?" What happens if you actually answer somebody by giving a health report or an emotional summary? Give your students the task of observing and analyzing some of the hidden communications that underlie greetings and farewells. Some questions that they might seek to answer: How do greetings and farewells differ depending on whether people are friends, enemies, strangers, or rivals? How do styles of ritual language differ with age? With culture or race? What happens when people violate the unwritten rules of ritual talk (e.g., by not making a ritual greeting before speaking or by answering in-detail when asked, "How 'ya doin'?")? This activity can help students become more aware that what we say is not always what we mean and can help them understand why we speak that way and how we use language to get out of uncomfortable spots.

6. Euphemism. George Orwell's 1946 essay "Politics and the English Language" remains a most effective attack on the use of euphemistic language to hide a person's true intent and purposes: phrases such as "sanitation engineer" for "garbage collector" or "military incursion" for "attack." After having them read the essay, send your students out to collect examples of euphemism at all levels of school and society. Simply analyzing and laughing at euphemism helps to make students more sensitive to it, but you can also encourage them to explore euphemism by such activities as translating clear prose into gobbledygook or writing instructions for a simple process—scrambling an egg—in euphemistic language: "Take an ovoid, shell-encased chicken product..."

You might also want to explore the protective aspect of euphemism so that students can see that we use language as a way to cover up what we can't or don't want to deal with. Students might write a short piece announcing someone's death without using the words "die" or "killed." Have the students role-play some scenes in a society where everyone is blunt, direct, forthright, and to the point. Does this become the best of all possible worlds? Explore so-called "politically correct" language as well. While reading stories and novels, look at how women and people of color are named. Create a survey with these words, asking respondents to explain the differences they perceive among these words. What's the difference between calling a female or woman a girl, a lady, a chick, a hot tamale, etc. Does it make a difference if we use "man" (as did Darwin in the quoted material) to mean *hu*man? What about calling "Indians" Native Americans or "Blacks" Afro-Americans? Does this make a difference?

7. Doublespeak. The National Council of Teachers of English has a committee whose sole purpose is to monitor doublespeak in current affairs. Their newsletter contains numerous examples of political language that deceives and conceals. The

newsletter (or any of the numerous books in the library on doublespeak and political language) will help you explore the use of political jargon and gobbledygook in the classroom. Why not have your students investigate the misuse of language through published statements in your area, then possibly present a set of Dubious Doublespeak Awards for the worst examples they find? Students can also look for samples of doublespeak in the literature they read in class, or they can create double-speak for specific situations they might meet in literature. For instance, if they are reading *Maniac Magee* by Jerry Spinelli, they might write up in doublespeak why Maniac isn't welcomed by the whole Black community to participate in their neighborhood picnic.

8. Dialect Study. Few people understand how or why dialects work, and too many adults are obsessed by dialect differences. To help bring enlightenment, engage the students in an informal examination of dialects. If you have speakers of different dialects in the classroom, set up groups in which the students learn about alternative expressions. Have the two groups prepare bidialectal dictionaries. Even if you don't have a rich mixture of dialects in a class, students can conduct a number of investigations around the school and community to explore dialects. One example: Have students listen for the nefarious "ain't" and chart its occurrences in speech. Television and radio are also an excellent source of dialects for your students to tape and examine.

9. Inventing a New Language. Many variations of this activity are possible. One is to "abolish" English and have the students design the theoretical model for a new, ideal language. What would be the most efficient way for this language to express relationships? What features of English would the students maintain? What aspects would they eliminate? How would the new language be written? The students might even develop samples of this language. Alternatively, students can create a new lexicon based on English syntax—that is, they can invent a new vocabulary for the existing word order. "Nadsat," the teen language in Anthony Burgess's *A Clockwork Orange,* provides one example. Orwell's essay on "Newspeak" in *1984* provides another. Students can also create "pig Latin" forms, systematically altering word structure so that only someone in possession of the code can translate. Developing sign languages offers additional possibilities.

10. The Language of Personal Space. Like body talk and the language of greetings and farewells, people have secret languages that involve the use of personal space. In two classic books, *The Silent Language* and *The Hidden Dimension,* Edward Hall investigated some of these cultural-linguistic uses of space. As a classroom activity, students can duplicate some of Hall's experiments with face-to-face conversation so they can experience firsthand communication without words. After pointing out that various cultures find different speaking distances comfortable, ask the students to discover what their own speaking conventions are. At what distance—two feet, one foot, eighteen inches—do students become uncomfortably close to one another? At what distance are they uncomfortably far away? How do we feel toward people who stand nose-to-nose with us in conversation? In *The Hidden Dimension,* Hall goes into more complex areas of the language of space, including such problems as overcrowding, the design and layout of floor space, the theft of urban space by automobiles, and the human's need for privacy. As with other physical languages, students can deduce much of the

structure of the language of space through simple experimentation and analysis. Again, photography and film-making projects can easily evolve from the class study.

11. Games and Puzzles. Games involving language are as old as humankind, and such games often help to develop a sense of language. Scrabble, for instance, is a game that many students enjoy, and it serves incidentally as a vocabulary builder. Crossword puzzles, diacrostics, and anagrams are enjoyed by other students. Such games and puzzles challenge students and make them want to stretch their vocabulary and find new or more precise words. Most bookstores carry dozens of paperback collections of word games, attesting to the popularity of this pastime. Purchase a half dozen of these books, tear them into individual sheets, and file them away to produce a game collection of several hundred activities.

12. Analyzing Handwriting. This activity won't necessarily improve penmanship, but it may produce a good deal more interest in it. Many handwriting analysis books are available in paperback stores and at supermarket checkout counters. Tell students about the basic principles of analysis, or let that be a topic for a small group presentation. and let them go. Students can analyze one another's writing, discuss signatures of famous personalities, experiment with disguising their own handwriting, or play guessing games about signatures.

13. Propaganda. An examination of World War II propaganda—German, Japanese, and Allied—makes a fascinating study. Examples are readily available— from tapes of Hitler's speeches to copies of leaflets dropped from planes on enemy troops. After a study of these materials and some discussion of how they work, turn the students loose to find examples of contemporary propaganda, often more subtle but seldom using new or different techniques.

14. Learning a Second Language. For years parents and teachers have rationalized the study of grammar on the ground that it was necessary for students engaged in the study of foreign languages. Not to miss a good bet, foreign language teachers have claimed utility for their discipline in helping students understand English. Both groups have little support for their positions. English teachers should not teach grammar simply because other teachers use a grammatical method. Teaching through grammar may not be any more successful in foreign languages than it is in English. Moreover, research has yet to show any direct correlation between skill in foreign languages and skill in English. However, when divorced from utilitarian teaching schemes, knowing—or better, using—a foreign language may well help people become more comfortable, competent users of their native language. In classes that include both native speakers of English and speakers of another language, let the two groups teach each other. Drill and exercises are not necessary. Often simply allowing the students to struggle with one another's languages over everyday concerns will be sufficient. If you don't have a mixed class of this sort, you might want to seek out tutoring opportunities for students who are interested in foreign languages and acknowledge their work as part of their regular English studies.

15. Learning Esperanto. A Polish linguist, L. L. Zamenhof, created Esperanto as an international language one hundred years ago. Firmly rooted in the Indo-European languages, it offers a simple and consistent grammar and a consistent spelling system. Millions of people speak Esperanto worldwide, and there are gen-

uine opportunities to speak it. Write to the Esperanto League of North America, El Cirrito, California, for more information.

16. Study of Names. The study of names can be an interesting class project. A common approach is for students to use a desk dictionary to find out the significance or meaning of their own name. Then the students move outward, first studying names around their city—names of streets, mountains, lakes—and then names around the state and country. An excellent resource is Alan Wolk's *The Naming of America,* which delves into place names. We especially enjoy studying the names created by developers for condominiums and malls: "Woodland Hills," which is a patch of asphalt; "Paddock Farms," which is a high-rise apartment. What do students see as the logic or hype behind such names?

17. Logotypes. A logotype or trademark is a self-contained message, a one-word visual language designed to identify a product or company and to project an image of it. Most industries spend a remarkable amount of time developing, testing, and marketing any new logo that they choose to use. Have students collect a number of logos (they can easily find hundreds in newspapers, magazines, and the yellow pages) and analyze the language. They can think about the impact of the shape and color and why this logo has appeal. Afterward, invite the students to develop some trademarks of their own, perhaps a new insignia or logo for the school, for your class, for fictitious companies, or for themselves. As a spinoff, have them look at the logotypes or icons widely used for computers. What does it mean when one can operate a computer through pull-down menus of icons rather than reading words.

18. Codes and Ciphers. -.-./-/-../.../...//.-/.-././/.-//--/-.—/.../-/./.-./-.—/// (Codes are a mystery.) Codes and ciphers are as old as history, and literally thousands of ways of sending secret messages have been generated. Books for young adult readers on the subject of codes, cryptology, international code breaking, and code design appear at regular intervals, so check your library.

19. Inductive Definitions. Few adults or young people know much about the process of dictionary making. They don't realize that definitions grow from popular usage rather than being created arbitrarily by a panel of wordsters. Assign the class a project of defining a word—just a single word. Students are not to consult dictionaries; rather, they should collect citations—examples of the word in use—and from that evidence work inductively toward a definition. Words like "break" or "fast" (or "breakfast") are a good choice because of their functions as different parts of speech. From this activity, you can help students understand some of the ways in which words take on meaning, while helping them realize that meanings are flexible and evolutionary.

20. Printing Processes. The printing of books and magazines is interesting for many students, and modern printing processes are nothing short of miraculous in their speed, quality, and accuracy. Let the students investigate printing processes, beginning with hand-set, single-sheet presses and working toward computer-set type, offset presses, and laser jet printers. A visit to a printing plant for the whole class or just for interested students would be appropriate. When young people learn how books, magazines, and newspapers are made, their reading interest in those publications seems to increase considerably.

21. Electronic Communications. The effect of modern electronics on communication systems has been as miraculous as the effect of printing. Encourage your students who have interests in science and engineering to study electronics and the communications field. Many nontechnical volumes have been written about such devices as the transistor or diode chip and their effect on communication systems. Other topics of interest might be computer technology, miniaturization, laser beams as a form of communication, television and radio, and the electronics of the telephone.

22. The Language of Advertising. Although teachers often deprecate the "bad grammar" of ads, many advertisements show extremely clever use of language through word play and puns. Huge sums of money are invested in slogans, captions, and the rhetoric of advertisements. It's little wonder ads are so effective. What makes their language work?

23. The Language of Science. Science books are filled with marvelous and curious terms. Where do they come from? What is the origin of such terms as *laser, biodegradable, black hole, quark, sea urchin, mollusk,* and *mesomorph?* Conduct an etymology unit on scientific words. As a variation, teach your students to read the ingredient labels on packages to learn what they are eating. Why must disodium EDTA be added to "prevent spoilage" in something that is labeled, "Fresh, Hometown, Hearth-Baked Bread"?

24. The Language of Law. Collect samples of legal documents: insurance policies, contracts, warranties, rules of the road. Help the students learn to decode the language, both through examining technical or specialized words and through studying the very careful wording that complicates legal writing. As a variation, have students study advertising and promotional claims and disclaimers and the use of "waffle" or "weasel" words, which guard a manufacturer from law suits.

25. Idioms. Explain to students that idioms are phrases or sayings which cannot be understood from the individual word meanings. Have students brainstorm in groups to create lists of idioms. Each student then chooses one to illustrate in a literal sense. "You're a real stick-in-the-mud." "She's got you wrapped around her little finger." Through this activity students come to be more aware that language isn't fixed in meaning and that it changes as new expressions are created.

26. Newspaper Headlines. Have pupils search for ambiguous and misleading headlines such as "Revolting Officers Shot" or "Giant Waves Down Liner's Funnel," metaphorical headlines such as "President Faces Storm" and "Bridge Designer Blasted," and headlines where choice of words is significant or there is a play on words. (This activity was shared with us by Ken Watson of Sydney University during his visit to the States.)

27. Comic-Cartoon Notebooks. Bobbye Goldstein studied the language used in comics and cartoons and found that difficult words were common. She also found that students were very willing to look at language through comics and cartoons. She suggests that you have students collect cartoons and comics and put them in notebooks in such categories as figurative language, colloquial expressions, and puns. The

students can identify palindromes and can even make lists of multiple meanings of some of the words. Contests can be held to see which student locates the most difficult words in the comics. (See "Looking at Cartoons and Comics in a New Way," by Bobbye S. Goldstein, in the *Journal of Reading*, April 1986, pp. 657–661.)

That's it. We quit at twenty-seven. But as you can sense, these twenty-seven activities barely begin to scratch the surface of possible language explorations for the English class. As interludes, they change the pace of the class. As valid linguistic activities, they heighten students' critical awareness of something they consume and produce in prodigious quantities: language.

TEACHING STANDARD ENGLISH

> Good English is that form of speech which is appropriate to the purposes of the speaker, true to the language as it is, and comfortable to speaker and listener. It is the product of custom, neither cramped by rule nor freed from all restraint; it is never fixed, but changes with the organic life of the language.
>
> —Robert Pooley
> *Teaching English Usage*

Figure 10.4   Defining Good English

Over a half century ago language scholar Robert Pooley offered what has become a classic definition of "good English," recognizing its nature as arbitrary and conventional— a "product of custom"—yet acknowledging the importance of a meeting of minds so that both speaker and listener feel comfortable with the language. This was an important statement in the history of English because it recognized the sociological nature of usage and dialects, and it helped to destroy the notion of a single standard form of the language. Pooley's definition allows for the linguistic fact that within specific language communities, people can be quite comfortable with language forms not generally found acceptable in broader circles, and it recognized that it would be quite unnatural for speakers to change their style of speaking within that language community.

Most linguists (and for that matter, most users of the language, just plain folks), recognize that each of us is master of many varieties of language. As part of our "home" or base dialect, we are masters of a variety of what linguists call "registers," ways of speaking differently in different situations: to authorities, to friends, to intimates, etc. From those ideas has emerged a philosophy of acceptance of dialect variety—in particular, the belief that the schools should not try to eradicate a natural home dialect but should encourage children to develop one or more additional dialects for use in other situations. The concept is an attempt to be humane and understanding about dialects, while at the same time allowing students to extend their linguistic capabilities.

That philosophy, is clearly at the heart of the Oakland Schools Ebonics program, but it has powerful implications for all students, not just those who come to school with a minority dialect. It is important to realize, too, that teaching standard English by whatever method will not automatically open new doors to children. As we showed in Chapter Two, language is learned in response to needs felt by the language user. Unless students recognize a real opportunity to participate in a standard English community, they will not willingly learn its dialect. The choice of dialects ultimately and appropriately resides with the language *user,* not the teacher.

Teachers might accomplish much more by approaching the standard English problem indirectly. For instance, by helping students participate as fully as possible in the community of language through a variety of experiences—reading and writing, speaking and listening—role-playing-teachers can ensure that students are comfortable users of language in many situations. When and if students are given a meaningful opportunity to participate in a standard English community—through school, employment, or housing—they will be better able to adapt their language use. Activities that can make students more aware of language differences include:

- Translating the dialect they find in the fiction they read into the dialect they speak.

- Choosing passages in fiction where young people are speaking to each other and showing how their language would be altered if they were speaking to a parent or a principal.

- Making lists of teen slang words that most adults don't use and often don't understand and discussing why such different vocabularies come into being.

- Writing a letter to a friend explaining a situation that occurred at school, then writing out the way the same situation would be explained to an adult and observing language differences.

- Writing short speeches presented to the class, explaining what should be changed in the school, then composing a letter or petition to the principal or school board explaining needed changes.

- Making dictionaries of terms and vocabulary used by specific groups of people: computer nuts, teenage girls, artists, school administrators, ministers, deep-sea divers, etc.

In addition, teachers ought to be concerned about destroying some of the old myths about good grammar, good usage, and upward mobility. If the schools spent as much time trying to end linguistic bias as they presently spend trying to enforce standard English, they might go a long way toward solving the problem. Certainly the teacher should concentrate on helping students—especially speakers of dialects other than standard English—understand what dialects are, where they come from, and what their effects on listeners are. Given such background understanding, students will be in a much better position to decide whether or not they want to change the way they talk or write.

OFFERING HELP WITH CORRECTNESS

We believe that the philosophy of writing (and, by implication, speaking) for the here and now, coupled with finding real audiences for student work (Chapter 9) offers the teacher a practical philosophy that can help resolve the dialects/correctness dilemma. The here-and-now approach strongly emphasizes the public use of language, recognizing that as students write and speak for audiences, they will realistically encounter situations where the use of a variant of standard English is appropriate.

How to do it? How do we provide the help students need to get their work into a form appropriate for their audience? One of our colleagues, Judy Kortright at Sexton High School in Lansing, Michigan, figured out a way to offer students a variety of approaches to correctness. She created a "correctness corner" in her classroom stocked with:

- Usage handbooks (both commercial materials and handouts created by the teacher).
- Teacher-made activity cards reviewing the basic and classic usage problems (lay-lie, sit-set, etc.).
- Posters and charts (both commercial and teacher-made that clearly and precisely explain particular usage items).
- Examples of good student writing.
- Reference books (dictionaries, thesauruses, spelling problem lists).
- Revision checklists (sequences of questions that guide students through editing and copyreading a paper).

The idea here is to give students multiple ways to solve their problems. In addition to the paper resources of the correctness corner, we also recommend the following:

- Continue to use peer response groups for writing, always beginning with response to content and ideas, but working toward polishing and surface correctness; continue, as well, to *train* peer groups in ways to respond to one another's work more and more helpfully.
- Have a usage "fair." Borrowing an idea from Celeste Resh at Mott Community College in Flint, Michigan, we've had students "adopt" a usage item that gives them particular problems, consult the handbooks in the correctness corner, conference with the teacher, prepare a poster or display on the item, and present or "teach" it to the class. Students who go through the process do, in fact, tend to learn specific items of usage, and the posters and displays become part of the equippage of the correctness corner.
- Encourage students to keep lists of troublesome spelling, punctuation, and usage problems in their writing folders. We've seen commercial notebook pockets nicely printed with the core rules of mechanics and recommend their use, but even better is for students to prepare their own lists based on their own writing.
- Give occasional mini-lessons on usage items. (See Weaver, Atwell.) Although our philosophy strongly emphasizes teaching particular students in the context

of particular papers, rather than common class lessons, there are times when one can efficiently and effectively give a short lesson on particular usage items. "Who/whom" is an item, for example, whose usage is often counter-intuitive: When *do* we put on that "m," or, as one of our students wrote following a fiction knock on the door, "Whom's there?"

OUR FINAL WORD ON LANGUAGE

It has been our experience that freed of the pressure of correctness, students naturally find language study engaging. They enjoy puzzling over puzzles, seeing the linguistic nature of riddles, and having the myths of correctness and "good" English explained and demystified. When their writing and speaking are placed in the context of actual audiences, they seem willing enough to include polishing and fine tuning as part of the process, for, after all, there's an *audience* awaiting. No teacher *at any level* will be likely to move his or her students toward the mythical ideal of 100% literacy (whatever that may be). But each of us can assume responsibility for recognizing our students' achievements in language, examining problem areas, and, through a rich and varied program of language exploration and on-the-job language use, move students along the language continuum. Our aim is not only literate students, but students who have come to acquire an understanding of this complex and amazing phenomenon called *language.*

◆ EXPLORATIONS

◆ If you want to be able to answer the students' questions about correctness matters, you need to have on hand a great deal of diverse material to satisfy different learners. You need the usual handbooks plus games, visuals, and self-instructional packets that present the material in many ways. Choose a skill that a student might want to master (say, how to proofread a page or how to use quotation marks) and develop a range of materials presenting it from several points of view. Field test your materials with students. If you are working with a group of people, each person can choose a different skill and reproduce the materials to share.

◆ Some issues centering on altering dialects:
Can a teacher honestly preserve the home dialect while teaching an alternative school dialect? Does possession of a standard dialect in fact give members of a society upward mobility?

◆ A broadly based skills program that puts grammar and correctness in their place is likely to run into some opposition from parents and administrators, who will cry "Neglect!" Interview some parents and administrators to explore the reasons for their concern. Develop some explanations that allow a teacher to run a broadly based language program while still providing satisfactory evidence that basics are being adequately covered.

◆ Create some materials for language interludes and explorations. These might be done as individual resource or activity packets, or as handouts for use with an entire class. Start with those of the twenty-seven that you found most interesting, then branch off into the recommended readings that follow and discover other possibilities.

RELATED READINGS

The most comprehensive text available on teaching grammar and teaching about grammar is Connie Weaver's *Teaching Grammar in Context.* On dialects and usage, despite its age, we recommend Robert Pooley's *Teaching English Usage* (originally published in 1946, now available as a reprint from the National Council of Teachers of English). Another classic is Martin Joos' *The Five Clocks,* a lucid explanation of how language usage shifts with various situations. To brush up on traditional grammar, we recommend a book whose title hints at its playfulness, Karen Elizabeth Gordon's *Deluxe Transitive Vampire: A Guide to Grammar for the Innocent, the Eager, and the Doomed* (a book that can also serve as a text or class reference for upper-level high school students). To brush up on modern grammar, our recommendation is Jeffrey Kaplan's *English Grammar: Principles and Facts,* which does an excellent job of presenting the essence of transformational generative grammar in accessible fashion. Steven Pinker's *The Language Instinct* is an eminently readable discussion of the nature of language, including the case made by the Chomskyites for language as an inherent part of the human mind. For fun reading, Anthony Burgess's *A Mouthful of Air* is filled with facts, statistics, and explanations of the play and joy of language. For an excellent discussion of Black English (Ebonics) and its origins, as well as consideration of implications for schooling, read Geneva Smitherman's *Black Talk* or Henry Louis Gates Jr.'s The *Signifying Monkey.* In the domain of language play, there are innumerable books available, but we especially like Herbert Kohl's *Book of Puzzlements.* Finally, another classic book on language that provides innumerable clever activities is S. I. Hayakawa's *Language in Thought and Action,* an explication of the principles of general semantics.

CHAPTER 11

CLASSROOM TALK, DRAMA, AND PERFORMANCE

Whether its form is conversation, lecture, gossip, discussion, or monologue, spoken English is one of the most central and ubiquitous skills that a member of the community of language masters. From birth, people acquire information, clarify their thoughts and beliefs, and transmit ideas and information to others principally by means of talk and conversation. By far the greatest part of our use of language involves oral English, either receptive or productive. Even nonreaders and haters of writing have been known to enjoy talking—over Coke or telephone—for hours. As James Britton has remarked, our lives are "afloat on a sea of talk."

Despite the pervasiveness of oral language in our lives, it has too seldom been given much attention in the schools. Neither has drama or performance. These are often seen as "add-ons" or something to do if time permits. In this chapter we intend to show teachers how talk, drama, and performance are ways to learn, to grapple with meaning, and to make sense of the world.

THE USES OF CONVERSATION

It is especially important that the teacher consider the underlying motivation behind speech activities. Through attempting to understand what happens when people talk, teachers are best able to structure a classroom setting that supports spoken language. For instance, conversation—chat, gossip, rappin', shootin' the breeze—has sometimes been seen as something outside the educational process. Teachers cut off students' conversations at the beginning of a class; "All right now, let's get down to business." The fact is, conversation is "business" of a very serious kind. Chat serves a great many functions in a person's life, many of which are not obvious at a superficial level of examination.

Most of us recognize that we use language for a wide range of reasons in our own conversations. We use chat and gossip in many ways to establish our own self-esteem, to make initial contact with others, to assess feelings, to form relationships, and to seek information—in essence, to structure our world and to compare it to the worlds of others. Chat is the spoken equivalent of the writing journal—a language form that operates on the border between a person's inner and outer worlds.

This is not intended to glorify chitchat or to suggest that teachers are doing a good job helping students become orally literate if they merely let them exchange trivia. However, a teacher must recognize the critical role of conversation in people's lives and support it—welcome it—inside the classroom. In fact, one of the major ways in which people will become good conversationalists instead of gossipmongers is for the school to allow them to talk about matters of more than a trivial nature. People can discuss complex ideas as comfortably as they gossip about sporting events. Through experiences in literature and composing, the teacher can provide students with a steadily expanding series of topics for conversation.

Students should feel free to discuss personal and academic problems, projects, books, television programs, films, one another, people, and world problems. When acknowledged as important, conversation will become the foundation for the entire spoken language program. Indeed, without students who are secure and competent conversationalists, other oral language activities will be dull, static, or ineffectual.

LEARNING THROUGH TALK

Teacher talk is usually seen as the most important talk in the classroom. In this view, student talk is seen as peripheral or disruptive. With no student talk allowed in the classroom, it is assumed that all learning comes from the teacher; that her voice, knowledge, and experiences are the only ones worth hearing.

But people talk to assimilate new knowledge, make sense of it, and integrate it into old knowledge. For example, if Friend A suddenly acts differently, the other friends talk about A's behavior, try to figure out what it means in the context of what they know about A, and then put the old and new knowledge together to figure out a course of action or a plan about how to respond to A. Humans use talk to solve life's most pressing problems; yet we as teachers often forget the opportunities talk can provide in our classes to further student learning.

Through talking, students show us that they can think and solve problems. But the richness of this talk, and its potential for learning, depends on the development of a learning community which is created through talk. Students need to feel safe and free from ridicule if they are to be active members of small groups.

So to tap into this richness, teachers need to shift their thinking and begin to value talk as another medium through which students learn. It may be helpful to ask yourself how learning happens in your classroom. Do you think meaning is made when students listen to the teacher, read a book, or view a video? What do students do to process that information and make sense of it, see how it fits together, see how

> Talk is not only a medium for thinking, it is also an important means by which we learn how to think. From a Vygotskian perspective thinking is an internal dialogue, an internalization of dialogues we've had with others. Our ability to think depends upon the many previous dialogues we have taken part in—we learn to think by participating in dialogues.
>
> From Curt Dudley-Marling and Dennis Searle, *When Students Have Time to Talk* (Portsmouth, N.H: Heinemann, 1991), p. 60. Reprinted by permission.

it fits in with what they already know? Do they ask questions of the teacher? of each other? write down their tentative thinking? answer already prepared questions? work in small groups on tasks related to the material?

In our rush to involve our students in stimulating experiences, sometimes we forget that students do need time to work with the information we are asking them to grapple with. We might race from having students read something to having them write analytically about it without building in time for them to explore topics and sort out their ideas with other students.

Because little has been written to help teachers use talk in their class to enhance student learning, we will sketch out ways the teacher can begin to do this, using some of the best work around—that of the National Oracy Project in England. Although teachers may not have recognized it as such, talk in small groups is multidimensional, meeting several goals we have for students. First, students will develop their understanding by explaining ideas to others and so will gain increasing control over these ideas. Second, through their ability to hold the attention of their listeners they will demonstrate the mastery of speaking skills. Third, they will show their control over a widening range of styles of talk such as giving explanations or instructions, narrating stories, presenting a summary or report.

So how does all this talk work? How can English language arts teachers use this source of learning effectively?

Involving and Engaging

When teachers begin new units they work to find ways to involve their students and encourage their engagement with new material. At this point students might brainstorm what they know about a topic they have read about, saw a video about, listened to, or the teacher introduced. At this stage the teacher is working to interest the students and get them to "buy into" the topic, to want to know more about it. By having students brainstorm or list or in some other way make a connection to the material in small groups, all students have a chance to be heard, all students can be active learners.

Exploring

After students have gotten further into the work, say the reading of a novel, they need time and a structure so they can make sense of the information themselves. In small-group discussion students can share their questions or puzzlements about the novel, list motifs or objects they notice are repeated frequently, talk about which characters they identify with the most.

Transforming

In this stage students have to start focusing their thinking, to sort their ideas into patterns, to make decisions. For instance, students can create a list of generalizations about what they think the author is trying to say through a novel. They can start developing ideas for ways they can present their understandings of the book to others. This kind of talk can begin very tentatively but as students receive feedback and listen to the ideas of others in their small group, their ideas become more developed. To again emphasize the importance of talk with others, think about how we as adults use talk with our friends and colleagues to sort through our own ideas, to help us think through a problem, and to listen to the ideas of others and mine their ideas before we decide on a course of action. Student talk can function in the same way when students are working towards new understandings.

Presenting

At this stage, groups do not have to make major presentations in front of the whole class. The important thing is to give students' work and thinking a broader audience so even more people can react to their ideas. Instead of throwing up your hands in despair thinking about how long it would take for each group of four to present to everybody, think small. Groups could present to other groups or tape record their ideas for others or a spokesperson could report to the teacher or to the whole class. By brainstorming all the ways students can present their ideas to an interested audience, it is surprising how many alternatives one can come up with.

Reflecting

In this stage the small groups get back together and talk metacognitively about what they have learned, how their learning was affected by interaction with other people. They also reflect on what groups have been doing, review the work, and make decisions about where to go next. The National Oracy Project concluded that "Pupils who are given opportunities to look back at what they have been doing, and to consider and to discuss what they have learned and how they learned it, are able to gain access to much deeper understandings of both the process and the content of their work. Implicit meanings are made explicit and become more accessible to conscious control" (p. 39).

(Stages are based on a learning model devised by Reid, Forrestal and Cook in their book *Small Group Learning in the Classroom*. Peta/Chalkface Press, Australia, 1989.)

FORMATS FOR CLASSROOM TALK

Dialogues and Partnerships

Since dialogue—a conversation between two people—is simple and direct, it is an especially efficient form for productive work. Unfortunately, the dynamics of the two-member groups has been neglected. Typically, students work together only to correct papers. While two-member groups have occasional problems with freeloading, inbreeding, or compounding of errors, they also avoid many of the problems that evolve in larger groups. Their use should be fully exploited in the classroom. The following are some good ways to launch partnership projects.

1. Collaborative Writing (version 1). Students work together as coauthors of a piece of writing—play, poem, story, or essay. For instance after reading a chapter of a novel they can compose a found poem (see Figure 5.3, #34) together, talking over why they selected the words and phrases they did, how the phrases and words should be arranged, and the impact they think their poem makes. This technique allows students to share writing skills with each other and to produce a stronger piece of writing than either could alone.

2. Collaborative Writing (version 2). Students work on their own writing in partnership with another person, who serves as a writing coach in:

Prewriting. (The students share ideas and talk over what they plan to write.)

Writing. (The partners coach each other through rough spots and listen to readings of the drafts.)

Post writing. (The collaborators serve as editors and proofreaders for one another, each taking responsibility for getting the other's work in the best possible shape.)

3. Response to literature. Partners read the same poem, story or novel and share what questions they have, which characters they identify with, which parts move them.

4. Connections to stories, videos, and other classroom material. After reading a story, students individually brainstorm any connections they can make between the story and their experiences or what they know of life. Partners share and compare their lists, explaining the connections they discovered. This kind of activity helps students see how others respond to stories as well as reinforces that school work relates to their lives and to the greater world.

The Small Group

Small-group work offers enormous potential to the teacher. Such groups have many of the advantages of whole-class talk activities without the disadvantages of large size and unwieldiness. The benefits of working in pairs and small groups include being able to explore a topic thoughtfully and to interpret and restate ideas so that student understandings are enhanced. Students in groups can also sort out their ideas first before presenting them to a more critical audience. When students talk their way into learning it seems to help pupils to learn in a qualitatively better way. The learning is more vivid and comes alive for them. Further, small groups encourage a conversational tone that the large class does not. Groups allow the sharing of ideas and common learning. They are more effective than the large group in pooling knowledge because the small group draws out the quiet people who do not contribute to the whole class. Above all, small groups foster conversational autonomy by keeping the teacher out of the picture; students must structure their own ideas and experiences. Although the teacher is not at the center of the learning in this kind of work, using small groups *is* teaching; not an avoidance of responsibility.

In order to begin small groups on a positive note, a few general considerations should be taken into account.

Group Size and Composition

To work well, a group must have compatible membership and be an appropriate size, two factors that are at best unpredictable. In our experience we have found that groups of three to five work well, but to begin small-group work the smaller size seems to work better. With time and experience teachers will discover what group size works best in which classes.

Group composition or makeup is equally difficult to give firm guidelines on. Should students be allowed to choose group membership themselves, or should the teacher make assignments? Should groups be permanent or rearranged regularly? Should one member of a group be selected as the leader, or can groups work their way to their own leadership patterns? Steve's experiences suggest that self-selected groups operate better than arbitrarily appointed or contrived groups, that leadership emerges without elections, that groups need to be rearranged from time to time. He has also had experiences that refuted each of those generalizations—assigned groups that worked well, groups that foundered until a chair was selected, groups that worked together successfully for long periods of time. Diana usually begins group work by selecting membership herself. This takes the burden off students who may feel pressured to work with friends but don't really want to or the students whom nobody picks. She also asks students near the beginning of the year to write down the names of students they would like to work with or those with whom they might have conflicts. Using this confidential information, she can appoint groups that will function successfully.

Another major consideration to keep in mind, especially at the middle school and high school level, is how gender roles can affect group work. Teachers have found that boys tend to dominate and girls tend to do more supporting, questioning, and listening. Some boys may try to exert greater influence over what happens in classroom talk—who talks, when, and about what—by being the ones who decide when to move from one topic to the next and when to finish a discussion. Other difficulties include some boys refusing to work with girls and vice versa, some girls adopting nonspeaking or subservient roles in group talk, and girls being subjected to verbal harassment. Teachers can deal with these concerns by allowing single sex groups and by making gender issues a part of the talk of the class so students are aware of how boys and girls behave linguistically.

The Group Task

Without a sense of task or purpose, any group will founder. Dividing students into small groups with the assignment insufficiently described is almost a sure recipe for failure. Without a clear aim, the students talk pointlessly. If students are clear about the purpose of the work, then small groups operate more effectively. Sometimes the task or goal can be as simple as reporting back to the class. It is also useful to have groups prepare something for presentation to the class: a discussion, perhaps, or a demonstration, role-play, or panel. Another element that helps groups function smoothly is to have some degree of pressure on the students to finish within a certain time or to present their findings to another group. Students also need to understand that there is a real reason for the group work, that diverse input is desired, that a variety of ideas will enhance what students are asked to do. If teachers put students in groups to answer questions that they have predetermined answers to, students' participation will at best be lackluster. Students can sense that their input and creativity aren't really being asked for. Small-group work should be intellectual work where students have to make some decisions. They may have to list their responses to a character in a story or find 15 quotations from a novel that best exemplifies their view of the character. But the input is theirs, they think about it and select it. The buy-in is much greater.

Small-group work can often be exploratory in nature, a coming together of tentative thinking that changes and is transformed as students work on tasks together. Teachers need to make sure that the task is a part of other learning so students don't see it as an add-on with no connection to anything else they do in the class.

The Teacher Role

The small-group dynamic is a naturalistic one, and teachers need to be cautious about trying to rigidly control group behavior. Nor can small groups be used to achieve ends that might not be worth achieving in the first place. For example, "separating friends" who talk too much in whole-class discussion will probably just lead to friends who talk across their separate groups. Nor will pedagogically unsound projects suddenly become workable—"Let's split up into small groups and diagram these troublesome sentences." Good luck to all.

The most satisfactory teacher group-role that we have discovered is simply teacher-as-coach, drifting from group to group, joining in when there is something substantial to contribute. This role is a difficult one to manage. More than once each of us has joined a dynamic group only to see the conversation wither because of our presence. Another role for the teacher is as gatherer of information on how well groups are going. This can be done through observation as well as through the tape recording of student sessions.

Teacher-Led Discussions

One of the most difficult skills for a teacher to master, and one that must be refined throughout a teaching career, is that of leading whole-class discussions. The teacher faces a collection of thirty or more students and somehow must get them to talk. In its weakest form teacher-led discussion is recitation, with students supplying answers to questions in order to demonstrate mastery of a text. One of our students described teacher-led discussions this way: "Too often in my experience these were exercises in getting to a predetermined conclusion with the teacher acting as the herder." But at its best, class discussion takes on a momentum of its own under the gentle guidance of the teacher, with talk helping to generate new knowledge and understanding.

The heart of the teacher-led discussion is the discussion question, and the quality and kinds of questions that teachers ask will make or break any class session. We have found that asking factual questions as anything more that a warm-up leads to a conversational dead end.

The basic advice we can give is: *ask open-ended questions to which the asker doesn't necessarily know the answer.* We encourage you to ask questions that interest you, questions that you want to think about and explore, questions that intrigue you. Asking students to generate the questions for class discussions also helps the teacher know the kinds of things students are ready and interested in discussing. Diana's tendency, like most teachers, is to jump to questions in Langer's Stance Four—asking students to objectify the experience of the novel and analyze it in some way. (See Chapter 5 for a discussion of these stances.)

Such questions include:

- From reading this would you say the author has an optimistic or pessimistic view of life?
- Which characters do you think the author really loves?
- What did you think about the ending? Did it work for you or frustrate you?
- Do you believe the characters were treated fairly by the author?
- Why do you think this character seems to have different values than her family?
- Could this story have taken place anywhere else?
- What themes and issues seem most important to the author?
- What do you think the author hopes readers might come away with after reading this story?
- Were males (females, Asians etc.) shown in a positive light through the characterization?
- Let's look at the characters' names. Do you think they are significant or symbolic in any way?

It takes work and practice to get away from jumping right to criticism and analysis questions. Teachers have to teach themselves to think from the reader's point of view. Readers usually want to start with Stance Two and Three questions. These kinds of questions are not the kind most teachers have been trained to ask. Diana usually has information on Langer's stances in front of her when she creates questions to begin a discussion so she'll remember to include questions on those two stances. Since in Stance Two students are very involved in the text world these kinds of questions can be asked:

- Which parts of the story are most vivid to you?
- Which characters did you most closely identify with or empathize with?
- Describe the town. What do you see, how do you imagine it?
- Who would you most like to say something to in the story? What would you tell him or her?
- Which event surprised or upset you?
- What kept you reading?
- What do you think happened in the incident the author mentioned but didn't explain?

When students seem willing to move to Stance Three questions and are ready to think about themselves in terms of the text, some of the following kinds of questions can be asked:

- From which character did you learn the most?
- Which action in the story would be hardest for you to perform?
- Which decision in the book would you have the most trouble accepting?
- Which feelings or emotions displayed by a character did you relate to the most?

These kinds of open-ended questions let students know that the teacher is interested in a real discussion, not in simple recitation.

But not all nonfactual questions are open-ended. Socrates is widely praised for his use of the questioning or inductive method, yet, for all his skill, he seldom asked open-ended questions. Like a trial lawyer (or a good many teachers), Socrates simply kept on asking questions until he had elicited the single statement or concept he had in mind, at which point the discussion came to a close. The "Socratic method" so widely praised in education is sometimes just another way of leading students to pre-determined answers.

But can one always ask open-ended questions? Aren't there times when the teacher will know the answer or lead the students toward an accepted concept? Of course there are, but here it is helpful to think in terms of personal interpretation of information. If teachers phrase questions in terms of the students' perceptions—"What did you think of the ending of the poem?" "What do you think are the most important facts in the case?"—then discussion flows, even if teachers have in mind some basic ideas and concepts of their own. Similarly, when academic concepts are phrased in Stance Three language and relate to students' lives, students assimilate knowledge: "How do you see the law of supply and demand operating in your own life?" "What are some of the ways you might be able to use Emerson's philosophy in your own life?"

One of the most useful ways for the teacher to avoid asking closed questions is to avoid taking sole responsibility for asking questions at all. As educators from John Dewey on have argued, learning how to ask a good question is even more difficult than learning how to answer one. The schools characteristically do very little to help students become good question askers. Perhaps the most important role a teacher can play in leading group discussion is not that of setting the agenda of questions but that of helping students channel and direct their own questions for investigation.

Other elements that lead to satisfactory whole-class discussions include: giving students wait time and allowing them the opportunity to think; asking small groups to develop the questions to be responded to in large group; arranging the room so students can see and hear each other; and providing time for reflection on both the processes of the discussion and its content.

MAKING IT WORK

Teachers might try to follow small-group guidelines to the letter and still find that group work is not going well. What else could be happening here? One possibility is that they are saying that group talk is valuable but all of their actions show that they don't value it. Another possibility is that group work isn't tightly woven into the work of the class. Our students are such masters of reading our nonverbal language and of figuring out the "real curriculum" i.e. what the teacher evaluates the heaviest, that they often don't hear our words as we mouth why small-group work is important.

Showing Students That Talk is Valuable

One way to begin to make group talk an effective learning tool in the classroom is to listen to what you say about talk. Do you start class by saying, "Quiet down so we can get to work," or "Stop talking and get to work," or "We're only working in small groups today." If we inadvertently make statements like these, students get the message that talk stops them from working; talk is not work; if they are allowed to talk the work is not important

Raising the status of talk takes real effort on the part of the teacher, since students have not been accustomed to regarding talking and listening as anything substantive. The teacher has to affirm and explain its importance, reviewing how talk helps people make meaning. Reviewing the functions of talking in Figure 11.1 may help.

If students are going to learn to value talk as a learning tool they also need to have opportunities to reflect and evaluate the talking and listening work they do. They need to see the ways that talking promotes learning and that the talking portion of their work will somehow be evaluated and counted by the teacher (see Evaluation Chapter 13). As part of the evaluative talk, students can also brainstorm a list of what they consider good or productive talk. Hopefully, the list students compile will include such things as acceptance of all opinions, supportive groups, time for each person to speak, being cooperative, being given clear guidelines. Students may struggle coming up with ideas because they've never been asked to think about this topic before. If this happens, encourage them to think about a discussion they've had with friends that they thought was productive. This might make the task clearer. Then to reinforce the importance of talk in the small group, students can rotate the position of observer, who looks at how students participate in the group. Attention can be paid to who listens well, who builds on the ideas of others, who asks questions, who is willing to change an opinion, who helps move the discussion forward. Students can

- We talk to make sense of the world and to try to exert some control over it.
- We talk in order to find out what others know, and to share what we know.
- We talk in order to develop our thinking.
- We use talk to entertain, to tell stories or recite poetry, to create new roles and imaginative worlds.
- We use talk to evaluate our work, achievements, and learning.
- We use talk to demonstrate and to describe what we know or have found out.

From *Teaching Talking and Learning* based on the work of the National Oracy Project. (York, U.K.: National Curriculum Council, 1991), pp. 7–8.

Figure 11.1

then be encouraged to take these observation skills outside the classroom and observe a conversation among friends or in their family. They can look at whether a real conversation is going on, or whether members simply take turns telling the other people what is on their minds without building on the remarks of others or even of taking them into account.

When students do have time to talk and do begin to accept the worth of talk, they can learn to use language as a tool for thought, for working to clarify and communicate ideas with others, and for becoming independent problem solvers. Be forewarned, this kind of understanding does take time and lots of metacognitive work such as reflective thinking, writing and talking about instances they learned through talk.

Building Talk into the Fabric of the Class

If students view talking to learn as a separate once-a-week activity seemingly unrelated to anything else, they will be less willing to commit themselves to making groups work. But if students see that talk can sometimes even be exhilarating and connected to other work, they are more willing to take it seriously. A good way to set the stage early in the year is for students to write a list of topics they would like to know more about or discuss. In small groups they share their lists, explaining why they are interested in the topic, then the group turns in a combined list of the consolidated topics on a note card. These cards can be easily stored in the teacher's desk drawer and are ready for use. Diana used this information to help her build these topics into the course. For instance her American Literature students were interested in talking about what the purpose of life was as well as what happens after death. When the class read William Cullen Bryant's poems "Thanotopsis" and "To a Waterfowl" these questions were built into the small-group work and students compared their views to what Bryant said.

When students participate in lively discussions that are important to them their ideas are often challenged. This is the opportune time to have them write reflections on what they learned through the talk, what they had never thought about before, and how the discussion made an impact on their thinking. Students can usually see that they were clarifying and expanding their thinking through these interactions.

Work talk into the structure of your class gradually. You can start by asking students at the beginning of class to talk briefly in pairs about what they had done in class the day before and what it made them think about or learn. Pairs can also be used during a lesson or towards the end of class to reflect and evaluate.

After the teacher and students are more comfortable using talk to learn, the teacher can look at the units students will be involved in and figure out in which topics, concepts, or stages in learning that talk can be most beneficial. Small-group work can then be structured into the unit.

Once students see that talk is valued they may feel free to raise issues that are of concern to them. It is often helpful to let them air their gripes and pet peeves, then let them discuss productive solutions and remedies in small groups. For example, if lunch hours are suddenly shortened or the absence policy is abruptly changed, hold a discussion or debate the issue in class. Frequently this sort of discussion will lead into writing, reading, and research activities, but even if it doesn't, students will have participated in the sorting out of ideas through talk.

OVERCOMING OBSTACLES

Using talk may seem frightening to some teachers because they worry about the noise level and fear disturbing other nearby classes. Often teachers who do a lot of small group and drama and performance activities become the educator of other teachers around them. Of course, in Diana's experience once students get used to working in small groups or other oral activities, and are very involved in what they are doing, they can work at a level that will not disturb other classes if the door is closed. One way to deal with disgruntled teachers nearby who complain about the noise, is to ask them how they know their students are involved and actually learning if they are not talking to others. Explain what you know about the value of talk and then ask those teachers for suggestions on how to get the same results without encouraging small-group work. No one method will work with all neighboring teachers, but in Diana's experience it was not much of a problem.

—to problem neighboring teachers

One of the bigger obstacles to using much oral work is the fear that the content won't get covered, that there is too much to do to allow time for students to process information through group work. No one can convince another teacher of the value of talk and small-group work. That teacher must experience it herself. Diana's advice to those unsure of whether talk should be a large part of their classroom, is to pay attention to what students are actually learning. Do your own informal research and watch and listen to your students. Ask them questions informally. You may be surprised to find that even though you "covered" the concept of the unreliable narrator that students have no idea what it means and gained little from the way the material was handled. Group work can allow for learning at a much deeper level.

Keeping track of pupils' talk and evaluating what they accomplish is also another obstacle for many teachers. Tape recording group sessions can of course be used occasionally, but for most secondary teachers who teach five classes each day, this could be unwieldy. Teachers can get a good idea of what is happening during group times by observing the groups. But one of the best ways for secondary teachers to evaluate group talk is to ask pupils to reflect in writing or to report back to the whole group on what they have been doing and saying. See Chapter 13 for further ideas.

STORYTELLING

Another way of integrating talk into the classroom is to encourage storytelling and structure time for it. Telling stories is the way we all deal with making sense of our lives. We tell and retell incidents to friends and acquaintances in our efforts to find places in our head to put things, to come to terms with experiences. The stories that we repeat have some kind of importance to us. Giving students opportunities to tell their stories taps into the richness of the experiences they bring to the classroom.

Stories can be told in many ways—speech and writing, in poetry, prose, and drama—but the most fundamental kind of storytelling is done face-to-face. Like conversation, storytelling is more easily promoted than taught, better encouraged than demanded. But a number of experiences can be provided to get it started.

Reminiscing is a natural starting point for storytelling. Without drifting to the summer vacation motif, the teacher can often lead off a class with a story about his or her own past that invites students to share some of their experiences.

Literature—especially stories by and about adolescents—provides innumerable starting points. Following the reading of a good story, the teacher can simply ask, "Has anything like this ever happened to you?"

Tall tales, boasting, and exaggeration have an important storytelling function since in creating an exaggerated tale, the students draw upon, expand, and develop their own view of the world.

Scary stories are among the common property of humankind: everyone has one and everyone wants to share one. After bringing in a book such as *Short Circuits: Thirteen Shocking Stories by Outstanding Writers for Young Adults* edited by Don Gallo (Delacorte 1992) or Alvin Schwartz's *More Scary Stories to Tell in the Dark* (Harper & Row, 1984) and reading a few stories, give students a chance to discuss the real and imaginary terrors of their lives.

Mary C. Savage a storyteller and family literacy program coordinator with the Henry Street Settlement in New York suggests that if stories do not flow because the group doesn't know each other or when the group does not yet feel like a safe place to tell stories, it is useful to try some of these devices to help people connect with their cultural background. You can ask them to:

- Draw a symbol for one of their grandmothers.
- Draw a picture of where they grew up or a landscape to which they feel attached.
- Tell how they played when they were children.
- Recall something they did that they never told their parents.
- Write about someone who influenced them.
- Explain a strength or limitation derived from having grown up in a particular ethnic or class culture.

Small groups or pairs can then tell their stories on the basis of these drawings, writings, or discussions.

Storytelling is a natural extension of conversation, and often the teacher can initiate it simply by saying "tell me more" when an incident or anecdote flashes by in informal conversation. In many classes, once the storytelling concept is introduced, the students become hooked on the idea and become habitual storytellers and story collectors. Encourage oral storytelling. Students are very willing to share a recurring dream, family myths and legends, school or community myths and legends. After the telling, students can write the stories or (lest writing be seen as punishment for volunteering to talk) tape-record them so that students in other classes can hear them.

DRAMA AND PERFORMANCE

Drama and performance are other ways to make meaning, other ways to get at the heart of what you are teaching. They require students to express themselves in new ways. We are not suggesting that students put on full-fledged plays although in

The power of drama lies in its ability to create contexts, to bring the world outside into the classroom, to enable pupils, in role, to broaden and extend their thinking and feeling, and to bring issues to life, to lift them off the page.

From Teaching Talking and Learning based on the work of the National Oracy Project. (York, U.K.: National Curriculum Council, 1991), p. 23.

drama classes there would be more room to do that. What we are suggesting is that the teacher create more active ways that students can interact with the material they are dealing with. This could involve role-playing, creating skits, scripting parts of novels, performing poems, and reading dramatically. We believe performing and dramatizing enhances students' learning for many reasons. First, there are many ways of knowing something; acting it out can heighten a student's understanding of a text or idea by forcing her to look at it in a new and different way. Second, students assume ownership of their own learning when they perform, for they become responsible for interpreting and creating a new representation of a text. Third, dramatic techniques are based upon active learning. Students must pull meaning "off the page" by entering and working through texts, looking both through the original writer's eyes as well as their own. A performed text comes alive and is no longer just a series of inanimate black and white marks on a page. Fourth, representing ideas orally helps students become better speakers and language users. Through speech performance they learn about formal presentation structures and how to more effectively communicate their ideas.

INITIAL EXPERIENCES WITH DRAMA

Students who have never even stood up next to their seat to read, may balk at getting up in front of the class and performing and interpreting a poem. To avert catastrophe, we never ask students to jump into performance cold. The first few times, students—especially those of high school age—may be edgy, nervous, and frightened, and the teacher must be very careful to make the activities pleasant and nonthreatening. Many experts in the field advocate beginning drama activities with informal warm-up exercises designed to release tensions and get people into the mood for drama. Typical warm-ups include:

- Pantomime. Participants imitate common actions: brushing teeth, talking on the phone, a person trying to keep from falling asleep at a lecture.
- Express moods. Give students a word to repeat in various ways to show joy, happiness, anger, sadness, or a kaleidoscope of moods.
- Creating a new use for an object. At their seats students can each use something common like a pencil in a new way. They might turn it into a razor blade, a hair pick, a cigarette, a cuticle shaper and so on.

If the teacher demonstrates what students are to do and participates enthusiastically, students will usually be much more willing to take risks. Asking students to wordlessly convey a major theme or idea or situation in a story and freezing the action is usually a good way to begin. For instance, as students read *Freak the Mighty,* they can be asked to do a "freeze frame" in which they freeze the action of an important scene which uses at least two people. Encouraging students in pairs to figure out how to enact a scene and having the other students guess what the scene is can involve students in the novel at a deeper level as it helps them overcome their fear of getting up in front of people.

PUPPETRY

In one of Steve's teacher education courses, a student did a project investigating puppetry as a way of introducing dramatic work. She constructed several simple glove puppets, wrote up some starter situations, and asked members of the class to put on the puppets and improvise. The two volunteers (draftees, actually) crouched down behind a table—a crude stage—and began improvising, a bit edgily at first but gaining enthusiasm as they entered into the play. Steve happened to be sitting to the side so that he could see both the puppets and puppeteers, and as the drama unfolded, an interesting thing happened: The puppeteers gradually became less conscious of the puppets and began to watch and speak to each other. A two-level drama emerged— one onstage, one behind stage.

This process intrigued Steve because these two students, seated on the floor, holding puppets in the air, shouting lines at each other, were among the shy members of the class; under no circumstances would it have been possible for Steve to get them this excited about an improvisation presented directly to the class. The puppets had released these students' dramatic talents.

Since then, Steve has used puppets with many groups at all age levels, and the results have been remarkably consistent. Puppets provide a mask—some basic protection— that allows people to open up to a high degree in dramatic work. Even older students, who Steve feared might see puppetry as juvenile, seem to enjoy it. Steve has even been forced to retire one set of classroom puppets that were demolished in a lively drama by two graduate students who had previously made a point of telling him what quiet, reserved people they were.

Secondary students react positively to using puppets, especially if they are used as a regular part of the course and not just brought out once a year. Puppets allow students to step outside themselves and become someone else. All eyes are focused on the puppet, not on the person, and this adds to the ease students feel when they use puppets.

Students can use puppets to:

- Introduce themselves at the beginning of the year.
- Read a poem that the puppet chose. After the poem is read, the puppet tells why it appealed to him or her or it.
- Talk to literary characters. One puppet might take on the persona of the Captain in *The True Confessions of Charlotte Doyle* and explain why he was so cruel to his men.
- Enact a dialogue. After reading Jonathan Edwards' "Sinners in the Hands of an Angry God," one student can write up the Puritan puppets' response to

the sermon while another student writes up responses from a puppet of the twentieth century. The puppets can then discuss their viewpoints with each other in front of the class.

- Be the characters in brief scenes they write to fill in gaps in a short story or a novel. As they read *Crazy Horse Electric Game* they can create a script based on what Kim said when Willie visited him in the hospital or what his girlfriend would say to Willie when he resurfaced after almost a year's absence. The puppets play the parts of the characters.

Teachers can also include puppetry as a part of the writing options or project activities. For example, students can create puppet characters to respond to characters in a novel or story or to verbalize a reaction to a poem.

The equipment for puppetry is simple. The puppets themselves can be made from paper bags, paper plates, cloth remnants, or papier-mache. They can be made in sizes ranging from finger puppets (simple tubes of cloth or paper) to the super puppet (a variation on the pillowcase that the puppeteer wears).

The sources of puppet plays are endless. Students can present puppet pantomimes, dramatic readings, ballets, plays, television programs, discussions, panels, debates, interviews, and conversations. Puppetry also makes a good road show, and students often enjoy taking a puppet repertory company to other classes, to other schools, or to libraries.

ORAL INTERPRETATION

Literature is a performing art, and we often overlook the dramatic excitement that oral reading—by individuals or groups—can bring to a class. Teachers have traditionally acted as if silent reading is the only proper kind, intimating that somehow students are cheating if they listen to literature. It is shocking to observe that all but a few of the best student writers are almost totally incapable of doing an equally good oral reading of what they have written.

Students need not be polished readers or have theatrical experience in order to do successful dramatic reading. What is essential is a message—a poem, story, play, essay—and a desire to communicate it to other people. In reading sincerely and naturally, most readers will be sufficiently dramatic to interest an audience.

The teacher can initiate an interest in oral interpretation simply by reading aloud regularly. Students of all levels seem to enjoy being read to, and it is unfortunate that oral experiences like story hour are abandoned after the early grades. A long novel, one that might be out of range for many students, can be read, a chapter at a time, over a period of several weeks or months. Literature to supplement a topical or thematic unit can be read to a class. Recordings of dramatic readings should be brought in as well, and all teachers should get a copy of the record and tapes catalog of Caedmon, a company that specializes in recordings of authors reading their own work.

The teacher should not be the only reader, of course, and students can be involved in oral interpretation. At first, the readings should be relatively short, and the student should have ample time to look over the material, though not necessarily to rehearse it, before reading aloud. By all means avoid "going around the class," having each student read a paragraph or two, in what often becomes a dull parade of uninvolved readings. If the teachers want to have students read aloud, they should organize it, prepare for it, and help the students do a polished job of it.

Having students read their own work is also a good oral interpretation project, since the reader begins by being familiar with the meaning of the work. Oral reading can also be encouraged by sponsoring activities like informal poetry readings or coffeehouse readings, in which writers come together to read and talk over their work. We like the idea of having a school-wide festival involving the reading of student work on an annual or a semester basis. Good writing from all over the school is collected, and either the writers themselves or good oral readers read the work to the entire school or to groups of parents. This kind of festival not only honors student writers but gives your good readers a chance for public recognition as well.

SCRIPTING AND PERFORMING

Put very simply, scripting is taking a piece of literature and turning part of it into a script after much thought about what to take out and what to include. It also usually requires that a narrator be added to set the scene, add necessary details, and generally move the action from place to place. Scripting, often called Reader's Theater, is versatile and can be used in many ways.

Scripting as an Alternative to the Book Report

Students have to learn how to write a script

As students read individually chosen novels, explain to them that they will each be writing a script from their novel that would make other students want to read their book. They have to carefully choose a chapter of their novel, write a script of it, and read/perform the script to the entire class. To help students understand the idea, it helps if the teacher writes a script on a novel she has just finished, makes enough copies for all the characters written into the script and has students perform it for the class. This usually promotes buy-in on the students' parts. They can see how much fun it is to choose readers for their scripts and so they are usually very interested in creating one. Next the teacher explains how to choose a chapter and how to decide what to put into the script by talking about action, dialogue, and suspense. It's usually necessary to talk about why it is important to include a narrator who could give details of setting, provide necessary background, move the action forward, and even report the thoughts of a character. Discussion of the functions a narrator serves also helps students see that the narrator can be the bridge between the scenes and events.

Through discussing what they find interesting in the script, students see that the script should have lots of dialogue and that it should have enough action to keep their classmates interested when it is performed.

As students finish their novels they begin to write scripts in class so they can get help if they need it. When the first script is ready, enough copies of the script for each character are made by the teacher. Performances are spaced out so only two or three novels are presented each day. Because the student who writes the script gets to choose the readers for that script, students see this as a privilege to be taken seriously. The more they read the scripts aloud, the better their oral reading became. The students who work hard to read with expression become readers who are asked to participate frequently. Because students like the performance aspect of this kind of assignment, it acts as a stimulus for them to read, as it encourages them to think about how they can interest others in their book. They like the assignment because they have the power to create a script that is representative of the novel. When every student has presented a script, each member of the class selects the five novels from the presentations that they most want to read. Thus students get more feedback on how well they succeed in interesting others in the novel they script.

As a Way into Themes, Characters, and Issues in Short Stories

Students write scripts to show their understanding of themes and characters in short stories. They usually do this by creating scripts to flesh out scenes that were alluded to but not developed. After reading such stories as "The Devil and Tom Walker" by Washington Irving, they develop scripts showing what they think happened in the woods when Mrs. Walker confronted the Devil. Students use what they know about characters to create dialogue that is "in character" as they use such clues as the tufts of hair scattered about in the woods and the discarded apron to create their view of how this clash played itself out. Working to be consistent with the tone of the story in these scripts, students try to make sure the character's language and attitudes are portrayed as they were in the story.

Students also create talk shows based on issues that unfold in short stories. For instance, in "She" by Rosa Guy in the short story collection, *Sixteen* edited by Don Gallo, the major conflict is between step-parent and step-child. Although the story is written from the point of view of the step-child, students often show both sides of the issue in their scripts. The Oprah Winfrey show has been a format students like to use. They invite to the show all four characters from the short story plus a psychologist (played by a student) as well as members of the class who felt they were experts on the issue because they lived with a step-parent. In this case, there is some use of scripts to keep the show on course and some use of ad-libbing. Through this activity students not only got more involved with the issues and characters in the short story but it also nudged them into reflecting on issues very close to some of their own lives.

As a Way to Increase Comprehension of More Difficult Literature

When students have trouble envisioning exactly what is happening in more difficult literature, it works well to have pairs of students turn a chapter into a script. They focus on meaning, on capturing the essence of the chapter, and then perform their script to other small groups or to the whole class. In scripting a novel like Crane's *The Red Badge of Courage* students could see that there is more of Henry's internal thoughts than dialogue, and they figure out that they might need more than one narrator to carry the heavy load of narration needed. The teacher can choose the chapters that seem important to an understanding of the novel or students can choose chapters they think might be important to script.

One group in Diana's American Literature class wrote the following as part of the script on Chapter XIII:

> *Narrator 1: The youth got up carefully, and Wilson led him among the sleeping forms lying in groups and rows. Presently he stooped and picked up his blankets. He spread the rubber one upon the ground and placed the woolen one about the youth's shoulders.*
>
> *Wilson: There now; lie down an' git some sleep.*
>
> *Henry: Hol' on a minute! Where you goin't' sleep?*
>
> *Wilson: Right down there by yeh.*
>
> *Henry: Well, but hol' on a minnit. What yeh going' t' sleep in? I've got your-*
>
> *Wilson: Shet up on' go on t' sleep. Don't be making a damn fool 'sa yerself.*
>
> *Narrator 2: An exquisite drowsiness spread through the youth. His head fell forward on his crooked arm and his weighted lids went slowly down over his eyes.*

Afterwards, students commented on how much more they got out of the novel by scripting it and then listening to the performances of the scripts. It seems that the emotions so often swallowed up by Crane's extensive descriptions came bursting through in these student-written scripts.

As a follow-up, small groups evaluate one or two scripts, answering questions like the following:

1. Briefly describe what each script emphasized.
2. What was particularly effective in any of the scripts?
3. Did any of the scripts include unusual narrative devices? Were they effective?
4. What made some scripts more interesting to read?
5. As a group, discuss what makes a script good. Now list all the advice you would give to someone about how to write a script.

As a Way to Evaluate Students' Ability to Synthesize What They Know About Authors and Characters

As a final exam activity, Diana has students write scripts which bring together nine characters and authors who had been read during the semester. Students bring the people together in any way they want, write it in script form and turn it in one week before the final exam period. The focus of the script must be on showing how the characters interact in terms of issues that will show what the characters or authors were like.

For instance in one script, the characters have this exchange as they talk about the death penalty.

Roger Chillingworth: I think all criminals should be killed.

Dr. Heidegger: I think we should use criminals in laboratory experiments.

Henry Thoreau: That's absurd. Whatever happened to human compassion? What about giving each other a second chance? We should do everything we can to rehabilitate our criminals. We must not give up on them.

Roderick Usher: Death! I dread the day I die! If I were to be murdered I'd want my killer tortured and then killed!

William Cullen Bryant: I think death is something to look forward to. It will be exciting and may be even better than life. Until we made sure we are punishing the criminals, we must not use capital punishment.

Several of these scripts, which showcase the thoughts and beliefs of the characters and authors, are then shared during the final exam time. Students have a wonderful time while knowledge about authors and characters from the semester is reinforced. Students in Diana's class have brought characters together in such places as on Ted Koppel's "Nightline," in a wax museum, on a golf course, and even in Dr. Heidegger's study.

Scripting works because scripts are student created; they have invested themselves in the product. Students share their insights through performance which expands the audience from just the teacher to the whole class, providing a more realistic and more interactive forum for their writing.

(A version of Scripting and Performing was published in Diana's Teaching Ideas column in the *English Journal* in October 1994, Copyright © 1994 by the National Council of Teachers of English. Reprinted with permission.)

DRAMA AS LITERATURE

In our eagerness to promote performance, we don't want to overlook the genre of drama which is usually part of any literature anthology. Many teachers, however, breathe a sign of relief that they can't get to the drama section (it's almost always at the end of the book) because they don't know what to do with a play besides having it read aloud. If drama is viewed as another kind of literature, the teacher will quickly see that students should be able to get involved with the characters, the issues, and the conflicts as with any other type of literature. Moreover, students can discuss the differences in action, language, and setting due to the performing nature of drama, as well as consider what drama does more or less successfully than other genres.

After plays have been read in the classroom, consider having students engage in some of the following kinds of activities, which represent a range of improvisational drama, scripted theater, and discussion possibilities:

- Change an element (plot, character, dialogue, setting) and write a bit, showing how this changes the play.
- Choose one character and then skim the play to find lines that character says that tell us a lot about him or her. Then go back through the play and find ten

lines that others say in reference to the character. Record these quotations. Now write a brief sketch of the character you chose, using the evidence you just collected. Then look at the character in terms of what you do and do not know about him or her.

- Compared to literature, does drama as a form let us know more or less about characters?

- Select two or three plays and look for symbolism in them. If symbolism exists, how is it present in drama (scenery, characters, language)? Discuss your conclusions.

- Sketch out the main events and conflicts in one or more plays; then rewrite the play in an oral form, the rap. Discuss what this new form adds to or takes away from the drama.

- Discuss themes present in the plays—are they similar to or different from themes we've discovered in the other literature we have read?

- From the anthology, pick out five poems and five short stories that deal with the same theme as one of the plays.

- Turn your play into a TV drama. How would it be different?

- Invite eight people from different plays to an imaginary dinner. What issues or themes would they talk about? What human concerns would they share?

- Choose a theme present in at least two of the plays and write a poem or an editorial about it.

- Write a folk tale or fairy tale based on a play.

- Write a dialogue between two major characters from different plays.

- Write a script for a talk show with three characters from different plays who can respond to a similar theme.

- Write a "Dating Game" episode with three male or three female characters. Compose the questions the members of the opposite sex would ask them and write the contestants' responses.

- Write a speech for one of the characters (such as Iago in *Othello*) as either a presidential candidate or a TV evangelist.

- You are in charge of creating Tony award categories and of awarding the Tonys to characters from the plays you have read. Explain your choices. Some suggestions: Strongest Female Character, Most Unfortunate Character, Most Mentally Disturbed Character.

- Write a letter to one of the characters whom you feel strongly about. Explain to him or her what bothers you about his or her behavior or what you find particularly appealing.

- Create a product that several characters might want or need and then write a commercial or advertisement enticing them to buy it. State which characters are your intended audience and why.

- Create and present an evening news show using incidents and characters from selected plays.

- Create a radio drama complete with an announcer and sound effects on a dramatic portion of one of the plays.
- Become characters from a play and let the class interview you.

PERFORMING POETRY

Since poetry often takes more than one reading to fully understand and appreciate its nuances, asking students to perform poetry provides a natural forum for this kind of close reading. When students perform poetry they usually do so in groups after having read the poem several times, figuring out how to break the poem into voices, and creating movement that makes the meaning of the poem immediately evident.

If students have had some experience in reading scripts to the class, this activity only asks for one additional thing—movement. Poetry performance can be worked into the classroom in many ways. If the teacher organizes the class around themes or around novels, having students hunt for poems that speak to the theme or novel is a natural way into poetry. While doing a unit on war that included both *Fallen Angels* and *The Red Badge of Courage,* Diana brought in several poems about war. But if the teacher doesn't know of poems on specific themes, bringing in batches of poetry books from the school library and having students locate the poems also works well. Encourage students to look for poems that would work well with several voices and for poems that will have a strong impact when read aloud.

Students divide the poem into parts with each part having one or more voices. Then they decide how it could be presented most effectively. One group in Diana's class performed "A Square Dance" by Roger McGough, a poem about the horrors of World War I. Since the poem has the rhythm of a square dance and uses a dance metaphor, the students decided to perform it as a square dance. The contrast between the words and actions created a chilling effect and students fell silent. The poetry performed moved them and involved them as it jumped to life. Another memorable performance was on "Carol with Variations 1936" by Phyllis McGinley. This poem intersperses Christmas song melodies with the naked facts about the carnage of WWII. The group that performed the poem had two students who were confident singers. They sang the words of the poem and then hummed softly while the other voices chanted the words of war. Both of these presentations showed an intimate understanding of the poems. To present the poem effectively the meaning had to be crystal clear to the presenters.

Another point in American Literature courses to use the performance of poetry is when reading Edgar Lee Masters *Spoon River Anthology.* Since the poems are spoken from the grave and usually refer to several other inhabitants of Spoon River, it is effective to have students work in groups and select one poem for each student that somehow speaks to or alludes to other people. Students perform these individually but part of their work is in deciding which order of reading will have the biggest impact because of the affect others' lives had on the person. Since all the characters are dead when they speak, candles or a small covered lamp can be brought in to make the room seem shadowed and eerie. Performing poems in these ways leaves indelible impressions upon the students.

◆ EXPLORATIONS

◆ Do some eavesdropping. Listen to people engaged in an argument and think over their skill in speaking with and listening to each other. Listen to politicians talking over their program with reporters. Reflect on what you have heard in terms of how much communication is going on. Consider the implications for teaching. What do kids need to learn to speak and listen well?

◆ Explore oral history and storytelling as a starting point for a spoken English unit. Have students or members of your collaborative group recall and tell significant stories from their past. Then have them do the same through interviews with their parents and grandparents, either taping or transcribing the tale and anecdotes. Bring a local storyteller to class!

◆ Bring a poem to class that your collaborative group can read dramatically.

◆ Keep a diary for a specified period of time (such as a day) of all the uses you make of conversation and what your purpose is in each interaction. Share with your group.

◆ Examine the implications of the questions you ask in class or plan to ask via your teaching notes or that a college literature teacher asks. In terms of questions about literature, figure out how many questions tap into student thinking in Stances One, Two , and Three and how many there are in Stance Four, which asks for more criticism and analysis. What are the implications for the kinds of discussions you (or your professor) will promote? It might also be interesting to divide the questions along other lines: into questions that catalyze *divergent* rather than *convergent* thinking (leading to original conclusions rather than coming to a fixed point), or into *cognitive* versus *affective* (questions that emphasize knowledge versus those that are concerned with values and subjective responses). Again consider the implications of your decision (or the professor's decision) in terms of what is being shown to students that the instructor values and in terms of the way student talk is likely to flow.

◆ Experiment with small-group patterns in this class proposing new techniques and structures. Try groups of three, four, five, and six. Test out leaderless groups, groups with appointed leaders, and groups that choose their own leaders. See what happens when groups do and do not have to report back.

◆ Some Australian teachers Steve met while on a teaching exchange said that their "methods" instructor in university told them never to assemble the class as a whole except for announcements. That is, the class was to make use of small groups and solo work exclusively. Evaluate that advice.

◆ In collaborative groups, brainstorm all the performance options your group can come up with on a novel you have all read. If time permits, develop one, and perform it.

◆ In collaborative groups create a script based on imagined students' negative reactions to being asked to perform a poem. Show how the teacher responds and tries to coax the students into participating.

◆ To experience a collaborative "composing" activity, bring a magazine to class and scissors. Cut out words and phrases that interest you or that you like. Pair up with another person who also has cut out a group of words or phrases. Spread out everything you both have cut out and begin to create a poem from this material. When you are finished, write a reflective paper on the process of what you did as well as the kinds of decisions you had to make about language.

RELATED READINGS

One of the best, most direct explanations of how talking enhances learning is in *Teaching Talking and Learning,* a booklet for teachers based on the work of the National Oracy Project in England. Teachers are also shown how to go about integrating the use of talk into their classrooms. *When Students Have Time to Talk* by Curt Dudley-Marling and Dennis Searle looks at talk in a comprehensive way although examples are from elementary classrooms. *Talking to Learn* edited by Patricia Phelan, Chair, and the Committee on Classroom Practices is a rich collection of articles that demonstrate talking and listening activities to expand students' understanding of literature as well as practical ways to work speaking and listening into the heart of the class.

For teachers who want to immerse students further in play building Carole Tarlington and Wendy Michaels offer *Building Plays* which focuses on how to go about getting students involved in writing their own plays. *Another 100+ Ideas for Drama* by Anna Scher and Charles Verrall and *Dramathemes* by Larry Swartz are both packed with ideas for involving students in meaningful drama activities.

Give a Listen: Stories of Storytelling in School edited by Ann M. Trousdale is a good place for teachers to start who want to learn more about storytelling and how it can be woven into the curriculum. *Keepsakes: Using Family Stories in Elementary Classrooms* by Linda Winton illustrates kinds of family stories that can be used at any level. Two books that can help teachers build confidence in their students' ability to tell stories are *The Storytelling Coach: How to Listen, Praise and Bring Out People's Best* by Doug Lipman and *Telling Your Own Stories: For Family and Classroom Storytelling, Public Speaking and Personal Journaling* by Donald David.

For teachers who need concrete examples of readers' theater scripts based on literature before they have students write their own scripts, Reader's Theater Script Service (P.O. Box 178333, San Diego, CA 92117) and Contemporary Drama Service (Box 7710-H4, Colorado Springs, Co 80933) offer a wide variety of such scripts. Write to the above addresses for catalogs.

CHAPTER 12

LANGUAGE: A MASS MEDIUM

[Much talk] seems to me like a commonplace entertainment to which a vulgar company have recourse; who, because they are not able to converse or amuse one another, while they are drinking, with the sound of their own voices and conversation, by reason of their stupidity, raise the price of flute-girls in the market, hiring for a great sum the voice of a flute instead of their own breath, to be the medium of intercourse among them: but where the company are real gentlemen and men of education, you will see no flute-girls, nor dancing-girls, nor harp girls; and they have no nonsense or games, but are contented with one another's conversation, of which their own voices are the medium, and which they carry on by turns and in an orderly manner, even though they are very liberal in their potations.

—Plato, *Protagoras*

Electricity has made angels of us all—not angels in the Sunday school sense of being good or having wings, but spirits freed from flesh, capable of instant transportation anywhere.

—Edmund Carpenter, *Oh, What a Blow That Phantom Gave Me*

Figure 12.1

One morning before school, Steve took a bit of time for the morning ritual of coffee, a bagel, and the morning newspaper. Removing the paper from its plastic sleeve (as a paperboy in his youth, of course, Steve *rolled* the newspaper and delivered it to a place out of the weather), and then removing the rubber band that clasped the news even more firmly, he was startled and disappointed when a bundle of advertising fliers fell out of the paper and tipped over his coffee. Mopping up the spilled coffee with one of the supplements (a Wal-Mart mini magazine that advertised great prices on perfume, garden mums, and some Intimate Moods lingerie modeled by a woman named Monica, who is reportedly a cashier at a nameless Wal-Mart store), he thought of Plato and the *Protagoras,* and, specifically, the lengths to which people go to conduct discourse in an age of mass media. (Does Monica, he wondered, play the flute?) One of the supplements lying on the floor turned out to be a small brown paper bag, and Steve kept it, thinking it would be useful for something or other. The bag was actually an advertisement for a new supermarket bakery, The Bread Store, and the bag was provided so customers could go to the bakery, pick up an unwrapped and unsliced loaf of Harvest bread (just like grandma used to make), insert it into the provided paper bag, and save 50 cents over the regular purchase price. Steve wondered what would happen if he took the plastic bag that had contained the newspaper and inserted an unwrapped and unsliced loaf of Harvest bread therein. Would he still save the four bits?

Still mulling these weighty matters (and wondering if he could sue for having burned himself on the hot coffee, just like the woman who successfully sued McDonald's Golden Arches for her own dropping of a hot cup of coffee in her lap while trying to drive and pry off the plastic lid), he tuned in public radio and heard musician Stevie Wonder declare, "The human voice is eternal," and that idea is the real source of his joy in writing music. But if the voice is "eternal," Steve the textbook author wondered, why was Stevie Wonder broadcasting his voice over public radio; why was he making music videos and CDs; why didn't he just stick his head out the window and let his "eternal voice" do its work? (Or why, for that matter, do Tchudi and Mitchell write a book instead of being content to preach their gospel of literacy to everyone within listening distance?)

And, to bring this parable to a close, Steve T. recalled the movie, *Network,* where (in a fantasy we'd all like to see happen) a disgruntled anchorman, sick of being just a puppet on the evening news, *did* stick his head out of his apartment window and shout, "I'm mad as hell and I'm not going to take it anymore." His voice reached hundreds of people on his New York street, and they joined in the chant. The news media picked up this event and broadcasted it nationwide. The newsman became a counter-culture hero and nearly brought the network to its knees before dying of a heart attack, which allowed the monolith, trademarked television network to continue its business of selling ideas, news, and products as usual.

This is a chapter about mass media, their role in our lives, and their role in the English language arts classroom. For practical purposes, we'll define a "mass medium" as "any *technology* or *strategy* designed to amplify the human voice." By and large people are *not* content just to have an intelligent conversation with their peers (as Plato did in his dialogues) or to sing their songs or play the flute in isolation: They want to reach a larger circle of people. By our definition, cupping your hands to shout over a longer distance is a form of "mass media"; so is using a megaphone or bullhorn or speaking on the radio. For that matter, Plato's dialogues are also a mass medium, for although they are presented as conversations, Plato was no mere note taker; he was preserving and publicizing the ideas of his mentor Socrates so that we can not only read, but be educated by them two thousand years later.

Part of our definition focuses on the *technology* of media and the ways in which we use technologies to magnify the voice. The printing press is a technology, as is the pencil; the megaphone is a technology, as is the computer word processor. Something like the newspaper actually involves multiple technologies: the radio, fax, and wire services that send in the news; electronic and film cameras that produce pictures; word processors and desktop publishing programs that turn writers' words into "camera ready" copy; more cameras that convert images into printing plates (or in some instances, computers that make the term "camera ready" obsolete by going from digital bits and bytes to a printing plate), and high-speed presses complete with folding and collating devices that can get out multiple thousands of copies of the paper by dawn. (If one wanted to go further, one could even argue that the newspaper delivery system—the trucks, the coin dispensers outside the donut shop, the paper delivery people, and maybe even their alarm clocks—are part of the multiple mass medium of the daily paper, since each is partly responsible for multiplying the human voice.

But as Marshall McLuhan reminded us, the technologies of media have powerful side effects: His claim, in fact, is that "Societies have always been shaped more by the nature of the media by which men communicate than by the content of the communication" (McLuhan and Fiore, p. 8). That is, McLuhan suggested that the technology itself has built-in advantages and limitations that affect the kinds of messages that it delivers. The common pencil, for example, will let you draw just about any shape you can imagine on a page and let you freely shape your letters and words any way you want to, but it limits you to one-of-a-kind productions (unless you multiply your effects with the technologies of carbon paper or a photocopy machine). A computer word processor, wonderful though it may be, actually limits your freedom to express yourself on paper: You are limited to the fonts and sizes stored in your computer memory, but you can fax your artwork and writing directly from your computer, upload it to a web site, or send it off to the printer—which gives certain advantages of publication. (It's also easier to draw a straight line on a computer than it is with a pencil.)

Television delivers some messages extremely well and others less well; seeing a movie in a theater has certain advantages over seeing it on your TV set; reading a book has advantages and disadvantages over seeing a novelization on screen; writing a paper yourself has advantages and disadvantages over plucking someone else's words and ideas off the world wide web. A major goal for the study of mass media in the English language arts, then, is to help students become aware of this interrelationship between technologies and the messages they carry; as McLuhan said, "The medium is the message."

The second aspect of our definition includes the notion of media *strategies.* We disagree with McLuhan, who felt that the technologies of media are more important than the content. To the contrary, we remain convinced that although technologies may shape content (you can't send a picture over the radio), what is especially interesting and important is for people to see how people use the medium to present the content they have in mind. The "medium" of the brown paper bag in the newspaper supplements seems, for example, to be a very clever strategy: It was memorable (something other than the usual printed supplements); it suggested usefulness (carry this bag—and its message—away with you); it was a concise and well organized message, including all you needed to know to understand a new bakery concept, the addresses of the new locations, and a coupon good for the reduced price on bread. Steve wondered, briefly, if poets might also insert brown paper bags in the newspaper for strategic effect. Then he recalled that in a number of cities, poets have displayed their work on public buses, up with the advertising placards—a very clever integration of a media technology and a strategy for amplifying one's voice. And he recalled the work of some writers in British Columbia who published a flier called "Two Cent's Worth," a broadside of short works that they placed near the "penny jar" at checkout counters, encouraging shoppers to take their change in poetry rather than pennies. We strategize interminably to get our words out to the public.

Another word for strategy is "rhetoric," a term that we sometimes hesitate to use because of its negative connotations: political rhetoric, sales rhetoric, rhetoric as puffery and hollow promises. Of course, much mass media is puffery: We suspect, for example that the The Bread Store™ and its Harvest™ bread are probably just the same old in-store bakery, and that the bakery and bread bear only slight resemblance to the stuff granny used to make in the farmhouse kitchen. (Indeed, the ad assures us that Honey Multi Grain Bread comes in a two-pound loaf while Honey Wheat comes in a twenty-four-ounce loaf; was granny ever that precise in her measurements?) At the same time, all media are *rhetorical:* the weather person uses wonderful electronic pointing devices and satellite photos to help us visualize the weather; the public broadcasting documentary on the civil war uses photographs, celebrity voices, interviews, maps and charts to get its message across; the soap operas contrive to leave us hanging at the end of each episode so we will tune in tomorrow. Rather than lamenting "rhetoric," we think it's important for youngsters (and oldsters) to be highly aware of its use and effects, to think not only about the content of media messages, but of the rhetoric being used to transmit a point of view and to shape the point of view of the respondent.

It is almost a cliché to say that ours is an electronic age or, as Edmund Carpenter observes, to say that electronic communications have made "angels of us all." As we look to the future, we can see that the fully functioning members of the community of language will draw on many media. They will continue to read and write, to consume and create print. They will be able to use the telephone (fixed-base, cellular, pay, videophone); they will be computer literate in ways undreamt of by their teachers (we're not far from the day where people will be able to dictate writing into a computer; where computers will become small enough that "laptops" become dinosaurs and boat anchors); they will use video (for both viewing and production); they may write paper letters sent by "snail mail" as well as by electronic mail. With their horizons expanded, young people need to be able to respond to the media creatively and critically and to use them to communicate with others successfully. These two aims—*responding to* and *using* the media are the two aims of this chapter.

Moreover, we want to point out the role of *language* as the central part of the process. One hears these days of such terms as "media literacy," "computer literacy," "television literacy," and "web literacy." Actually, these are a metaphorical use of "literacy" to mean "competence," the ability to "read and write" (perceive and produce) in that medium. But the English language arts teacher will quickly recognize that these "literacies" are, in fact, based on a prior literacy: the ability to use language itself. Speaking and listening skill is certainly prior to any other media use—you gotta *be* literate to become *computer* literate. Literal reading and writing are also pretty fundamental to these other literacies—we communicate with our computers by typing on alphanumeric keyboards and by studying the printed words that appear on the screen. Any media project is thus an "English" project, and virtually any responding or creating project we can imagine can also be justified as helping to develop the quintessential skills of language that underlie all media. Although we have, in a sense, isolated our discussion of mass media in its own chapter, we want to continue to emphasize the need for curriculum integration, for the English language arts teacher to introduce media not as one-shot novelties, but as tools/strategies for communication that we employ every day of our lives.

THE TERRIFYING ANGEL: TELEVISION

What *are* we to do with television? Its worst critics blast it as being not only destructive but downright evil, creating a false set of standards and values for its watcher-victims. Others point to the informational and instructional value of many television programs, not just limited to public television and non-prime time viewers, and counter argue that there is plenty of good stuff on TV if people are willing to search for it. Depending on one's point of view, cable and satellite television have either compounded the misery or opened new doorways, and it's clear that in our students' futures the choices will multiply. Television is predicted to merge with the world wide web (which we'll discuss in detail later), and as phone companies enter the cable/video/computer market, we are increasingly seeing the television set as containing media within media and conceivably replacing the refrigerator as the most ubiquitous appliance in the household. The activities that follow can help students of many ages sharpen both their response to television and their understanding of it as a medium of communication. (Many of these activities, by the way, could be conducted on the household refrigerator as well.)

TV-Watching Log

We've all read statistics on the number of hours students spend in front of the television set. Let your students analyze their own tube time by having them keep a complete log of their viewing for a single week. How many hours do they watch? How many hours on school days? On weekends? Have them discuss planned versus unplanned watching. How often do they turn on the set just to see what is happening? Encourage the students to break their watching into categories: news, adventure, comedy, docudrama, cartoons, sports, movies, and so on. Put your categories and figures on the chalkboard or a large sheet of paper to produce a graphic demonstration of the dominance of this medium in students' lives. This activity will generate all kinds of follow-up discussion. Often young people will show considerable savvy as they discuss their viewing. Students can also consider alternative ways of spending their time. Steve thinks he had some impact on a middle school class by pointing out that if they cut their TV viewing in half until the time they graduated from high school, they would have time to jog 12,000 miles, to read a couple thousand books, or to earn enough by baby sitting to pay cash for a car!

TV Review Sheet

As a follow-up to the TV log, students can begin to critique the shows they watch. On a page or two in their journals, students can review, say, the five best and five worst shows for a given week. The journals can then be discussed in small groups, with a fresh group of critics being assigned each week. Students might also want to send their reviews to the managers of local television stations. "Criticism" in this case can be as informal or formal as the teacher and students wish. At first, it may be best simply to let students react informally, but as the term or year progresses, they should be more and more skilled at explaining just what triggered their reactions.

Study TV Conventions

Because of its domination by commercial interests, television is highly repetitive. Once a new show succeeds, others follow the pattern. Have your students investigate a TV genre: police shows, situation comedies, cartoons, space operas, superhero shows, soap operas. Encourage them to look at the stereotypes of character and plot and conventions. As a follow-up, let the students write satires of the genres they have been studying. These satires might even be presented for the class through improvised drama or video.

The Image of America on TV

Stereotypes are not limited to characters in the TV genre shows. Television also creates stereotypes of Americans. Have the students keep track of stereotypes for a week or more. Have them look at the roles of men and women, children, husbands and wives, singles, racial minorities, lawyers, doctors, blue-collar workers, and so on. It has been said that TV is a revolutionary movement because it shows the lower economic classes what the upper crust owns and how it lives. It has also been argued that despite the efforts of people in the women's movement, television offers stereotypes of women as homemakers and/or sex objects. Do your students agree? Are their families like the families on TV?

Commercials

Some people feel that TV ads are both better and worse than the programs: better because they are developed with great skill to achieve high impact through brief exposure; worse, because they are highly exploitative, frequently verging on the dishonest. Conduct a TV commercial unit with your students; have them watch, analyze, and critique the commercials they see. This too, is a unit that can be followed with a video or stage production, with students writing and taping their own commercials, serious or satirical.

In a positive vein, in recent years promoters have discovered the TV tie-in, in which a novel is made over for television or a popular television program is turned into a novel. While the quality of the by-product—either TV show or book—varies considerably, in general the tie-ins spur interest in print literacy. Many paperback bookstores now have a "TV novels" section with a hundred or more titles that have been on television. Draw on the interest that the tie-ins produce by teaching some of the books or by assigning the shows for discussion and analysis.

Learning Via the Tube

With your students' help compile a list of the educational or documentary channels available in your area: PBS, Arts and Entertainment, Discovery, the History Channel, and so on. Such sources are an especially rich complement to an interdisciplinary unit and can provide all sorts of opportunities to see how television can be used rhetorically as a medium of communication, not just entertainment.

Video Production

Producing a video can be immensely satisfying for students, a visible and tangible product. Because of the high quality of contemporary equipment, video making often produces results that are apparently more professional than those of other modes of composition (that is, a video "looks" better than, say, a written short story or a term paper). However, to do quality videos, students need to do a great deal of preparation, planning, and practice. Waving a camera around without forethought produces material to which kids apply the curse of all curses: "boring." We favor lots of writing and talk prior to, during, and after taping and editing. Before beginning a video, students might want to spend some time studying the techniques of commercial television (even while understanding that fortunes are spent achieving effects on TV). Topics for student videos are limitless: Almost any idea, feeling, poem, play or song can lead to a short video. Thematic units can culminate in a video project, as can the traditional research "paper" project. Some video projects your students might find interesting are:

- improvised drama. Replay a taped session for discussion. Then do the improvisation a second time.

- the video documentary. Have students find an issue, problem, or topic around town or school and report on it.

- tape a staged play, either a chamber theater presentation or a fully produced play. Have students discuss how their taping can actually enhance or accentuate the meaning of the play.

- create a file of student writers on tape: reading, responding to questions from an audience, talking about how and why they write.

- prepare a video on a favorite author, with a student costumed as the writer.

- start or participate in a school's closed-circuit television network. Many schools now have kids do the morning news and announcements, and student video projects are played on the big screen in the lunchroom.

- explore local cable television as an outlet for student video productions.

EXPLORING FILM AND VIDEO

Almost as soon as "moving pictures" were developed, *The English Journal* carried articles on "photoplay appreciation," suggesting that English language arts teachers rightly recognized that this new medium belonged in their classrooms. But until recently, it was difficult to use film in the classroom. The projectors were bulky and balky; films came in multiple reels and had to be ordered months in advance. Bulbs fried the celluloid or burned out in the middle of showings (a standard piece of advice in traditional English "methods" class was always to have a spare projector bulb in your desk). The development of video players and the explosion of video stores has dramatically altered that. For a dollar or two you can rent hot new releases or the classics. What used to be called the school library is now the media center, suggesting that both the technology and the content are now a standard part of the schools' educational materials. Some activities to explore film:

Independent Judgments

One of the big problems with film viewing today is that enormous public relations efforts discourage independent judgment. Instead of seeing a movie and responding to it in personal terms, the viewer is predisposed to take a particular stance toward it. Public relations departments begin to hype a film as an Academy Award winner even before a single scene has been shot! Have your students study the promotion strategies behind new films. How is a film represented? marketed? What claims do the theaters make about it? Does the film live up to the hype?

Evaluating and Rating Films

Have students develop their own evaluation system for films, e.g. "stale popcorn," "not enough salt," "hot and buttery." Set aside a corner of the bulletin board or a spot on the classroom web site for recent film reviews. Also discuss film rating and censorship issues. Who rates films? What are the criteria for a rating? How do filmmakers get around rating systems (e.g., by using lots of violence and four-letter words, but avoiding a nude scene that would get a picture an adult rating)? Compare film and television rating systems. Do students concur with the ratings? Should anybody be rating films at all?

Filmgoers Polls

With permission of the theater owner, students can interview people going into and leaving the theater. Why are people going to the movie? What do they expect to see? Where did they first hear about the film? Do they already know how it ends? Are they pleased or disappointed afterward? Will they recommend the picture to their friends? Such interviews can yield statistical data for tabulation or material for a student-written feature article about film. Both kinds of writing are a natural for the school paper. If interviewing at the theater is not possible, students can conduct similar polls around school, asking fellow students what they watch and why.

Fads and Fancies in Film

Encourage your students to study film types or genres, particularly the more faddish sorts. Disaster films are ever popular (subdivided into their own genres: plane crashes, deep sea calamities, earthquakes, fires, meteor plunges, and so on.) The super robo-type cop films escalate in technological wizardry. Serial killer films make their rounds. Remakes of sixties TV comedies come to the fore. Have your students seek out the formulae of such films and try to explain the appeal they have for viewers.

Deepening Response

Teachers can use film to help students to become more aware of how they respond to film (and to literature and to life). Instead of settling for the one-word response, "great," "awful," or the stock response, "I loved the ending," teachers can nudge students toward making fuller, richer responses to the media. The questions following any film—or for that matter, television program—might run as follows:

1. *Response.* What is your response? How did you react? What did the film or video make you think or feel? Where did the film touch your own life, your

Often neglected in an age of TV, *radio* is the medium that set off the modern era of electronic communications/entertainment. Classroom projects centering on responding to and communicating by radio include:

- studying radio history: the technology of radio, the early radio stations, the establishment of "networks," the effect of radio on live entertainment (e.g., vaudeville, Chautauqua)
- listening to the old tyme radio programs, now widely available on tape: *Fibber McGee and Molly, The Lone Ranger, The Shadow*
- listening to great moments in history as captured on radio: the crash of the Hindenberg, Franklin Delano Roosevelt's fireside chats
- comparing the "visual" effects of radio drama with those of television
- creating a classroom sound effects studio and creating radio dramas
- comparing and contrasting present day FM and AM radio stations—what niches do they occupy?
- investigating the content and social effects of talk radio
- creating a "talk radio" show using the school intercom system
- surveying niche radio in our town: how do radio stations identify and attract specific audiences?
- meeting with a radio advertising specialist to discover how radio ads are sold and how they support the cost of programming
- visiting the local public broadcasting station to learn about radio technology as well as content and programming; serving as phone answerers during the next PBS fund raising event

Figure 12.2   Exploring the Radio

own experience? Did you relate to any of the characters in the film? Were any of the problems or characters just like you?

2. *Discussion.* Let's look at the film itself. Why did you react the way you did? Was it the action? the characters? the visuals? How did the director of the film control and elicit your reactions and responses?

3. *Evaluation.* Did the film have an impact on you *skillfully?* Were the characters realistic? Did they need to be? Did the film hold together as a whole? How would *you* have directed it?

4. *Technology and Content.* What was the interaction between the technology or medium of the film and the content portrayed? How did the director use the camera to direct your attention? How were visual effects achieved? How did the background music enter into the "picture"?

An especially interesting genre for film study is the sci-fi outer space "opera," for it represents the whole history of film and nicely illustrates the interplay between technology, film content, and culture. Students can study:

- Early efforts at representing space in film, the adaptation of Jules Verne's *Voyage to the Moon,* where a rocket jabs the man in the moon in the eye through primitive but ground breaking cartoon effects.

- The classic sci-fi films, serials, and television programs: Buck Rogers, Tom Corbett, etc. What now appears as comic special effects were once seen as "realistic." How can that be?

- The Star Wars revolution: How did the *Star Wars* trilogy revolutionize not only the sci-fi industry, but the film industry as a whole?

- The series films: *2001, 2010, 2064; Star Trek; Star Wars* of the 1970s and the '90s remakes.

- The evolution of special effects in science fiction films, from creation of critters to the representation of outer space.

- And especially: The cultural, social, political, and economic issues represented in science fiction films. In what ways are sci-fi films not about the future at all, but about today?

Figure 12.3   Space Operas

THE PRINT MEDIA

Despite periodic worries that the visual media will be the death of print, and despite the fact of the decline of newspapers in the U.S. and worldwide, print media are in most respects holding their own. The American Bookseller's Association boasts that more books than ever are being published, and the success of the big bookstore chains—Dalton's, Waldenbooks, Barnes and Noble, Border's—even while they may have driven smaller shops out of business, provides testimony to the vibrancy of the book industry. Equally notable is the phenomenon of magazine publishing, which has taken up some of the slack created by newspaper decline by offering a dazzling array of highly specialized glossy publications on just about any topic one could name. In a media-blitzed world, print remains relatively inexpensive and, in contrast to film and television, requires no special equipment, no electric plug or batteries, to operate—people *read* in all sorts of places where they can't watch visuals, and many still choose the privacy and flexibility of print to the controlled content and technology of TV.

The Newspaper

Elsewhere we have argued that the daily paper—any daily paper, *today's* paper—provides enough material that it can be the backbone of the English language arts classroom. Students can:

- read and respond to everything from the lead stories to the classifieds, from the "style" section to the comics.
- analyze and critique presentation of the news, comparing coverage in various newspapers (too often, nowadays, the same coverage based on wire sources), and comparing that to television coverage of the same stories.
- analyze the newspaper as a vehicle for advertising: How is your daily paper designed to accommodate ads?
- examine the visual/print relationship in the paper. In particular, as the newspaper world learned from the successes of *USA Today*, increasingly "readers" like their newspaper to resemble television in both graphics and content. How does our daily paper use graphics to make itself reader- (or viewer-) friendly?
- create their own newspapers. (See Figure 12.4)

[handwritten note in margin:] Students can make some sort of paper

---

Contemporary computer and photocopy technology make it possible for classrooms, elementary through college, to be a beehive of newspaper activity. Students can produce:

1. a weekly or monthly class paper, featuring news, student writing, games, letters to the editor.
2. a newsletter for parents explaining what is going on in the English language arts classroom.
3. broadsheets or fliers: one page "extras" dealing with controversial issues, current happenings, important events.
4. *competing* papers: with small groups putting out news sheets they think will gather a readership, with the class computing statistics on the papers that are most successful.
5. advertising sheets as fund raisers—get support from local businesses and industries by putting out advertising fliers on their behalf.
6. poster papers: one-of-a-kind newspapers prepared on poster board and mounted on the bulletin board (thus saving printing and paper costs).

Figure 12.4   The Class Newspaper

THE COMPUTER

The *uses* of computers in the English language arts classroom are perhaps more obvious than solutions to the problem of how to get computers into the classroom. Some day, we imagine, and perhaps in the not too distant future, youngsters will be issued computers along with or instead of textbooks—inexpensive laptop units that can be linked by phone or the nearest wall jack into a central school system that holds the software, individual student files or accounts, class reading materials, library access, links to the web, and so forth. Even today we seem to be fast approaching a point where there is at least one computer in every classroom, which is enough to make computer literacy a natural part of the mass media of the English language arts program.

Desktop Publishing

To show you how much and how rapidly things have changed, the first edition of this book included a section on classroom magazine and newspaper publishing using the long-vanished "ditto" or spirit master or the mimeograph machine (including instructions on how to type a mimeograph stencil with "justified" type to make it look more like real print). Today a variety of pagemaker programs, linked to clip art collections, digital scanners, and plugged into color laser or inkjet printers turn classrooms into fully equipped print shops. Kids can do newsletters, brochures, articles, leaflets, fliers, posters, banners with amazing ease and simplicity. They can take a Polaroid or electronic snapshot, digitize the image, and have photos in their news sheets in minutes. Student artwork can be scanned, edited in an art program,

---

Many of the kinds of activities suggested for newspaper exploration can also be conducted on magazines. Some possible explorations for the classroom:

- conducting a survey of the range and kind of magazines offered by the local news agency or bookstore (no doubt steering kids away from the adult section, which they have probably investigated on their own time anyway). Who is catered to by magazines?

- looking at the interrelationship of magazine content and advertising. Ski and bicycle magazines, for example, are candidly acknowledged to be mostly a way of getting product information to consumers, to whom the actual content of the magazine may be less important than news of new gizmos and gadgets.

- analyzing the audience of a magazine through the content of articles; then analyzing the audience through the content of the ads.

- discussing the relationship of visuals to print in a magazine, including the use of "visual print," words and headlines presented in flashy or novel type styles.

- looking at the classifieds and personals in many magazines as well as the small print ads at the back and discussing the consumer image created by those magazines.

- designing and producing a specialized magazine for the students' own age group. If you were starting a magazine to sell to kids just like yourself, what would it include?

Figure 12.5 Exploring Magazines

scaled and resized, run beneath print or presented with print running around it, making integration of art and writing increasingly easy. We've stressed the value of publication in earlier chapters of this book; the computer makes production of highly professional materials for real-world distribution a snap. We hasten to caution, however, that for us, the quality of the work being produced must always remain more important than the glitz and flash and intrinsic appeal of computer design and layout. Weak writing is still weak writing, even if gussied up with clip art, multiple type fonts, and some clever shading and shadowing. Computer enhancements should be just that: *enhancements* of already excellent work.

Web Sites

The evolution of the World Wide Web has altered the whole conception of "publishing." While desktop publishing and the producing of products on paper undoubtedly has a long and vigorous future, the production of media texts on the web has enormous potential and appeal. Here the technology is changing very rapidly to put webbing within the reach of anyone who wants to go on the net. By contrast, when Steve first had students produce web sites, just two years before this was written, the students had to master "HTML"—hypertext markup language—and type in codes for every boldface or italic character, for every change in print size, for every cross reference. Already word processing and pagemaking programs are including those codes within their machinery so that essentially anything one writes in standard format can be automatically translated for uploading to a web site. Because of that rapidly changing technology, we won't explore the "how to" of these matters; in fact, our experience suggests that in any English language classroom there will be plenty of kids who have mastered the how-to or are willing to do so as part of the class, so the nontechie teacher needn't worry about the fine details. It's the larger details that matter to us, the teaching of composing for the web:

- What is it that we have to say? Why are our ideas important? Whom do we want to reach?
- What kind of material do we need to develop? Who in our class wants to tackle particular parts of the project? Where will we go to get information?
- How do the parts of our project fit together? Web site design is a particularly useful way to encourage students to see the relationships of part to whole.
- How do you write for the web? For example, because of the possibility of doing cross-linkages, the web favors short, paragraph-length writings, and, as one student explained to us, "You don't use very many transitions, because you put in a cross link instead." While we might worry about the demise of writing that goes beyond paragraph length (as well as the death of the transition), the fact is that students need to keep such matters in mind.

Surfing the Web

Perhaps even prior to designing a web site is exploring the Internet to see what it has to offer and how it offers it. While casual surfing is a fun thing for kids and adults to do, we recommend that for educational use, exploration of the net be done systematically, to help kids know how to find and to evaluate materials. Activities we've explored include:

- The scavenger hunt. Choose four or five relatively obscure or difficult questions (or have the students develop them): Where will the national bowling championships be held next year? How much does it cost to send airmail *from* England? What's today's newspaper headline in Moscow or Johannesburg? Use this activity to help students learn to use "search engines" to mine the web.

- Internet research projects. As the scavenger hunt reveals, one can often get results from the web much more quickly than one can by trying to look things up in the library. On the other hand, our experience with such projects suggests that sometimes web research tends to shape the content of a project; that is, students are inclined to write about what they happen to find rather than searching for answers to specific questions. But unquestionably web research projects—web exclusive, or linked to library research—give students the potential to inquire much more deeply into topics than was ever possible in the days of the term paper.

- Critical evaluation of the web. The web makes every computer owner a potential publisher with an audience of millions. But where print media have traditionally enjoyed a kind of editorial control (if only because of the cost of publication), the webmaker is his/her own editor-in-chief. You can find almost anything on the web (and to teachers' dismay, students do): from pornography to propaganda, from serious journalism to fringe group ravings. How can we tell the difference between quality information and garbage? (We leave it to the individual teacher to set the boundaries of what kids are permitted to study. In our experience, youngsters will stay within boundaries if good explanations are offered, e.g., "If you look up pornography on school time, the administration will definitely pull the plug on our Internet connection.") Extremely valuable as a critical analysis is to search out a range of sites on a controversial issue—women's rights, Ebonics, education—and to have the students critically discuss what they find, including what is presented, what sort of support or research is offered to buttress opinions, and the rhetorical style used to present material (whether rant and rave or composed and discursive. Such an exploration is usefully done with newspapers, magazines, CD rom archives, and library sources.)

Electronic Mail, Discussion Groups, Bulletin Boards

These aspects of the Internet can turn the classroom into a global village. The professional literature is filled with examples of classrooms that have used the net to create pen pal groups, to develop international forums on issues, to make contact with experts and specialists who would ordinarily be far beyond the access range of elementary and secondary school students. We've been especially impressed by the user friendliness of some of the commercial on-line services in catalyzing such contact through kids chat rooms, bulletin boards, publishing centers, and so on.

MULTIMEDIA

Boundaries between media are increasingly being blurred. Films are produced, never shown in theaters, and packaged for video sale. Films are "made for TV." Computerized special effects create film images that look more real than real. Stage shows and sporting events are packaged and staged for television viewing. Computer programs include "slide shows" and "movies." What we're calling multimedia here will increasingly come to be centered on a crossing over of technologies. In the twenty-first century, young people and adults will need to be critically literate consumers of what comes packaged for their consumption.

One project we've used successfully with students of all ages is to explore the mass media of persuasion by having students develop a multimedia campaign to promote an *issue* or *idea*. Choosing a topic they think is important to the school, the community, or world, they identify a target audience and create a multimedia campaign for that audience. Thus the students might campaign for more student privileges or the right to ride skateboards on school grounds; they could lobby for improvements around the school or for increased parental involvement; they might start a community cleanup campaign or urge the city council to create more services and activities for young people.

After helping the students identify a topic and a target audience, the teacher then lists the following as some of the ways in which we use a variety of "media" to promote our ideas and point of view:

buttons	placards	bumper stickers
promotional videos	editorials	radio spots
laws	oratory	petitions
debates	letters to politicians	letters to editors
advertisements	public hearings	photo displays
computer web sites	posters	t-shirts
web sites	simulations	drama
rumors	threats	blackmail

Some teachers are bothered by seeing unconventional or "unethical" persuasion forms like "threats" and "blackmail" on a list of the media of persuasion. Are these, in fact, "media"? We claim they are since they are essentially persuasive strategies designed to amplify the sound of one's voice. Do we advocate teaching kids to use rumors and blackmail to get their way? Of course not, but we do feel it's important for them to recognize that when media are employed, the users often show no mercy in using any strategy they think will successfully bring about an action they wish to support.

In conducting the unit, we give the students several weeks to develop their material. Sometimes we'll have four or five small groups working up campaigns on separate issues; sometimes the whole class will be working on the project. Sometimes the actual presentation will be mostly for us, the class, but we encourage students to take up real-world issues and to present their campaign to its intended audience.

The discussions during and following this campaign are both highly contemporary and rhetorically classic:

- What media are most successful in delivering your message?

- Is it possible to be immoral or unfair when promoting your point of view?

- Is telling the whole truth a successful way to campaign?
- What effects did your campaign have on the audience?
- Did you achieve what you intended? why or why not?
- Can the common citizen have a voice in public affairs? What do you need to do to make that voice heard?

Extending Multimedia

Beyond "the campaign," we urge you (and your students) to consider a wealth of possibilities for multimedia work in the classroom. For example, your class can create:

- Documentaries: perhaps slide presentations (computerized or with traditional transparencies projected) coupled with a written script and background music to explore dramatically an issue or problem.
- Literature presentations: reading of, say, a dozen poems or the works of a dozen poets accompanied by photographs and slides, or possibly integrating recorded readings of literature by the artists themselves. Add to that samples of art—slides, reproductions, copies downloaded from the web—to connect writers with other art forms of the eye and ear.
- Reading of student work: elevated with the accompaniment of music, art, photographs, possibly done "live," perhaps done as an interactive audio/video web site.
- Reader's theater: a literary work read aloud, with lighting and sound effects, appropriate background music, written guides or other texts to introduce a work to an audience.

POPULAR CULTURE AS MASS MEDIA

TV, films, newspapers, the web, magazines, these are all a part of what is called "popular culture," the culture of the moment, the culture of the people. Although there has long been some snobbishness toward popular culture as distinguished from the "high" culture, we think such elitist biases are inappropriate and unhelpful. Much of what now passes for the high culture was once intended for large mass audiences: the plays of William Shakespeare, the stories and tales of Charles Dickens, the music of Bach, Vivaldi, and Mozart. We don't mean to propose a kind of critical relativism that would claim, say, that pornography is fine art or that letters on e-mail have the same quality as the correspondence of Eloise and Abelard, but we do see a bridge between what is popular and widespread and what eventually becomes ensconced in museums and anthologies. We suggest that periodic examinations of popular culture as a mass medium are useful for kids of all ages.

More classroom activities with a multimedia twist:

- Examine music television as a multimedia phenomenon, including not only sound and sight, but *personality* as a medium of communication. Also explore music TV as a force in shaping values, beliefs, and attitudes.
- Have students imagine their multimedia future. What do they expect will be the dominant modes of communication twenty-five and fifty years from now? What will happen to the media they use now? How can they prepare themselves to be intelligent media consumers?
- In a classic article, Janet Emig argued that *writing* is a unique mode of communication because it involves the eye (seeing what we write), ear (as we silently hear the words we compose), and hand (as we guide pencil or pen across paper). One could also add that even though it has no video screen, writing generates all sorts of images. Invite your students to explore the concept of writing as a multimedia phenomenon.
- Explore magic as multimedia: What are its "technologies"? What are its rhetorical or persuasive "strategies"? Bring a magician to class.
- Explore church as a multimedia phenomenon. How many different media go into a church service? What are the technologies? What are the strategies?
- Explore school as a multimedia phenomenon. How many media go into an ordinary day at school? What are the technologies? What are the strategies? How can teachers be perceived as both technologies and rhetorical strategizers?
- Ask students to imagine a nonmedia society. If we took away phones, TV, computers, etc., how would life differ?

Figure 12.6   A Multimedia Potpourri

You can:

• examine fads and trends in television and music. What's hot and what's fading? Why? Where do these trends come from? How do they appeal to broad numbers of people?

• examine fads and trends in dress, clothing, language. These manifestations of popular culture are, in their own way, mass media: technologies and strategies for communicating messages. With little preparation at all your students can probably develop a very articulate description of the hierarchies of style for people of their own age group: What's "standard," what identifies you as a member of another group, what sorts of statements do various dress modes make?

• examine franchises. Franchises are at the heart of our popular culture: To become a franchisable entity a product, company, or service needs to appeal to a wide range of people in a national or international market. This quest can start with the fast-food franchises: What do Burger King, McDonald's, Taco Bell, Pizza Hut "communicate" to us about what we value? How are these popular culture values merchandised to us as well? What's the difference between a Burger King and a McDonald's regular? Who chooses Godfather's over Pizza Hut? Why? Then move on to look at other franchises: doughnuts, brake linings, carpet cleaning, home furnishings, hardware stores. Students can make a study of the local Home Depot or Stanley Steemer franchise—often the managers will be delighted to talk to kids—to learn about how this franchise operates and why it is successful. From this, students can draw their own conclusions about franchises as mass media of popular culture.

• iconography. What symbols, logotypes, brand names are immediately recognizable by your students? Include in this study everything from road signs and markers to television network logos. How do logotypes communicate as elements of the mass media? How do they appeal to large numbers of people? What is their language or rhetoric? Have students design logos: for themselves, for the class, for the school, for your community, for an imaginary product, for a laudable idea or goal.

• architecture. Buildings make statements. The architecture of any era makes a statement about the values of people who are creating structures. Begin with the architecture of the school. When was the school built? How does its architecture speak about conceptions of education. Does the school look like a college campus? a factory? a prison? Enhance this unit by digging out pictures of elementary and secondary schools in your town fifty, seventy-five, or one hundred years ago. What changes do students see? Then branch out. Look at public buildings, small businesses, shops in the mall, light and heavy industry, houses in suburban neighborhoods, urban houses, public parks, libraries. How do all these buildings communicate as forms of mass media?

THE FINE ARTS AS MASS MEDIA

We've consistently advocated integrating the fine arts with English language arts. Youngsters can come to see music, dance, photography, sculpture as "languages," as media of communication. Although the "fine" arts are often seen as part of the elite or high culture, in every century, in every generation, artists have made efforts to reach larger and larger audiences: Michelangelo paints the ceiling of the Sistine Chapel; Alexander Calder creates a huge sculpture for a public square in Chicago; the Metropolitan Opera Company brings open-air productions to Central Park. By way of studying the fine arts as mass media, students can look at:

• technology: How do forms of painting differ? What can you do in the medium of acrylics that is unavailable to you as a water colorist? How does the technology of an eighty-six piece symphony orchestra differ from that of a jazz combo? What can you do sculpting in metal that you can/can't do hacking and hewing a sculpture out of marble? What are the limits and advantages to dance as a way of bringing your message to the public? How has the technology of photography developed and improved over the years? What can you do with a modern camera that Matthew Brady couldn't do? What future technologies will be available to photographers and how will this affect their work?

• strategy: How does a painter try to engage you in his/her work? How does the strategy of realism differ from that of abstract art? Is there a problem if you cannot "understand" exactly what an abstract piece of art is all about? How can a static sculpture reach out and engage an audience? Why do some sculptures move? Take a theme or issue of current importance and imagine how you could present your point of view through dance or sculpture or painting. Select a current breaking news event and compare its visual presentation in newspapers, the weekly news-magazines, network television, public broadcasting, and the twenty-four hour news networks.

Above all, we urge you (as does Peter Abbs in his book *English Among the Arts)* to be a gap bridger: between the notions of high and low culture or elitist and mass culture, between the isolation of English from the other fine arts. You can do this by having your students be active *producers* as well as *consumers* of popular culture/fine arts in your classroom, so that even as they focus their attention on the language arts of reading, writing, listening, and speaking, they are constantly perceiving the world through other forms and media and feel comfortable extending their print work to include a rich variety of sights and sounds from other fields.

LITERATURE AS A MASS MEDIUM

We'll conclude this chapter by briefly returning to our favorite mass medium: literature. We do this to make a connection, to suggest, once again, that at its best literature is in the thick of the popular culture human experience, dealing with love and hate, brawling and bawling, making love and war. Any theme, topic, or issue that affects your students' lives can be found in literature, including literature for children, young adults, and adults. While it may be tempting to isolate mass media in units of their own—the art unit, the photography unit, the computer unit—we remind you of the emphasis in this book on the students' experience at the core of things. We learn about mass media to explore ourselves: our experiences, concerns, perceptions, and desires. Although such experiences can be found in any medium, most of us teachers of English do what we do because of a belief that books and print are the most effective mass medium of all, perhaps a little less flashy than films and computers, but promoting development of the soul in unique and contemplative ways.

Moreover, many of the critical questions that we've raised about mass media can be applied to literature as well to give students a new perspective on books and prints. Poets, after all, do not write merely to amuse themselves or to make life difficult for English language arts students. They want to sell their poetry, reach audiences, change lives and worlds. (Recall Percy Shelley's claim that poets are the "unacknowledged legislators of the world.") Taking this perspective adds a new dimension to traditional classroom questions:

- What do you think the writer was trying to accomplish here?
- How did the writer use "technology"—words, genre forms, even typography—to try to get the message across to you?
- How did the writer "strategize" to win you over? Was it successful?
- What makes a great book great?

◆ EXPLORATIONS

◆ Using media effectively in a class depends in part on how comfortable you are using them. If you have never done so, make a video tape or slide presentation to learn the intricacies of using the cameras. Get a book or take a class on web site design and technology. Do your next handout or course plan as a newsletter to get to know a desktop publishing program well.

◆ Like learning language, media use is also "developmental," meaning that (without being Procrustean) we can see that different skills are appropriate for different kids at different times. Consider a range of classroom media that are available to you (a chart is given below). What sorts of media uses and applications do you see as appropriate for the students at your level? Even better, do this project collaboratively with a group of elementary, secondary, or K–12 teachers to develop a profile of media skills and applications:

Medium	Applications
Television (viewing)	
Video (production)	
Still photography	
Phones	
The Internet	
Desktop publication	
Other computer uses	
Radio	
Pen, pencil, paper	
Literature	
The arts	
Music	
Dance	
Graphic arts	
Other important media. . .	

◆ For that same list of media, develop ways of encouraging students to think critically about media effects. Engage them in an examination of media "messages." Some questions for exploration:

What does this medium do best (e.g., spread news, present literature, inform, amuse, entertain)?

What does it do worst?

In what ways does a message have to be bent or shaped to fit the medium? For example, what *can't* you do with a telephone. (Clue: Why are people interested in developing videophones?) What can you say in dance that you cannot say with a sculpture?

An interesting variation of this activity is to consider how the various literary genres function as media. Ask the same questions about, say, a poem, a short story, and an essay.

◆ Choose a theme, issue, or topic for exploration and imagine that you were to teach it without textbooks, but with reasonably prolific availability of media. How would you design the unit? Then consider how you could use print in the same unit possibly including textbooks and printed literature.

◆ Develop an art/crafts/media calendar for some students with whom you work—a list of coming events for young people in your area. Find ways to incorporate those events in your work, perhaps as extra-credit topics, possibly as class field trips. (Be sure to check with your local arts and humanities councils to explore the programs they have developed to engage young people in the arts.)

RELATED READINGS

One of the most prolific and energetic writers about media has been Neil Postman an English education and "media ecology" specialist at New York University. It's interesting to trace a sequence of Postman books to see an evolving view of the relationship of language and mass media. He began writing with Charles Weingartner in 1966 with *Linguistics: A Revolution in Teaching,* arguing that new, scientific ways of looking at language provide important critical tools for students to employ. Postman and Weingartner wrote several other books together, including *Teaching as a Subversive Activity* (1969), where a central argument is that youngsters need to develop their "crap detectors" to survive in society. By 1976, Postman was concerned about *Crazy Talk, Stupid Talk: How We Defeat Ourselves by the Way We Talk,* which dealt with ways to talk sense in a world increasingly dominated by media values, and in 1982, he lamented *The Disappearance of Childhood,* due in part to *Technopoly: The Surrender of Culture to Technology* (1992). His most recent book describes *The End of Education: Redefining the Value of School* (1995), where he calls for approaching education through broad, multicultural, multimedia themes such as "Spaceship Earth," "The Fallen Angel" (dealing with the imperfections of knowledge), "American Experience" (a critical assessment of our culture), "Diversity," and "Word Weavers," the last coming back to Postman's and our home base in language, the root of all media.

Innumerable books have been written about the effects of media on society and education. A few of our favorites include: *Literacy at the Crossroads* by Regie Routman, which discourages the heavy use of media in the classroom and argues for the English language arts classroom as a bastion of print literacy; *Creativity and Popular Culture* by David Holbrook, discussing the loss of young people's individual voices in an age of mass media; *Bonfire of the Humanities* by Marc David, lamenting the evolution of a couch potato culture; *Advertising and a Democratic Press* by Edwin Baker, exploring how advertising interests distort the flow of news; and *Radical Artifice* by Marjorie Perloff, which discusses poetry writing in an age of media and the competition between the natural language of poetry and the "natural language" of the typical talk show. Especially useful for teaching is Alan Teasley and Ann Wilder's *Reel Conversations,* which connects films to the language arts class and viewing assignments to writing assignments, with lots of concrete ways to use films.

Just for fun, we entered "media education" into an Internet search engine and came up with three *million* hits, including a number of web sites that include media units for the classroom. Happy hunting.

Finally, we'll simply note that we have not included any "how-to" books in this brief list—no "how to" make a video or "how to" create a web site. Such materials are readily available and change with the technology. You can find them easily at your school, university, or public library, or in many cases at technology stores: the camera shop, the computer shop, the art museum.

CHAPTER 13

ASSESSMENT, EVALUATION, AND GRADING

We all evaluate ourselves as part of daily living. We wonder if we can lift heavier weights, if our cholesterol count is going down, if our savings balance is going up. We wonder if we can jog longer than we used to, if our relationships are as satisfying as we'd like them to be, if our life is in balance or too heavily skewed towards work-related or school-related activities. Assessment and evaluation are a part of life and mark off steps in our progress towards our life goals.

However, if some outside force graded us on our progress, we might not take kindly to it. If a banker told us our savings plan merited a C− or a psychologist said our relationship capacity only fell into the B+ range, we might take offense. So it is in the schools. Evaluation and assessment help both teachers and students see if they are reaching their goals, but placing a letter grade on that progress only seems to encourage competition and comparison. Thus the focus of this chapter will be on evaluation and assessment, while a smaller part will suggest ways to deal with the problem of grading.

ASSESSMENT AND INSTRUCTION

The kind of assessment we advocate is an on-going part of instruction, not just something done the last week of a marking period when the teacher is aware that grades are due. Assessment should be related directly to learning activities and to the work done; it should be based on a broad range of evidence, not just a few quickly constructed multiple-choice tests. In the best of all classrooms, assessment includes observations of students in action, finished work, and students' own self-assessment.

> Assessment serves instruction by continually informing teachers both about the progress of their students' language development and about the effect their language teaching has on that development. Good assessment begins with an inquiring stance and a belief in the ability of children. Children are brilliant language learners. Our needs and theirs are best served when we recognize this.
>
> From Curt Dudley-Marling and Dennis Searle, *When Students Have Time To Talk* (Portsmouth, N.H.: Heinemann 1991), p. 91. Reprinted by permission.

The process of assessment is best started by sharing our goals with students. What is it we want them to do? Learn to write a fable? Learn to listen and build upon others' ideas in small groups? Read in a new genre? Learn to draw from a variety of resources for information on a topic? Once we no longer have a hidden agenda and students can see what they're being asked to do, they can begin to evaluate the extent to which they have achieved specific goals.

Assessment that is responsive to how students learn will include elements that focus on learning processes. Since we are asking students to learn a process or ways of approaching a task or a problem, this should be included in what we evaluate in the class. As part of assessing writing, students can describe their own process of revision and why they made the changes they did. Including how students learn and how they use their own processes of learning in assessment also validates the importance of the process and the reasoning they use.

While the pressures build on teachers to be accountable, there are workable alternatives to multiple choice and "fill in the blank" assignments. Valid measures of progress through process evaluation can substantiate a grade and yield valuable information for instructional needs.

We want to develop an approach to assessment that, as McGregor and Meiers in *Telling the Whole Story* explain: "reflects a view of English teaching in which the major aims are to help all students to become competent makers and users of language for a wide range of purposes, and to communicate effectively in many different situations" (p. 13). We also want our approach to assessment to reflect that our program is built on an awareness that language learning is an interactive, social process, and that therefore English classrooms must create learning environments in which it is natural for language to be used for real purposes and for real audiences.

ASSESSMENT TASKS—TEACHERS GATHER DATA

The first part of assessment is gathering data or evidence of student learning. What tasks are we asking students to do or become involved in? This is what we refer to as assessment tasks—activities that help us know what the student knows. By looking at what students do, we are incorporating informal and ongoing procedures for evaluation as well as the more formal procedures. So what are some valid measures of progress? We like to think of these measures in terms of the processes of talking, listening, reading, and writing as well as the finished work or product.

> The foremost goal of evaluation is self-evaluation, that is, the analysis of our own attitudes and processes so that we can use the information to promote continued growth and learning. The purpose of self-evaluation is the purpose of education—to enable an individual to function independently, intelligently, and productively.
>
> From Regie Routman, *Invitations* (Portsmouth, N.H.: Heinemann 1991), p. 342. Reprinted by permission.

Process assessment tasks or data include:

1. Students' oral responses. How do students respond in oral discussions? What kinds of questions do they ask? Do they build on the responses of others? This kind of information gives us a good sense of how they are interacting with the material as well as how their speaking and group skills are developing.

2. Reading or literature logs. Through response logs we can see if students are involved in reading, how extensively they are reading, whether they can make connections to their own lives, whether they can give opinions about books, whether they can interact and interpret a book after reading it silently.

3. Journals. In this unedited work students can show fluency, how they organize their thoughts, which conventions they have probably mastered and which ones they are working on, what topics they think are significant, and give teachers insights into student thinking and processing of information.

4. Conferencing. Short conferences can give teachers a good peek at students' writing strengths and the problems they are encountering. Information gathered in conferences may give teachers information on what kind of instruction or modeling they need to do to further student growth.

5. Self-evaluation. Routman in *Invitations* explains that reflection logs, a place for students to think about and comment on their learning, can be important tools for fostering self-evaluation. Having to put thoughts into writing seems to help clarify what has, or has not, been learned (p. 349). Not only do students think about their learning; teachers have an opportunity to understand what concepts have been understood and what needs to be retaught. Routman suggests that teachers start by asking some guiding questions such as: What did I learn today? What am I still confused about? What would I like to know more about?

Asking students to talk and write about what they are learning also makes teachers constantly aware of whether or not they are making clear to students why they are doing what they are doing and how it relates to learning. If we are to assess in new ways, we have to teach our students the worth of the kinds of assessments we are using. When students write about what they got out of a book or what they learned from another student's presentation, they begin to see that learning isn't something they just do for the teacher, it's something they do for themselves.

Students can also be asked to do self-evaluations on their work in small groups. Figure 13.1 is a questionnaire developed for small-group work that focused on brainstorming themes and motifs in the novel *The Adventures of Huckleberry Finn.*

Small Group Work Questionnaire for theme, motif, and generalization work on *The Adventures of Huckleberry Finn*

Name_____

Group members: _____   _____

Directions: This questionnaire lets you know what is expected of you in a small group and gives you a place to reflect on your participation. Put a check (✓) in the space below if you can answer yes to the question, put a check plus (✓+) in the space if you feel this is an area you excelled in, put a check minus (✓−) in the space if you answered no.

	Day 1	Day 2	Day 3
1. Did you help keep the group on task?	—	—	—
2. Did you respond thoughtfully to the views of others?	—	—	—
3. Did you suggest helpful ways to approach the task?	—	—	—
4. Were you prepared well enough (by finishing the novel) to contribute meaningfully?	—	—	—
5. Did you ask relevant questions of your group?	—	—	—
6. Did you demonstrate an awareness and knowledge of issues from the novel?	—	—	—
7. Did you show initiative in offering suggestions on possible themes, motifs, generalizations?	—	—	—
8. Were you able to develop, sustain, and defend your point of view when persuading group members of your ideas?	—	—	—
9. Did you express, through actions and words, appreciation or acceptance of the ideas of others?	—	—	—
10. Did you pay close attention to the views of others?	—	—	—

Divide the pie (circle) below into the part you think each person in your group, including yourself, played.

Day One   Day Two   Day Three

Figure 13.1   Small Group Work Questionnaire

Generalizations about the author's intent were then formulated. It is important to "count" process tasks so students understand that they are learning by being involved in the process, and that this learning is a valued part of the class.

The more familiar type of assessment tasks revolve around student products, usually viewed as finished pieces of work. These tasks can be much broader than just asking students to write papers or take a test, as we hope the following suggestions demonstrate. Product assessment tasks or data include:

1. Written tests:

   A. Word test. To elicit what students know about a piece of literature instead of finding out what they don't know, a word test works well. The teacher picks out twelve to fifteen words that are central to the story. Students choose the ten to which they wish to respond (by giving them choice they are not tied to extracting exactly the same things from the reading that the teacher did), or they may add other significant words. They then explain what each word means in the context of the story. For instance in *The True Confessions of Charlotte Doyle* students could explain the place "the brig" had in the story. What a "round robin" was in terms of the story or how the word "unnatural" was used. If students paid attention to other parts of the story, they write about the ideas or concepts they noticed.

   B. Short-answer essay questions. Students compose a response which can demonstrate their understanding of a concept or an event. These questions should not simply be recall questions where students parrot back what their teacher told them. For instance, after finishing *The Watsons Go to Birmingham—1963* students could be asked to write about the kinds of hatred characters encountered and which instance of hate was hardest for them to understand. After reading *Spite Fences* students can be asked to write about what they learned through the confrontation at the drugstore.

   C. Creating a written text. Students can be asked to write in interesting ways to show what they know. They can, for instance, be asked to connect one piece of literature to another through this type of directive: Choose a character from each of the two novels who either have a lot in common or who would have a lot to say to each other. Create a conversation between the two characters that demonstrates not only your knowledge of the characters but also your understanding of issues or themes involved in the novels. In this type of test, students are asked to create new knowledge to demonstrate their understandings. This kind of test has an up-side for teachers—the tests are very interesting for the teacher to read and the teacher can learn from the students' perceptions.

   D. Collaborative test-making. In groups students construct questions that they think would show a deep understanding of a novel or other kind of material. Of course, the teacher must explain that these should not be recall questions but questions that cause students to show what they know. The questions the groups hand in are then evaluated.

   E. Reaction or response to a story. Oftentimes this makes a good final exam option. Students read a story they have never read before and respond to it in ways similar to what they have been doing in class. For instance, if the class was looking at gender, race, and class stereotypes, the students can be asked to write in terms of those. If you have emphasized Langer's reading stances as ways for students to think about their reading, students can write a response and then describe the stances included in the response. If students have studied characterization so they can incorporate new strategies into their own writing, they can describe all the methods of characterization used in the story.

2. Stories or papers. These are the kinds of products teachers are used to evaluating. We encourage teachers to extend their view of what "counts" as a paper and suggest they especially look at Figure 5.3 in Chapter 5 which includes a plethora of ways students can write about novels.

3. Writing for real audiences. Letter exchanges between schools, submitting an editorial or letter to the editor to the school paper, a request for information from a company, and so on are sent out of the classroom. This kind of writing can also be viewed as an assessment task, especially since it is probably in final draft form and has been edited and proofread.

4. Literature extension projects, including performances. Scripting (described in Chapter 11), selecting and reading aloud poems that relate to a novel, and other formats suggested throughout the literature chapters are also assessment tasks which show a student's reaction to a novel. The way children respond to literature through art, drama, and music also demonstrates their perceptions and interpretations and are assessment tasks.

5. Portfolios. Much has been written on the use of portfolios in the classroom (see Related Readings) and sometimes portfolios are seen by teachers as writing folders where drafts, revisions, final copies, work in progress, and conferencing feedback are kept. Portfolios, though, imply selection. Students select work to place in the portfolio to demonstrate achievement in learning. Portfolios are an example of an assessment task when students write about their selection process.

It takes time and effort to make portfolios a workable and valuable part of the classroom. Before portfolios make sense, a writing program must be in place, in which students get choices in what they write, and opportunities to learn to talk about their work. Usually, teachers do a lot of modeling on the overhead, showing students ways to talk about writing and helping them learn to articulate qualities of good writing. Once a writing program is under way and has become a valued part of the class, then the teacher can begin to introduce the idea of portfolios.

Portfolios seem to work best when students feel ownership in their own writing and care about it and when students have a say in what's included and excluded. To make anything work well, students have to see it as part of class. The teacher refers to the portfolio and encourages students to think about it and how they will select work that is a record of their achievements.

The selection process is one of the most important pieces of portfolio use since students have to think about what they value, what they think their work shows, and how they have changed and grown as writers. During the self-selection process students can be involved in deciding what areas should be represented in the portfolio, what the criteria for pieces should be, and how the reasons for their selections should be recorded.

Robert Tierney et al in *Portfolio Assessment in the Reading/Writing Classroom* (p. 113) tells us that students might want to include favorite stories, reports they thought were interesting, papers done with others, favorite journal entries, papers that were their best work, papers that were difficult, and pieces that show the trail of their development.

At this point the teacher also encourages and provides time for students to obtain comments from others about what they are planning to include. Having whole-class activities and assignments such as this make the portfolio a part of the class experience and thus students see that it is important.

Robert Tierney also points out that in writing and reading there is increased interest in student decision making. Students are asked what they want to read, what they want to write and what they want to revise. What he believes is missing is involving students in assessing and evaluating their own work. Tierney reminds us that student self assessment is one of the major principles undergirding the use of portfolios. So using portfolios provides a natural avenue into student self-evaluation.

Although many books on portfolio use give examples of elaborate checklists and/or rubrics to help students in assessing their own work and in selecting it, keeping this part of the process simple in the beginning seems to work best. Students can explain why they selected the piece, what merits they see in it, and some information about its origins. Teachers often complain that students are not very good at responding to others' writings and to assessing their own writing. But Tierney tells us that preliminary findings indicate that students' self-assessments mature over time, that the number of comments they make increases, that the comments focus on more aspects of writing, that students begin to notice growth through comparisons with previous work; and that students' ability to evaluate their total performance increases (p. 122). Portfolios seem to be a wonderful place to foster growth in writing, especially since students can compare one semester's work with another.

Other possibilities for assessment tasks or activities that focus on a product are included in Figure 13.2. As the reader can see, all of the assessment tasks ask students to construct meaning, not just repeat back the teacher-given information. It should be pointed out that teacher-given information can be incorporated into assessment tasks when students are asked to do something with the information and create something with it. As teachers set assessment tasks for their students, the guidelines in Figure 13.3 can help them stay focused and use assessment tasks to find out what students know, not what they don't know.

skit	time line	diagram	flowchart
poetry	sculpture	research	manual
role play	essay	illustration	display
diary	bibliography	"how to" instructions	blueprint
written report	letter to editor	debate	experiment
painting	photo essay	family tree	action plan
museum exhibit	scrapbook		

Figure 13.2   More Product Assessment Tasks or Activities

ASSESSMENT TOOLS—TEACHERS INTERPRET DATA

After gathering data on student process and product, the next step is to figure out how to evaluate what you have collected. For every assessment task you create, there are a number of assessment tools that can be used. When we refer to assessment tools we use the term to mean ways to collect data (portfolios, frequency counts, participation charts, anecdotal records) and ways to evaluate data (rating scales, rubrics, checklists, point systems).

Developing Indicators of Achievement

Whatever assessment tasks and tools you use, it is important to begin to make explicit what you believe is being achieved by students. To do this it helps to describe the criteria on which judgments are based. We have found it helpful to make a collection of descriptive statements that are continually expanded. This list of statements can be called "Signs of Development" and "Signs of Achievement" (as Robert McGregor and Marion Meiers call their work in this area), or indicators. There are several books that talk about growth and development in literacy and give lists of what can be found at different grade levels (see Related Readings). Included in some of these books are a breakdown of what these "signs" look like in different areas of literacy. We find these useful because it reminds us how complex each task is that we ask students to do, and how many parts each seemingly simple task includes. We hope that teachers will find ways to acknowledge the importance of the parts that make up student tasks, and find ways to include some of these signs in their evaluation of student work. Through the creation and addition to lists such as the one in Figure 13.4, our job of explaining what we expect of our students and of evaluating their work becomes easier.

Assessment Tools include:

1. Holistic scoring. In this type of scoring, papers are read quickly and given a single score which includes evaluation of the content, mechanics, and style. Holistic scoring usually implies that the teacher does not make "corrections" on the paper but simply responds to the overall impact of the piece. Generally in this scoring, content

---

Does the task meet some or all of these guidelines?

1. Does it produce knowledge rather than reproduce it? (Is it worthwhile?)

2. Does it have an aesthetic, utilitarian or personal value apart from its value in documenting the competence of the learner? (Is it meaningful?)

3. Does it tap into prior knowledge, in-depth understanding of an issue or problem and ask students to organize, synthesize and integrate information in new ways? (Is it significant?)

4. Does it foster self-evaluation and students' awareness of their learning?

5. Does it reflect the actual learning and instructional activities of the classroom?

6. Are the criteria known and valued by the student?

Figure 13.3 Guidelines for Constructed Assessment Tasks

In speaking:
- is willing to express ideas and feelings
- shows awareness of issues raised in discussions
- initiates new and related issues
- can develop and defend a point of view
- can recognize the assumptions on which a speaker's argument is based
- responds to what the speaker says and extends the idea

In writing:
- is willing to explore new genres in writing
- creates a mood and atmosphere through description
- is able to write clearly on complex topics
- organization makes the piece easy to follow
- can elaborate on ideas

In reading:
- can find examples of bias or propaganda
- can read on one issue from many sources and give a good overview
- can create thoughtful responses to the literature read
- can recognize and describe the purpose and structures of different genres

Figure 13.4   A Sampling of Indicators of Growth

and organization play a big role. Although some teachers may feel uncomfortable scoring papers this way, we would like them to consider that students need to write as much as possible and if the teacher responds to every error on every paper, then students probably will not be asked to write often. To increase your confidence in doing a good job with this kind of scoring, work with a few other teachers to score a group of student papers. It is surprising to us how frequently there is agreement. Diana remembers a time when she was scoring articles in school newspapers for a state-wide competition. Groups of teachers quickly read stacks of the same articles, rating them from one to four. Then a first place, second place, and honorable mention winner had to be selected from the top group. If there was disagreement, the article was talked about and each person explained the elements he was responding to. But in a whole morning of scoring, agreement was reached very easily.

Generally, rubrics are created to inform the scoring. In Figure 13.5 a rubric is shown that was developed to holistically score a narrative piece of writing on the high school proficiency test in Michigan. Different rubrics were developed to reflect the kind of writing the students were asked to do. For example, if the piece was persuasive there would be a statement in the rubric about how convincing the piece was and how well support was used for the stand or argument.

Narrative Writing Rubric for Holistic Scoring

4. The writing is engaging, original, clear, and focused. Ideas and content are richly developed and supported by details and examples where appropriate. Control of organization and transitions move the reader easily through the text. The voice and tone are authentic and compelling. Control of language and skillful use of writing conventions contribute to the effect of the presentation.

3. The writing is generally clear, focused, and well-developed. Examples and details support ideas and content where appropriate. The presentation is generally coherent, and its organizational structure is functional. The voice, tone, diction, and sentence structure support meaning. Use of writing conventions is not distracting.

2. The writing has some focus and support; ideas and content may be developed with limited details and examples. The presentation shows some evidence of structure, but it may be artificial or only partially successful. The tone may be inappropriate or the voice uneven. Sentence structure and diction are generally correct but rudimentary. Limited control of writing conventions may interfere with meaning some of the time.

1. The writing has little focus and development; ideas and content are supported by few, if any details and examples. There is little discernible shape or direction. The writing demonstrates no control over voice and tone. Faulty sentence structure and limited vocabulary interfere with understanding. Limited control of writing conventions (such as spelling, grammar/usage, capitalization, punctuation and/or indentation) makes the writing difficult to read.

Figure 13.5   Michigan Educational Assessment Program

While it may seem overwhelming to develop different rubrics, there is overlap in all of them. Once student papers are in front of you it is easier to see exactly what you are responding to in the writing. As teachers enter the profession, they often develop the rubrics after they have received the papers from students. This way you can see concrete examples of good and not-so-good writing and more easily articulate the qualities of both excellent and mediocre writing.

2. Checklists. If students have completed a long project or assignment, one way to assess it is through a checklist. Checklists can include whether a certain number of resources have been used; if anecdotes were included; if interviews were carried out. Checklists can also be used to note student achievement through such categories as *consistent* and *nonconsistent* when reviewing strides made in reading and writing. For instance statements on writing could include: shows creativity by expanding assignment; shows effort in editing; works to use sentence variety; takes risks by trying a variety of forms and topics; tries many kinds of beginnings, and so on. Of course, checklists work best if students have either helped to create them or are aware that these are the goals they are to work towards.

3. Completion of task. This assessment tool is usually accomplished through observation. We look for such widely varying things as: Were students engaged in their reading? Did they search for web sites that could help them on a research project?

Did they listen and participate in their small-group work? Did they write a reflection of what they learned? Were they attentive to a classmate's presentation? Did they contribute to a peer response of another student's writing? Regie Routman raises important points about observation in the boxed quote below. It is important that teachers become aware of what is valuable in what their students are doing. Again, having lists of indicators of development and achievement in literacy is especially important here to help us begin to "see" what our students are accomplishing. We often jump to the final project and only judge that and miss a lot of indicators that the student is learning along the way. McGregor and Meiers mention that such things as being resourceful in gathering information, participating in the making and revision of group/class stories and poems, and giving constructive assistance to other students are markers of development. These are the kinds of things it is difficult to see if we only look at the final product.

> The difficult part is that good observation, the most critical component in evaluation, is only as good as the teacher's knowledge base. We have to be able to observe and value strengths more than deficits. We have to know what to look for: What are the developmental markers we are seeing or not seeing? Most of all, we need to value observation as integral to evaluation and be willing to risk adding it to our literacy programs.
>
> From Regie Routman, *Invitations* (Portsmouth, N.H.: Heinemann 1991), p. 303. Reprinted by permission.

4. Rubrics. Rubrics are scoring guides developed for an individual task or classes of tasks. They describe the features student products are expected to include for each specific score. There is a chosen scale, with a range of choices for scoring student performance.

Often the rubric is embedded in the assignment or task. For instance if the assignment is to present a collection of poems to the class accompanied by background music and recorded on a tape, many of the elements of the rubric are already there. When a contributor to Diana's Teaching Ideas Column in *English Journal* submitted such an assignment, Diana created a scoring guide to go along with it (see Figure 13.6). From the guide the assignment could easily be reconstructed because the rubric includes each part of the assignment.

Another scoring guide was created for that same *English Journal* column on an assignment that asked students to script and perform scenes from the novel *1984* (Figure 13.7). When Diana sat down to construct this rubric, she basically took each point from the assignment and made a statement about it. One tricky part of creating guides is in the way the statements are worded. You must be able to respond to all with the same sentence stems. Again, it is easy to almost write out the directions of what students were asked to do from the scoring guide. We include these here, not only to show what one looks like, but to demonstrate that oral activities and performances can be evaluated as easily as papers. Constructing scoring guides is not difficult, it just takes time and practice.

To construct rubrics that describe the features the student product must contain for each specific score, such as the one shown in Figure 13.5, these steps can be followed.

Respond to the following items by selecting: not at all (1); a little (2); somewhat (3); a lot (4); or a great deal (5). Add up the points and construct a grading scale.

1. It was easy to understand how all the published poems read fit into the theme.
2. The way the published poems were read made the meaning clear.
3. The artistic representation on the tape cover enhanced the viewer's understanding of the theme.
4. The connections between poems added to the impact of the tape.
5. The poetry composed by the students was strong and had clear images.
6. The poetry composed by the students on this tape showed a variety in form.
7. The poetry composed by the students on this tape provided the listener with new insights or thoughts.
8. The tape was composed in such a way that it kept the listener's interest.
9. Vocal variation added to the impact of the tape.
10. Creative touches enhanced the effect the tape had on the listener.
11. It was obvious from the way the tape was put together that a large amount of time was spent on this project.

Figure 13.6   Sample Rubric or Scoring Guide on Poetry Performance

Respond to the following items by selecting: not at all (1); a little (2); somewhat (3); a lot (4); or a great deal (5). Add up the points and construct a grading scale.

1. The details of the arrest were clear.
2. All arrested parties had biographies given with all pertinent information included.
3. Interviews kept Julia, Winston, and Big Brother's characters consistent with how they were portrayed in the novel.
4. New insights into characters were shown through the way they were portrayed.
5. The visual elements enhanced the presentation.
6. The creative elements enhanced the presentation.
7. The presentation was fast-paced and kept the viewer's interest.
8. The presentation showed an excellent understanding of the themes presented in the novel.
9. The presentation showed an excellent understanding of the time in which the novel was set, and the oppressive nature of the society.

Figure 13.7   Sample Rubric or Scoring Guide on *1984* Script and Performance

1. Choose a scale along which you will place student work. Will it be a four-point scale, a six-point scale? Even amounts of numbers work best because they don't allow for the hedging that a middle number provides.

2. Think about what you would consider the best possible response to the task. Describe this response.

3. Describe a slightly less accomplished response. Which characteristics will be different? You can use words that indicate a scale such as always, sometimes, occasionally, never, or consistent and so on.

SOME ASSESSMENT DEFINITIONS

Many terms are bantered about, especially in the area of assessment. In this short section we will provide definitions for a few terms currently being used and explain how we see them in our assessment scheme.

Performance assessment requires students to demonstrate their level of competence or knowledge by creating a product or a response. (Performance assessment may or may not be authentic.) Performance assessment is a different kind of assessment, a direct demonstration of students' skill and knowledge which reflects a different kind of teaching. It requires students to respond with their own words or constructions to questions or prompts involving complex tasks rather than selecting preconstructed answers. Asking students to create scripts, to make videos, to draw in response to literature, to write the conversation between two characters from different novels are examples of performance assessment.

Authentic assessment involves activities or projects that represent the literacy behavior of the community and workplace and reflect the actual learning and instructional activities of the classroom and out-of-school worlds. Pamphlets written by students to alert others to the dangers of factory emissions in their community, or library exhibits that include text, graphics, and artifacts on an issue or problem, are examples of literacy in the community and workplace. Another example of authentic assessment would be all the pieces involved for a class to create a school campaign. They could use P.A. announcements, posters, pamphlets, and buttons to get their message across. The poetry tapes and video mentioned above are other forms of authentic assessment.

Constructed response assessment involves pencil and paper tasks which students answer in their own words using their own ideas. The word tests, short-answer tests as described earlier, are examples of this kind of response.

Selected response assessment involves paper and pencil tasks to check if the students know what the teacher knows. Answers are predetermined and the student is expected to explain what was in a book or in class notes.

STUDENTS AND GRADES

The main concern of many students when they are asked to do an assignment or a task in class is "does this count?" Their concern is not as often focused on "will this be graded" as on "will this be worth something?" Anything they view as not helping them toward their goal of eventually getting a grade in class becomes meaningless to them. Students are very efficient. They have busy lives and so want to know exactly how each assignment will count toward their grade. Students will infrequently do something for their own enrichment or pleasure. This is the kind of attitude the grading system has brought us. So in classes students need to know what checks, or credit, or grades are given for each scrap of work they do, or they see no reason for doing it. They have learned to "play the game," and we must take this into account in our response to their work.

If we decide to try alternative systems, part of our job is to explain to students what we're doing, why we're doing it, and how this will help them grow as learners. We may also need to explain our views on learning as we wean them away from the idea that a good grade on a multiple-choice test is evidence of real learning.

GRADING

Does an "A" mean a student does everything almost perfectly or does it mean the student has shown tremendous growth? This is the kind of question that teachers everywhere struggle with as they sit down to try to capture all their students' growth in literacy in a single grade.

Too often grades deal with trivial matters; students may be graded down as easily for their failure to "show respect for school property" as for their propensity to "talk too much" (especially ironic is this happens in a class dealing with language). Grades induce a false competitiveness in many children, producing students skilled at playing the grading game and unskilled at meeting the more substantial goals of education. Worst of all, grades are often used as mere binder for straw that ought to be blown away, supporting poor educational practice by threatening to fail those who do not acquiesce or perform.

Grades are also difficult to give. Sally Brown puts her finger on the problem very nicely in Figure 13.8: "How could anyone get a 'C' [or an 'A' or 'B']?"

At best, grading is a narrow, arbitrary measuring system, but it's the way teachers have traditionally had to report student progress—especially at the secondary level. Many elementary schools have more enlightened systems that use narrative reports and inclusion of the student's actual work to show to parents at conferences.

Unless teachers are in an extremely rare situation, they will have to somehow come to terms with *how* to assign a letter grade to their students' work. Let us say at the outset that *no* system is ever completely satisfactory. Diana found herself in her thirty years of secondary school teaching, changing her grading system every year. One piece might work very well, but there was always some kind of growth that didn't seem to be reflected in whatever system she used.

It seems that the first thing the teacher must do to prepare to assign grades is to think about and write down how class time is spent and how much emphasis is placed on such things as group work, writing, reading and literature, and independent projects.

Next, the teacher needs to think about how her expectations were made clear. Was something stated once and never brought up again? For instance, a teacher may tell students they must each read two novels on their own each marking period or write daily reflective notes. If encouragement and explanation and continued reference to these expectations is not given, students will assume they are not important and the teacher really doesn't expect them. Basing a large part of the grade on such subtle expectations will not be fair to the students.

Finally, everyone has to grapple with *how much* each part of the class activities and work will count in the overall grade. Will group work and process work be 35 percent or 50 percent? Will daily assignments and reflective journals or literature logs count

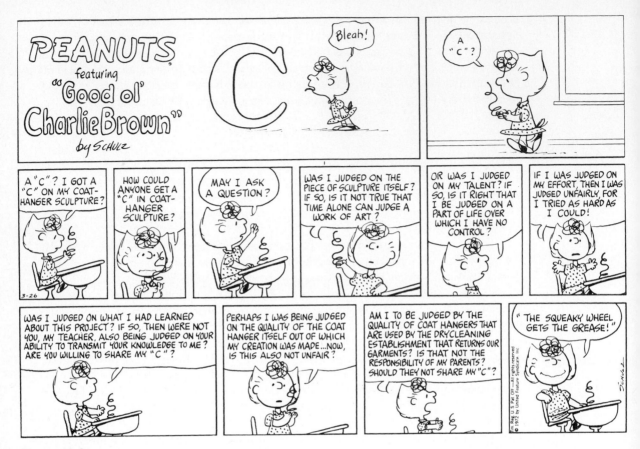

Figure 13.8

(From Charles Schultz, "Peanuts," March 6, 1972. © 1972 by United Feature Syndicated, Inc. Reprinted by permission.)

30 percent? Will finished projects that took up a lot of class time be worth 25 percent? How about the writing in students' writing folders or portfolios? Will it be worth 25 percent? 40 percent? What about reading and literature? Will books and literature-based assignments be worth 25 percent? 40 percent? How about more formal kinds of tests? Will they be worth 10 percent?

None of this kind of "divvying up" is easy. The best the teacher can do is to closely align the time spent on tasks and time given for tasks with the percent assigned to that work. This kind of rough division by percentage will be useful to almost any grading scheme the teacher uses.

The Point System

One popular way to give grades is based on a point system. Everything the student does is translated into a certain number of points. Participation in a small group discussion may be worth up to 5 points (these points can be based on such tools as the student questionnaire shown in Figure 13. 1). Drafts of stories may be worth 10 points and polished pieces worth even more. Completing a novel and orally recapping it for the teacher or a small group could be worth 20 points and a project on the novel might be worth 15 more. The positive thing about the point system is that students are rewarded for trying a great many things, they don't have to have mastered a form or genre to get high grades. Through the points assigned, the teacher can often get students to try more difficult work such as writing in a genre the student has never tried before. This approach lets students start at their own ability level and work up, it does not impose what the supposed ability level is. Of course, once all these points have been amassed, the teacher has to decide how many points are worth an A, how many for a B and so on. Point systems are usually understandable to students and they tend to like this kind of grading.

Percentages

Some teachers like to use percentages and translate everything done into percentages. Although we know language arts teachers who happily use this system, it seems difficult to use for many aspects of the work done in a language arts classroom. However, we also know teachers who simply change the grades they have assigned to student work into percentages because it is easier to "add up" into a final grade.

We have to say here, that no matter how valiant the attempt to create "objective" grades through the use of such things as percentages, there is no way to be totally objective, since even what we select to weigh the most in our grading is not objective. Diana has worked to create "fair" scales but has found that there is always some student whose work doesn't seem to be fairly reflected with that particular scale. For instance if a student poured a lot of energy into one particular project and exceeded all expectations but also did not complete work in another area, and each area has an equal weighting in the grading scheme, that student's effort may not be reflected in a final grade. Thus in the end, we all take into account effort, involvement, and where that student started from.

Contract Grading

This type of grading can work well at all levels of schooling. Two main components are involved:

1. The amount of work a student must do to achieve a given grade.
2. The quality of acceptability for that work.

Because secondary teachers often don't know everything they will be asking students to do for a whole semester or marking period, it can be difficult to be as specific as is usually needed for this system to work. However this system is very flexible, especially when students would like to design a project or a program of work. Teachers can use contract grading to differentiate the amount of work needed for each grade. When Diana used this system in a university course, students who wanted to work towards a higher grade had to read more young adult novels, work in a group to create a project on a novel, and attend an all-day conference. Since its often easier to set standards of quantity rather than quality, Diana solved the problem of students turning in papers done in a cursory manner by giving each paper a check if it was satisfactorily completed, a check plus if it was more than satisfactory, and a check minus if it didn't meet expectations. Then by a quick glance at her grade sheet she could see if students were meeting the class expectations. Papers that received a check minus (plus questions to help them develop responses or comments) did not meet the expectations. Through this kind of feedback students could clearly see the kind of depth their responses needed to have.

Although some teachers who begin to use contract grading ask students which grade (and work) they will be contracting for, we have found that it also works well just to assume every student will aim for the top grade. Later if they find they don't have the time to fulfill all of those requirements, they just don't turn in the work required for the higher grade.

Student Self-Evaluation

Steve has experimented widely with a form of self-evaluation in both college and high school classes. He believes it may be more important for students to learn to judge their own work than for them to understand teacher's assessments. Thus he provides many opportunities for self-assessment. After students complete a paper, he asks them to describe their "pleasures and pains" in writing—in effect, describing what they think they did well and what they did badly. At the end of the term, he has them write an informal "intellectual history" of themselves in the course, summarizing what they have read, thought about, talked about, and achieved.

We think that this kind of self-assessment program is valuable for two reasons:

- First, it gives students a true sense of their achievement in a course, so that no grade can substitute for their deeper understanding of what they have done.
- Second, it provides a more solid basis for grading than any simple numerical system. If the only form of evaluation in a course is a series of numbers in the teacher's grade book, it is not surprising that students become grade conscious. In a self-evaluation system the foundation is far more solid, so the grade comes as a confirmation of what the student already knows through self-examination.

Students can even be involved in the grading process. At the end of the term, they can be asked to review the criteria that the teacher has established for the course and to suggest how they see themselves as measuring up. On that basis, students can *recommend* a grade (not "pick one"), and the teacher takes final responsibility for assigning a grade. When Steve uses this system he usually states that he will accept any recommendation that is written "in good faith"—that is, that makes an honest attempt at evaluation. Bad faith recommendations, described in advance for the class, include such problems as comparative grading ("All the rest of those people want an 'A' so why shouldn't I have one?"), task avoidance ("I really don't know what to say, so I'll ask for a 'B'."), or failure to discuss concrete accomplishments ("They say that you get out of a course what you put into it. Well, I must have put a lot into this course because I sure got a lot out of it!"). Steve also spends time discussing the range of grades that might be possible, given the basic expectations and requirements of the course. On the whole, the recommended-grade system works well. Occasionally students try to take it for a ride, recommending unreasonably high grades, but Steve has had more problems with students recommending a low grade out of false modesty.

Here are other variations on the self-evaluation plan:

• *Matched grades.* The student and the teacher make up grade recommendations independently and compare notes. If the grades match (which they often do), all is well. For mismatches, a difference of opinion of one grade or more, a conference is called to work out the difference.

• *Conferences.* The student and the teacher meet to work out the grade. The student brings along samples of the work for the term, and the two arrive at a grade.

• *Journal Evaluation.* The student keeps a detailed log of accomplishments in the class, a kind of running record in support of a grade recommendation.

TEACHER SELF-ASSESSMENT

Since this chapter has dealt with evaluation of student work it seems a good place to encourage teachers to evaluate their own work, especially in terms of what they are asking students to do. Usually we are so involved in what we are doing in the classroom that it is difficult to see if our instruction is addressing all the significant areas of literacy. The standards work done around the country focuses on naming and explaining all the areas a strong English language arts program would probably have in place. That's why we think that for teachers who want to see the big picture, to "problematize" their own teaching, looking at state or national standards can be helpful. In Diana's work with teachers who were learning about the Michigan Language Arts Content Standards, the teachers found it helpful to look at their own classrooms in two ways. One way was to bring in a vignette of a lesson or assignment and look through the content standards to see which standards were being met. The other way was to begin with the content standards, see what kind of work would be going on in the classroom to meet it, and then see if they were addressing that standard in their classes.

Figure 13.9 illustrates how teachers looked at their classrooms through the vignette approach. First they read the vignette, read the content standards and then figured out which content standards were being addressed through this activity. Then because one major concern of the standards work is to closely tie assessment to instruction, after teachers elicited elements of best practice from the vignette, they also drew out the assessment tasks embedded in the vignette. Lastly they created assessment tools that could be used to judge the work.

This idea of "best practice" comes from the work of teachers in classrooms. Because these practices help students achieve, because they are based on sound developmental theory (learning theory), and demonstrate an understanding of motivation and the psychology of students, these practices, strategies, and activities have been labeled as models of "best practice." Teachers can look at these elements in terms of

<u>SUMMARY OF HIGH SCHOOL VIGNETTE #1</u>

High school students in small groups brainstorm themes and motifs that they believe exist in a novel. Next, using all the themes and motifs the class has written down, they create generalizations about what the author is trying to show through the book. They evaluate and rate the validity of the generalizations through a rubric they have devised.

<u>EVIDENCE OF CONTENT STANDARDS AND BENCHMARKS:</u>

Since the teacher was striving to get students to grapple with and construct their own meaning as they worked with the text, **Content Standard 3 (All students will focus on meaning and communication as they listen, speak, view, read, and write in personal, social, occupational, and civic contexts)** is being addressed. Students wrote, responded to each others' ideas, listened, and interacted to demonstrate that *Benchmark A (Use speaking, listening, viewing, reading, and writing for multiple purposes in such a way that each enhances the other)* was operating here. Since group reports involved students in speaking to the whole class while others listened and interacted appropriately, *Benchmark B (read and write fluently, speak confidently, listen and interact appropriately in situations)* was being addressed. Parts of *Benchmark C (describe and use a communication model that highlights effective listening strategies—attending, assigning meaning, evaluating, responding—and elements of effective speaking)* are exhibited also.

Content Standard 4 (All students will use the English language effectively) was addressed mainly through discussions and whole-class presentations, so *Benchmark A (demonstrate how language usage is related to successful communication in different spoken and written contexts)* was in action there.

This assignment drew heavily on **Content Standard 5 (All students will read and respond to a wide variety of classic and contemporary literature and other texts to seek information, ideas, enjoyment, and understanding of their individuality, our common heritage and common humanity, and the rich diversity in our society).** Students showed evidence of meeting *Benchmark A (read and respond thoughtfully to both classic and contemporary literature recognized for quality and literary merit)*; *Benchmark B (describe and discuss archetypal human experiences that appear in literature and other texts from around the world)*; *Benchmark C (analyze how the tensions among characters, communities, themes and issues in literature and other texts are the substance of the literary experience)*; and *Benchmark D (analyze how cultures interact with one another in literature and describe the consequences of the interaction)*.

Content Standard 9 (All students will demonstrate understanding of the complexity of enduring issues and recurring problems by making connections and generating themes within and across texts) is also addressed. *Benchmark A (analyze and reflect on universal themes and substantive issues from oral, visual and written texts)* was certainly present as was *Benchmark C (develop and extend a thesis)*. *Benchmark D* was evident mostly in discussions *(use themes and central ideas in literature and other texts to generate solutions to problems and formulate perspectives on issues in their own lives)*. By creating their own criteria, students addressed **Content Standard 12 (All students will develop and apply personal, shared, and academic criteria for the enjoyment, appreciation, and evaluation of their**

(continued)

Figure 13.9 Content Standards in Action

own and others' oral, written, and visual texts). *Benchmark B (Evaluate their own and peers' texts using both individually and collaboratively developed standards)* was also at work.

SAMPLE ASSESSMENT TASKS

1. In small groups students brainstorm recurring themes and motifs in the novel.

2. From the themes and motifs, students compose ten generalizations about the novel that illustrate what the author might be trying to show readers.

3. Students present what they consider to be the ten best generalizations produced and explain the reasons for the choices.

SAMPLE ASSESSMENT TOOLS

1. Students respond to a questionnaire about what they contributed to the group. Teacher can also judge productiveness of group by observation.

2. Quality of the generalizations can be judged by a student-developed rubric.

3. Evaluation can be based on a checklist.

THIS VIGNETTE ILLUSTRATES THE FOLLOWING STANDARDS FOR BEST PRACTICE:

The Students. . .
- have some choices
- collaborate and share their thinking with others

This Instructional Activity. . .
- has strategies that involve students
- values student contributions
- encourages students to construct meaning
- involves students in discussing and sharing what they know
- gives students opportunities to work in small groups to help each other make meaning through speaking and writing
- aims at expanding and/or challenging student thinking
- involves students in discussing and developing criteria or rubrics
- gives students opportunities to justify and defend their own thinking
- integrates reading, writing, speaking, and listening
- encourages students to look for common threads in human interaction and human behavior and concern
- starts with student understanding of the novel and builds from there
- allows room for students' originality
- has clear, specific directions

Figure 13.9

what they do in the classroom and form lessons around ideas in this "best practice" section. By naming these elements, it may be easier to think about how the principles can be applied to other learning situations.

Another way the teachers got a look at their own classrooms was to begin with the content standards, see what kind of work would be going on to meet them, and then see if they were addressing these standards in their classes.

Since the Michigan Frameworks and the Standards developed by NCTE and IRA are based on a belief in the necessity of involving students in their own learning, another category suggested itself, "Classroom Opportunities to Achieve." This category described what was happening in the classroom to foster the active learning necessary to reach high levels of literacy. This section also offers teachers ideas about implementing the content standards by describing specific activities that can get at the heart of that specific content standard. Figure 13.10 shows the content standard, the benchmarks for two grade levels, opportunities to achieve, and assessment tasks and tools. Both of these procedures can help teachers understand the kind of instruction they are providing for their students.

CONTENT STANDARD #4:

All students will use the English language effectively. When we use the English language, we use it in many different ways and forms. Many times the forms of language that we use depend upon the audience and the type of message we want to communicate. Our language is much different when we use it in a formal setting such as speaking to an assembly or writing to apply for a job as opposed to talking with friends about a recent event or writing in a diary. As we grow in our ability to use language, we learn what forms and types of language are best suited for different situations. As we experience language in many different settings, we become better able to use the forms of language that will suit our own purposes.

CLASSROOM OPPORTUNITIES TO ACHIEVE

Do students have opportunities to:

1. experiment with different ways to express the same idea in writing and in speaking?
2. write from different perspectives and discuss how word choice and style affect the writing?
3. become involved in activities that focus on investigating word origins?
4. read or view and discuss texts that use different language patterns?
5. compare language use across generations or neighborhoods?
6. see models of, talk about, and use a variety of language patterns in their writing?
7. become aware of idiomatic phrases through discussion and activities aimed at identifying and gathering samples?
8. write in many formats and talk about how language changes depending on the format (friendly letter, explaining how to do something)?
9. participate in oral activities in the classroom which involve them in using language in many contexts?   *(continued)*

Figure 13.10

10. participate in activities that encourage them to analyze language use in different situations?

11. write reflections on their composing processes which can include why they selected specific words?

12. create group compositions, noting how they came to consensus on phrasing and word choice?

13. create cross-disciplinary presentations?

BENCHMARKS FOR MIDDLE SCHOOL:

A. Compare and contrast spoken, written, and visual language patterns used in various contexts within their own environment. Examples include community activities, discussions, mathematics class, science class, and the workplace.

B. Investigate the origins of language patterns and vocabularies and their impact on meaning in formal and informal situations.

C. Investigate idiomatic phrases and word origins and how they have contributed to contemporary meaning.

D. Demonstrate how communication is affected by differences in word choice and why one particular word is considered better or more appropriate than others.

E. Recognize and use levels of discourse appropriate for varied contexts, purposes, and audiences, including terminology specific to a particular field. Examples include community building, an explanation of a biological concept, comparison of computer programs, commentary on an artistic work, analysis of a fitness program, and classroom debates on political issues.

SAMPLE ASSESSMENT TASKS

1. Create a slang dictionary.

2. Select a specific number of words and create a survey. Ask respondents to rank each word from 1 to 5 from very positive to very negative. The same survey could be given to teens and parents to see how each group responds to the same words.

3. Each student selects a different area and generates 10 to 20 vocabulary words specific to that area (art, computers, cars, biology, math, soccer, volleyball, insurance, music). He or she looks up the words in the dictionary to find the country or culture where the word originated. Findings are presented to the class and students make generalizations about why some areas have so many words of foreign origin.

SAMPLE ASSESSMENT TOOLS

1. Rubric that focuses on completeness, whether or not words are slang, and if definitions adequately explain the word.

2. Completion of survey, administering of it, and completion of a written or oral explanation of the findings.

3. Completion and a rubric based on presentation qualities, quality of generalizations, etc.

(continued)

Figure 13.10

4. Choose an idiomatic expression and illustrate it. One example is "he's a stick in the mud."

4. Completion and if the illustration conveys the meaning of the idiom.

5. In groups of two or three, students tape-record a conversation about a common topic such as TV, a favorite singer or fashions. Then they play the tapes and transcribe what they have said, noting areas that were difficult to turn into written speech. After discussing these differences they write up a group report of their findings on the differences between spoken and written language.

5. Another group listens to the tape, reads the transcription of it and the report on the findings, and uses a rubric the whole class has developed to evaluate the work.

BENCHMARKS FOR HIGH SCHOOL:

A. Demonstrate how language usage is related to successful communication in different spoken, written, and visual contexts. Examples include job interviews, public speeches, debates, and advertising.

B. Show an understanding of how language patterns and vocabularies transmit culture and affect meaning to communicate effectively in formal and informal situations.

C. Explore and explain how the same words can have different usages and meanings in different contexts, cultures, and communities.

D. Demonstrate ways in which communication can be influenced through word usage. Examples include propaganda, irony, and humor.

E. Recognize and use levels of discourse appropriate for varied contexts, purposes, and audiences, including terminology specific to particular fields. Examples include community building, presentations integrating different disciplines, lessons comparing fields of study, promotional material created for an interdisciplinary project, and videos designed to inform or entertain diverse audiences.

SAMPLE ASSESSMENT TASKS

1. Create an ad campaign in the context of another discipline.

SAMPLE ASSESSMENT TOOLS

1. Rubric based on such elements as how persuasive and convincing the ad was, how much information on the other discipline was conveyed etc.

2. Read and analyze joke collections in terms of what creates the humor.

2. Rubric based on such elements as how thorough the analysis was, how many elements of humor are mentioned, etc.

3. Compare two distinct examples of language use (political speeches, sermons, teen talk, movie reviews etc.) in terms of vocabulary use, speech patterns (repetition, dialect, slang etc.), and purpose.

3. Rubric based on such elements as the thoroughness of the comparison, how many elements are mentioned, and whether readers gain new insights from the comparison.

4. Through library, computer research, or human interviews find out how different ethnic,

4. Rubric based on elements of good writing as well as on thoroughness of

(continued)

Figure 13.10

religious, or age groups identify themselves and what words they use to describe themselves. Also find out what phrases or questions they feel stereotypes them. Write up your findings. Example: people with roots in Mexico have definite feelings about being called Hispanic, Chicano, Latino, and Mexican-American. See what name is acceptable to which groups.

research/interviews, type of information uncovered, etc.

5. So students can see how levels of language change depending on the age of the intended audience, bring in a series of informational videos such as those used in drug or sex education at the elementary, middle school, and high school level. Students analyze the films in terms of how language differs, how explanations differ and how complexity of information differs depending on the age of the intended audience.

5. Rubric based on thoroughness of analysis and number of elements mentioned.

12. After research on the time period explain why the characters acted as they did in the time period and situation.

12. Rubric that includes accuracy about the time period, whether the explanation is logical etc.

Content Standards and Benchmarks were developed under the auspices of the Michigan Department of State. The other parts are from materials developed during the Ingham County Curriculum Review Project for Language Arts, directed by Kathy Dewsbury-White, Jan Kakela, and Diana Mitchell. Reprinted with permission.

Figure 13.10

◆ EXPLORATIONS

◆ Practice holistic scoring. Get a batch of student papers written from one prompt or assignment. Invite two teachers or classmates to learn to score with you. Begin by reading each paper quickly and just assigning it a high, medium, or low. Compare the results with the other two readers, working to explain what caused you to react to the paper as you did. During the next round, try scoring them from a high of 4 to a low of 1.

◆ Articulate the qualities of good writing. Using the same or different set of papers, rank them from 4 to 1 and then write short, descriptive statements that explain all the elements you were looking for or that you noticed.

◆ Construct a rubric. Using an assignment you have created, construct a rubric, use it to evaluate the assignment, and then reflect on how well the rubric addressed the important pieces of the assignment.

◆ Choose a unit or lesson you have created. Using Figure 13.9 as a model, unearth the elements of best practice embedded in your unit or lesson.

◆ Choose a novel you could use in the classroom and create assessment tasks and tools you could use with it.

◆ Reflect on how you've been graded as a student. Talk with your group about instances where you felt the evaluation and grade were fairly given and instances where you felt it was unfairly given. List the methods used and explain why you viewed the experience as negative or positive. Draw some conclusions.

◆ Assess your own stance on the process assessment tasks included in this chapter. What problems do you see including students' oral response in the evaluation scheme, reading or literature logs, and so on. Discuss with your group your views on process assessment tasks and how you view inclusion of this in evaluation and grading.

◆ Try creating some of the product assessment tasks. For instance, from a novel construct a word test, a short-answer essay test. Or in a group create a collaborative test. Reflect on your experiences and draw some conclusions.

RELATED READINGS

Although aimed at elementary teachers and discussing a whole literacy program *Transitions* by Regie Routman has a chapter on evaluation which provides good solid workable suggestions and a philosophical framework for the secondary teacher.

To broaden your view of assessment and to see lots of assessment tools in action in the classroom, take a look at *Literacy Assessment in Practice* developed by the Assessment of Writing and Reading Inservice Teacher Education project team; *Invitations* by Regie Routman; *Responsive Evaluation* edited by Brian Cambourne and Jan Turbill; and *Transitions* by Regie Routman.

Two resources for not only looking at assessment issues but also to get lists of indicators for development and achievement are *Telling the Whole Story* by Robert McGregor and Marion Meiers and the *First Steps* series which includes titles in Reading, Writing, Oral Language, and Spelling.

A book that maps out the assessment process in a step-by-step manner is *Learning in Overdrive: Designing Curriculum, Instruction, and Assessment from Standards* by Ruth Mitchell, Marilyn Willis, and The Chicago Teachers Union Quest Center.

Two books published by the Association for Supervision and Curriculum Development that focus on aspects of assessment are *Communicating Student Learning* edited by Thomas R. Guskey and *Assessing Student Outcomes* by Robert J. Marzano, Debra Pickering, and Jay McTighe.

Fran Claggett's *A Measure of Success* brings together the best that is known about assessment in rich, meaningful ways without simplifying this very complex area.

Many excellent books on portfolios exist. Two of the best we've found are *Portfolio Portraits* edited by Donald H. Graves and Bonnie S. Sunstein, and *Portfolio Assessment in the Reading/Writing Classroom* by Robert J. Tierney, Mark A. Carter, and Laura E. Desai.

Notes from a Kidwatcher: Selected Writings of Yetta M. Goodman edited by Sandra Wilde has only one section devoted to evaluation but almost all of Goodman's writing enriches our understanding of children's literacy and so informs us about how we should be evaluating our students. *Alternatives to Grading Student Writing* edited by Stephen Tchudi, already mentioned in Chapter 9, is also full of useful advice and ideas.

IDEA(L)ISM AND SUCCESSIVE APPROXIMATION

We want to end this book with what, in classical rhetoric, would be the *peroration*, the rousing appeal that sends an audience into the streets to take public action or to seize arms or to overthrow the emperor. But we've chosen the more modest title of "coda" for this section; "coda" is a term from music, often a *reprise* of the main themes with a few *new motifs*.

It is important for us to place this book into the context of actual teaching situations. For instance, although current theory promotes integrated curriculum, and interdisciplinary, experience-centered programs that enlarge the range of literacy, powerful forces in society would push the English language arts teacher toward isolation and fragmentation. The back-to-basics people want more parts of speech and drill; parents want control over their children's reading matter and are objecting to new books; class loads are increasing; small-group learning is frowned upon as "noisy"; testmakers often have more to say about curriculum matters than do teachers; textbook adoption has more to say about curriculum matters than do teachers; and education takes place in a climate where, arguably, teachers and educators are far less respected and honored than they used to be.

Teachers have a variety of ways of coping with these external realities. We recall once meeting a dour high school teacher who told us, "I really hate this place, and I'd rather be working on my flower gardens. I only have ten more years to go before retirement." Such a reaction is clearly unprofessional, an abandonment of responsibility, and there is, candidly, not much that any of us can do about it.

Of greater concern is a second kind of teacher, represented by a group we worked with for a year. In September, the teachers were bright and enthusiastic, ready to try anything. They plunged into their teaching with vigor, and their optimism was reflected in the tone of excitement in their workshop sessions. As the year progressed, however, the meetings seemed to grow less interesting, and toward the end of the year, everyone realized that a negative pall had fallen over the group. Whenever one member proposed an idea, five others would instantly offer reasons why "It'll never work." Their optimism was gone. Exploring deeper, we found their discouragement could be traced to a range of mildly negative experiences that they were having daily. Nothing traumatic like a student leaping out of a window or the principal chewing out the teacher in front of the students. Little things: no supplies; not enough photocopy paper; too much red tape; too many students; too many absence reports, tardy slips, admits, and hall passes; no books; gloomy classrooms. Many of these teachers also felt very much alone in their schools because of little things like mild disapproval on the part of colleagues, occasional tut-tuts from the assistant principal about discipline or decorum, lack of support for new programs, and department meetings that failed to deal with substantive issues.

These teachers realized that they were becoming victims of "teacher burnout." Once this problem was identified, the group was able to renew itself and managed to end the year on as high a note as they began. But we feared for their survival the following year. "The schools," as one cynic has remarked, "are an awful place for people to have to teach."

But many teachers maintain their enthusiasm and energy. Teaching next door to that burned out would-be-gardener history teacher was a 62-year-old woman who could present Shakespeare in ways that deeply excited students. The schools are filled with teachers who have learned, to paraphrase Faulkner, not only to *survive* but, to *prevail.* We hope the readers of this book are among such people and that this book has played a modest role in helping develop your enthusiasm for our profession and your determination to prevail and succeed in it. Such people seem to us to have two main characteristics:

First, they have a clear, stable sense of self and purpose. They are what psychologists call "self-renewing" persons, people who do not stagnate, whose interests and ideas are always at least two or three stages beyond their present accomplishments. Self-renewing English language arts teachers may take home some student themes for response, but they don't let theme grading cancel or blight a planned trip to the theater or the opera. They may read mystery novels as well as children's literature and professional magazines. They believe that the human mind is a pretty extraordinary thing and that there are few limits to what it can perceive and know; thus they constantly push their own minds into new directions, new skills, new courses, new experiments.

Second, such teachers know how to function within an institution. They recognize that institutions are by nature impersonal (although they may be administered by highly personable people), that bureaucracies seem to spring up by nature and of their own accord, that one has to understand the nature of the institution and work creatively within it. Some teachers, we fear, come to see the institution as a barrier to or even as an excuse for not achieving their aims and goals. The best teachers we know just don't allow institutional problems and pressures to place them on the defensive; they are alert to problems and aggressively work to take positive, even anticipatory, action.

Such teachers are, in a very real sense, "idealistic."

"Idealism" we think, is a badly understood educational concept. Too many people take it to mean "naïve optimism," the kind of thinking traditionally engaged in by liberals, free thinkers, and professors of education. We can't tell you how many times teachers have argued against progressive education by saying, "That's so *idealistic*," as if idealism itself is an argument *against* making progress! In fact, "idealism" simply means having a set of ideas—a vision, if you will —a set of idea(l)s about the way things can and should be.

Our advice to teachers: *Keep your idealism.* (Please note that we didn't say "youthful" idealism. Any teacher—twenty to sixty-five—needs to have ideals.) Further, we suggest: Define your ideals carefully and don't let "them"—circumstances, clerks, administrators, and frustrations—force you to reject valid ideals.

Already we seem to hear a voice muttering at the back of the lecture hall: "Who are they kidding? It's not realistic to be idealistic!" To the contrary, we submit that it is actually not practical to be narrowly "realistic." If teachers do not have an idealized vision of what they want their teaching to be, if they cannot see the remotest possibility of meeting that ideal by hook or by crook in the near or distant future, then the only "realistic" thing for them to do is abandon teaching in favor of a "practical" profession like spot welding or steam fitting—or gardening.

It would be naïve to base one's idealistic vision on the assumption that next year unlimited funds will be available to every teacher for any teaching purpose, that in September all students will trot into classes eager to learn and capable of plunging into independent self-directed work. It would be equally naive to base a vision on the belief that a revolutionary storm is about to sweep across this country to dissolve the present system of education and to lead to something better. But it is both realistic and idealistic to visualize good, imaginative classes being taught under the present, less-than-ideal conditions.

Reality limits the ease and potential for accomplishing one's ideals overnight. Nevertheless, too few teachers are aggressive in fighting the limitations of their situation. They limit themselves by making false assumptions about their school. They assume they will be fired if they don't teach *the noun,* but they never investigate whether or not the school actually checks up on teachers; they assume that the principal will not provide funds for student writing awards, but no one has ever submitted a proposal; they assume that students aren't interested in books, but nobody has actually tried a full-scale individualized reading program.

We'll close this book—this *coda*, this *peroration*—by sharing a strategy that we've used in our own teaching with, we think, pretty good success. We call it:

Idea(l)ism and Successive Approximation

It suggests that we need to state our idea(l)s clearly and then to approximate them as best we can, getting as close to realizing them as possible within the parameters of the institution:

Step I. State the idea(l) clearly, without limiting your vision by the perceived limits of reality.

Example: I want a classroom library. An excellent one. I want one thousand brand new paperback titles, subscriptions to twenty-five newspapers and magazines, and a pamphlet file of five hundred up-to-date monographs on every conceivable subject. And I want a comfortable display and lounge area where the students can browse and read.

Step II. List all the obstacles to that ideal. Don't leave any out. (This procedure, by the way, is an excellent way of releasing tension.) But be careful not to list any false or imagined obstacles. Make certain the barriers *do* exist.

Example: Barriers to a classroom library.

1. There's practically no money in the book budget.
2. The district just adopted a new anthology that is consuming the rest of the budget.
3. The curriculum committee has a very short list of approved supplementary books and worries about censorship cases.
4. I have no place to store books; I don't even have my own classroom, much less furniture or space for a reading center.

And so on. You can probably add ten more obstacles to the list, all of them valid.

Step III. Systematically design ways of approximating your goal, attacking the obstacles one by one, aggressively seeking ways to leap past them to approximate the ideal.

Solutions for obstacles 1 and 2: You simply will have to look elsewhere for books. First, of course, you can bring in titles from your own paperback collection, a hundred or more that have accumulated over the years, tomes that simply build up dust and moving expense. You can ask the students to bring in books (with their parents' approval, of course). Some of your friends may be willing to contribute, and you can accost the manager of the paperback bookstore for samples, damaged stock, and leftover magazines and newspapers. You can get the students to join a paperback book club, knowing that they always have some loose change. You can start a paperback cooperative with other teachers in order to pool your meager resources. You can also help the student council set up a paperback bookstore. And so on. Any teacher can quickly build up resources of this sort in reasonable—though not ideal—quantities.

Obstacle 3, the curriculum committee, presents a greater challenge.

First, you should do a little precensorship of the titles you have accumulated to pull out some harmless but censorially dangerous literature, like the romance novel with a bosomy cover or even a U.S. Department of Agriculture Bulletin on sheep breeding. Having removed the most obvious sore spots, you can skim some professional book lists (see our reference sources for Chapters 5–7), looking for references to the titles you have accumulated. It's unlikely that the curriculum committee will raise too many objections if books are recognized in nationally approved guides for reading.

Obstacle 4, not having storage, is relatively easy to overcome. You could turn the problem over to the students.

Some high school students to whom we posed this problem suggested:

- A book cabinet on wheels.
- Using the Internet as a source of reading.
- Putting the books in the trunk of your car and letting students check them out at the parking lot (a not altogether serious proposal, but not altogether a bad idea, either).

- Putting books on reserve in the library.
- Publishing a list of available books and bringing in a box of selected titles, say, once each week for students in need of more reading.

We don't mean to suggest that these are complete or foolproof solutions to the classroom library problem, but you catch our drift: The creative teacher, one who can keep his/her spirit and idea(l)s in place, can always think of just one more possible solution, one more approximation, to get closer to the ideal.

It is also crucial for teachers to form networks and support groups with like-minded folks. There are times to argue and debate issues with people of opposing viewpoints, but there are also times to settle in with friends who will voice strong and positive support for what you are doing. For us, much of that support comes through professional organizations: We've both been active in the National Council of Teachers of English for years and find its annual convention a time of great renewal. We've been active in our statewide organizations as well, spending perhaps too many hours in executive board meetings, planning conferences, editing newsletters and journals, figuring out how to enhance membership. But we've found our work with state organizations to be among the most rewarding of our careers.

You could start a reading group in your school or community, a group of people who read a book a month—school related, best seller, or pure fun—and get together to talk about it. You can start a writing group where everybody agrees to bring a draft of a new piece to each session. You can get on the Internet, finding the education groups that share your interests and joining chat rooms and bulletin boards. Have coffee with a colleague. Meet a colleague and go shopping or out to dinner. Organize a theater party. Go to a summer institute or travel abroad. Take a course in physics or astronomy or automotive repair. Learn to play a musical instrument. In each of these ways you'll be enlarging your participation, not simply in the community of teachers, but in the community-at-large, which, after all is what literacy, what teaching the English language arts, is all about.

BIBLIOGRAPHY

Abbs, Peter. *English Within the Arts*. London: Hodder and Stoughton, 1982.

Allen, Janet. *It's Never Too Late: Leading Adolescents to Lifelong Literacy*. Portsmouth, N.H.: Heinemann, 1995.

Applebee, Arthur. *Tradition and Reform in Teaching English*. Urbana, Ill.: National Council of Teachers of English, 1974.

Armstrong, Thomas. *Multiple Intelligences in the Classroom*. Alexandria, Va.: Association for Supervision and Curriculum Development, 1994.

Atwell, Nancie. *In the Middle: Writing, Reading, and Learning with Adolescents*. Portsmouth, N.H.: Boynton/Cook, 1987.

———. *Side by Side: Essays on Teaching to Learn*. Portsmouth, N.H.: Heinemann, 1991.

Baker, Edwin. *Advertising and a Democratic Press*. Princeton, N.J.: Princeton University Press, 1994.

Barbieri, Maureen. *Sounds from the Heart*. Portsmouth, N.H.: Heinemann, 1995.

Beach, Richard. *A Teacher's Introduction to Reader-Response Theories*. Urbana, Ill.: National Council of Teachers of English, 1993.

Benton, Michael, and Geoff Fox. *Teaching Literature—Nine to Fourteen*. London: Oxford University Press, 1985.

Berlin, James. *Writing Instruction in Nineteenth Century American Colleges*. Carbondale, Ill.: Southern Illinois University Press, 1984.

Bizzell, Patricia and Bruce Herzberg. *The Rhetorical Tradition*. New York: St. Martin's, 1989.

Black, Laurel, Donald Daiker, Jeffrey Sommers, and Gail Stygall. *New Directions in Portfolio Assessment*. Portsmouth, N.H.: Boynton/Cook, 1994.

Boomer, Garth. *Metaphors and Meanings*. Sydney: Australian Association for the Teaching of English, 1988.

Bosma, Betty. *Fairy Tales, Fables, Legends, and Myths: Using Folk Literature in Your Classroom.* New York: Teachers College Press, 1987.

Braddock, Richard, Richard Lloyd Jones, and Lowell Schorer. *Research in Written Composition.* Urbana, Ill.: National Council of Teachers of English, 1963.

Britton, James. *The Development of Writing Abilities, 11–18.* London: Macmillan Educational, 1975.

———, Douglas Barnes, and Mike Torbe. *Language, the Learner, and the School.* Portsmouth, N.H.: Boynton/Cook, 1990.

———, Robert Shafer, and Ken Watson, eds., *Teaching and Learning English World Wide.* Clevedon, U.K.: Multilingual Matters, 1990.

Brooks, Jacqueline Grennon, and Martin G. Brooks. *The Case for Constructivist Classrooms.* Alexandria, Va.: Association for Supervision and Curriculum Development, 1993.

Brown, Jean E. *Preserving Intellectual Freedom.* Urbana, Ill.: National Council of Teachers of English, 1994.

———, and Elaine C. Stephens. *Teaching Young Adult Literature.* Belmont, Calif.: Wadsworth, 1995.

Cambourne, Brian, and Jan Turbill. *Responsive Evaluation.* Portsmouth, N.H.: Heinemann, 1994.

Carpenter, Edmund. *Oh What a Blow That Phantom Gave Me.* New York: Bantam, 1976.

Cart, Michael. *From Romance to Realism: 50 Years of Growth and Change in Young Adult Literature.* New York: HarperCollins, 1996.

Carter, Candy, and Zora Rashkis, eds. *Ideas for Teaching English in the Junior High and Middle School.* Urbana, Ill.: National Council of Teachers of English, 1980.

Chomsky, Noam. *Language and Mind.* New York: Harcourt Brace Jovanovich, 1972.

Christenbury, Leila. *Books for You—a Booklist for Senior High Students.* Urbana, Ill.: National Council of Teachers of English, 1995.

———. *Making the Journey: Being and Becoming a Teacher of English Language Arts.* Portsmouth, N.H.: Boynton/Cook, 1994.

Claggett, Fran. *A Measure of Success.* Portsmouth, N.H.: Boynton/Cook, 1996.

———, Louann Reid, and Ruth Vinz. *Learning the Landscape: Inquiry-Based Activities for Comprehending and Composing.* Portsmouth, NH: Boynton/Cook, 1996.

———. *Recasting the Text: Inquiry-based Activities for Comprehending and Composing.* Portsmouth, N.H.: Boynton/Cook, 1996.

Clifford, John, ed. *The Experience of Reading: Louise Rosenblatt and Reader-Response Theory.* Portsmouth, N.H.: Boynton/Cook, 1991.

Cook, Leonora, and Helen C. Lodge, eds. *Voices in English Classrooms: Honoring Diversity and Change.* Urbana, Ill.: National Council of Teachers of English, 1996.

Corcoran, Bill, Mike Hayhoe, and Gordon Pradl, eds. *Knowledge in the Making: Challenging the Text in the Classroom.* Portsmouth, N.H.: Boynton/Cook, 1994.

Courts, Patrick. *Multicultural Literacies: Dialect, Discourse, and Diversity.* New York: Peter Lang, 1997.

Creber, J. W. Patrick. *Sense and Sensitivity.* London: University of London Press, 1965. Revised edition: Exeter, U.K.: St. Luke's College of Education, 1987.

———. *Thinking Through English.* Milton Keynes, U.K.: Open University, 1990.

Daniels, Harvey. *Literature Circles: Voice and Choice in the Student-Centered Classroom.* York, Maine: Stenhouse, 1994.

Darwin, Charles. *The Descent of Man*. New York: Hurst and Company, 1874.

David, Donald. *Telling Your Own Stories: For Family and Classroom Storytelling, Public Speaking, and Personal Journaling*. Little Rock, Ark.: August House, 1993.

David, Marc. *Bonfire of the Humanities*. Syracuse, N.Y.: Syracuse University Press, 1995.

Day, Frances Ann. *Latina and Latino Voices in Literature*. Portsmouth, N.H.: Heinemann, 1997.

———. *Multicultural Voices in Contemporary Literature*. Portsmouth, N.H.: Heinemann, 1994.

Delpit, Lisa. *Other People's Children*. New York: The New Press, 1995.

Dewey, John. *School and Society*. Chicago: University of Chicago Press, 1956.

Dillard, J. L. *Black English: Its History and Usage in the United States*. New York: Vintage, 1973.

Dixon, John, *Growth Through English*. Urbana, Ill.: National Council of Teachers of English, 1967, 1969, 1975.

Donelson, Kenneth L., and Alleen Pace Nilsen. *Literature for Today's Young Adults*. 5th ed. New York: Longman, 1997.

Dudley-Marling, Curt, and Dennis Searle. *When Students Have Time to Talk*. Portsmouth, N.H.: Heinemann, 1991.

Education Department of South Australia. *Literacy Assessment in Practice*. Urbana, Ill.: National Council of Teachers of English, 1991.

Education Department of Western Australia. *First Steps*. Melbourne: Longman Australia, 1994.

Elbow, Peter. *Writing without Teachers*. New York: Oxford, 1973.

———. *What is English?* New York: Modern Language Association, 1990.

———, Pat Belanoff, and Stacy Farait, eds. *Nothing Begins with N: New Investigations of Freewriting*. Carbondale, Ill.: Southern Illinois University Press, 1991.

Enciso, Pat. *The Nature of Engagement in Reading: Profiles of Three Fifth Graders' Engagement Strategies and Stances*. Unpublished doctoral dissertation. Columbus, Ohio: The Ohio State University, 1990.

Ernst, Karen. *Picturing Learning*. Portsmouth, N.H.: Association for Supervision and Curriculum Development, 1994.

Fader, Daniel *Hooked on Books*. New York: Berkeley Medallion, 1966.

Farrell, Edmund J., and James R. Squire, eds. *Transactions with Literature: A Fifty-Year Perspective*. Urbana, Ill.: National Council of Teachers of English, 1990.

Finders, Margaret J. *Just Girls: Hidden Literacies and Life in Junior High*. New York: Teachers College Press, 1997.

Fleischer, Cathy. *Composing Teacher-Research: A Prosiac History of the Teacher Research Movement*. Albany: State University of New York, 1995.

Fletcher, Ralph. *What a Writer Needs*. Portsmouth, N.H.: Heinemann, 1993.

Flood, James, Julie M. Jensen, Diane Lapp, and James R. Squire, eds. *Handbook on Teaching the English Language Arts*. New York: Macmillan, 1991.

Freeman, David E., and Yvonne S. Freedom. *Between Worlds: Access to Second Language Acquisition*. Portsmouth, N.H.: Heinemann, 1994.

Fuller, R. Buckminster. *An Operating Manual for Spaceship Earth*. Carbondale, Ill.: Southern Illinois University Press, 1969.

Gardner, Howard. *Multiple Intelligence*. New York: Basic Books, 1993.

Gates, Henry Louis, Jr. *The Signifying Monkey*. New York: Oxford University Press, 1988.

Geller, Conrad. "Guarding the Innocence: English Textbooks Into the Breach." *The English Journal 65*(December 1974): 71–75.

Goldstein, Bobbye. "Looking at Cartoons and Comics in a New Way." *Journal of Reading* (April 1986): 657–661.

Goodman, Ken. *On Reading*. Portsmouth, N.H.: Heinemann, 1996.

Gordon, Karen Elizabeth. *The Deluxe Transitive Vampire: A Guide to Grammar for the Innocent, the Eager and the Doomed*. New York: Random House, 1994.

Graff, Gerald. *Beyond the Culture Wars*. New York: W. W. Norton, 1992.

Graves, Donald. *A Fresh Look at Writing*. Portsmouth, N.H.: Heinemann, 1994.

———. *Writing: Teachers and Students at Work*. Portsmouth N.H.: Heinemann, 1988.

———, and Bonnie S. Suntein, eds. *Portfolio Portraits*. Portsmouth, N.H.: Heinemann, 1992.

Guskey, Thomas R. *Communicating Student Learning*. Alexandria, Va.: Association for Supervision and Curriculum Development, 1996.

Hale-Benson, Janice E. *Black Children, Their Roots, Culture, and Learning Styles*. Baltimore, Md.: The Johns Hopkins University Press, 1986.

Hall, Edward. *The Hidden Dimension*. Garden City, N.Y.: Doubleday, 1966.

———. *The Silent Language*. Greenwich, Conn. Fawcett Premier, 1962.

Harmin, Merrill. *Inspiring Active Learning*. Alexandria, Va.: Association for Supervision and Curriculum Development, 1994.

Hayakawa, S. I., and Alan Hayakawa. *Language and Thought in Action,* 5th ed. San Diego: Harcourt Brace, 1990.

Heald-Taylor, Gail. *Whole Language Strategies for ESL Students*. San Diego, Calif.: Dormal, Inc., 1989.

Hill, Bonnie, Nancy J. Johnson, and Katherine Noe, eds. *Literature Circles and Response*. Norwood, Mass.: Christopher-Gordon Publishers, 1995.

Hillocks, George. *Teaching Writing as Reflective Practice*. New York: Teachers College Press, 1995.

Hipple, Ted, ed. *Writers for Young Adults*. New York: Scribners, 1997.

Holbrook, David. *Children's Writing*. Cambridge: Cambridge University Press, 1967.

———. *Creativity and Popular Culture*. New York: Farleigh Dickensen University Press, 1994.

Hook, J. N. *A Long Way Together*. Urbana, IL: National Council of Teachers of English, 1980.

Hubbard, Ruth Shagoury, and Karen Ernst, eds. *New Entries*. Portsmouth, N.H.: Heinemann, 1996.

Hudelson, Sarah. *Write On! Children Writing in ESL*. Old Tappan, N.J.: Alemany Press, Prentice Hall, 1991.

Illich, Ivan. *Deschooling Society*. New York: Harper & Row, 1971.

Jacobs, Heidi. *Interdisciplinary Curriculum*. Alexandra, Va.: Association for Supervision and Curriculum Development, 1989.

Jackson, David. *Continuity in Secondary English*. London: Methuen, 1982.

Jean, Georges. *Writing: The Story of Alphabets and Scripts*. London: Thames and Hudson, 1992.

Jones, Richard Lloyd, et al. *Democracy in Education*. Urbana, Ill.: National Council of Teachers of English, 1988.

Joos, Martin. *The Five Clocks*. New York: Harcourt, 1967.

Kaplan, Jeffrey. *English Grammar: Principles and Facts*. 2nd ed. Englewood Cliffs, N.J.: Prentice Hall, 1995.

Kaywell, Joan, ed. *Adolescent Literature as a Complement to the Classics*. Norwood, Mass.: Christopher Gordon, 1993.

Knoblauch, Cy, and Lil Brannon. *Critical Teaching and the Idea of Literacy*. Portsmouth, N.H.: Boynton/Cook, 1993.

Kohl, Herbert. *Basic Skills*. Boston: Little, Brown, 1982.

———. *A Book of Puzzlements*. New York: Schocken, 1981.

———. *36 Children*. New York: New American Library, 1967.

Kohn, Alfie. *Beyond Discipline—from Compliance to Community*. Alexandria, Va.: Association for Supervision and Curriculum Development, 1996.

Kozol, Jonathan. *Death at an Early Age*. Boston: Houghton Mifflin, 1967.

Ladson-Billings, Gloria. *The Dreamkeepers*. San Francisco: Jossey-Bass, 1994.

Lane, Barry. *After the End: Teaching and Learning Creative Revision*. Portsmouth, N.H.: Heinemann, 1993.

Langer, Judith. *Envisioning Literature: Literary Understanding and Literature Instruction*. New York: Teachers College Press, 1995.

———. *Literature Instruction*. Urbana, Ill.: National Council of Teachers of English, 1993.

Langer, Susanne. *Philosophy in a New Key*. Cambridge, Mass.: Harvard Paperback, 1980.

Lawson, Bruce, Susan Ryan, and Ross Winterowd, eds. *Encountering Student Texts*. Urbana, Ill.: National Council of Teachers of English, 1989.

Leonard, George. *Education and Ecstasy*. New York: Delacorte, 1968.

Lerner, Max. *America as Civilization.* 30th anniversary edition. New York: Holt, 1987.

Lipman, Doug. *The Storytelling Coach: How to Listen, Praise, and Bring Out People's Best*. Little Rock, Ark.: August House, 1995.

Mager, Roger. *Preparing Instructional Objectives.* Belmont, Calif.: Fearon-Pitman, 1962.

Marshall, James D., Peter Smagorinsky, and Michael W. Smith. *The Language of Interpretation: Patterns of Discourse in Discussions of Literature*. Urbana, Ill.: National Council of Teachers of English, 1995.

Marzano, Robert J., Debra Pickering, and Jay McTighe. *Assessing Student Outcomes*. Alexandria, Va.: Association for Supervision and Curriculum Development, 1993.

Mayher, John. *Uncommon Sense*. Portsmouth, N.H.: Boynton/Cook, 1990.

McCormick, Kathleen. *The Culture of Reading and the Teaching of English*. New York: Manchester University Press, 1994.

McCracken, Nancy Mellin, and Bruce Appleby, eds. *Gender Issues in the Teaching of English*. Portsmouth, N.H.: Boynton/Cook, 1992.

McGregor, Robert, and Marion Meiers. *Telling the Whole Story*. Sydney: Australian Council for Educational Research, 1991.

McLuhan, Marshall. *City as Classroom*. Agincourt, Ontario: Book Society of Canada, 1977.

McLuhan, Marshall, and Quentin Fiore. *The Medium is the Massage.* New York: Bantam, 1967.

McNeil, Robert, et al. *The Story of English*. New York: Penguin, 1986.

Mearns, Hughes, *Creative Youth*. New York: D. Appleton, 1925.

Millers, Brenda Power. *Taking Note*. York: Maine Stenhouse, 1996.

Milner, Joseph, and Lucy Milner, eds. *Passages to Literature*. Urbana, Ill.: National Council of Teachers of English, 1989.

Mitchell, Ruth, Marilyn Willis, and the Chicago Teachers Union Quest Center. *Learning in Overdrive: Designing Curriculum, Instruction, and Assessment from Standards*. Chicago: North American Press, 1995.

Moffett, James, and Betty Jane Wagner. *Student-Centered Language Arts, K–13*. 4th ed. Portsmouth, N.H.: Boynton/Cook, 1992.

Monseau, Virginia R. *Responding to Young Adult Literature*. Portsmouth, N.H.: Boynton/Cook, 1996.

————, and Gary Salvner, eds. *Reading Their World: The Young Adult Novel in the Classroom*. Portsmouth, N.H.: Boynton/Cook, 1992.

Morris, Paul, and Stephen Tchudi. *The New Literacy: Beyond the 3Rs*. San Francisco: Jossey-Bass, 1996.

Murray, Donald M. *A Writer Teaches Writing*. Boston: Houghton Mifflin, 1985.

Myers, Miles, and Elizabeth Spalding, eds. *Assessing Student Performance in Grades 9–12*. Urbana, Ill.: National Council of Teachers of English, 1997.

National Council of Teachers of English. *An Experience Curriculum in English*. New York: D. Appleton, 1935.

————. *A Correlated Curriculum*. New York: D. Appleton, 1939.

————. *The English Language Arts*. 5 volumes. New York: Appleton-Century-Crofts, 1952–55.

————. *The National Defense and the Teaching of English*. Urbana, Ill.: National Council of Teachers of English, 1961.

————. *Standards for the English Language Arts*. Urbana, Ill.: 1996.

National Oracy Project. *Teaching Talking and Learning*. York, U.K.: National Curriculum Council, 1991.

Newell, George E., and Russel K. Durst. *Exploring Texts: The Role of Discussion and Writing in the Teaching and Learning of Literature*. Norwood, Mass.: Christopher Gordon, 1993.

Oakland Unified School District. *Policy on Standard American English Development*. December 18, 1996.

Orenstein, Peggy. *School Girls*. New York: Doubleday, 1994.

Orwell, George. "Politics and the English Language." *Shooting an Elephant and Other Essays*. New York: Harcourt Brace, 1950.

Perloff, Marjorie. *Radical Artifice: Writing Poetry in the Age of Media*. Chicago: University of Chicago Press, 1991.

Peterson, Ralph. *Life in a Crowded Place*. Portsmouth, N.H.: Heinemann, 1992.

Peyton, Joy Kreefl, and Leslee Reed. *Dialogue Journal Writing with Nonnative English Speakers: A Handbook for Teachers*. Alexandria, Va.: TESOL, 1990.

Phelan, Patricia, ed. *Literature and Life Making Connections in the Classroom*. Urbana, Ill.: National Council of Teachers of English, 1990.

————. *Talking to Learn*. Urbana, Ill.: National Council of Teachers of English, 1989.

Piaget, Jean. *The Language and Thought of the Child*. Cleveland: World Publishing, 1966.

Pinker, Steven. *The Language Instinct*. New York: Penguin, 1994.

Pipher, Mary. *Reviving Ophelia*. New York: Putnam, 1994.

Pooley, Robert. *Teaching English Usage*. Urbana, Ill.: National Council of Teachers of English, 1946.

Postman, Neil. *Crazy Talk, Stupid Talk: How We Defeat Ourselves by the Way We Talk*. New York: Delacorte, 1976.

———. *Technopoly: The Surrender of Culture to Technology*. New York: Knopf, 1992.

———. *The Disappearance of Childhood*. New York: Delacorte, 1982.

———. *The End of Education: Redefining the Value of School*. New York: Knopf, 1995.

———, and Charles Weingartner. *Linguistics: A Revolution in Teaching*. New York: Delacorte, 1966.

———. *Teaching as a Subversive Activity*. New York: Delacorte, 1969.

Pradl, Gordon. *Literature and Democracy*. Portsmouth, N.H.: Boynton/Cook, 1996.

Probst, Robert. *Response and Analysis—Teaching Literature in Junior and Senior High School*. Portsmouth, N.H.: Boynton/Cook, 1988.

Public Broadcasting System. *The Story of English*. London: Penguin, 1985.

Purves, Alan, Theresa Rogers, and Anna O. Soter. *How Porcupines Make Love III*. New York: Longman, 1995

Reed, Arthea J. S. *Comics to Classics: A Guide to Books for Teens and Preteens*. New York: Penguin, 1994.

———. *Reaching Adolescents: The Young Adult Book and the School*. New York: Macmillan, 1994.

Reid, Forrestal, and Cook. *Small Group Learning in the Classroom*. Sydney, Australia: Primary English Teaching Association/Chalkface Press, 1989.

Romano, Tom. *Clearing the Way*. Portsmouth, N.H.: Boynton/Cook, 1988.

Rose, Mike. *Possible Lives*. New York: Penguin, 1995.

Rosenblatt, Louise. *Literature as Exploration*. New York: D. Appleton, 1938. 5th ed., New York: Modern Language Association, 1996.

———. *The Reader, the Text, and the Poem*. Carbondale, Ill.: Southern Illinois University Press, 1978.

Routman, Regie. *Invitations*. Portsmouth, N.H.: Heinemann, 1991.

———. *Literacy at the Crossroads*. Portsmouth, N.H.: Heinemann, 1996.

———. *Transitions*. Portsmouth, N.H.: Heinemann, 1988.

Ruhlen, Merritt. *Voices from the Past: The Origin of Language*. New York: John Wiley, 1984.

Russell, David. *Writing in the Academic Disciplines 1870–1990*. Carbondale, Ill.: Southern Illinois University Press, 1991.

Samuels, Barbara G., and G. Kylene Beers, eds. *Your Reading—An Annotated Booklist for Middle and Junior High*. Urbana, Ill.: National Council of Teachers of English, 1996.

Santayana, George. "The Life of Reason." *The Genteel Tradition*. Cambridge, Mass.: Harvard University Press, 1905.

Scher, Anna, and Charles Verrall. *Another 100+ Ideas for Drama*. Portsmouth, N.H.: Heinemann, 1987.

Scholes, Robert. *Textual Power, Literary Theory, and the Teaching of English*. New Haven, Conn.: Yale University Press, 1985.

Sherrill, Anne, and Terry C Ley, eds. *Literature IS . . . : Collected Essays of G. Robert Carlsen*. Johnson City, Tenn.: Sabre, 1994.

Simons, Herbert W. *The Rhetorical Turn*. Chicago: University of Chicago Press, 1990.

Smagorinsky, Peter. *Standards in Practice Grades 9–12*. Urbana, Ill.: National Council of Teachers of English, 1996.

Smith, Ernie A. *the Historical Development of African American Language*. Los Angeles: Watts College Press, 1994.

Smith, Frank. *To Think*. New York: Teachers College Press, 1990.

Smitherman, Geneva. *Black Talk*. Boston: Houghton Mifflin, 1994.

Steller, Arthur W. "Foreword." James Bean, ed. *Toward a Coherent Curriculum*. Alexandria, Va.: Association for Supervision and Curriculum Development, 1995: v.

Stein, Gertrude. "Poetry and Grammar." *How to Write*. Los Angeles: Sun and Moon Classics, 1995.

Swartz, Larry. *Dramathemes*. Portsmouth, N.H.: Heinemann, 1988.

Tarlington, Carole, and Wendy Michaels. *Building Plays*. Portsmouth, N.H.: Heinemann, 1995.

Tchudi, Stephen, ed. *Alternatives to Grading Student Writing*. Urbana, Ill.: National Council of Teachers of English, 1997.

————. *Planning and Assessing the English Language Arts*. Alexandria, Va.: Association for Supervision and Curriculum Development, 1989.

————, and Susan Tchudi. *The English Language Arts Handbook*. Portsmouth, N.H., Boynton/Cook, 1991.

————, and Susan Tchudi. *The Young Writer's Handbook*. New York: Scribner's, 1984.

————, and Susan Tchudi. *The English Teacher's Handbook*. Portsmouth, N.H.: Boynton/Cook, 1990.

————, and Stephen Lafer. *The Interdisciplinary Teacher's Handbook*. Portsmouth, N.H., Boynton/Cook, 1996.

Tchudi, Stephen, ed. *Language, Schooling, and Society*. Portsmouth, N.H.: Boynton/Cook, 1986.

Teasley, Alan, and Ann Wilder. *Reel Conversations*. Portsmouth, N.H.: Boynton Cook, 1996.

Tierney, Robert J., Mark A. Carter, and Laura E. Desai. *Portfolio Assessment in the Reading/Writing Classroom*. Norwood, Mass.: Christopher Gordon, 1991.

Trousdale, Ann M., ed. *Give a Listen: Stories of Storytelling in School*. Urbana, Ill.: National Council of Teachers of English, 1994.

Vygosky, Lev. *Thought and Language*. Cambridge, Mass.: Cambridge University Press, 1962.

Weaver, Connie. *Teaching Grammar in Context*. Portsmouth, N.H.: Heinemann, 1996.

—————. *Understanding Whole Language: From Principles to Practice*. Portsmouth, N.H.: Heinemann, 1990.

Weinstein, Carol Simon. *Secondary Classroom Management*. New York: McGraw-Hill, 1996.

Wells, Gordon, and Gen Ling Chang-Wells. *Constructing Knowledge Together*. Portsmouth, N.H.: Heinemann, 1992.

White, Edward. *Teaching and Assessing Writing*. San Francisco: Jossey-Bass, 1994.

Wigginton, Eliot. *The Foxfire Book*. Garden City, N.Y.: Doubleday, 1962.

Wilde, Sandra, ed. *Notes from a Kidwatcher: Selected Writings of Yetta M. Goodman*. Portsmouth, N.H.: Heinemann, 1996.

Wilhelm, Jeffrey D. *"You Gotta BE the Book": Teaching Engaged and Reflective Reading with Adolescents*. New York: Teachers College Press, 1995.

———. *Standards in Practice Grades 6–8*. Urbana, Ill.: National Council of Teachers of English, 1997.

Winton, Linda. *Keepsakes: Using Family Stories in Elementary Classrooms*. Little Rock, Ark.: August House, 1995.

Wolk, Alan. *The Naming of America*. New York: Thomas Nelson, 1997.

INDEX